JFK Day by Day

A Chronicle of the 1,036 Days of John F. Kennedy's Presidency

FEATURING PHOTOGRAPHY FROM THE WHITE HOUSE COLLECTION
OF THE JOHN F. KENNEDY PRESIDENTIAL LIBRARY

Terry Golway
Les Krantz

RUNNING
PRESS

Copyright © 2010 Facts That Matter, Inc.

First published in the United States in 2010 by Running Press Book Publishers
All rights reserved under the Pan-American and International Copyright Conventions
Printed in China by PWGS

9   8   7   6   5   4   3   2   1
Digit on the right indicates the number of this printing.

Library of Congress control number: 2010922445

ISBN: 978-0-7624-3742-9

This book was created by
Facts That Matter, Inc.
N2826 Wildwood Dr.
Lake Geneva, WI 53147
PUBLISHER: Les Krantz
EDITOR: David Aretha
DESIGNER: Jensie Lauritsen Miksich
CONTRIBUTING WRITERS: David Aretha, Christy Nadalin, Chris Smith, and Marci McGrath
PHOTO RESEARCHERS: Marilyn Farnell and Jane Martin

Running Press Book Publishers
2300 Chestnut Street
Philadelphia, PA 19103-4371

Visit us on the web!
www.runningpress.com

EDITOR'S NOTE

The articles in this book were written in present tense to capture the immediacy of the events. The writers relied on numerous reliable sources for their articles, including Associated Press, United Press International, *The New York Times*, *The Washington Post*, other newspapers, JFKLibrary.org, official U.S. government Web sites, and many books on President Kennedy and the issues of his day.

PHOTO CREDITS

All photos in this book were culled from the archives of the John F. Kennedy Presidential Library except for the following images:

Associated Press: 4, 6, 8 left and right, 11, 14, 24, 25, 30, 38, 40, 73, 84, 86, 91, 92, 98, 99, 101, 103, 111, 137, 139, 142, 153, 155, 184, 200, 212, 222, 245, 272, 279, 280, 285

Library of Congress, Prints & Photographs Division: 68 top, 82, 209, 233 bottom; A. Philip Randolph Papers: 28; Gunnison Housing Corporation: 72; Historic American Buildings Survey/Historic American Engineering Record: 181; Lawrence E. Spivak Collection: 241; Look Magazine Photograph Collection: 35, 123, 132, 152, 165, 205, 206; NAACP Records: 77 top; New York World Telegram and Sun Collection: 36, 39, 46, 48, 49, 52, 67, 77 bottom, 94, 95, 97, 115, 122, 129, 147, 170, 177, 178, 179, 180, 186, 215, 216 right, 220, 224 left, 225, 232, 233 top, 247, 248, 255, 267, 274, 283; U.S. News & Report Magazine Photograph Collection: 136, 230 bottom

Eisenhower Archives: 74

Facts That Matter Collection: 104, 110

NASA: 44, 51, 120, 134, 141

U.S. Air Force: 34

President Kennedy goes over notes at his desk
on January 18, 1962.

CONTENTS

1961: BEARING THE BURDEN   PAGE 10

The youngest president ever elected, John F. Kennedy stumbled in April by botching the Bay of Pigs invasion in Cuba. Yet JFK accepted responsibility for his blunder and persevered. Two of his programs, the Peace Corps and Alliance for Progress, proved popular and strengthened America's ties with foreign nations. Nevertheless, the Cold War remained a troublesome battle. Soviet Premier Nikita Khrushchev browbeat the rookie president at their June summit, and the pro-Soviet East German government eroded East-West relations by constructing the Berlin Wall.

1962: PROFOUND CHALLENGES   PAGE 102

Facing a series of crises in 1962, President Kennedy responded with boldness and finesse. He resumed nuclear testing in response to the Soviets' detonations, scolded "Big Steel" for their price hikes, upped the military presence in Vietnam, and sent federal troops to Mississippi in response to racial strife. The greatest challenge of his presidency arose in October, when the Soviets placed offensive nuclear missiles in Cuba. Kennedy wisely avoided calls for a Cuban invasion but demanded that the Soviet Union remove its missiles. In the end, the Soviets backed down.

1963: THE FINAL YEAR   PAGE 198

With tensions easing in the wake of the Cuban missile crisis, Kennedy signed a nuclear test-ban treaty with the Soviet Union—a major breakthrough in the Cold War. The President looked to move the nation forward in 1963. He railed for a tax-cut bill that would spur the economy, championed civil rights causes like never before, and vowed to fight a war on poverty. JFK was beginning his reelection campaign in November 1963 when an assassin ended his life in Dallas, Texas. Millions of people worldwide, who had grown to respect and love the progressive young president, mourned the heavy loss.

Kennedy arrives in Los Angeles for the 1960 Democratic National Convention.

RISE TO THE PRESIDENCY

Could a Catholic with chronic health problems ascend to the White House?
He could if he had smarts and ambition and the name of Kennedy.

e was born into power and influence, the grandson of a Boston political legend, the son of an ambitious businessman intent on seeing his children reach heights he believed were denied him because of his religion and ancestry. If the young John Fitzgerald Kennedy, the second son of Irish Catholics Joseph Kennedy and Rose Fitzgerald Kennedy, born in Massachusetts on May 29, 1917, dreamed of becoming president, he could hardly have chosen a better family setting. Great things were expected of young Jack and his siblings.

But young Jack Kennedy did not, in fact, dream of winning the presidency. As a young man, he envisioned himself as a journalist—not, to be sure, a fedora-wearing, whiskey-besotted wretch banging out crime stories on deadline, but a suave political commentator, moving and mixing easily in the company of presidents, prime ministers, and statesmen. Elective politics, campaign oratory, and whistle-stop tours would be reserved for his older brother, Joseph P. Kennedy, Jr. Brother Joe was the chosen one, an ebullient, outgoing young man who combined the charm of his material grandfather, Boston Mayor John "Honey Fitz" Fitzgerald, with the drive of his father and namesake, a banker and movie executive. Jack, on the other hand, was thin and sickly, unsuited, it seemed, for the rigors of campaign politics. His illnesses, which included stomach ailments, digestive woes, and back pain, often landed him in the hospital for days and even weeks at a time.

His health, however, did not prevent him from enjoying the privileges that came with being a Kennedy in the late 1930s. He attended Harvard University, traveled to Europe, and visited Great Britain in 1939, while his father served as U.S. ambassador to the Court of St. James. That following year, he published his first book, *Why England Slept*, an analysis of Britain's failed attempt to appease German dictator Adolf Hitler in the mid-1930s. The success of Why England Slept indicated that Kennedy was a journalistic star in the making.

After graduating from Harvard in 1940 with a degree in international relations, Kennedy postponed his career ambitions to enlist in the Navy, a task that required all of his father's political pull. Kennedy was so unhealthy that he flunked physical exams for both the Army and Navy in 1941. His father, however, arranged for a friendly doctor to administer another physical. This time he passed, and he was admitted into the Navy's intelligence office months before the Japanese attack on Pearl Harbor.

As the U.S. engaged the Japanese across the wide expanse of the South Pacific, Kennedy was assigned to command a small motor torpedo boat, more commonly known as a PT boat. His vessel, PT-109, was rammed and cut in half by a Japanese destroyer during an engagement near the Pacific island of South Georgia on August 1, 1943. Kennedy and 10 other crewmembers survived the crash—two crewmembers were killed on impact—but they were adrift in dangerous, shark-infested waters. Kennedy coolly led his men on a five-hour swim to a nearby island, with Kennedy towing a badly burned sailor too weak to swim on his own. The survivors of PT-109 eventually were rescued, and Lieutenant John F. Kennedy was an authentic war hero.

On the other side of the world, older brother Joe was gaining a reputation as a skillful and courageous Navy pilot in the European theater of operations. In late 1944, Joe, his crew, and his plane disappeared over the English Channel while on a bombing mission. There would be no brilliant postwar career in politics for Joseph P. Kennedy, Jr.

When the war ended, Jack Kennedy resumed his interest in journalism. He wrote a magazine piece about Soviet-American relations in the postwar world, and he covered the initial conference of the new United Nations organization in San Francisco in late 1945. Within a few months, however, John Kennedy took up his older brother's fallen mantle, declaring his candidacy for Congress in the 1946 midterm elections.

Twenty-year-old John Kennedy poses with his father, Joe Sr., and brother, Joe Jr., in 1937.

The young representative (D-MA) reads on Capitol Hill in 1946.

As a candidate, he lacked his brother's panache and his grandfather's back-slapping geniality. His would-be constituents were blue-collar Bostonians, not the well-tailored diplomats he mingled with during the UN conference. But he managed to exude charm and empathy to go along with his impressive war record, leading to victory on Election Day. It was the beginning of his historic journey to the White House.

Politics may not have been his first career choice, but Kennedy's ambition led him to seek higher office after just two undistinguished terms in the House of Representatives. He ran for a U.S. Senate seat in 1952 and defeated Henry Cabot Lodge, scion of one of New England's oldest and most-fabled families. At the age of 35, John Kennedy took his place in one of the world's most exclusive clubs, a place that revered tradition, experience, and discretion.

Kennedy's youth, connections, and ambition set him apart from many of his colleagues, and inspired a good deal of envy among them. Although Kennedy was a relative newcomer to Washington politics, reporters and columnists began touting him as a future presidential candidate. It did him no harm when he married a beautiful young photographer, Jacqueline Bouvier, in 1953. The press could hardly get enough of the handsome couple. They were smart and glamorous; the rest of Washington seemed dull and pedestrian.

The young senator seemed the picture of vitality. In reality, however, he continued to suffer from severe back pain and from Addison's disease, a failure of the adrenal gland. This illness could be managed with cortisone shots, but it could not be cured. Kennedy decided to risk surgery on his back in 1954 against the advice of doctors, who thought the operation might kill him because of complications with Addison's disease. Before the operation began, Kennedy received last rites from a Catholic priest.

JFK became the first patient with advanced Addison's disease to survive such a major operation. While recuperating, Kennedy collaborated with his aides, chiefly a young speechwriter named Theodore Sorensen, on a new book about courage in politics. *Profiles in Courage* became a bestseller when it was published in 1956 and won Kennedy a Pulitzer Prize, although historians agree that Kennedy was not the book's sole author. Some of Kennedy's colleagues were not so impressed, suggesting privately that the author would do well to demonstrate less profile and more courage. The jibe may have been inspired in part because of Kennedy's absence from the Senate when Senator Joseph McCarthy, a family friend, was formally censured for his anti-Communist witch hunt in 1954.

Kennedy's own profile became even more prominent with the book's success. When Democrats gathered for their presidential convention in the summer of 1956, Kennedy sought to capitalize on his name recognition, declaring himself a candidate for vice president when the party's presidential nominee, Adlai Stevenson, announced that he would let the convention's delegates decide on his running mate. Kennedy miscalculated, for his support among the party's rank and file was not nearly as strong as he thought. Kentucky Senator Estes Kefauver won the vice presidential nomination on the second ballot. Kennedy delivered a gracious concession speech, asking the convention to declare Kefauver's nomination to be unanimous.

The Stevenson-Kefauver ticket was doomed anyway, as incumbent President Dwight Eisenhower and his vice president, Richard Nixon, won a resounding victory in November. Kennedy spent much of the next year preparing for his own reelection campaign in Massachusetts. Once safely returned to the Senate in 1958, he and his aides and family began plotting his next, most-audacious, move: a presidential campaign in 1960.

No Roman Catholic had ever won the presidency. Indeed, only one had ever won a major-party nomination, Alfred E. Smith in 1928. And Smith, a Democrat, was soundly defeated. His religion was one of the campaign's major issues.

But John F. Kennedy was no Al Smith. He was urbane; Smith was urban. Kennedy was polished; Smith was rough-hewn. Kennedy attended the finishing school for the nation's elite, Harvard; Smith dropped out of grade school to support his widowed mother, and joked that his "diploma" read "FFM"—Fulton Fish Market, where he spent his adolescence.

But even if Kennedy seemed less alien than Smith, he faced other questions. He was very young—he turned 43 in 1960—and was relatively inexperienced. At least two Democratic contenders, Senator Hubert Humphrey of Minnesota and Senator Lyndon Johnson of Texas, had far more substantive records on Capitol Hill. Some members of the party's old guard, including former president Harry Truman and former first lady Eleanor Roosevelt, opposed him.

Kennedy put together a first-rate team of advisers, including Kenneth O'Donnell, Pierre Salinger, Stephen Smith, and speechwriter Sorensen. Presiding over the campaign as its chief enforcer was Robert Kennedy, the senator's younger brother. The Kennedy team steamrolled over opponents during the primaries and wrapped up the nomination at the party's convention in Los Angeles.

John Kennedy went on to confront the religion issue with a speech to a group of Baptist ministers in Texas in September. He and his Republican opponent, Vice President Richard Nixon, engaged in four historic debates. The debates were televised, giving Kennedy, with his good looks and cool demeanor, a decided advantage.

On November 8, 1960, John Fitzgerald Kennedy was elected president of the United States, becoming the first Catholic to achieve the nation's highest office. His father's dream was realized. He took office on January 20, 1961, after delivering perhaps the finest inaugural address of the 20th century.

A new era—the New Frontier, as Kennedy called it—had begun.

BEARING THE BURDEN

The Peace Corps symbolizes the young president's idealism, but Communists prove a thorn in Kennedy's side—in Cuba, Berlin, and Southeast Asia.

John Kennedy's margin of victory in the 1960 presidential election was one of the smallest in U.S. history—he won only 49.7 percent of the vote. Eager as he was to assume the powers of the presidency, he and his aides understood that voters had not handed them a mandate. Accordingly, the new president did not attempt to raise expectations during the early months of his administration. There would be no attempt to imitate Franklin Roosevelt's fabled first 100 days, during which the new administration proposed a huge array of new programs and reforms.

Still, there were pressing issues facing the new president, at home and abroad. He inherited a plan to assist a band of Cuban exiles determined to overthrow Fidel Castro's Communist regime on the island nation. Communists fighting a civil war in the Asian nation of Laos threatened the rest of Southeast Asia, as did Communist activity in Vietnam.

Meanwhile, the domestic economy was a concern after several years of stagnant growth. The boom that followed the end of World War II was sputtering, as demand at home peaked and European competitors reemerged from the war's ashes. Kennedy had little interest in economics and was bored by domestic policy. But he campaigned on a promise to get the country moving again. For most Americans, that meant a return to the days of growth and prosperity.

Kennedy kicked off his administration with policy initiatives that spoke to the idealism of his inaugural address and his famous call to public service: "ask not what your country can do for you—ask what you can do for your country." In early March, JFK announced the formation of the Peace Corps, which would send thousands of young Americans into the developing world to build schools and hospitals, teach poor villagers about modern farming techniques, and otherwise spread American values around the globe. The second initiative, the Alliance for Progress, was designed to soften Washington's image in Latin America. It would emphasize partnership in development rather than simple dictation from Washington.

Fears that Kennedy was too inexperienced seemed to be realized early in his presidency. The Bay of Pigs invasion in April, intended to bring down Castro, was a monumental failure. JFK took full responsibility for the fiasco in a televised address to the nation.

Two months later, Kennedy met with Soviet leader Nikita Khrushchev in a much-anticipated summit meeting between the two leaders in Vienna, Austria. The result was another disaster, as Khrushchev browbeat Kennedy about Laos, Berlin, and other trouble spots. The Soviet leader accused the U.S. of reasserting colonial control over the developing world. Kennedy did a poor job defending America's position, and left Vienna fearful that the U.S. and the Soviets were on the road to nuclear war.

Kennedy during his inaugural address.

The new president delivered his fabled inaugural address in howling winds and temperatures in the low 20s.

THE TORCH IS PASSED

Jan 20 Kennedy Sworn In as President; Delivers Powerful Address

WASHINGTON—Except for a cordial visit with President Dwight Eisenhower, John F. Kennedy's Inauguration Day got off to a bumpy start. So much snow had fallen the night before that officials considered postponing the outdoor ceremony. But the show went on, despite frigid temperatures, howling winds, and sunshine that reflected blindingly off the pure white snow.

Scheduled to start at noon, the inaugural ceremony outside the Capitol ran late. The wind and sun's glare prevented 86-year-old Robert Frost from reading a poem on the platform, despite Vice President Lyndon Johnson's attempt to shade the paper with his hat. Another gaffe followed when Kennedy's hand slipped from the Bible as Chief Justice Earl Warren swore him in.

However, the new president righted the ship when he delivered his inaugural address. He quickly grabbed the nation's attention when he announced: "Let the word go forth from this time and place, to friend and foe alike, that the torch has been passed to a new generation of Americans—born in this century, tempered by war, disciplined by a hard and bitter peace, proud of our ancient heritage...."

His 1,300-word speech was brief but powerful. Exuding extreme confidence, he frequently jabbed his finger into the air for emphasis. The 43-year-old president, the second youngest ever to take the oath, pledged loyalty to America's allies and support for those nations who hungered for democracy. He did not mention the Soviet Union, but he strongly alluded to

> *"And so, my fellow Americans, ask not what your country can do for you—ask what you can do for your country."*
> *— KENNEDY, IN HIS INAUGURAL ADDRESS*

the rival superpower when he declared: "Finally, to those nations who would make themselves our adversary, we offer not a pledge but a request that both sides begin anew the quest for peace, before the dark powers of destruction unleashed by science engulf all humanity in planned or accidental self-destruction."

Kennedy urged Americans to work together in "defending freedom in its hours of maximum danger." In words meant to inspire and motivate, he declared: "The energy, the faith, the devotion which we bring to this endeavor will light our country and all who serve it—and the glow from that fire can truly light the world." He followed with a more succinct declaration: "And so, my fellow Americans, ask not what your country can do for you—ask what you can do for your country."

Kennedy concluded his speech amid raucous applause, and spirits ran high over the rest of the event-filled day. From a reviewing stand near the White House, Kennedy and his wife, Jacqueline, waved to the 32,000 marchers in the inaugural parade. Various receptions, balls, and parties followed in one of the most festive days Washington had ever seen. After decades marked by economic hardship, war, and uninspiring leadership, a "new generation of Americans" was excited about their future—and their president.

FROM THE INAUGURAL ADDRESS

HIGHLIGHTS FROM PRESIDENT KENNEDY'S HISTORIC SPEECH

"The torch has been passed to a new generation of Americans—born in this century, tempered by war, disciplined by a hard and bitter peace, proud of our ancient heritage...."

■ "Let every nation know, whether it wishes us well or ill, that we shall pay any price, bear any burden, meet any hardship, support any friend, oppose any foe, in order to assure the survival and the success of liberty."

■ "Let us never negotiate out of fear. But let us never fear to negotiate."

■ "In the long history of the world, only a few generations have been granted the role of defending freedom in its hour of maximum danger. I do not shrink from this responsibility—I welcome it."

20 John F. Kennedy is inaugurated on the steps of the Capitol, along with Vice President Lyndon Johnson. At 43, Kennedy is the youngest, and first-ever Roman Catholic U.S. president. In a 10-minute address, he appeals to Americans to unite against the common enemies of man: tyranny, poverty, disease, and war.

21 Key players in JFK's foreign policy team are sworn in, including Dean Rusk, secretary of state; Robert S. McNamara, secretary of defense; and Robert F. Kennedy, attorney general.

22 The President establishes the Government Ethics Committee to examine the ethical standards of government agencies.

23 Kennedy chooses Frank Burton Ellis of Louisiana to direct the Office of Civil and Defense Mobilization.

24 The President postpones nuclear test-ban talks with Britain and the Soviet Union, originally set for February.

25 During the first live telecast of a presidential news conference, Kennedy announces that the Soviet Union has freed two surviving crewmen of a U.S. reconnaissance plane shot down over the Barents Sea in 1960. He praises Soviet Premier Nikita Khrushchev's efforts to establish better relations between the superpowers.

26 Vowing swift action to impede the nation's economic decline, Kennedy announces plans to extend unemployment benefits.

27 The President assigns the problem of Cuban refugees to the Department of Health, Education and Welfare.

Jackie Kennedy shares a laugh with her husband at one of the five balls.

Jan 21 FIVE PARTIES TOO MUCH FOR JACKIE

WASHINGTON—Jackie Kennedy took an afternoon nap at the White House on Inauguration Day, but when she awoke she was still exhausted. A doctor quickly provided her with Dexedrine, a psycho-stimulant, which gave her just enough pep to get through the evening.

At least she *looked* great, which was all that mattered to the hordes of photographers who would cover the five upcoming inaugural balls. When Jackie met her husband in the Red Room prior to the night's festivities, she was wearing a white chiffon dress, a white gossamer cape, and white gloves laced with pearl buttons. "Darling," Jack said, "I've never seen you so lovely."

The couple attended three inaugural balls together, but they never did dance due to the throngs of supporters who swarmed them at each stop. At the second party, Jack snuck away to a private party thrown by Frank Sinatra, at which Hollywood beauties Angie Dickinson and Kim Novak were in attendance. After the third ball, at 1 A.M., Jackie could no longer continue, and Naval officer Godfrey McHugh escorted her home.

The President attended two more balls alone, and after more partying finally called it a night. But it was almost 4 A.M., and a full slate of presidential duties would await him in just a few short hours.

"There is an economy of style and a controlled power about the new President."

— THE ATLANTA CONSTITUTION

28 As a condition for expanded U.S. assistance to Vietnam, the President approves a plan that calls for government reform and military restructuring in that country.

29 Jack and Jackie Kennedy invite staff members and their families to a White House party, where many children see their fathers sworn into office.

30 In his first State of the Union address, JFK asks Congress to include health insurance in the Social Security program. He challenges lawmakers and the nation to meet perils abroad and a worsening recession at home.

31 In a Mercury test flight, a 37-pound chimpanzee named Ham is recovered alive in the Caribbean after he rocketed 155 miles into space from Cape Canaveral.

February

1 The U.S. Strategic Air Command launches the first test of a Minuteman intercontinental ballistic missile.

2 President Kennedy asks Congress to increase benefits for the aged and jobless. Next week he will call for an increase in the minimum wage to $1.25 per hour.

3 Reflecting concern over military readiness for multiple international challenges, Defense Secretary McNamara launches an accelerated building program of long-range cargo and troop carrier planes.

4 After consulting with Secretary of Health, Education and Welfare Abraham Ribicoff, the President authorizes $4 million in aid for Cuban refugees who have fled to the United States.

Jan 21 — INAUGURAL SPEECH DUBBED A "MASTERPIECE"

WASHINGTON—From all corners of the nation, cheers rang out for President Kennedy's inaugural speech. In just ten minutes, Kennedy inspired America with his message of peace, possibilities, and personal responsibility.

Newsday called the speech "a masterpiece of brevity," and the *Times Union* in Albany declared that the "Inaugural will be recalled and quoted as long as there are Americans to heed his summons." Praised the *New York World-Telegram and Sun*: "Now we have a new Administration, a new man with a freshness in look, in some ways a freshness of ideas, a new President of eloquence…of spirit attuned to our times."

The Associated Press reported: "It was an utterly serious speech, seriously delivered and seriously received. Time and again, it sparked applause." Undeterred by the frigid temperatures, many were emotionally moved by the speech. Tears streamed down the face of Ethel Kennedy, wife of new attorney general Robert Kennedy.

Even in the Deep South, where trust often runs thin for members of the New England elite, journalists were inspired by Kennedy's message and delivery. "There is an economy of style and a controlled power about the new President," opined *The Atlanta Constitution*. "Perhaps he really can lead us to light our country with such a faith that 'the glow from the fire can truly light the world.'"

But the most supportive words of all came from the lips of the new first lady, Jackie Kennedy. "It was soaring," Jackie said. "I put my hand on his cheek and said, 'Jack, you were so wonderful!'"

Kennedy hosts the swearing-in of his Cabinet in the East Room of the White House.

A busy man during his first morning on the job, JFK met with former president Harry Truman from 10:02 to 10:10.

Jan 21 THE NEW PRESIDENT GETS TO WORK

WASHINGTON—After only about four hours of sleep, President John F. Kennedy ripped himself out of bed at 8 A.M. on Saturday and began his first full day as president. Soon afterward, staffers were marveling about how much Kennedy was accomplishing in so few hours. In fact, he took a major step toward eliminating hunger in the United States before many Americans had started making breakfast.

Shortly after conferring with his staff aides at 9 A.M., Kennedy issued his first executive order. He directed that "a greater and wider variety" of surplus food be distributed "to all needy families." The order would provide such food as flour, corn meal, rice, dried milk, and eggs to approximately four million Americans.

Former president Harry Truman, who hadn't entered the White House in eight years, looked forward to his meeting with the new boss. Truman said that Kennedy's inaugural address was the greatest ever—and that he knew, because he had read all of them. However, the Truman-Kennedy meeting lasted just eight minutes. JFK had other things to do. According to *The New York Times*, "the White House was bustling with action today."

Kennedy saw each of his new Cabinet members sworn in. They included Robert F. Kennedy, attorney general; Dean Rusk, secretary of state; J. Edward Day, postmaster general; C. Douglas Dillon, Treasury; Robert S. McNamara, Defense; Stewart L. Udall, Interior; Orville L. Freeman, Agriculture; Luther H. Hodges, Commerce; Arthur J. Goldberg, Labor; and Abraham A. Ribicoff, Health, Education and Welfare. Also, Adlai E. Stevenson was sworn in as chief delegate of the United Nations.

Rusk, McNamara, and Bobby Kennedy will be the Cabinet members in the spotlight. Rusk and McNamara will focus their energies on the Cold War, which is manifesting itself in Cuba and Southeast Asia (Laos and Vietnam). Kid brother Bobby, 35, is expected to crack down on organized crime as well as racial injustice in the southern states.

Also on Saturday, Kennedy spoke to the Democratic National Committee, designated six major appointments to the Agriculture Department (including Charles F. Murphy as under-secretary); and sent to the Senate for confirmation 38 previously announced sub-Cabinet posts.

Kennedy even made plans for his "day of rest." For Sunday, he scheduled lunch with poet Robert Frost and dinner with Mr. and Mrs. Franklin D. Roosevelt, Jr. As for White House staff members, they were scheduled to meet with the President on Monday morning at 9:15—sharp.

STOCKING HIS CABINET

Aside from Robert Kennedy, the President's attorney general, Defense Secretary Robert McNamara would become the most high-profile member of the Kennedy Cabinet. Like many other Cabinet secretaries, McNamara was an unknown quantity from Kennedy's perspective, but he came highly recommended. He was 44 years old in 1960, a graduate of Harvard, a World War II veteran, an intellectual, and a Republican, one of two in Kennedy's Cabinet (Treasury Secretary Douglas Dillon was the other). As president of the Ford Motor Company, he was one of the nation's most prominent business leaders.

Kennedy originally offered McNamara the leadership of the Treasury Department, which he declined. JFK came back with an offer to run the Defense Department, which McNamara accepted after insisting he would have complete control over the department, a demand that impressed Robert Kennedy.

McNamara would preside over the military's buildup in Vietnam, which is his most lasting legacy. But he also was a voice of moderation during the blockade of Cuba during the missile crisis in 1962; he ordered the Navy to do nothing without checking with him first.

Given Kennedy's intense focus on foreign affairs, it was hardly surprising that the other Cabinet secretary to become a household name during his presidency was Secretary of State Dean Rusk. The native of Georgia was president of the Rockefeller Foundation, a pillar of the Northeast establishment. Kennedy selected him because he intended to run the nation's diplomatic efforts himself, and he believed Rusk would accept his role as facilitator rather than as a creator of policy.

5 The USSR accepts Kennedy's request for a six-week delay in the Geneva nuclear test-ban talks in order for the U.S. team to consider new proposals.

6 Inventing a protest tactic that will draw national attention and crowd jails in several southern states, nine civil rights demonstrators in Rock Hill, South Carolina, opt for "jail, no bail."

7 Less than one month after taking office, JFK bans most trade with Cuba.

8 Federal housing chief nominee Dr. Robert C. Weaver runs into fierce opposition from southern Democrats. Despite blocking elevation of the post to Cabinet status, the Senate will confirm Weaver, making him the highest-ranking black government official in U.S. history.

9 The President urges Congress to improve health programs for older Americans.

10 The administration urges Soviet restraint on contentious East-West issues and warns of a tougher U.S. approach than in the Eisenhower years.

11 Angered by American support for Cuban counter-revolutionaries, Fidel Castro claims the right to promote revolution throughout Latin America.

12 Word that the death in January of former Congo Prime Minister Patrice Lumumba was a murder adds another foreign crisis to the new administration's agenda.

13 Talks begin on counterinsurgency strategy with reluctant South Vietnamese President Ngo Dinh Diem. Despite U.S. pressure, Diem will resist giving up centralized decision-making powers.

Jan 22 KENNEDY AIMS TO RAISE ETHICAL STANDARDS

WASHINGTON—On his first Sunday as president of the United States, John F. Kennedy went to work. His biggest order of business: clean up Washington. The President established a three-member Government Ethics Committee, whose purpose will be to conduct a "thorough examination of present ethical standards and regulations" in federal government agencies.

The committee will try to rectify conflict-of-interest matters, such as owning stock in corporations. Currently, federal government workers are not allowed to own certain stock, but the standards are unclear and inconsistent.

According to a White House press release, the panel "has been asked to recommend approaches to strengthening the conflict-of-interest laws so as to maintain the highest standards while, at the same time, not unduly impact the effectiveness of agency and department operation or the recruitment of qualified personnel."

Calvert Magruder, retired chief judge of the United States Court of Appeals, will head the small committee. The other members will include Dean Jefferson B. Fordham of the University of Pennsylvania Law School and Professor Bayless Manning of Yale Law School.

Jan 24 JFK EXPANDS AMERICA'S FOOD FOR PEACE PROGRAM

WASHINGTON—President Kennedy made good on his promise to help feed the hungry of other nations, as he moved today to expand America's Food for Peace program. Signing an executive order, the President expanded the authority of George S. McGovern, 38, director of the program. Kennedy also accepted a 30-page report by a White House task force that advocated an expansion of the plan.

Kennedy hoped that the Food for Peace program would "narrow the gap between abundance here at home and near-starvation abroad." Under President Dwight Eisenhower, the U.S. exported well more than $1 billion worth of food a year to some 60 countries. However, the task force report called for a dramatic increase in food giveaways.

"Our attitude is that we have been blessed with abundance," said McGovern, "which we are glad to share with those less fortunate." McGovern added a political motivation, stating, "If wisely used, our agricultural abundance will be a major instrument of our foreign policy."

The first Food for Peace survey mission will embark soon for Latin America. Other missions will head to Southeast Asia and Africa. Kennedy said he is willing to send food to Communist China, should its leaders request. Such a scenario, however, is unlikely.

The President takes a question during the first regular presidential press conference ever televised live.

14 President Kennedy, Vice President Johnson, and Cabinet officers seek a "full-fledged alliance" with the national Industrial Conference Board to coordinate efforts on economic growth, plant modernization, and price stability.

15 The President warns that the U.S. will oppose any interference by the Soviets with a United Nations pacification campaign in the Congo.

16 Kennedy establishes a labor management advisory committee charged with improving federal wage and price policies.

17 The administration plans to combat the recession by speeding up the awarding of military contracts, accelerating reclamation projects by the Interior Department, and proposing legislation to boost farm income and to control a surplus of corn and feed grains.

18 A compromise in the House Ways and Means Committee improves chances for Kennedy's proposal for 13 additional weeks of emergency unemployment compensation.

19 On the heels of a January rise in housing starts, the Federal Home Loan Bank announces a new anti-recession measure. It adds more than $1 billion to the nation's available home-building credit.

20 Kennedy asks Congress to provide $5.6 billion in federal aid for education.

21 In the face of spiraling violence in the Congo, the United Nations Security Council approves the use of force by UN troops to prevent civil war. The council rejects Soviet calls to withdraw the troops and oust UN Secretary General Dag Hammarskjold.

Jan 25 PRESIDENT DELIVERS NEWS ON LIVE TELEVISION

WASHINGTON—Children who were expecting to watch *Popeye the Sailor Man* on Wednesday evening were in for a surprise. President John Kennedy (a sailor himself!) took over the airwaves at 6 P.M. for a well-orchestrated press conference. In fact, it was the first regular presidential news conference ever televised live.

In front of four hundred people in a State Department Building auditorium, Kennedy delivered breaking news. He announced that the Soviet Union had released two surviving Air Force crewmen from an RB-47 jet that had been shot down over the Barents Sea on July 1, 1960. The new president proved adept at answering questions. He offered insightful details about the incident while carefully sidestepping questions related to foreign policy. The conference lasted for 38 minutes.

After previous presidential news conferences, newsmen had raced to the nearest phones in order to call in their stories—hoping to be the first to report on the President's announcements. There was no need for that on Wednesday. The American public had already heard it all.

Jan 27 WOULD-BE KENNEDY ASSASSIN RECEIVES SENTENCE

WASHINGTON—Richard Pavlick, who had been arrested for plotting an assassination of President-Elect John F. Kennedy in December, was sentenced to a mental hospital on Friday.

Federal Judge Emmett C. Choate ordered that Pavlick be committed to the U.S. Public Health Service's mental hospital in Springfield, Missouri, until he was deemed mentally competent to face charges for transportation of high explosives.

Pavlick, 73, hails from Gilmanton, New Hampshire, the pleasant but scandalous town that inspired novelist Grace Metalious to write *Peyton Place*. A slightly built retired postal clerk and former mental patient, Pavlick had been shadowing Kennedy with the intention of committing a murder-suicide. "The Kennedy money bought him the White House," Pavlick said. "I wanted to teach the United States the presidency is not for sale."

Pavlick planned to drape himself in explosives and blow himself up in Kennedy's presence. He went so far as to case JFK's homes in Washington; Hyannisport, Massachusetts; and Palm Beach, Florida. At each home, Pavlick said, "the security was lousy."

However, the Secret Service got its hands on a letter by Pavlick in which he boasted about his ambition. On December 15, police arrested the suspect in Palm Beach, Florida.

Jan 28 JFK BRIEFED ON VIETNAM

WASHINGTON—A week after his inauguration, President Kennedy called his first National Security Council meeting today. The situation in Vietnam was the topic of the conference, and the news was sobering.

Air Force Brigadier General Edward Lansdale, fresh from a fact-finding mission to Vietnam, briefed Kennedy on the startling increase in Vietcong guerrilla and terrorist activity in South Vietnam. According to Lansdale, the Communists are closing in on their goal of absorbing South Vietnam into their bloc.

Lansdale thoroughly endorses the U.S. Embassy in Saigon's Basic Counterinsurgency Plan for Vietnam. The plan is critical of the South Vietnamese government's response to the insurgency. Lansdale feels, and Kennedy agrees, that guerrilla tactics need to be employed against the North, both to weaken the Vietcong and to discourage North Vietnam's leaders and citizenry from cooperating with the insurgents.

A serious JFK greets officials prior to his sobering State of the Union address.

> *"The American economy is in trouble. The most resourceful industrialized country on earth ranks among the last in the rate of economic growth."* — KENNEDY

Jan 30 STATE OF THE UNION
President Addresses Congress on Economy, Cold War

WASHINGTON—In his first State of the Union address, President Kennedy struck a somber tone as he discussed the many challenges the country faces, both domestically and abroad.

"I speak today in an hour of national peril and national opportunity," Kennedy said. "Before my term has ended, we shall have to test anew whether a nation organized and governed such as ours can endure. The outcome is by no means certain. The answers are by no means clear. All of us together—this administration, this Congress, this nation—must forge those answers."

The President painted a bleak economic picture, saying: "The American economy is in trouble. The most resourceful industrialized country on earth ranks among the last in the rate of economic growth. Since last spring our economic growth rate has actually receded. Business investment is in a decline. Profits have fallen below predicted levels. Construction is off. A million unsold automobiles are in inventory. Fewer people are working—and the average workweek has shrunk well below 40 hours. Yet prices have continued to rise—so that now too many Americans have less to spend for items that cost more to buy."

Kennedy said that over the next two weeks, he would ask Congress to ensure "a prompt recovery" that would pave "the way for increased long-term growth."

Despite the nation's financial woes, Kennedy declared that the U.S. needs to bolster its military to remain strong during the Cold War. In that regard, he said, he has ordered a strengthening of U.S. missile, airlift, and Polaris submarine programs.

While escalating defense spending, Kennedy said he simultaneously wants to reach out to the Soviet Union in space and science initiatives. "On the Presidential Coat of Arms, the American eagle holds in his right talon the olive branch, while in his left he holds a bundle of arrows," he said. "We intend to give equal attention to both."

22 In a personal message to Soviet Premier Khrushchev, President Kennedy expresses hope for improved U.S.-Soviet relations.

23 The President proposes new federal measures to address water needs, flood-control, and other natural resource challenges.

24 White House employees are asked to pledge that they will not seek to profit by writing or talking about their experiences, even after retirement.

25 Kennedy names Henry Kissinger national security adviser, and prepares to name Adlai Stevenson as U.S. ambassador to the United Nations.

26 At a Civil Rights Commission conference, the President praises the "quiet intelligence and true courage" of educators in a desegregation fight in New Orleans. The Justice Department had sued for more than $350,000 in federal aid that Louisiana is withholding from the schools.

27 After an alleged Soviet spy ring is discovered in Britain, Congress cools to the idea of closer nuclear weapons cooperation with NATO allies.

28 Kennedy asks the House to raise taxes on the trucking industry to fund a $37 billion interstate highway system.

Kennedy concluded his eventful day by hosting a party for Washington higher-ups and their families.

Jan 30 WHITE HOUSE PARTY CAPS DAY OF GREAT AMBITIONS

WASHINGTON—The Kennedys entertained in the White House for the first time yesterday evening. Invited guests included members of the President's administration, Congress, and campaign staff, as well as their families.

In contrast to the more staid Eisenhower parties, which did not feature hard liquor, the Kennedys set up full bars in both the East Wing and the family's personal dining room. The President's brothers and their wives also attended. According to one of the few invited reporters, brother Ted "spent an awful lot of time at the East Wing bar."

Festivities for the evening included the swearing-in of several members of the administration—a special treat for the children in attendance, who were able to witness the important event in their fathers' lives.

The party and ceremony capped an extraordinarily eventful day for the new president. Prior to his first State of the Union address, Kennedy met with Vice President Lyndon Johnson and NASA Administrator James Webb. Although the details of the meeting were not disclosed, Kennedy's views were likely ambitious. He stated during the address: "I now invite all nations, including the Soviet Union, to join with us in developing a weather prediction program, in a new communication satellite program, and in preparation for probing the distant planets of Mars and Venus, probes which may some day unlock the deepest secrets of the universe."

Meanwhile, the President is forging ahead on civil rights issues. The Associated Press reported today that Kennedy directed the Coast Guard Academy to provide admission opportunities for qualified Negroes. During the inaugural parade, the President had noticed that all of the marching Coast Guard cadets were white.

22

Jan 31 | CHIMP SHOT INTO SPACE

CAPE CANAVERAL, FLA.—A chimpanzee went on the ride of its life today—a ride much farther than NASA had hoped.

A 37-pound male chimp named Ham was strapped into an 83-foot rocket and shot into space by a Redstone booster. The rocket was supposed to reach an altitude of 115 miles into space and then drop the capsule into the Atlantic Ocean 290 miles away. Instead, Ham shot 155 miles high and landed 130 miles past his target.

Despite traveling at 5,000 mph instead of the intended 4,200 mph, Ham survived the journey, suffering only a bruised nose. The chimp had been trained to push levers during the trip whenever certain lights went, which he accomplished. That he performed such tasks nearly as quickly in space as he did during training indicated that astronauts' reaction times likely would not suffer during space travel. The excessive force of the Redstone booster, however, is cause for concern.

The Soviet Union is currently winning the "space race." Last year, Soviet dogs Belka and Strelka orbited the earth and returned successfully.

Feb 2 | PRESIDENT STRIVES TO AID THE POOR AND ELDERLY

WASHINGTON—President Kennedy put his money where his mouth is today in his efforts to help America's poor and aged.

Agriculture Secretary Orville Freeman's task force has agreed to move forward on a new food stamp program. The needy would receive—apparently through local welfare offices—books of food stamps that have monetary value, such at 10, 25, and 50 cents. Citizens could then use these stamps to buy food. Currently, people can only receive packaged surplus food from the government, such as flour and dried milk. The new program would allow individuals to purchase a variety of foods, giving them the opportunity to improve their diets.

The Kennedy administration presented to Congress today a program for national growth that focused largely on Social Security. Through a Social Security tax increase, the President aims to improve the program's benefits in several different ways.

First, the minimum monthly benefit for a retired worker would jump from $33 to $43 a month. Also, men would have the option of receiving Social Security benefits if they retire early, as young as 62. These benefits would be less than if they retired at 65. (Currently, women can receive benefits at age 62). In addition, Kennedy recommends that insured workers begin to receive disability insurance if they have been totally disabled for six months.

1 By executive order, Kennedy establishes the Peace Corps, which is designed to temper revolutionary and anti-American ideas in developing African and Asian countries. Headed by his brother-in-law, Sargent Shriver, the program will have more than 7,300 volunteers in 44 countries within two years.

2 Pentagon officials advise the President to pursue "general strengthening of our armed forces," including some increase in support for unconventional military programs.

3 Tensions rise between Congolese leaders and UN forces amid reports of massacres of civilians. UN Secretary General Hammarskjold asks for men and money to continue a UN presence there through 1961.

4 The House Appropriations Committee rejects President Kennedy's request for a $150 million increase in foreign-assistance lending authority for the Development Loan Fund.

5 The President curtails overseas spending of U.S. dollars by military personnel in order to help ease an American balance-of-payments problem.

6 President Kennedy establishes the Committee on Equal Employment Opportunity, headed by Vice President Johnson. It is charged with stopping racial discrimination in hiring by the government and its contractors.

7 The President's Council of Economic Advisers predicts a noticeable improvement in the U.S. economy "in the next few months."

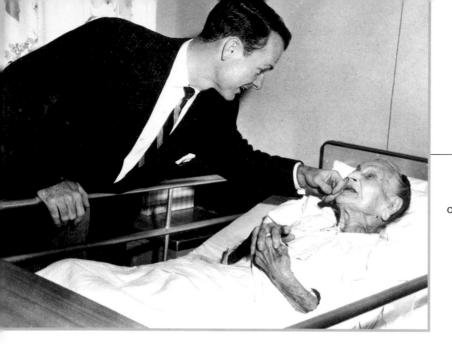

Doctor and humanitarian Thomas Dooley comforts cancer patient Carolyn Fischlein, 89, in Parma, Ohio.

Feb 9 KENNEDY PROPOSES AFFORDABLE HEALTH CARE FOR SENIOR CITIZENS

WASHINGTON—Though younger voters vaulted John Kennedy to the White House, the President today displayed his concern for the needs of America's senior citizens. In a special message to Congress, Kennedy outlined a social welfare proposal meant to provide affordable health care to citizens 65 and older.

According to the President's proposal, the government would pick up the tab for much of a senior citizen's hospital and nursing home care. In particular:

• If a senior citizen spends up to 90 days in the hospital, that patient would pay only $10 a day for the first nine days. Insurance would cover the other costs on those days and would cover all costs after that.

• Nursing home care would be provided for several months after the patient left the hospital.

• For outpatients, clinical diagnostic costs in excess of $20 would be covered.

Kennedy's plan would not cover surgical costs and other medical costs. However, the price tag for the covered services would be steep—in excess of $1 billion a year. The President proposes to pay the bill with a Social Security tax increase—.25 percent for both the employer and the employee.

The proposal will face stiff opposition in Congress. Both Everett McKinley Dirksen and Charles A. Halleck, the Republican leaders of the Senate and House, respectively, strongly voiced their displeasure with the proposed program.

Kennedy also made the following recommendations, which would be financed by general treasury revenue:

• Establishment of the National Institute of Child Health and Human Development.

• Grants for the construction of medical and dental schools.

• Federal scholarships for medical and dental students.

• Money for the construction of nursing homes.

Republicans are expected to resist these proposals, too.

Feb 15 JFK to Khrushchev: Don't Threaten the Congo

WASHINGTON—President Kennedy responded to Soviet Premier Khrushchev's threats with his own stern warning today: Stay out of the Congo.

A day earlier, in response to events in the Congo, the Soviets had demanded that Dag Hammarskjold be withdrawn as secretary general of the United Nations. More alarmingly for Kennedy, the Soviets yesterday threatened to support a rebel, pro-Communist regime in the Congo. Currently, UN troops are trying to keep the peace in the strife-ridden country.

Kennedy would not stand for the Soviets' saber rattling. He announced his staunch opposition to such threats and said it would be disastrous if the UN pulled its troops out of the Congo. Kennedy tried to rally the support of other UN members. "The United States can take care of itself," he said, "but the United Nations system exists so that every nation can have the assurance of security. Any attempt to destroy this system is a blow aimed directly at the independence and security of every nation, large and small."

That said, Kennedy also discussed the possibility of a summit with Khrushchev in the upcoming months, in which they would work on improving relations between the two superpowers. Consistent with the themes of his inaugural address, Kennedy is trying to take a hard stance against Communist aggression while avoiding exacerbating tensions between Washington and Moscow. It has been, and will continue to be, a difficult balance to maintain.

Soldiers guard the residence of pro-Western Moise Tshombe, president of the Congolese province of Katanga, whose secession was causing chaos in the Congo.

8 The national employment picture is mixed, with unemployment rising to 5.7 million in February, highest in 20 years, while total jobs reached 64.6 million, a record for the month.

9 President Kennedy proposes that Congress create a program to improve housing for middle- and low-income families and the elderly, while boosting the building industry.

10 Supported by a covert Soviet airlift of supplies, pro-Communist rebels launch a new offensive against the government in Laos.

11 The Port Authority of New York supports construction of the World Trade Center in Manhattan, an ambitious project that will become a symbol of American financial power.

12 Moving to put his own stamp on federal policy, Kennedy abolishes 17 interdepartmental advisory and policy-making committees dating from the Eisenhower years.

13 JFK invites Latin American nations to join the Alliance for Progress, a 10-year, $20 billion social and economic development program designed to encourage democratic reform.

14 Continuing the week's hemispheric theme, President Kennedy asks Congress to appropriate $5 billion in authorized funding for the Inter-American Fund for Social Progress.

15 Frederick Nolting, Jr., the Kennedy administration's new ambassador to the Republic of Vietnam, replaces outgoing envoy Elbridge Durbrow.

Feb 20 More Money Needed for Education, Kennedy Says

Washington—President Kennedy today sent an open letter to the members of Congress, detailing his plan to bolster education in America. Claiming that "our progress as a nation can be no swifter than our progress in education," Kennedy proposed both an increase in educational standards and providing the resources to make educational excellence available to all who pursue it.

Due to the postwar baby boom, the President said, America stands to gain a million students a year over each of the next 10 years. His missive calls for new, fully certified teachers as well as the money to offer them competitive salaries. Noting that inadequate space is an issue, he suggested that an additional 600,000 classrooms will be needed nationally to accommodate the influx of new students.

In addition to blanket aid for education at the elementary and secondary levels, Kennedy asked Congress for funds to support higher education, especially with regard to housing, general infrastructure, and tuition assistance for students. Finally, Kennedy wants to convene an advisory board to review and evaluate the existing National Vocational Education Acts. Kennedy characterized his commitment to education not "merely to compare our achievements with those of our adversaries," but "to educate better citizens as well as better scientists and soldiers."

Feb 22 JFK Stresses Harmony to Soviet Leader Khrushchev

Washington—A personal message from President Kennedy was delivered to Soviet Premier Nikita Khrushchev today, continuing the ongoing dialogue between the two world leaders.

Kennedy reiterated his hope, shared with the Premier, that the two superpowers might find some common ground on which to work in cooperation with each other. The President said there will be many areas in which the two leaders will not see eye to eye, and will have to agree to disagree. However, he suggested that the willingness to recognize these differences will help their negotiations.

President Kennedy expressed the hope that the continued opening of the diplomatic channels will lead to greater mutual understanding. He assured Khrushchev that "I intend to do everything I can toward developing a more harmonious relationship between our two countries."

"[Peace Corps volunteers] will be expected to work and live alongside the nationals of the country in which they are stationed—doing the same work, eating the same food, talking the same language." —KENNEDY

Kennedy shares a smile with Sargent Shriver, director of the Peace Corps.

Mar 2 ENTHUSIASM BUILDS FOR KENNEDY'S PEACE CORPS

WASHINGTON—Excitement for the Peace Corps, in which Americans will voluntarily help the needy in other nations, is gathering momentum. Nancy Gore, daughter of Senator Albert Gore (D-TN), arrived at the new corps headquarters today ready to get to work. "We're all very enthusiastic," she said.

Yesterday at his news conference, President Kennedy announced the establishment of a temporary Peace Corps. He also submitted a special message to Congress that would make the Peace Corps a permanent program. Kennedy hopes to have 500 members of the program working overseas by the end of this year.

According to Kennedy's vision of the Peace Corps, the federal government or private organizations would send skilled volunteers to other countries. The volunteers would be expected to work for no pay. The rewards would be intangible—honorable service for America and helping fellow human beings. The President said the life would not be easy. "Men and women will be expected to work and live alongside the nationals of the country in which they are stationed—doing the same work, eating the same food, talking the same language."

Prominent Americans have signed up for the Peace Corps. They include Sally Bowles, daughter of Undersecretary of State Chester Bowles, and Olympic decathlon champ Rafer Johnson.

Said Kennedy: "The initial reactions to the Peace Corps proposal are convincing proof that we have, in this country, an immense reservoir of such men and women—anxious to sacrifice their energies and time and toil to the cause of world peace and human progress."

16 Kennedy proposes that farmers, rather than lawmakers, develop farm production and marketing programs. Congress could veto but not create programs affecting the production of commodities.

17 The United States votes with the majority of the UN General Assembly in denouncing the racial policies of the South African government.

18 Secretary of State Dean Rusk and Soviet Foreign Minister Andrei Gromyko meet for lunch to exchange view on crises in Laos and the Congo. Rusk warns of the potential for wider conflict.

19 Departing from past practice of requesting foreign aid one year at a time, the White House proposes $8 billion over five years for economic assistance, to be distributed by a single federal body.

20 The U.S. Supreme Court declares unconstitutional Louisiana laws aimed at stopping school desegregation.

21 American, British, and Soviet teams gather in Geneva, Switzerland, to resume three-power nuclear test-ban talks.

22 Kennedy sends a proposal to Congress for a long-term foreign aid program. It emphasizes the importance of self-reliance by recipient nations.

23 Kennedy uses a televised news conference to warn that the United States will not tolerate a pro-Communist Laos, nor will the U.S. support negotiations before a cease-fire in that conflict.

24 The President's budget message to Congress asks for an increase of $2.3 billion for nonmilitary items in the next fiscal year.

JFK's executive order aimed to end discrimination by government contractors based on race, creed, color, and national origin.

Mar 6 JFK Demands Equal Employment Opportunities

WASHINGTON—President Kennedy took his first bold initiative in the field of civil rights today with the issuance of an executive order. Kennedy established a 12-member committee that would examine hiring and firing discrimination within the United States government as well as companies that have contracts with the federal government.

Executive Order 10925 established the President's Committee on Equal Employment Opportunity. The order declares that government contractors "will not discriminate against any employee because of race, creed, color, or national origin." The order included potential penalties, including the possible cancellation of government contracts. In addition, the order stated that all government agencies broaden employment opportunities for minorities.

Vice President Lyndon Johnson, a strong advocate of civil rights issues, was named chairman of the committee. Secretary of Labor Arthur Goldberg will serve as vice chairman. The executive order demanded that the committee submit a status report on minorities in the federal government to the President within 60 days.

"Through this vastly strengthened machinery," the President stated, "I intend to insure that Americans of all colors and beliefs will have equal access in employment within the government, and with those who do business with the government."

Kennedy, who rarely discussed civil rights issues during the campaign for fear of losing the South, now seems on the progressive path.

"We as a nation have before us the opportunity—and the responsibility—to remold our cities, to improve our patterns of community development, and to provide for the housing needs of all segments of our population." —KENNEDY

Mar 9 Kennedy Urges More Housing, Urban Renewal

WASHINGTON—President Kennedy today presented a far-reaching and ambitious housing proposal to Congress. Ideally, the plan would provide more housing for low- and middle-income citizens while revitalizing the construction industry and combating America's economic slump.

In a special message to Congress, the President proposed a 10-point program. Highlights include:

• Forty-year mortgages, with no down payment, for moderate-income families—a plan that would surely spur home buying and new construction.

• The construction of 100,000 units of public housing, half for the elderly.

• The purchase of open land for the purpose of creating parks and other facilities.

• A massive urban renewal program that would involve slum clearance and slum rehabilitation, the acquisition of land for development, and compensation to small business owners who would be displaced. Kennedy asked Congress to authorize $2.5 billion in grants and loans over a four-year period for this part of the program.

"Our communities are what we make them," the President stated in his message to Congress. "We as a nation have before us the opportunity—and the responsibility—to remold our cities, to improve our patterns of community development, and to provide for the housing needs of all segments of our population. Meeting these goals will contribute to the nation's economic recovery and its long-term economic growth."

Kennedy plans to submit a proposal to Congress for the creation of the Department of Housing and Urban Affairs. The new Cabinet-level department would oversee the program.

25 The President blames recession, mistaken Eisenhower budget estimates, and urgent defense needs for a likely $2.2 billion federal deficit in 1961 and a larger one in 1962.

26 JFK and British Premier Harold Macmillan meet for the first time. They issue a joint appeal to the Soviet Union to give "a positive and constructive" reply to peace plans for Laos.

27 The American Civil Liberties Union supports Kennedy's view that federal loans to church schools are unconstitutional.

28 Congress receives a revised White House defense budget aimed at the biggest peacetime military buildup in U.S. history. It includes rapid development of long-range missile and bomber capabilities.

29 At the request of Jackie Kennedy, Lorraine Pearce is appointed as the first-ever curator of the White House.

30 The 23rd Amendment to the Constitution gathers a decisive 38th state ratification, thanks to Kansas. Thus, residents of Washington, D.C., receive the right to vote in presidential elections.

31 Kennedy signs legislation designed to continue Eisenhower's effort to withhold sugar trading quotas and their economic benefits from Rafael Trujillo, dictatorial leader of the Dominican Republic.

TROUBLES IN LAOS

The Cold War was truly a global war, with hardly a region in the world immune to the jockeying for position between the U.S. and Soviet Union. Certain places became associated with the sparring between the two superpowers during the Kennedy years, including Cuba, Berlin, and Vietnam.

But before any of the familiar flash points dominated the news, there was Laos, a small, landlocked kingdom in Southeast Asia that was among President Kennedy's top priorities during the early months of his tenure. Laos was enmeshed in a brutal civil war among three contending parties—the Communist Pathet Lao movement, the pro-American government of King Savang Vatthana, and Laotians who wanted nothing to do with either side. The royal government received hundreds of millions of dollars in U.S. support, but a Communist victory in the civil war seemed very likely. If Laos fell, the Kennedy administration feared for the rest of Southeast Asia.

During his first few months in office, Kennedy was deeply concerned about a Communist takeover in Laos. But he was reluctant to commit ground troops to defend the king's regime, especially after the Bay of Pigs disaster. He decided, then, to support a neutral Laos, as opposed to a pro-American Laos. And he moved 10,000 Marines from Okinawa to neighboring South Vietnam and Thailand as a show of force.

A cease-fire was declared in April 1961. The following year, 14 nations, including the U.S., signed a document recognizing Laotian neutrality. But Laos continued to worry policymakers as conflict broke out nearby, in Vietnam.

A mother wounded during fighting in Laos

Mar 11 COMMUNIST FORCES ATTACK GOVERNMENT TROOPS IN LAOS

VIENTIANE, LAOS—Pro-Communist troops in Laos celebrated today after a devastating attack against the Laotian government's defenses. Assault troops of the Pathet Lao movement blasted through defenses in central Laos. The Leftists cut off highway access between the country's administrative capital and royal capital. According to a rebel radio broadcast, 300 government troops had been killed or wounded.

The Pathet Lao troops were able to mount their heavy attack thanks to Soviet trucks and Soviet-built transport planes. The rebels reportedly shot down several American-supplied airplanes. The United States supports the pro-Western government of Laotian Prime Minister Boun Oum.

Just yesterday, General Phoumi Nosavan of the Laotian regime and former premier Souvanna Phouma, a neutralist, had agreed on a peace plan to end the country's civil war. That plan is now in jeopardy. Today's attack also puts a further strain on U.S.-Soviet relations.

Mar 11   KENNEDY OFFERS "ALLIANCE FOR PROGRESS"

WASHINGTON—Fourteen years after the United States offered the Marshall Plan to European nations, President Kennedy offered a similar deal to Latin American countries. He called it an "alliance for progress."

After hosting a White House reception for Latin American diplomats last night, Kennedy today asked Congress to appropriate $500 million for their homelands. The funds would promote economic development, social progress, and political freedom. The President wants the countries to "lift the people from poverty and ignorance and despair," he said, as well as resist the temptations of communism.

In addition to the $500 million, Kennedy asked Congress for $100 million in aid for earthquake-ravaged Chile. Moreover, he stated, hundreds of millions of dollars more would be needed for Latin America in years ahead.

The President insisted that the money was not a handout. The nations will have to show evidence that they are making social progress before the U.S. gives them aid.

In Havana today, Cuban Premier Fidel Castro mocked Kennedy's gesture. The Soviet-backed dictator declared, "We'll see whether the conscience of Latin America can be bought for $500 million, as Kennedy intends, or whether, as we contend, it cannot be bought at any price."

Mar 22   PRESIDENT SERIOUS ABOUT LAOS NEUTRALITY

WASHINGTON—In a nationally televised news conference—complete with maps for all to see—President Kennedy discussed the seriousness of the political situation in Laos. Currently, the country is mired in a civil war between its present, pro-Western regime and pro-Communist Pathet Lao rebels.

Kennedy warned that the United States would not tolerate the loss of Laos to rebel forces. The President did not give an ultimatum. However, he did say that the U.S. and its allies in the Southeast Asia Treaty Organization must consider military options. Kennedy urged a prompt end to hostilities and the urgent need for negotiations.

"I want to make it clear to the American people and to all the world that all we want in Laos is peace and not war, a truly neutral government and not a Cold War pawn, a settlement at the conference table and not on the battlefield," Kennedy said.

Since early in the Eisenhower administration, Washington has been worried about the "domino effect" in Southeast Asia, in which one country after another would fall to communism.

1 After some of the worst flooding in eastern Iowa since 1929, the President declares parts of the state affected by the Cedar River to be a major disaster area.

2 The first Roman Catholic president and his family attend Easter mass in Florida.

3 An official statement from the U.S. State Department holds that Cuba is a satellite state of the Soviet Union.

4 At a foreign policy conference hosted at the State Department, Kennedy speaks to delegates and answers questions from the audience.

5 British Prime Minister Macmillan visits the White House again for talks on the deteriorating situation in Southeast Asia and other issues affecting foreign policy cooperation between the U.S. and Britain.

6 President Kennedy recommends American support for UN preservation of Egypt's Nile Valley antiquities, which are threatened by construction of the Aswan High Dam.

7 The administration prepares to announce the elimination of more than 40 government agencies as part of an executive branch reorganization. A bill awaiting the President's signature will give him the authority to make the changes.

8 Kennedy approves a bill reinstating the 1949 act that granted the President power to reorganize the executive branch. Ten days later he will submit a proposal to create a Cabinet-level department of urban affairs and housing.

9 Ngo Dinh Diem is reelected president of the Republic of Vietnam.

Mar 22 KENNEDY ASKS FOR AID FOR UNDERDEVELOPED NATIONS

WASHINGTON—In a special message to Congress today, President Kennedy proposed a development plan of global proportions. Kennedy asked for legislation that would authorize development loans to countries in Africa, Asia, Latin America, and the Middle East. Specifically, the President asked for the establishment of a foreign aid agency that would be authorized to borrow $7.3 billion from the Treasury over five years.

Kennedy wants to slightly reduce the amount of American military aid to foreign countries and substantially increase the amount of economic aid. In the first year of the program, the U.S. would give $2.4 billion in loans and grants to underdeveloped nations. Up to $900 million would be for development loans. Some $1.5 billion would go to education, institutional development, social progress programs, and emergency assistance in those countries—as well as to the Peace Corps.

Said Kennedy: "There exists, in the 1960s, an historic opportunity for a major economic assistance effort by the free industrialized nations to move more than half the people of the less-developed nations into self-sustained economic growth."

The President indicated that the massive foreign aid initiative would be good for American business, as it would open new markets all across the globe.

Mar 23 JFK TAPS WILKINSON TO HEAD NEW FITNESS PROGRAM

WASHINGTON—With television luring more and more American kids to the living room couches, President Kennedy is hoping to reverse the trend. Today he named Bud Wilkinson, the longtime successful football coach at the University of Oklahoma, as his special consultant on physical fitness. He will continue to coach the Sooners.

"Pure spectatorism is a vicarious thrill all right," Wilkinson said, "but participation is more beneficial, win or lose."

Wilkinson will work to establish a youth fitness program. He said he would ask government agencies as well as private groups, such as the Boy Scouts, for help in developing the program.

A presidential committee on youth fitness currently exists. However, Wilkinson will not be involved with that government body.

April

10 Adolf Eichmann sleeps in a Jerusalem prison cell the night before his war crimes trial begins in Israel.

11 Singer and songwriter Bob Dylan enjoys a successful debut at Folk City, the leading Greenwich Village folk club.

12 Yuri Gagarin is the first human to successfully orbit the Earth, highlighting Soviet leadership in space exploration. Meanwhile, President Kennedy pledges no U.S. intervention aimed to overthrow the Castro government in Cuba.

13 Kennedy and German Chancellor Konrad Adenauer conclude two days of meetings with a pledge to strengthen military and economic cooperation.

14 U.S.-supplied aircraft based in Florida bomb numerous military targets in Cuba, the prelude to a secret invasion campaign.

15 Cuba's foreign minister calls the aerial attacks on his country an "act of imperialism" on the part of the U.S.

16 A CIA-trained invasion force of 1,400-plus Cuban exiles sails aboard five freighters toward a planned landing on Cuba's southern coast. Unknown to them, Kennedy calls off further air strikes.

17 The Bay of Pigs invasion force encounters fierce Cuban army resistance, and all but 26 exiles are captured or killed within 72 hours. Initially, the U.S. denies involvement in the operation.

18 Soviet leader Nikita Khrushchev urges an end to U.S. "aggression" and offers assistance to Cuba. Kennedy warns the Soviets that the U.S. will not tolerate outside military intervention.

Mar 26 MACMILLAN, KENNEDY URGE TRUCE IN LAOS

KEY WEST, FLA.—President Kennedy and British Prime Minister Harold Macmillan met today for the very first time. They focused not on the United States or Britain but on a small kingdom in Southeast Asia: Laos. The two leaders are determined to end the civil war between the Royal Laotian government and the pro-Communist rebels.

In a joint statement, Kennedy and Macmillan declared that "the situation in Laos cannot be allowed to continue to deteriorate." They urged Moscow, which has supported the rebels, to accept a cease-fire proposal. "They strongly hope," their press secretaries declared, "that the Soviet Union will make a positive and constructive reply to these proposals."

Britain has proposed that a truce be arranged by the International Control Commission, which is composed of representatives from Canada, Poland, and India.

JFK and Macmillan did not discuss the use of force to solve the crisis.

The President is asking for more long-range missiles and more troops—but fewer B-70 bombers (pictured).

Mar 26 PRESIDENT CALLS FOR BIGGER, DIFFERENT DEFENSE BUDGET

WASHINGTON—President Kennedy today submitted a defense budget to Congress that stressed an increase in long-range missiles and a reduction in B-70 supersonic bombers. Overall, the President's proposed defense budget for fiscal year 1962 was $43.8 billion, nearly $2 billion more than President Dwight Eisenhower's request for 1961.

Kennedy proposed to reduce the number of B-70 bombers, whose viability has been questioned, from 12 to four by the late 1960s. Eisenhower also spoke against the B-70 program last year, but opposition from Congress forced him to yield his position. Kennedy should expect similar opposition this year.

JFK also proposed to drop the nuclear plane project. However, he called for more funds for Minuteman intercontinental ballistic missile bases and an increase in Polaris submarines (to 29 by 1964). He also requested an increase of 5,000 troops for the Army and 3,000 for the Marines.

Kennedy said he wants the United States to prepare more for "small wars" as opposed to a nuclear showdown. Despite the increase in defense spending, he emphasized that the U.S. would not be a belligerent nation.

"Our interest, as I have emphasized, lies in peaceful solutions, in reducing tension, in settling disputes at the conference table and not on the battlefield," he said.

Lorraine Waxman Pearce will help the First Lady renovate the White House with museum-quality furnishings.

19 Laos announces that its army will welcome the arrival of U.S. military advisers.

20 The Cuban government announces the defeat of the invasion force. Although he privately blames CIA leaders for the failure, Kennedy prepares to publicly accept responsibility for the disaster.

21 Glad to focus on a topic other than Cuba, the President announces the first project of the Peace Corps, a road-building project in Tanganyika.

22 After meeting with Kennedy at Camp David, Maryland, to discuss the Cuban crisis, former president Eisenhower expresses support for the President. Kennedy appoints General Maxwell Taylor to lead a probe of the CIA's role in the Bay of Pigs campaign.

23 Five weeks before his first state visit to France, Kennedy praises President Charles de Gaulle's quick actions to prevent an attempted coup by French generals in Algeria.

24 The White House issues a statement that President Kennedy accepts "sole responsibility" for the American role in the attack on Cuba.

25 The President orders defense and intelligence agencies to plan for a possible Berlin crisis, and to report on the extent of Soviet assistance to Cuba.

26 Kennedy sends a congratulatory message to the people of Sierra Leone. They are set to gain independence at midnight after more than 150 years of British rule over the African state.

Mar 29 — PEARCE WILL HELP JACKIE RENOVATE WHITE HOUSE

WASHINGTON—First Lady Jackie Kennedy today named Lorraine Waxman Pearce to the office of Curator of the White House. Pearce, a graduate of the Winterthur Program in Early American Culture, is the first person to occupy the newly created post.

Reportedly disappointed by the lack of period furnishings in the White House, the First Lady has launched a drive to restore the interior of the house in a historically relevant fashion. Last year, the Eisenhowers were given several Federal-style pieces dating to the early 19th century with which to furnish the diplomatic reception room. Jackie Kennedy is clearly keen to similarly outfit the White House in historically correct, museum-quality pieces.

With the creation of both Waxman's post and the White House Fine Arts Committee, the First Lady's ambitious White House renovation is on course to be perhaps the most extensive since the historic structure was burned by the British in 1814.

Apr 2 — KENNEDYS ENJOY EASTER SUNDAY IN PALM BEACH

PALM BEACH, FLA.—The First Family spent Easter far away from Washington today, opting to celebrate instead in their "winter White House" in Palm Beach, Florida. Purchased by the President's father, Joseph Kennedy, in 1933, the Mediterranean-style estate is a favorite family gathering spot for winter vacations and holidays.

The family attended an Easter mass at St. Edward's Church in Palm Beach. The President also conducted some business today, including a meeting with veteran news correspondents Marvin Arrowsmith and Merriman Smith. Kennedy also managed to spend some time on the links, squeezing in 14 holes of golf at the Seminole Country Club.

Yuri Gagarin's unprecedented journey gives the USSR a leg up in the "space race."

Apr 12 GAGARIN FIRST TO ORBIT THE EARTH

Moscow—Russians beamed with pride today while welcoming a Soviet cosmonaut back from space. Hours earlier, Yuri Gagarin became the first human being ever to enter outer space and the first to orbit the Earth.

Excited and seemingly in perfect health, Gagarin told reporters about his unprecedented journey, which lasted an hour and 48 minutes. "One's legs, arms weigh nothing, objects float in the cabin," he said. "While in the state of weightlessness, I ate and drank, and everything occurred just as it does here on Earth."

Since the Soviets first launched a satellite into space in 1957, American officials have been nervous about the military edge that the Soviets might gain. As then-Senator Lyndon Johnson said at the time, "Soon, [the Soviets] will be dropping bombs on us from space like kids dropping rocks onto cars from freeway overpasses."

In Washington today, President Kennedy acknowledged that the United States continues to lag behind the Soviets in the space race, adding that the "news will be worse before it is better."

Apr 12 KENNEDY INSISTS NO DIRECT FORCE WILL BE USED AGAINST CUBA

WASHINGTON—In his news conference yesterday, President Kennedy tried to put an end to rumors that the United States would invade Cuba and overthrow the government of Communist-leaning dictator Fidel Castro. "There will not under any conditions be an intervention in Cuba by the U.S. armed forces," Kennedy said.

"The basic issue in Cuba is not one between the United States and Cuba," he added. "It is between the Cubans themselves. I intend to see that we adhere to that principle."

Kennedy did not confirm or deny whether the U.S. is helping Cuban exiles stage a coup against Castro's regime. Multiple reports have indicated that such exiles are training in the southern U.S. and in Guatemala.

There is no doubt that the administration is displeased and uncomfortable with the Castro government. Since rising to power in 1959, Castro has seized about $1 billion worth of American property on the island. U.S. officials are also nervous that a Soviet-backed country sits just 90 miles from U.S. soil.

"There will not under any conditions be an intervention in Cuba by the U.S. armed forces." —KENNEDY

JFK's Ambivalence About Cuban Invasion

John Kennedy inherited a plan to support a small, armed band of Cuban exiles determined to overthrow Fidel Castro's Communist regime in Havana. CIA officials urged a skeptical JFK to act quickly, before Castro tightened his grip on the island. But other voices in the new administration, including that of special assistant and historian Arthur Schlesinger, Jr., warned him that he would lose the world's goodwill if he backed the violent overthrow of a neighboring regime.

Kennedy and his aides debated the pros and cons of the invasion through the winter of 1961. JFK clearly was ambivalent. At one point, when Schlesinger asked him what he thought of the plan, he replied, "I think about it as little as possible."

The President naturally regarded the presence of a Soviet-backed Communist regime 90 miles off the Florida coast as a security threat. Yet he was not entirely convinced that a small number of exiles would succeed in overthrowing Castro's government.

Still, there was something romantic, something admirable, about the exiles' plan. Nobody had forced them to put their lives on the line. Their sense of idealism and patriotism appealed to the man who had told Americans to ask how they could serve their country.

So, on April 15, 1961, President Kennedy gave his final approval for an invasion in the Bay of Pigs the following morning. Some 1,400 men sailed from Nicaragua to the landing beach, on the southwest coast of the island, on April 16. Castro responded with 20,000 troops supported by tanks and warplanes.

John Kennedy suddenly had a full-fledged disaster on his hands.

Cuban Premier Fidel Castro jumps from a tank as he arrives at Giron, Cuba, near the Bay of Pigs.

Apr 18 REBELS INVADE CUBA

They Battle Castro's Army; Unclear if United States Is Involved

WASHINGTON—Foes of the Castro regime invaded Cuba yesterday morning at the Bay of Cochinos (Bay of Pigs). The armed rebels, numbering in the hundreds, maybe more, landed on the southern coast before dawn. Cuban Premier Fidel Castro's military arrived, and a battle was fought yesterday in Las Villas Province. There is no word yet on the number of casualties.

The Bay of Cochinos is located on Cuba's southern coasts. Rebel spokesmen declared that invaders have also landed in the provinces of Oriente (eastern Cuba) and Pinar Del Rio (western Cuba).

The United States' role in the invasion is not yet clear. However, Castro has insisted for months that the U.S. has been arming and training rebels to invade his Communist-leaning country. Rebels have been training in Guatemala since last summer, and the Revolutionary Council was formed about three weeks ago.

The invasion was well coordinated. Yesterday's marine landing was supported by air support, and paratroopers were dropped inland. The rebels are outnumbered by an army that is believed to be 400,000 men strong. However, the Revolutionary Council hoped that the rebels would inspire a revolution among the Cuban people and spark army personnel to desert in large numbers. It does not appear that anything like that has happened yet.

Fidel Castro (above) eyes his strongest ally, Nikita Khrushchev.

Apr 18
JFK, KHRUSHCHEV, ESCALATE RHETORIC

WASHINGTON—President Kennedy and Soviet Premier Nikita Khrushchev exchanged tense missives today regarding each nation's involvement in Cuban affairs.

Khrushchev fired the first shot, warning Kennedy that the President's "little war" against Cuba will result in an "incomparable conflagration between the United States and the Soviet Union." Kennedy's response was swift and sure. He let the Soviet leader know that he has "taken careful note of your statement that the events in Cuba might affect peace in all parts of the world." He added, "I trust that this does not mean that the Soviet Government, using the situation in Cuba as a pretext, is planning to inflame other areas of the world."

While denying that the United States plans direct military intervention in Cuba, Kennedy inferred to Khrushchev that America supports efforts by Cuban rebels to overthrow the Castro regime. JFK stated that "the people of the United States do not conceal their admiration for Cuban patriots who wish to see a democratic system in an independent Cuba. The United States Government can take no action to stifle the spirit of liberty."

ROOTS OF A FIASCO

The Bay of Pigs invasion did not lack for enthusiasm on the part of the small invading force. The plan did, however, lack just about everything else. The exiles were few in number, inexperienced, and lightly armed, and they had no air support.

The invasion was supported by men Kennedy trusted, including Richard Bissell, deputy director of the CIA. Bissell and his boss, Allen Dulles, believed a small invasion could succeed because the U.S. would have no choice but to support the exiles once they were fighting Castro's troops.

Kennedy, however, insisted from the start that he wanted no direct U.S. involvement in the invasion. Aware of the political implications of the invasion, he wanted to be able to tell the world that the U.S. had nothing to do with it, that it simply was a matter of Cubans fighting Cubans. JFK approved a quick U.S. bombing raid on Cuba's small air force, but insisted on no further American action. The CIA men assumed—incorrectly—that JFK would change his mind once the battle was joined.

5 The President signs into law an increase in the minimum hourly wage from $1 to $1.15 this year and $1.25 in two years. The bill also adds 3.6 million additional workers to those already covered by minimum wage rules.

6 George McGovern, director of Kennedy's Food for Peace program, applauds the President's creation of a new council to assist McGovern and the UN Freedom from Hunger campaign.

7 Communist leader Ho Chi Minh wins reelection as president of the Democratic Republic of Vietnam (North Vietnam).

8 President and Mrs. Kennedy welcome astronaut Alan Shepard to the White House to receive NASA's Distinguished Service Medal. Half a million people cheer Shepard's ensuing parade down Pennsylvania Avenue.

9 Despite six pending civil rights bills in Congress, White House Press Secretary Pierre Salinger reports that Kennedy does not think it is "necessary at this time to pass civil rights legislation."

10 At an outdoor reception at the White House, the President tells 1,000 foreign students that in America's open society, diversity, division, and even "dissension" are a source of strength, not weakness, for the nation.

11 President Kennedy authorizes the deployment of 400 U.S. special-forces troops to Vietnam to train South Vietnamese soldiers.

12 The President and First Lady leave Washington for a two-day vacation with friends in Florida.

13 Vice President Johnson continues his tour of Vietnam, after which he recommends to JFK a "strong program of action" in that country.

Apr 19   AMERICAN "ADVISERS" WILL AID LAOTIAN SOLDIERS

VIENTIANE, LAOS—The United States is taking a diplomatic risk in Laos by sending military "advisers" to the Laotian battlefields. In making the announcement today, U.S. Embassy officials added that the U.S. is determined to support Laos against Communist rebels.

Uniformed U.S. soldiers will provide technical and tactical advice to Laotian troops. They will be part of the Military Assistance Advisory Group, which the Laotian government had requested from the United States. The U.S. made the move after the Soviet Union refused to respond to Britain's request for a cease-fire in Laos.

The Kennedy administration has been trying to show that it will not tolerate the spread of communism in Southeast Asia. Yet today's action is risky, since the U.S. does not want to provoke the dangerous superpower.

Apr 20   KENNEDY: U.S. TO STAND STRONG AGAINST COMMUNISM

WASHINGTON—Three days after the failed invasion of the Cuba, President Kennedy addressed the issue on television today. Speaking to the American Society of Newspaper Editors, the President was very careful in the words he chose.

Kennedy did not say whether or not the United States was involved in the invasion. Instead, he said that "we made it repeatedly clear that the armed forces of this country would not intervene in any way."

The President said any "unilateral American intervention, in the absence of an external attack upon ourselves or an ally, would have been contrary to our traditions and to our international obligations." But he added that "our restraint is not inexhaustible."

His following remark indicates that the United States would take military action against Communists if it felt threatened, even if the U.S. was not attacked: "Should it ever appear that the inter-American doctrine of non-interference merely conceals or excuses a policy

Kennedy said that Americans "are not complacent about Iron Curtain tanks and planes" in Cuba.

"Together we must build a hemisphere where freedom can flourish." — KENNEDY

of non-action if the nations of this hemisphere should fail to meet their commitments against outside Communist penetration, then I want it clearly understood that this government will not hesitate in meeting its primary obligations, which are to the security of our nation."

An anti-Casto rebel force of more than a thousand men landed in Cuba on April 17. Many were captured and others killed (precise numbers are not known), and some escaped to the Escambray Mountains. Castro's military subdued the threat.

Kennedy's speech focused largely on the spread of communism and his determination to stop it. Regarding communism in Cuba, he said, "American people are not complacent about Iron Curtain tanks and planes less than 90 miles from their shore."

The President used strong, but again unspecific, language when discussing the Soviet influence in the Western Hemisphere. "We and our Latin friends will have to face the fact that we cannot postpone any longer the real issue of survival of freedom in this hemisphere itself," he said. "On that issue, unlike perhaps some others, there can be no middle ground. Together we must build a hemisphere where freedom can flourish; and where any free nation under outside attack of any kind can be assured that all of our resources stand ready to respond to any request for assistance."

Apr 21 | PEACE CORPS IS UP AND RUNNING

WASHINGTON—President Kennedy's dream of a Peace Corps is coming to fruition. Today the President announced that the corps' initial project will be in Tanganyika, where volunteers will help local technicians build roads.

Meanwhile, support for the Peace Corps is sky-high. Volunteers have been applying at a rate of 1,500 a week, and other Americans are offering to donate money to the cause.

Thomas Quimby, who is in charge of recruiting for the Peace Corps, said that volunteers need to possess a serviceable skill but do not need to be college graduates. "We want surveyors, people to lay out access roads, farm roads, and drainage systems." He also said that those with farming skills will be helpful, as will teachers—especially those who can teach the English language.

Why are so many people volunteering for the Peace Corps? "I think it springs from a desire to be significant in the development of a peaceful world," Quimby said.

14 Racial violence erupts in Alabama as Ku Klux Klan-led mobs attack "Freedom Riders" in Anniston and Birmingham. A mob burns one of two buses used by the civil rights activists; several are beaten.

15 After returning from Florida, the President meets with adviser McGeorge Bundy and the Foreign Intelligence Advisory Board for an update on several political hot spots around the world.

16 Kennedy begins a two-day state visit to Canada, his first foreign trip as president. During a welcome ceremony in Ottawa, he experiences intense back pain.

17 The President tells members of Canada's parliament that "what unites us is far greater than what divides us." He urges the North American allies to support NATO and to oppose Communist influence in the hemisphere.

18 After returning from Canada, the President holds a coffee hour at the White House for members of Congress.

19 As a national rail strike looms, Kennedy uses a provision of the Railway Labor Act to impose a two-month delay on the union action.

20 More chaos erupts in Alabama as a mob in Montgomery attacks Freedom Riders (and John Seigenthaler of the U.S. Justice Department) shortly after local police abandon their security assignment outside the Freedom Riders' bus.

21 Federal marshals, among hundreds sent to quell violence in Alabama, use tear gas to disperse a white crowd that is breaking windows at a church where Martin Luther King, Jr., is speaking.

Kennedy talked with President Eisenhower at Camp David, presumably about the Cuban invasion.

Apr 22 JFK KEEPING HIS COOL IN REGARDS TO CUBA

CAMP DAVID, MD.—In the wake of the Bay of Pigs fiasco, the first significant failure of his political career, President Kennedy has kept his ego in check. Though the United States has the military means to follow the colossal failure with an emphatic victory, Kennedy is taking time to reason out the situation.

Earlier today, the President conferred with his predecessor, President Dwight Eisenhower, at Camp David. The two men talked alone for 90 minutes in the presidential cabin while lunching on fried chicken. The CIA had drawn up the invasion plan during the Eisenhower administration. The content of the luncheon conversation was not revealed.

Earlier in the day, Kennedy met with his National Security Council to discuss the Cuba situation. The President also announced that he had named retired Army general Maxwell Taylor to launch an inquiry into military intelligence and American preparation for "paramilitary" operations. Kennedy has said that he does not plan to fire anyone who was involved in the failed invasion.

Apr 24 KENNEDY ON CUBA: POINT THE FINGER AT ME

"...as president he bears sole responsibility for the events of the past few days."

—WHITE HOUSE STATEMENT

WASHINGTON—President Kennedy wants to be clear: He and no one else is the one to blame for the ill-fated invasion of Cuba.

Tonight, the White House released a statement that read: "President Kennedy has stated from the beginning that as president he bears sole responsibility for the events of the past few days. He has stated it on all occasions and he restated it now so that it will be understood by all."

A small rift between the two parties had developed recently when Secretary of the Interior Stewart Udall, a Democrat, said that the Eisenhower administration had initially planned the invasion. Republicans took umbrage. But according to the White House statement, "The President is strongly opposed to anyone within or without the administration attempting to shift the responsibility."

Taking the Blame

For days after the failed invasion of Cuba, President Kennedy was heard muttering to himself, "How could I have been so stupid?"

Nearly everything about the invasion had been botched, including America's denials of involvement at the United Nations. Cuba had accused the U.S., correctly, of attacking its warplanes two days before the invasion. U.S. Ambassador to the UN Adlai Stevenson denied the charge. He had not been told that U.S. planes had, in fact, carried out a raid.

JFK's political honeymoon was about to end, or so it seemed. Before the disaster, polls showed that more than 70 percent of Americans thought he was doing a good job. But the Bay of Pigs threatened to expose his administration as incompetent, inexperienced, and less than truthful.

JFK decided to confront the disaster head on. He called former president Eisenhower and former vice president Richard Nixon—the man he defeated in the 1960 election—to brief them and solicit their advice. The White House issued a statement in which JFK took sole responsibility for the fiasco.

On April 20, Kennedy delivered a speech to the American Society of Newspaper Editors in which he once again took full blame for the failure, but warned the Soviets that the U.S. would continue to oppose any attempts to interfere with American national security.

JFK's handling of the first crisis of his administration won him surprising public acclaim. His approval rating actually went up, to an amazing 83 percent, a week after the invasion.

May 1 — CASTRO BANS ELECTIONS IN "SOCIALIST" CUBA

HAVANA—During a large, spirited May Day rally, Cuban Premier Fidel Castro declared Cuba a Socialist state today. Moreover, in a chilling pronouncement, he declared that elections were no longer needed in his country, meaning his rule will be nothing short of a dictatorship.

"Do you need elections?" he asked the crowd. "No!" they shot back.

Castro also announced that severe restrictions will be imposed on the Catholic Church in his country.

In Washington, officials were troubled by the news. The State Department issued a statement saying that Cuba is firmly a Communist country, adding that only the Soviet Union and Czechoslovakia call themselves "Socialist republics." The statement also called attention to the termination of suffrage, saying that other Communist countries at least go through the charade of elections.

22 Kennedy announces a new Peace Corps initiative that will send 300 members to the Philippines as teaching assistants.

23 The Cabinet meets with the President for a briefing on his upcoming trip to several European capitals.

24 The President asks Americans to contribute to the non-governmental Tractors for Freedom Committee, which was established to swap farm equipment for Cuban rebels imprisoned after the Bay of Pigs failure.

25 In a message to Congress, Kennedy reveals a lofty goal: "I believe that this nation should commit itself to achieving the goal, before this decade is out, of landing a man on the moon and returning him safely to Earth."

26 The administration proposes to combine all foreign aid programs, other than the Peace Corps and Food for Peace, into one agency at the State Department. It would be called the Agency for International Development.

27 Kennedy signs a bill that contains $600 million in reconstruction and other non-military aid to Latin America.

28 The President attends mass in Hyannisport, Massachusetts, and stays overnight at the home of his father, Joseph P. Kennedy.

29 During a Boston dinner marking his birthday, Kennedy says he will travel to Vienna as "leader of the most revolutionary country on earth." There, he will meet Soviet Premier Khrushchev.

30 Kennedy asks Congress to make the Peace Corps program permanent and fund $40 million for its 1962 activities.

President Kennedy and more than 100 American mayors are thrilled with the new legislation.

May 1 NEW LAW COULD LEAD TO MORE JOBS

WASHINGTON—President Kennedy was beaming today after signing a bill that will help America's depressed urban areas. Under the new plan, more than 100 U.S. cities will be able to ask for loans and grants for the purpose of attracting industry and training unemployed workers. The legislation, which the President himself had pushed for, sets aside $394 million for the initiative.

"There's no piece of legislation which has been passed which gives me greater satisfaction to sign," said Kennedy, who used 18 pens to sign the piece of legislation. "This bill will help make it possible for thousands of Americans who want to work to work. It will be of special help to those areas which have been subjected to chronic unemployment for many months, and in some cases for many years."

William L. Batt, Jr., Pennsylvania's secretary of labor and industry, will head the new program.

Washington hopes that the new legislation will impede the rising unemployment rate, which has been approaching 7 percent—a figure not seen in the U.S. since 1958.

May 4 AMERICAN SHEPARD ENTERS SPACE

CAPE CANAVERAL, FLA.—Astronaut Alan Shepard today became the first American to leave Earth's atmosphere and enter outer space. After rocketing 115 miles above Earth, Shepard and his space capsule splashed into the Atlantic Ocean, 300 miles from the Cape Canaveral launching pad.

"Boy, what a ride!" he exclaimed.

Propelled at 9:34 A.M. by a Redstone rocket booster, the 37-year-old Navy commander reached 5,000 mph and traveled for 19 minutes. He landed safely, without any noticeable physical problems. Project Mercury officials declared that the rocket and capsule systems worked as planned. Shepard became the second person to journey into space, matching the April 12 feat of Soviet cosmonaut Yuri Gagarin.

President Kennedy, who watched the historic feat on television, called Shepard afterward. Kennedy told him that he looked forward to meeting him when he arrives in Washington, where he will receive a hero's greeting.

Had Shepard's flight not been pushed back from March 6, he'd have been the first man in space.

President Kennedy presents NASA's Distinguished Service Medal to Alan Shepard, the space program's first nationwide hero.

May 8 SHEPARD HONORED WITH MEDAL, PARADE

WASHINGTON—In a Rose Garden ceremony today, President Kennedy presented Mercury astronaut Alan Shepard with NASA's Distinguished Service Medal, in recognition of his first successful space flight three days ago.

One of the original "Mercury 7" astronauts, Shepard was selected, along with six colleagues, from an initial group of 110 of the finest test pilots and aviators in the United States Armed Forces. A naval pilot and graduate of Annapolis, Shepard became the first American in space with his successful completion of his *Friendship 7* mission on May 5. The U.S. was beaten into space by the Soviets by a matter of days, when cosmonaut Yuri Gagarin orbited the Earth on April 12.

The President called Shepard's flight an "outstanding contribution to the advancement of human knowledge of space technology, and a demonstration of man's capabilities." Kennedy acknowledged that this flight was made possible through the efforts of a great many men. He recognized several of them, including NASA officials Robert Gilruth, Walter Williams, Hugh Dryden, and (NASA head) James Webb. He added that "the other members of this team who are astronauts know that our pride in them is equal." The President remarked that "it does credit to [Shepard] that he is associated with such a distinguished group of Americans…his companions in the flight into outer space."

Still, the day belonged to Shepard. Nowhere was that more evident than along Pennsylvania Avenue, where the heroic astronaut was feted with a parade attended by perhaps a half-million cheering well-wishers.

May

31 French President Charles de Gaulle greets the Kennedys at Orly Airport in Paris. During the state visit, the two men will express solidarity in opposing any Soviet aggression in France.

June

1 Upon seeing the enthusiastic response to the First Lady's love for French language and culture, the President introduces himself at one event as the "man who accompanied Jacqueline Kennedy to Paris."

2 Kennedy and de Gaulle end three days of talks and declare their agreement on the defense of Berlin, which is expected to be a hot topic in Kennedy's upcoming talks with Khrushchev.

3 In Vienna, Kennedy and Khrushchev hold inconclusive talks on nuclear testing, Laos, and the brewing crisis in Berlin and Germany, which are still divided by the major powers.

4 The Kennedys get a warm welcome at Buckingham Palace, where they later have dinner with Queen Elizabeth II and Prince Philip.

5 British Prime Minister Macmillan and President Kennedy meet at Admiralty House and issue a joint statement on "the rights and obligations of the allied governments in Berlin."

6 The Kennedys return to Washington, where the President speaks to the nation by radio and television. The talks with Khrushchev, he says, have lessened chances of a "dangerous misjudgment on either side."

May 10 PRESIDENT WELCOMES FOREIGN STUDENTS TO WHITE HOUSE

WASHINGTON—The President and Mrs. Kennedy welcomed some 1,000 foreign students from 73 countries to a special reception on the South Lawn of the White House today. Speaking from an erected bandstand, Kennedy stated that many world leaders were educated, at least in part, in the United States.

In his brief address, the President highlighted the fact that the United States, perhaps unlike the countries many of the visiting students hailed from, is a completely free and open society. Kennedy told the students that in America "all of our strengths and all of our weaknesses are on display…and I hope that those of you who study here will come to realize that this diversity, this division, in some cases this dissension, is not a source of weakness but is a source of strength."

In closing, the President expressed the wish that the students would take what they will learn about American-style democracy back to their home countries. He added: "We want you to know that we are proud to have you here."

"I hope that those of you who study here will come to realize that this diversity, this division, in some cases this dissension, is not a source of weakness but is a source of strength." —KENNEDY, TO FOREIGN STUDENTS ABOUT THE UNITED STATES

May 15 BUSLOADS OF FREEDOM RIDERS ATTACKED IN ALABAMA

Freedom Riders gasp for breath after their bus was set on fire by an angry mob in Anniston, Alabama.

BIRMINGHAM, ALA.—"Freedom Riders" on two different buses were viciously attacked as they ventured into Alabama yesterday. As one bus approached the terminal in Anniston, it was ambushed by some 200 white segregationists, who firebombed the vehicle. The other bus was surrounded in Birmingham by a mob of whites, who beat the Freedom Riders with metal pipes.

The Congress of Racial Equality (CORE) is sponsoring the Freedom Rides, a southern journey that began on May 4 in Washington, D.C. The interracial riders have been using the restrooms and eating at the restaurants of southern bus terminals. Segregation at such facilities has been banned by the Interstate Commerce Commission and ruled unconstitutional by the U.S. Supreme Court.

Alabamans demonstrated today that they are not ready to accept integration. In Anniston, whites slashed the bus's tires and smashed its windows before someone threw a bundle of flaming rags into the bus. "Fry the goddamn niggers!" someone yelled. Members of the mob

THE FREEDOM RIDERS

On a May morning in 1961, as the Kennedy White House was dealing with the after-effects of the Bay of Pigs fiasco, the President was startled to learn that white mobs had attacked two busloads of civil rights workers in Alabama. The President and his brother, Attorney General Robert Kennedy, didn't know in advance that a civil rights group, the Congress for Racial Equality, planned to defy the South's segregated transport system by ignoring the separation of restrooms and other facilities by race.

It was the beginning of the Freedom Ride movement, a biracial effort to show that transportation facilities in the South remained segregated despite a Supreme Court decision ordering the practice to stop. President Kennedy was not pleased. He was preparing for a summit meeting with Soviet leader Khrushchev. Civil rights agitation would only distract from the business of Cold War management.

The Kennedy brothers tried to persuade the Freedom Riders to get off their buses and fight their battle another day. Robert Kennedy sent an assistant, John Seigenthaler, to plead with Alabama Governor John Patterson to crack down on the white mobs. Seigenthaler himself was beaten and left unconscious near the state capitol in Montgomery.

The President no longer had a choice. He sent in hundreds of federal marshals to protect the Freedom Riders from continued attacks, hoping the protesters would cease their agitation. They did not.

John Kennedy knew that the Freedom Riders had the law on their side. But, in the spring of 1961, he could not acknowledge that they had right on their side as well.

leaned against the door so that the passengers couldn't escape. Only when the fuel tank exploded did the whites run from the bus. Passengers escaped through the door and windows, with many in need of hospital care.

In Birmingham, about 20 Ku Klux Klansmen and segregationists attacked black and white Freedom Riders as well as journalists and bystanders. Freedom Riders James Peck and Walter Bergman were severely beaten.

President John Kennedy responded to the crisis this morning with an emergency meeting at 8:30—while still in his pajamas. The President and Attorney General Robert Kennedy have decided to put federal marshals on call. The marshals will go to Alabama if the violence escalates. Meanwhile, Alabama Governor John Patterson, a segregationist himself, refused to take Robert Kennedy's phone call. His aides said he was out fishing.

7 The administration proposes a Youth Employment Opportunities Act to give employment and training to young workers (ages 16 to 22) through public service and works projects.

8 On a day when Kennedy meets with Congolese President Fulbert Youlou on economic development plans, the White House reveals that the President is suffering from a strained back.

9 President Diem requests additional American troops for training purposes in the South Vietnamese army. Vice President Johnson says the U.S. will support Diem's government.

10 Kennedy travels to the home of friend Paul Wrightsman in Palm Beach, Florida. There, the President swims to alleviate his back pain.

11 Soviet Premier Khrushchev sends the White House a written offer to hold an immediate conference on a German peace treaty and on efforts to make West Berlin a free city.

12 Kennedy asks Congress to reorganize the Federal Home Loan Bank Board, and to replace the federal maritime board with a maritime commission reporting to Commerce.

13 Continuing his series of meetings with European leaders, the President welcomes Italian Prime Minister Amintore Fanfani for two days of talks on the defense and economic issues for the Atlantic Community.

14 Fidel Castro says he will accept 500 tractors valued at $28 million, instead of the bulldozers he had demanded, in exchange for more than 1,200 captured Cuban rebels.

Members of the press surround Freedom Riders outside a bus in Montgomery, Alabama.

May 20 — FREEDOM RIDERS BEATEN AFTER ENTERING MONTGOMERY

MONTGOMERY, ALA.—Just six days after Freedom Riders were attacked in Anniston and Birmingham, Alabama, another busload of Freedom Riders was ambushed today in the state capital of Montgomery.

Attorney General Robert Kennedy had successfully talked Greyhound officials into transporting the Freedom Riders on their latest journey. Moreover, Alabama Public Safety Director Floyd Mann promised to protect the riders from Birmingham to Montgomery. A police caravan escorted them to Montgomery, but when the bus reached the city limits, the patrol cars abandoned the bus.

When the bus pulled into the terminal, a mob of approximately 300 segregationists—some armed with clubs and metal pipes—attacked the bus. More than a dozen whites beat Jim Zwerg, a white Freedom Rider, and others severely beat Negroes John Lewis and William Barbee. John Siegenthaler, an aide to Robert Kennedy in the Justice Department, was knocked unconscious. Some bystanders also suffered serious injuries. Montgomery police eventually arrived to subdue the mayhem.

In an issued statement, President Kennedy said he has "instructed the Justice Department to take all necessary steps." He called on Alabama Governor John Patterson and state officials to exercise their lawful authority to prevent any further outbreaks of violence.

May 22 MARSHALS STRUGGLE TO PROTECT NEGROES

MONTGOMERY, ALA.—Racial violence continued in Montgomery last night despite the presence of 600 federal marshals.

Attorney General Robert Kennedy had dispatched the marshals to the Alabama capital after segregationists had attacked a busload of Freedom Riders in Montgomery on May 20. Last night, the marshals struggled to curtail the violence at the First Baptist Church.

Reverend Martin Luther King flew to Montgomery yesterday in support of the Freedom Riders. But while King spoke at First Baptist, several thousand whites surrounded the church despite the marshals' presence. The segregationists set fire to cars, injured some of the marshals, and threatened the Negroes.

To control the mob, the marshals unleashed tear gas, which wafted into the church. Coughing and teary-eyed, the Negroes feared for their lives. At around 3 o'clock in the morning, King phoned Robert Kennedy, urging immediate help. King was uncharacteristically angry, asking the attorney general if law and order existed in the United States.

Robert Kennedy then contacted Alabama Governor John Patterson, who lashed out at RFK about the federal government's intrusion in his state. Nevertheless, Patterson ordered police and the Alabama National Guard to disperse the mob.

U.S. Justice Department official John Seigenthaler wears cotton in his ear due to a beating when he tried to rescue a Freedom Rider.

15 By a 323-77 vote, the House rejects Kennedy's plan to reorganize the Federal Communications Commission.

16 Speaking while seated due to back pain, Kennedy tells the Eighth National Conference on International Economic and Social Development that foreign aid is essential to counteract Communist-backed wars of liberation worldwide.

17 The President spends the weekend recuperating from back pain at Glen Ora, a retreat in Middleburg, Virginia, that is favored by the Kennedys.

18 Admiral Hyman Rickover, sometimes called the "Father of the Nuclear Navy," complains that a plastic toy modeled on the real Polaris submarine has unwittingly given the Russians priceless intelligence about the American warship's design.

19 Kennedy signs an agreement for the administration of aid to Latin America through the Inter-American Social Progress Trust fund.

20 At a time of rising tensions in Southeast Asia, Japanese Prime Minister Hayato Ikeda and his advisers arrive in Washington for three days of talks on trade and defense issues.

21 The Senate rejects Kennedy's proposal to reorganize the Securities and Exchange Commission. However, it passes a bill designed to increase travel to the United States by foreigners.

22 Kennedy and Japanese Prime Minister Hayato Ikeda announce greater cooperation between their nations, including a Joint U.S.-Japan Committee on Trade and Economic Affairs.

Kennedy announces to Congress his goal of putting a man on the moon. His ambition appears to be a reaction to losing the race to space this spring.

"I believe that this nation should commit itself to achieving the goal, before this decade is out, of landing a man on the moon and returning him safely to Earth." —KENNEDY

May 25 JFK Shoots for the Moon
Requests Funds for Moon Landing and Other Programs

WASHINGTON—In what he termed his "second State of the Union address" of 1961, President Kennedy dropped a bombshell on the American people today. The President said he was determined to send a man to the moon.

"I believe that this nation should commit itself to achieving the goal, before this decade is out, of landing a man on the moon and returning him safely to Earth," he declared. "No single space project in this period will be more impressive to mankind, or more important in the long-range exploration of space; and none will be so difficult or expensive to accomplish."

Whether or not it can be accomplished at all, it will certainly be expensive. In his televised address to Congress, Kennedy said the new space program would cost between $7 billion and $9 billion over the next five years. The President proposed several new programs for Congress to consider. All told, they would cost $1.8 billion over the next fiscal year.

The proposals include:

• A space initiative, costing $679 million, that would include the moon project, nuclear rocket development, and weather and communications satellites

• Increased foreign economic and military aid, costing $535 million

• $130 million for the Small Business Administration

• $75 million for the retraining of unemployed workers

• More than $200 million for federal participation in the construction of civilian fallout shelters (in case of a nuclear attack)

The new programs, if passed, would up the federal budget to nearly $85 billion, creating a deficit of nearly $3.5 billion. President Eisenhower had achieved a balanced budget in three of his eight years in office.

Kennedy drew the biggest applause of the night when he discussed his upcoming meeting with Soviet Premier Khrushchev in Vienna.

"No formal agenda is planned and no negotiations will be undertaken," he said. "But we will make clear America's enduring concern is for both peace and freedom; that we are anxious to live in harmony with the Russian people; that we seek no conquests, no satellites, no riches; that we seek only the day when [quoting a Bible verse] 'nation shall not lift up sword against nation, neither shall they learn war any more.'"

A MAN ON THE MOON

John F. Kennedy's name is indelibly linked to America's space program, so it seems hard to believe that the President entered office skeptical of the nation's exploration efforts. In his inaugural address, he suggested that both sides in the twilight struggle work together to "explore the stars." But in March 1961, he eliminated funding for NASA's Apollo program, which was developing plans to put a man on the moon. His own science adviser, Jerome Wiesner, argued that it was pointless to send men into space—he thought such exploration should be done by machines alone.

Although Alan Shepard (pictured) entered space on May 4, 1961, he did not orbit the Earth—like Yuri Gagarin did weeks earlier.

Kennedy seemed inclined to agree, until, that is, the Soviet Union launched a cosmonaut named Yuri Gagarin into orbit around the Earth on April 12, 1961. The fantastic achievement made news around the world. Kennedy's competitiveness, his loathing of the Soviet system, and his nationalism combined to change his mind about American space travel. Vice President Lyndon Johnson encouraged these instincts. Johnson, a Texan who was well aware that NASA was based in his home state, told Kennedy that it was important to beat the Soviets in space exploration. Neutral nations would be watching, Johnson said, and they inevitably would judge America based on its leadership in the race to the moon.

Kennedy appreciated challenges, and he longed to get the better of the Soviet Union. So, on May 25, 1961, Kennedy told a joint session of Congress that he wished to put an American on the moon "before this decade is out."

It was an outlandish ambition. And it was realized.

23 Hours after hosting Japanese visitors during a rainy, cold outing on the Potomac aboard the presidential yacht, Kennedy develops a fever and cancels his meetings for the day.

24 Khrushchev unveils a special seven-year economic plan that he says will transform the USSR into the world's richest country.

25 Still feeling the effects of his recent virus, the President attends mass in Middleburg and swims that afternoon at Glen Ora.

26 Responding to a strike that has idled a quarter of U.S. merchant ships for 11 days, Kennedy uses the Taft-Hartley Act to order a formal inquiry into whether he should intervene.

27 The President signs a bill that authorizes nearly $900 million for Defense Department construction projects.

28 Kennedy tells the executive council of the AFL-CIO that the country has emerged from the recession.

29 The President proposes the creation of a U.S. Disarmament Agency for World Peace that would formulate disarmament and report to him and the secretary of state.

30 Kennedy signs sweeping legislation to extend Social Security to more than four million more people, allow early retirement with reduced benefits, expand urban renewal and federal housing programs, raise the national debt ceiling, and continue corporate taxes previously set to expire.

Police officers look on as Freedom Riders arrive on a Trailways bus in Jackson, Mississippi.

May 25 KENNEDY MUM AS FREEDOM RIDERS ARE SENT TO PRISON

JACKSON, MISS.—After making international news all week, the Freedom Riders may have reached their final destination today: the Mississippi state prison.

Yesterday, an interracial group of 27 Freedom Riders boarded two buses in Montgomery. Their plan was to stop in Jackson and continue to their final destination, New Orleans. Escorted by 16 highway patrol cars, containing patrolmen and National Guardsmen, the Freedom Riders arrived at the Jackson terminal. When they entered a whites-only waiting room, they were immediately arrested—even though federal law permits Negroes admission to such facilities.

Wasting no time, a judge heard the Freedom Riders' case today and sentenced them (for trespassing) to 60 days in the state penitentiary.

Despite the alarming verdict, and the barrage of news coverage surrounding the Freedom Riders in recent days, President Kennedy did not address the issue today. Instead, in this afternoon's "second State of the Union address," he focused on economic and military issues as well as his goal of putting a man on the moon.

May 29 PRESIDENT CELEBRATES BIRTHDAY

BOSTON—President John F. Kennedy celebrated his 44th birthday this evening with a dinner at the Boston Armory. Several of New England's Democratic leaders as well as Richard Cardinal Cushing, archbishop of Boston, attended the event.

President Kennedy wishes he saved room for dessert while eyeing his enormous birthday cake.

By way of explaining his pending trip to France, Kennedy entertained the gathered dignitaries with an eloquent recitation of the history of Franco-American relations. The President intends to meet with French President General Charles de Gaulle to nurture "the close relationship which must exist between France and the United States if the cause of freedom in the Atlantic community is to be preserved."

Kennedy looks forward to traveling to France "with the good wishes of all of our citizens of our country as we pay a visit to an old friend." However, his subsequent trip to Vienna will lack the same spirit of diplomatic bonhomie. In Vienna, Kennedy intends to sit down with Soviet Premier Khrushchev, with whom Kennedy has been exchanging increasingly tense communications. Relations have become strained over such issues as Cuba and the Congo. On President Kennedy's part, he intends to "go as the leader of the greatest revolutionary country on earth."

The President concluded with an expression of thanks to the crowd, which included some of his staunchest supporters. He also quoted orator William Lloyd Garrison, copping a sentiment he will carry with him on his trip overseas: "I am in earnest, I will not equivocate, I will not excuse, I will not retreat a single inch, and I will be heard."

Jun 2 JFK, DE GAULLE REACH CONSENSUS ON BERLIN

PARIS—President Kennedy and French President Charles de Gaulle concluded their summit in Paris today. The long-time allies discussed a range of issues, including Third World aid, the strength and security of the Atlantic Alliance, and their relationship with the Soviet-led Communist bloc. In addition, Kennedy and de Gaulle reaffirmed their strong and equal commitment to their respective roles in Berlin, and in doing so, also reaffirmed the strong bond between their two nations.

During an earlier press luncheon at Paris' Palais de Chaillot, Kennedy expanded on their brief joint statement. He expressed his warm regard for the President and Mrs. de Gaulle, the French people, and the kind hospitality that the French afforded the Kennedys during their visit.

Following his statement, the President took questions from the audience on several issues, including Kennedy's impending meeting with Premier Khrushchev in Vienna. Kennedy asserted: "I go to Vienna with a good deal of confidence."

1 President Kennedy intervenes personally in stalled disarmament negotiations by meeting with Valerian Zorin, chief arms negotiator for the USSR.

2 Responding to the death of Ernest Hemingway, JFK says that the author "almost single-handedly transformed the literature and the ways of thought of men and women in every country in the world."

3 After the Board of Inquiry reports on a nearly three-week-old strike by maritime workers, the White House announces an injunction against the strike under the Taft-Hartley Act.

4 A month after their first meeting in Vienna, President Kennedy and Soviet Premier Khrushchev send each other greetings on U.S. Independence Day.

5 The first in Theodore White's series of books analyzing U.S. elections is published. *The Making of the President, 1960* will win the Pulitzer Prize for nonfiction in 1962.

6 Continuing his outreach to organized labor groups, President Kennedy speaks to the Executive Board of the United Steelworkers of America at the White House.

7 Kennedy signs legislation authorizing more than $1 billion in home loans to veterans of World War II and the Korean War.

8 The President's Committee on Equal Employment secures agreement from eight leading military contractors on racial equality in their hiring and promotion actions.

Jun 2 PARIS LOVES JACKIE

PARIS—Despite her French maiden name of Bouvier, Jackie Kennedy is only one-eighth French. Yet Parisians have adopted her as one of their own during the First Couple's three-day stay in the City of Lights.

Since their arrival on Wednesday (May 31), the press and the public have fawned over Mrs. Kennedy, who has enthralled the masses with her fluent French and knowledge of French culture—as well as her sophistication and beauty. Charles de Gualle, the normally stoic French president, reportedly "melted" while conversing with Jackie during a luncheon.

The Kennedys pose with French President Charles de Gualle, who was reportedly smitten with the First Lady.

For Wednesday night's state dinner at the Palace of Versailles, Jackie wore a pink and white straw-lace gown with diamonds in her hair. Officials said that no guest of honor at the Palace had ever caused such a sensation. When some 2,000 onlookers surrounded the Kennedys during an after-dinner reception, President de Gaulle ordered that a path be cleared for the couple.

President Kennedy accepted the attention on his wife with good humor. "I am the man who accompanied Jacqueline Kennedy to Paris," he quipped, "and I have enjoyed it."

"I am the man who accompanied Jacqueline Kennedy to Paris...."
—KENNEDY, SPEAKING FACETIOUSLY

Jun 3 KENNEDY, KHRUSHCHEV BEGIN LONG-AWAITED SUMMIT IN VIENNA

VIENNA—Round one of the historic summit between U.S. President John F. Kennedy and Soviet Premier Nikita Khrushchev was uneventful today. The two men appeared cordial during their four hours of talks at the U.S. Embassy, an event covered by hordes of reporters from around the world. Yet it appeared that little if any progress was made.

Reportedly, such critical issues as Berlin and nuclear testing were not discussed. Only Laos was discussed in detail, but neither Kennedy nor Khrushchev—while talking through translators—yielded their positions.

At issue was the International Control Commission (ICC), which is trying to enforce a cease-fire in Laos between the present government and the pro-Communist rebels. The ICC is comprised of representatives from Canada, India, and Poland—the latter a Soviet bloc country. The USSR wants the ICC's decisions to be unanimous, so that Poland isn't consistently overruled.

Kennedy greeted his Cold War rival warmly at 12:45 P.M, then joked with the Premier during a late lunch. After several hours of closed-door discussions, Kennedy walked Khrushchev to his car at 6:45 P.M. Spokesmen from both nations briefed reporters afterward. The two men will resume negotiations tomorrow.

Kennedy and Khrushchev were cordial with one another, but they didn't discuss such crucial issues as Berlin and nuclear disarmament.

SPARRING WITH KHRUSHCHEV

John Kennedy flew to the Austrian capital of Vienna in early June 1961 to meet with the Soviet leader, Nikita Khrushchev, for a highly anticipated summit meeting. Hovering over the summit's agenda was increased tension concerning Western access to the divided city of Berlin. For Kennedy, continued access to the former German capital was non-negotiable. For Khrushchev, the presence of American forces in West Berlin, deep in Soviet-dominated East Germany, was both provocative and embarrassing.

Many Americans believed that their young, confident, and articulate president would have little trouble negotiating with the bulky, crude Soviet leader. But as the talks proceeded, Kennedy found himself on the defensive as Khrushchev browbeat him over the Berlin situation. The Soviet leader also pressed an argument about the inevitability of socialism, positioning Kennedy as the defender of a failed imperial system.

The two men continued to spar over geopolitical issues such as Laos, Cuba, and colonial wars in Africa and Asia, where the Soviets openly supported Communist insurgencies. Khrushchev continued to assail Kennedy, prompting weak responses from the President. Khrushchev told his advisers that while he liked the American leader, he thought he was weak and inexperienced.

The two-day conference ended worse than it began. As they said goodbye, JFK reasserted America's interest in access to West Berlin. Khrushchev made it clear that he could not tolerate the status quo. Then, Kennedy said, there will be war. "It will be a cold winter," he warned.

After his return to Washington, Kennedy advised Americans to begin building bomb shelters.

9 Khrushchev suspends previously announced reductions in Soviet defense, saying he is compelled by American actions to boost the USSR's defense budget by $3.5 billion. Soviet troops will remain in East Germany, he says.

10 On the same day the Soviet military displays new supersonic bombers in Moscow, President Kennedy calls the pending U.S. mutual security legislation the year's "most vital piece of legislation in the national interest."

10 Pakistan President Mohammad Ayub Khan begins a three-day visit to Washington by attending a state dinner at Mount Vernon, hosted by President and Mrs. Kennedy.

12 Kennedy speaks to leaders of the National Association for the Advancement of Colored People, who urge him to issue a "clear call" for civil rights legislation.

13 The White House sends Congress proposed legislation to authorize greater federal and state coordination on managing rivers and other water systems around the country.

14 In his encyclical *Mater et magistra,* Pope John XXIII condemns materialism and calls on prosperous nations to give more aid to underdeveloped ones.

15 British and American delegations ask the UN for urgent consideration of Soviet opposition to a nuclear test-ban treaty.

16 U.S. negotiators insist they are willing to continue talks with the Soviets on nuclear testing, but they reject Moscow's demand for a joint test-ban directorate comprised of Soviet, Western, and "neutral" parties.

The Kennedys dined at Buckingham Palace on June 5 with Queen Elizabeth and her husband, Prince Philip (both pictured).

Jun 4 PRESIDENT, FIRST LADY VISIT ENGLAND

LONDON—The President and Mrs. Kennedy arrived today in London, where they were greeted at the airport by Prime Minister Harold Macmillan. In his brief remarks on the tarmac, Kennedy noted that two of his sisters are married to Englishmen, and that one of the highlights of his visit will be "to become the godfather of a new English citizen." The President was referring to the young niece of the First Lady, whose baptism is to be celebrated tomorrow.

In addition to family obligations, President Kennedy is looking forward to discussions with Prime Minister Macmillan about the Soviet Union and its intentions in Berlin and Laos, as well as the ongoing concern of nuclear testing and disarmament. The President and Mrs. Kennedy are expected to conclude their visit tomorrow evening with a private dinner at Buckingham Palace. Queen Elizabeth II and Prince Philip will be their hosts.

Jun 7 KENNEDYS RETURN TO STATES AFTER EVENTFUL EUROPEAN TRIP

WASHINGTON—President and Mrs. Kennedy returned to Washington yesterday after a successful trip to Europe. The President enjoyed convivial meetings with French President Charles de Gaulle in Paris and British Prime Minister Harold Macmillan in London. He also met with Soviet Premier Khrushchev in Vienna, holding a four-hour conversation on the first day of their two-day summit that Kennedy described as "sober and intensive." They followed up their private meeting with a state dinner at the majestic Schonbrunn Palace, during which Khrushchev, when asked if he would consent to a photo shaking Kennedy's hand, gestured toward the First Lady, saying, "I'd like to shake her hand first."

The next day, the two world leaders met again, reaching some accord on Laotian independence but disagreeing sharply on the Berlin issue and nuclear disarmament. Still, their talks were heralded by Moscow radio as "a good beginning."

Yesterday evening, Kennedy addressed the American people on radio and television, from the Oval Office. He described his meeting with Khrushchev as a "full and frank exchange of views…a very sober two days." According to the President, "there was no discourtesy," but also, apparently, "no advantage or concession was either gained or given…no spectacular progress was either achieved or pretended."

Still, the President found great value in his time spent with the Soviet leader, and getting to know his personality and policies one-on-one. Kennedy discovered that the two leaders have "wholly different views of right and wrong…of what is aggression…of where the world is and where it is going. Our views contrasted sharply, but at least we knew better at the end where we both stood."

Jun 8 JACK'S BACK FLARES UP AGAIN

WASHINGTON—The White House disclosed today that President Kennedy is suffering from a bad back—an ailment of significant concern considering the serious back problems he endured in the 1940s and '50s.

Kennedy strained his back on May 16 during a tree-planting ceremony in Ottawa. He felt immediate pain while digging a hole with a silver-plated shovel. The White House had concealed the ailment until this afternoon.

Today, Kennedy left for a three-day respite in Palm Beach, Florida, where he was expected to swim in a heated pool and relax his back. Reporters noticed that the President was limping as he boarded his plane.

Kennedy suffered a ruptured disk as a football player at Harvard, and he underwent back surgery months after the Japanese destroyed his PT boat in 1943. Following another back surgery in 1954, Kennedy almost died from an infection. A successful surgery followed in 1955.

Despite wearing a surgical corset, Kennedy seemingly has been fine over the last six years. Dr. Janet Travell has treated his recent injury with hot pads and shots of novocaine, a pain-relieving drug.

Doctors are taking extra care in treating Kennedy's back due to the serious injuries he suffered as a young man.

July

17 A proposed network of communication satellites should be privately owned, not government-owned, according to the U.S. National Space Council. Vice President Johnson heads the council.

18 Kennedy asks Congress to authorize new public research on maternal and child health issues through the creation of a National Institute of Child Health and Human Development.

19 Five years after the creation of the President's Council on Youth Fitness, JFK urges more emphasis in American schools on "all programs that contribute to the physical fitness of our youth."

20 Reflecting increased public concern over the Soviet threat, the President orders the Defense Department to create a national fallout shelter program.

21 President Kennedy joins millions watching on television as astronaut Gus Grissom completes the second U.S. suborbital space flight. Grissom is recovered but his Mercury capsule sinks.

22 Canadian Prime Minister John Diefenbaker and President Kennedy speak via a new defense communication system. The system is designed to coordinate North American efforts to detect Soviet missile activity.

23 A state-run Soviet news service compares recently launched U.S. weather and missile-detection satellites to U-2 spy planes, saying, "a spy is a spy, no matter what height it flies."

WASHINGTON TO HELP SOUTH VIETNAM FEND OFF COMMUNISTS

Jun 9

WASHINGTON—The Kennedy administration is determined to prevent countries in Southeast Asia from falling to communism. Today, Vice President Lyndon Johnson discussed plans to aid South Vietnam, which is being threatened by Communist forces from North Vietnam.

Speaking with reporters today, Johnson said a special task force has been established within the U.S. government to address South Vietnam's problems and recommend ways that the United States can help. The U.S., he said, will be sending health experts to South Vietnam to deal with sanitation and public health issues. Johnson added that South Vietnam is currently trying to expand its army.

On June 16, a U.S. economics team plans to head to Saigon to determine what South Vietnam needs to maintain its independence. Johnson said the U.S. will take the needed steps "to maintain the freedom of the nations that have not fallen under the Communist yoke."

Though ailing, Kennedy met with his advisers on West Berlin and conferred with Japanese Prime Minister Hayato Ikeda (pictured).

JFK AILING, BUT BUSINESS GOES ON

Jun 23

WASHINGTON—President Kennedy got through an eventful day today despite suffering from fever and a bad back.

Kennedy did seem better today after his temperature had spiked at 101.6 yesterday. He also walked without the crutches he had been using to alleviate his back strain. Today the President concluded his third and final day of high-level talks with Japanese Prime Minister Hayato Ikeda.

Kennedy received some good news yesterday, as the House voted to pass his multibillion-dollar plan for housing and urban improvements. Only one of the President's major proposals was shot down: The House did not approve FHA insurance of 40-year, no-down payment loans on homes costing $15,000 or less.

Meanwhile, Cuban Premier Fidel Castro today rejected the United States' offer of 500 bulldozers in exchange for some 1,200 captured rebels. The Tractors for Freedom Committee, headed by Eleanor Roosevelt, has been negotiating with the Cuban government for a month. The fate of the rebels remains up in the air.

The new legislation aims to help everyone from school children to senior citizens, and give a jolt to the economy.

A BETTER AMERICA

Jun 30
President Signs Multiple Bills Designed to Improve Americans' Quality of Life

WASHINGTON—President Kennedy signed an omnibus bill today intended to provide affordable housing, resurrect cities, and beautify the nation. The President signed several bills in all today before he left with his family for Cape Cod to enjoy the Fourth of July holiday.

The omnibus bill covered nearly of all of the housing and urban renewal programs that the President had requested earlier this year. Congress added other provisions.

Highlights of the bill include:
- $2 billion in grants to cities for slum rehabilitation, redevelopment, and land purchase
- $450 million in loans to cities to improve infrastructure, such as sewers and waterworks
- $50 million in loans to cities to improve their bus, rail, and subway facilities and equipment
- $50 million in grants to states and local authorities to acquire vacant land for conservation, recreation, and other purposes
- $1.2 billion in loans for the construction of college dormitories
- $200 million in loans for housing in rural areas
- $75 million in loans to public agencies to build housing for senior citizens
- Authorization for 40-year rental subsidies of low-rent public housing
- Federally insured 35-year mortgages for buyers of homes that are $15,000 or less

The President signed into law several other bills today, including a bill that will liberalize Social Security benefits for 4.4 million Americans and allow men to retire at age 62. Even children were not forgotten: Kennedy signed into law a bill to authorize $105 million for the nation's school milk program.

24 The White House releases a presidential statement on satellite research and development. Kennedy invites "all nations to participate in a communication satellite system in the interest of world peace and closer brotherhood among peoples throughout the world."

25 In a nationally televised speech on the Berlin crisis, the President asks Congress to provide more than 200,000 troops to respond to Soviet threats around the world.

26 Six months after launching a government ethics review, the administration announces a new code of conduct for federal employees that bans disclosure of "official information."

27 Congressional leaders from both parties support the President's call for increased defense spending in the face of growing international tension over Berlin. The administration will increase its draft target for August from 8,000 to 13,000 conscripts.

28 The Kennedys travel home to Massachusetts to celebrate Jackie's 32nd birthday.

29 Tensions rise in Tunisia after UN Secretary General Dag Hammarskjold tells the Security Council that he witnessed French soldiers violating Tunisian sovereignty and a UN-backed cease-fire.

30 The Soviet newspaper *Pravda* carries Khrushchev's vision for Soviet communism. Highlights of the report include a prediction of capitalist downfall, a determination to avoid nuclear war, and the belief that peaceful coexistence with the West is "an objective necessity."

Jul 4 JFK, Soviets Share July 4 Greetings

HYANNISPORT, MASS.—The Kennedy administration has released the contents of an exchange of messages between President Kennedy and the Soviet Union's top leaders—Premier Nikita Khrushchev and Supreme Soviet President Leonid Brezhnev.

In a message dated July 3, the Soviet leaders expressed their congratulations to the President and the American people on the 185th anniversary of American independence. Further, they expressed hope that Kennedy and Khrushchev's meeting in Vienna will help the two nations work together to build "bridges of trust, of mutual understanding, and of friendship," and to promote global peace.

In response, Kennedy thanked the Soviets for their good wishes and remarked that the United States remains committed to the revolutionary principles of personal liberty that birthed this nation. He agreed that the Soviet Union and the United States share a special responsibility for global peace in this age, and he assured the people of the Soviet Union of "our desire to live in friendship and peace with them."

Jul 12 Kennedy Meets with NAACP Leaders

WASHINGTON—President Kennedy met with Negro leaders affiliated with the National Association for the Advancement of Colored People (NAACP) in his White House study today. The civil rights leaders are unhappy with Kennedy's lack of action in promoting civil rights legislation before the current Congress. They let the President know how they felt, citing "a lack of White House support" as well as the "absence of a clear call" from Kennedy.

The President was allegedly unable to offer any assurances or other words likely to satisfy the 60-member NAACP contingent, which was headed by Washington bishop and Chairman of the Board Stephen G. Spottswood and Executive Secretary Roy Wilkins. The group wants legislation that grants permanent status for the Civil Rights Commission, fair employment practices, and school desegregation assistance.

According to White House Press Secretary Pierre Salinger, President Kennedy believes that existing civil rights legislation, if properly enforced, should be sufficient.

Despite this cordial greeting, NAACP leaders are dissatisfied with President Kennedy's perceived foot-dragging on civil rights issues.

WHAT HE LEARNED ON CAPITOL HILL

John Kennedy spent 14 years on Capitol Hill before becoming president, which was 14 more years than Dwight Eisenhower spent in politics before becoming commander-in-chief. Ironically, though, one of the biggest obstacles Kennedy faced as a candidate in 1960 was his perceived inexperience. His opponent that year, Richard Nixon, had served eight years as vice president, a heartbeat away from the presidency at a time when the health of an aging president was a serious concern.

Kennedy's record on Capitol Hill was not particularly distinguished. Unlike contemporaries such as Lyndon Johnson and Hubert Humphrey, Kennedy was neither a leader nor a noteworthy legislator. His name was not attached to a landmark law. Liberals and elder statesmen, people such as Eleanor Roosevelt and Harry Truman, thought he lacked character and courage when he refused to condemn disgraced senator Joseph McCarthy of Wisconsin, a onetime family friend.

But JFK was not without accomplishment. In the late 1950s, he led a campaign to rid organized labor of corruption, which angered union leaders. As a member of the Senate Foreign Relations Committee beginning in 1957, he addressed numerous crises around the world with his speeches and well-received articles. He called on Americans to assist emerging nations to achieve independence from colonial rule and obtain economic freedom. This was a far-sighted proposal at a time when U.S. foreign policy focused almost exclusively on the Cold War with the Soviet Union.

John Kennedy's years on Capitol Hill taught him how Washington worked. That knowledge gave him the confidence to envision a bold, energetic presidency.

Jul 18 | JFK URGES CREATION OF CHILD HEALTH INSTITUTE

WASHINGTON—In a pair of letters directed to Vice President Lyndon Johnson and Speaker of the House Sam Rayburn, President Kennedy has asked Congress to fast-track a bill authorizing the surgeon general to create a National Institute of Child Health and Human Development within the Public Health Service.

Citing the success of the seven existing institutes within the Public Health Service, Kennedy expressed his hope that the same attention, research, and resources can be brought to bear for health issues that relate specifically to children.

According to Kennedy, "the proposed legislation will enable the Children's Bureau to carry out more effectively its responsibilities pertaining to the welfare of children."

July

31 The House overwhelmingly approves the President's request to activate a quarter-million Army reservists and extend the length of active duty training.

August

1 The President signs the newly granted call-up authority, although disarmament adviser John J. McCloy reports that Khrushchev insisted in recent talks that he did not want war over Berlin.

2 Despite some disagreement regarding tactics with National Chinese Premier Chen Cheng, JFK restates American opposition to the seating of Communist China at the United Nations.

3 Although he disagrees with Congress over how many long-range bombers the U.S. should build, the President signs a bill authorizing nearly $1 billion in equipment designed to improve non-nuclear defense capabilities.

4 Kennedy commends FBI and immigration service agents who the previous day foiled an attempt by two men to fly a hijacked Continental Airlines jet to Havana.

5 In a message to the Inter-American Economic and Social Conference in Uruguay, Kennedy pledges $1 billion "to meet the human and material problems" of the Americas.

6 U.S. and South Vietnamese leaders agree on a security strategy designed to create a "self-sustaining economy and a free and peaceful society in Vietnam." The following week, American special forces teams will be in southern Laos, interdicting the flow of supplies from North Vietnam.

Jul 19 JFK: Kids Need to Get Fit

WASHINGTON—Concerned that America's youth are not getting the proper exercise, President Kennedy today called for better fitness programs in the nation's schools.

"To members of school boards, school administrators, teachers, the pupils themselves, and their parents, I am directing this urgent call to strengthen all programs which contribute to the physical fitness of our youth," Kennedy said at a news conference. "I strongly urge each school in the United States to adopt the three specific recommendations of our National Council on Youth Fitness."

The council's first recommendation, Kennedy said, is to identify "physically underdeveloped" pupils and work with them to improve their physical capacity. Secondly, he wants schools to allot "a minimum of 15 minutes of vigorous activity every day" for all students. And thirdly, he called for "valid fitness tests" to determine students' physical abilities and to evaluate their progress.

"The vigor of our country," Kennedy said, "its physical vigor and energy, is going to be no more advanced, no more substantial, than the vitality and will of our countrymen."

Jul 20 JFK Signs Clean-Water Bill

WASHINGTON—Under the new administration, the federal government is doubly serious about purifying America's water. At least that seems to be the intention, as today President Kennedy signed a bill that would allocate more than twice as much federal money for water purification projects.

The legislation calls for the allocation of $570 million in grants over the next four years for the construction of sewage-treatment plants. Just $262 million had been allocated over the previous four years.

If state and local governments want to clean their streams and lakes for better fishing, drinking water, and/or recreational reasons, the federal government will help out more than ever. The U.S. government will give $3 for every $7 that state and local governments spend for such water-pollution projects. The limit on federal grants to each community will be raised from $250,000 to $600,000.

Kennedy has expressed a commitment to environmental projects. In March, he declared: "It is our task in our time and in our generation to hand down undiminished to those who come after us, as was handed down to us by those who went before, the natural wealth and beauty which is ours."

The President signs a bill to raise funds for sewage-treatment plants and cleaner lakes and streams.

Jul 20 PRESIDENT CALLS FOR FALLOUT SHELTER PLAN

WASHINGTON—Recognizing the very real possibility of a nuclear attack on the United States, President Kennedy today charged the secretary of defense with the responsibility of fast-tracking a national fallout shelter plan.

In addition to the shelters themselves, the program is required to include a communications system to alert authorities and civilians about an impeding chemical, biological, or radiological attack on the United States as well as emergency assistance to help state and local authorities deal with the aftermath of such an attack. In addition, a contingency plan to provide for continuity of government is to be devised.

This executive order is to take effect on the first of August.

THE NEW FRONTIER

Before 1960, only three Democrats had won the presidency in the 20th century, and each had something in common. Woodrow Wilson, Franklin Roosevelt, and Harry Truman had what we would call today a "brand name" for their programs. Wilson called his the New Freedom. Roosevelt implemented what he called a New Deal, and Truman built on FDR's achievements with his Fair Deal.

John Kennedy followed this branding tradition, summoning Americans to follow him on a journey to what he called the New Frontier. He coined the phrase during his acceptance speech at the 1960 Democratic National Convention, when he invoked the settling of the American West. Now, he said, Americans confronted a new frontier, "the frontier of the

1960s—a frontier of unknown opportunities and perils, a frontier of unfulfilled hopes and threats."

Kennedy's New Frontier was not a list of specific programs. Rather, it was a summons to renewed national greatness, a challenge to explore "the uncharted areas of science and space...unanswered questions of peace and war."

Although the space program would lead to exploration of a truly new frontier, Kennedy entered office skeptical of manned space missions. He very briefly considered abolition of NASA in his first budget, but he changed his mind when the Soviet Union sent a cosmonaut into orbit in April 1961. A month later, Kennedy challenged the nation to put a man on the moon by 1969.

7 By signing the Cape Cod National Seashore Act, JFK creates the first national seashore park and makes the first major addition to the National Park System in 16 years.

8 U.S. officials analyze the previous day's televised address by Khrushchev in which he emphasized his intent to conclude a treaty with East Germany, with or without the West.

9 The President appoints James B. Parsons a U.S. justice of the Northern District of Illinois. Parsons thus becomes the first black American to hold a seat on a federal district bench in the continental United States.

10 One week after the foiled El Paso hijacking, Kennedy confirms reports that armed border police are being used as air marshals on some commercial flights.

11 The President signs new legislation capping at $100 the total value of duty-free goods that Americans can bring into the country from abroad.

12 The crisis deepens in Berlin as the East German government approves "measures" to check the flight of refugees. Approximately three million have escaped to the West since 1949.

13 With Soviet assistance, East Germany seals its border and begins construction of the Berlin Wall. Roads and commuter lines are blocked, and guard posts are established at the Brandenburg Gate and other key crossing points. Concerned about Allied unity, President Kennedy opts not to directly challenge the action.

Jul 25 KENNEDY RESPONDS TO THE LATEST SOVIET THREAT

WASHINGTON—Troubled by recent rancor in Moscow, President Kennedy wants to bolster the U.S. military. He expressed his concerns and proposals this evening during a nationally televised speech.

"Seven weeks ago tonight I returned from Europe to report on my meeting with Premier Khrushchev and the others," Kennedy said. "His grim warnings about the future of the world…his threats which he and his agents have launched, and the increase in the Soviet military budget that he has announced, have all prompted a series of decisions by the administration and a series of consultations with the members of the NATO organization. In Berlin, as you recall, he intends to bring to an end, through a stroke of the pen, first our legal rights to be in West Berlin and secondly our ability to make good on our commitment to the two million free people of that city. That we cannot permit."

To deal with the Soviet threat, Kennedy proposed that the U.S. military add 217,000 men, including 125,000 for the Army, 63,000 for the Air Force, and 29,000 for the Navy. He also requested that $1.8 million be earmarked for new weapons, equipment, and ammunition. Kennedy said that although the budget deficit for this year would exceed $5 billion, he does not intend to raise taxes at this time.

The President said that if the Soviets "have proposals—not demands—we shall hear them. If they seek genuine understanding—not concessions of our rights—we shall meet with them. We have previously indicated our readiness to remove any actual irritants in West Berlin, but the freedom of that city is not negotiable."

To underscore the seriousness of the situation, Kennedy closed his speech with a spiritual appeal. "In meeting my responsibilities in these coming months as president," he said, "I need your goodwill and your support—and above all, your prayers."

"We have previously indicated our readiness to remove any actual irritants in West Berlin, but the freedom of that city is not negotiable." —KENNEDY

Jul 29 — JACKIE TURNS 32, CELEBRATES WITH FAMILY

HYANNISPORT, MASS.—President Kennedy arrived in Hyannisport last night to celebrate Mrs. Kennedy's birthday with family and friends. After arriving at approximately 6:15, the President took three-year-old Caroline out to a local store for a lollipop and a Tootsie Roll.

Birthday festivities included a cruise aboard *The Marlin*, the 52-foot motor yacht that the Kennedy family has owned for the past decade.

Mrs. Kennedy, who celebrated her 32nd birthday on the 28th, is one of the youngest first ladies in U.S. history. However, she is considerably older than Frances Folsom, who was 21 when she married sitting president Grover Cleveland in 1886.

Aug 7 — PRESIDENT SIGNS BILL TO PRESERVE CAPE COD

WASHINGTON—When the Kennedys venture to their home on Cape Cod, they can be guaranteed of natural beauty. Today, President Kennedy signed a bill today creating the Cape Cod National Seashore. More than 26,000 acres of land and freshwater ponds will be preserved, he said, "for the inspiration and enjoyment of people all over the United States."

Millions of East Coast citizens live within a short drive of Cape Cod, Massachusetts, a beach-lined peninsula and tourist haven. In recent years, new construction and commercialism has threatened the beauty of Cape Cod. The new legislation will put restrictions on further development. This is the first national seashore created since Cape Hatteras National Park in 1937.

Proving himself an environmentalist, the President signed the Cape Cod bill less than three weeks after signing the clean-water bill.

14 To discourage unrest, the Soviets position two armored divisions around Berlin and conduct maneuvers with other divisions across East Germany. Meanwhile, President Kennedy writes to Sir Winston Churchill on the 20th anniversary of the Atlantic Charter.

15 Allied governments formally protest Soviet action in Germany, calling it the "most flagrant violation" of the four-power agreement since the Berlin blockade in 1948.

16 West Berlin Mayor Willy Brandt tells a large crowd that he has written to President Kennedy demanding political action, "not merely words." Elsewhere, West German Chancellor Adenauer and Khrushchev express agreement on avoiding any worsening of the crisis.

17 Kennedy signs a defense bill appropriating more than $46 billion for fiscal year 1962, including most of what he had requested during his July speech on the Berlin crisis.

18 The administration sends symbolic and armed responses to West Berlin. Vice President Johnson flies to the city, and 1,500 additional U.S. troops enter Berlin by convoy.

19 Despite attention on the worsening situation in West Berlin, including panic food buying, there are reminders of other hot spots: Africans launch a general strike in Rhodesia and French forces in Tunisia battle rioters with fire hoses.

20 Reflecting concern over proposed British membership in the European Common Market, Kennedy orders his economic and diplomatic advisers to conduct an extensive study of the potential impact.

The new bill states that the U.S. government will buy surplus wheat and grain, allowing farmers' income to rise.

Aug 8 WASHINGTON TO HELP AMERICAN "FAH-MAHS"

WASHINGTON—During the 1960 presidential campaign, John Kennedy—with his New England accent—asked a group of farmers in Sioux City, Iowa, "What's wrong with the American fah-mah today?" From the balcony, a man yelled, "He's *stah*-ving!" Today, Kennedy signed a bill designed to help the nation's farmers.

The new legislation, which the President had urged Congress to pass, will trim surpluses of farm products, which will help farmers financially. Midwestern farmers have been hurt by the nation's overproduction of wheat and grain, which has led to low prices and, hence, low income for the farmers. With the new legislation, the government will acquire large amounts of the surplus wheat and grain and sell and donate it to other countries.

The new bill includes other provisions to help America's agricultural workers. For instance, the Department of Agriculture will have greater authority to give loans to struggling small farmers and to those farmers distressed by natural disasters.

Aug 9 KENNEDY PICKS PARSONS IN LANDMARK JUDICIAL APPOINTMENT

WASHINGTON—President Kennedy today named James B. Parsons to a lifetime appointment as a federal district judge. Parsons thus becomes the first Negro jurist to be offered the post with life tenure.

Born in Missouri and raised in Decatur, Illinois, Parsons was a 1934 graduate of Millikin University who earned his law degree from the University of Chicago in 1949. Professionally, he has been a professor of music, political science, and constitutional law; served as an assistant U.S. district attorney; and sat on the bench of the Cook County Superior Court. He is also a war veteran, having served in the U.S. Navy from 1942 to 1945.

While at his summer home in Lakeside, Michigan, Parsons was notified of his historic appointment with an early-morning phone call from President Kennedy.

West Berliners fume over the construction of the border fence, which eventually will become a wall.

21 Two days after promising Berliners that the U.S. will never forget its obligations to them, Vice President Johnson reports to President Kennedy. Defense officials are preparing contingency plans in case of a full Soviet blockade.

22 The President and First Lady host a symphony concert for disabled children on the South Lawn of the White House.

23 Just seven months after the Kennedys moved in, a tourist from Georgia becomes the one millionth visitor to the White House in 1961. It is the first time that a million visitors have toured the site in any year.

24 A day after 1,000 troops and 10 U.S. tanks were deployed along the East Berlin border, the President warns that the Soviets will bear responsibility for any interference with access to West Berlin. The East Germans had warned that "all persons" stay at least 110 yards away from the border.

25 According to Secretary of Defense Robert McNamara, 76,500 reservists must report for active duty within two months.

26 While vacationing on Cape Cod, Kennedy monitors Allied efforts to gain greater involvement from France. A French spokesman promises Western unity against Soviet threats to block air access to Berlin.

27 Even as Western powers demand the reopening of Berlin's border, East German leaders further restrict the movement of citizens. Some face forced relocation to other parts of East Germany.

Aug 13 BERLIN DIVIDED
East Germany Will Build Wall to Separate Beleaguered City

WEST BERLIN—Berlin is officially a city divided. East Germany today sealed its frontiers and began construction of a wall that will bisect Berlin and serve as a border between East and West Germany. Commuter traffic between the two halves of the city has also ceased, and guard posts have been established to prevent residents from crossing from one side of Berlin to the other.

Yesterday at 4:00 P.M., East German leader Walter Ulbricht signed the fateful orders. The wall is the unfortunate result of the steady deterioration of diplomatic relations between the Soviet Union and the West since the end of World War II. The Potsdam Agreement divided defeated Nazi Germany, and its capital Berlin, into four occupation zones. These zones are controlled individually by the British, French, Americans, and Soviets. Postwar tensions have led to the unification of the western-controlled zones into the capitalist Federal Republic of Germany, while the isolated Soviet zone formed the Communist German Democratic Republic.

When the clear success of the West German style of government began to starkly contrast with the authoritarian East German rule, the population of the Eastern bloc began to defect in droves. In the first half of the 1950s, some one million East Germans fled to the West. Unable to retain its citizens, the failing Communist society is determined to do so by force.

West Berlin Mayor Willy Brandt, who met the President at the White House on March 13 (pictured), desperately needs America's support.

Aug 16
BERLIN'S MAYOR URGES U.S. TO TAKE ACTION

WEST BERLIN—West Berliners are seething over the Communists' recent border closing with East Berlin, and West Berlin Mayor Willy Brandt urged President Kennedy to step forward. Brandt sent Kennedy a letter today, stating, "Berlin expects not merely words but political action."

Also today, Brandt addressed a crowd of a quarter-million West Berliners. The city's residents believe the Soviet Union is encroaching too much on their freedoms and that the Western governments—including West Germany and the United States—are letting the Soviets get away with it.

Brandt compared the West's alleged appeasement with Britain's cave-in to Adolf Hitler in 1938, when the German dictator demanded control of the Rhineland and got what we wanted. Emboldened, he made further encroachments in Europe. Brandt said that the West cannot allow the Soviets to follow that pattern.

"Woe to us if through indifference or moral weakness we do not pass this test," Brandt declared. "Then the Communists will not stop at the Brandenburg Gate. They will not stop at the zonal border. They will not stop on the Rhine."

The United States did take some action today. General Bruce Clarke, commander of U.S. forces in Europe, arrived in West Berlin to address the situation.

Aug 17
UNITED STATES, LATIN NATIONS SIGN ALLIANCE

PUNTA DEL ESTA, URUGUAY—While the Soviets are threatening freedom in West Berlin, Latin American nations are banding together with the United States in the name of democracy. Today, the U.S. and 19 Latin American nations (excluding Cuba) signed the Alliance for Progress, which Kennedy had proposed back in March.

According to the terms of the alliance, the U.S. will provide financial assistance to the Latin American countries over the next 10 years. The money will be used to promote economic development, social progress, and political freedom. Kennedy had said he wanted to help the impoverished citizens of these nations rise up from poverty.

Politically, the United States wants to avoid another situation like the one in Cuba, where Premier Fidel Castro—hostile to the U.S.—has formed an alliance with the Soviet Union.

Kennedy speaks about the Alliance for Progress upon his return home from Uruguay.

Aug 17 TENSIONS HIGH IN BERLIN

WEST BERLIN—It has been a dramatic week in Berlin, as the city has found itself in the position of ground zero in the Cold War between the East and the West. Berlin's three million-plus citizens have lost the right to move freely within their city. They are cut off from jobs, friends, and even family.

The border closure has occurred in violation of existing agreements. In an ominous show of force, two battle-ready Soviet armored divisions have surrounded the city. Meanwhile, Soviet Premier Khrushchev has concluded a separate peace treaty with East Germany.

Yesterday, the governments of France, Great Britain, and the United States formally protested East Germany's actions. The Kennedy administration has portrayed the situation as a clear indication of the failure of communism.

West Berlin Mayor Willy Brandt strongly warned the West about the potential implications for world peace. The West appears to be unwilling to take a stronger stand, however, as it is wary of escalating the tense situation to the brink of war.

ALLIANCE FOR PROGRESS

The Cold War was not just an East-West struggle. John F. Kennedy saw it as a North-South battle as well, especially with a Soviet-sponsored regime in Cuba. Latin America, with its history of instability and poverty, was potentially fertile ground for Communist insurgencies. The President was determined to head off that possibility by extending his hand to the region's people.

Three months into his presidency, Kennedy invited Latin American diplomats to the White House, where they heard him unveil a new initiative he called the Alliance for Progress. He described the Alliance as a North-South partnership to share the riches of the Americas. But the Alliance, like so many other Cold War programs, was not born simply of philanthropy. Kennedy believed that by acting as a good neighbor, the U.S. could counter the influence of Castro and the Soviets. He asked Congress for $500 million to fight poverty, illiteracy, and land reform south of the border.

Critics saw the Alliance for Progress as a way for U.S. business interests to extend their reach into Latin America. But even Fidel Castro praised the program, and in December 1961, Kennedy was cheered wildly during state visits to Venezuela and Colombia. The Colombian president, Alberto Lleras Camargo, told his visitor why the crowds cheered him so.

"It's because they believe you are on their side," he said.

August

28 Despite a personal appeal to him from President Kennedy, French President de Gaulle refuses to sign an Allied note to the Soviet Union inviting all parties to discuss the Berlin crisis at the United Nations.

29 In a pre-Labor Day message to Americans—given heightened meaning by recent tension between Communist and free-market nations—JFK calls labor "an expression of individual personality and will," not something the state or a ruling party should exploit.

30 The administration's education policy takes a hit when the House defeats a bill for public-school construction.

31 Kennedy accuses the Soviet Union of "atomic blackmail" for its intention to resume testing nuclear weapons. In a related move, he approves a task force designed to safeguard nuclear weapons in NATO-member countries in Europe during the Berlin crisis.

September

1 Days after announcing it would resume testing, the Soviet Union detonates a nuclear device in Central Asia.

2 The cover of this week's *Life* magazine features a photograph of Jacqueline Kennedy and the headline "The First Lady: She Tells Her Plans for the White House." Inside, she tells writer Hugh Sidey of her intention to redecorate the White House with antiques in the style of past presidents.

3 Changes go into effect for the federal minimum wage law, which now covers several million additional workers.

President Kennedy spoke only briefly to the children, but it was a moment they undoubtedly will never forget.

Aug 22 JFK, First Lady Host Concert for Handicapped Children

WASHINGTON—The President and Mrs. Kennedy today welcomed handicapped children from the District of Columbia for a special concert on the South Lawn of the White House.

This was the first of a series of White House concerts by and for young people, planned and sponsored by Mrs. Kennedy. It featured the symphony orchestra of the Brevard Music Camp of Transylvania County, North Carolina. Dr. James Christian Pfohl, camp director, served as conductor.

The President appeared briefly on stage to welcome the musicians and assembled guests. He referred to the musicians as "a great national cultural asset" before returning to work in the Oval Office.

Aug 24 President Issues a Warning to Soviet Union About Berlin

WASHINGTON—President Kennedy today responded to a note from the Soviet government accusing the West of "provocative" actions in Berlin. In a written statement, Kennedy responded sharply to what he characterized as "attempted intimidation designed to distract attention from failures of the Soviet government and to heighten world tensions."

Following recently enacted restrictions on travel to East Berlin by "foreigners," and an East German warning that all individuals are to keep 110 yards from both sides of the border, the West mobilized troops and tanks along the border in a show of force.

Kennedy accuses the Soviets of violating existing agreements to "cooperate with the Allied governments to mitigate the effects of the administrative division of Germany and Berlin." His warning to the Soviets is unmistakable. He asserted that the "peaceful commitment to freedom of the people of West Berlin and the restraint of their leaders under great provocation have never been demonstrated more plainly than in recent days."

The President appears to be especially concerned about the impact Soviet actions may have on Allied air routes to and from West Berlin. He claimed that "any interference by the Soviet Government or its East German regime with free access to West Berlin would be an aggressive act for the consequences of which the Soviet government would bear full responsibility."

Aug 25 76,500 CALLED TO DUTY

WASHINGTON—With tensions brewing in Berlin, the Defense Department today called up 76,500 reservists and National Guardsmen to active duty. Secretary of Defense Robert McNamara announced the decision after President Kennedy approved the measure. The breakdown of the 76,500 call-ups includes 46,500 for the Army, 23,600 for the Air Force, and 6,400 for the Navy.

One month ago today, the President proposed that the U.S. increase its military might by 217,000 men due to the Soviet pressure in Berlin. Western-Soviet relations have since soured, with the Communists closing borders that divide East and West Berlin.

McNamara would not say how many of the new call-ups would be shipped overseas, nor would he predict how long the reservists would stay on active duty. "I can't predict the length of the Berlin crisis," he said. He did say that at least a portion of the call-ups would remain permanent.

Sept 1 ADMINISTRATION REACTS TO SOVIET WEAPONS TESTS

WASHINGTON—President Kennedy met with his National Security Council yesterday morning in the wake of the decision by the Soviet Union to resume nuclear weapons testing. According to the Kennedy camp, the Soviet move is nothing more than "atomic blackmail, designed to substitute terror for reason in the present international scene."

According to Ambassador Arthur Dean, "these events, at a time when the world could have had a workable treaty banning nuclear explosions, show a determined Soviet purpose to rest its future policy on the terrorization of humanity…but the Soviet government underestimates the people of the world, if it thinks they will capitulate to a strategy of blackmail and terror."

The Kennedy administration was quick to reassure the public that in spite of Soviet efforts to test "the will and determination of the free world," the defense needs of the United States and its allies are adequately met with existing stockpiles of weapons and delivery systems. The President, while disappointed with the current state of affairs, is more than prepared to defend American interests. Some 75,000 NATO reserves have been activated, along with ships and aircraft, and plans to safeguard nuclear weapons in NATO member countries are already well established.

4 Congress passes the Foreign Assistance Act, which authorizes more than $4 billion in military and economic assistance for the next fiscal year. The bill also creates a separate agency to handle economic aid.

5 Kennedy orders resumption of U.S. underground nuclear testing. He also signs a new law that stipulates the death penalty for convicted airline hijackers.

6 The President commends officials in several southern states for peacefully integrating their public school systems.

7 Kennedy works to influence leaders of major U.S. steel companies to hold prices level, despite persistent inflationary pressures on the economy.

8 The Department of Defense prepares an announcement that the U.S. will send an additional 40,000 troops to Western Europe. Kennedy asks State and Defense to report to him on the effect of the buildup on the Berlin situation.

9 Test-ban talks are suspended. It is a mere formality since the negotiations had broken down shortly before the Soviets had announced that they would resume nuclear weapons tests.

10 President Kennedy and British Prime Minister Macmillan issue a joint statement of regret over Khrushchev's recent declaration. Khrushchev stated that the Soviets will end nuclear testing only when the West accepts a German peace treaty and complete disarmament.

11 Congress extends for two years the work of the federal Civil Rights Commission, which was created by the Civil Rights Act of 1957.

Kennedy, who understands that an extra 15 cents an hour is a paltry raise for U.S. laborers, had hoped for a 25-cent hike.

Sept 3 JFK Dismayed Over Minimum Wage

WASHINGTON—When the clock struck midnight last night, millions of Americans got a raise. However, it wasn't as much as they or President Kennedy had hoped for.

The President had urged Congress to raise the minimum wage from $1 an hour to $1.25. Instead, the agreed-upon legislation calls for an increase to $1.15 beginning today and $1.25 starting two years from now.

Kennedy also wanted the minimum wage law to cover 4.3 million more workers than it had previously. Instead, Congress—after much wrangling over the bill—agreed to expand the coverage by 3.6 million people. Many retail workers, construction workers, and other laborers now must be paid a minimum wage.

This is the third time since 1938 that the Fair Labors Standards Act has been amended to raise the minimum wage. However, this is the first time that the law has been altered to cover more workers.

Sept 3 U.S., Britain Support Test Ban

HYANNISPORT, MASS.—Two days after the Soviet Union detonated a nuclear bomb over Soviet Central Asia, President Kennedy and British Prime Minister Harold Macmillan have called for a global ban on atmospheric nuclear testing.

Said a White House spokesman: "Their aim in this proposal is to protect mankind from the increasing hazards from atmosphere pollution and to contribute to the reduction of international tensions."

Until Friday, the Soviet Union had not exploded a nuclear weapon in the atmosphere in nearly three years. Friday's blast caused outrage worldwide. The unleashed radioactivity contaminates dust, which can blow for miles and make people and animals ill.

Currently, the USSR, United States, and Great Britain are the only nations with nuclear weapons. Kennedy and Macmillan want Moscow to respond to their atmospheric test ban proposal by September 9. They want representatives of the three nations to meet in Geneva to discuss the matter.

Sept 5 HIJACKING NOW PUNISHABLE BY DEATH

WASHINGTON—President Kennedy today signed a bill meant to dissuade Cubans from hijacking U.S. commercial airplanes. The new law states that hijacking is an act of piracy that can be punishable by death.

The new legislation calls for up to a year imprisonment for carrying a concealed weapon on an aircraft. Also, a person can now get five years for providing false information about a hijacking. New penalties for hijacking a plane range from 20 years to life in prison, as well as death in certain instances.

On several occasions over the last three years, Cubans have hijacked airplanes that were either en route to Miami or had departed Miami.

Sept 9 KHRUSHCHEV RESPONDS TO TEST-BAN PROPOSAL

Moscow—Soviet Premier Nikita Khrushchev today responded to the American and British requests to ban atmospheric testing. Khrushchev called for not a test ban but complete nuclear disarmament—but only if the U.S. and Britain agreed to his peace proposal for Germany.

Western leaders are not willing to accept the Soviets' German peace proposal, which calls for the Allies to end its occupation of West Berlin. Moreover, the Western nations consider Khrushchev's call for complete nuclear disarmament disingenuous.

Cold War tensions have escalated since August, when East German officials closed border crossings between East and West Berlin. They then began building a wall to separate the two sides of the city. Due to the Berlin crisis, the U.S. has since ramped up its military preparedness.

Khrushchev claimed that he ordered the September 1 atmospheric nuclear test because Western nations had been threatening war over Berlin. "Weighing all the pros and cons," he stated, "the Soviet government with an aching heart had to resume test explosions."

After asking for a global ban of atmospheric testing on September 3, President Kennedy ordered the resumption of underground nuclear testing.

Kennedy meets with Brigadier General William Yarborough at Fort Bragg, North Carolina.

12 The President greets Indonesian President Sukarno and Mali President Keita for discussions on the recent conference of nonaligned nations in Belgrade.

13 Kennedy signs a crime bill that approves $30 million of funding over three years and emphasizes efforts to reduce crime by unemployed juveniles.

14 As American steel industry leaders criticize the White House for "assuming the role of informal price setters for steel," the President urges labor leaders in the industry to reach a settlement with management.

15 The Nevada desert rumbles as the United States tests a low-yield, underground nuclear device, ending the country's three-year moratorium on testing.

16 U.S. officials claim that East Germany, with Soviet backing, is preparing to arrest and deport large numbers of people living near West Berlin.

17 In his strongest public criticism since leaving office, former president Eisenhower sees "indecision and uncertainty" in White House actions on Cuban and Laotian problems.

18 Despite recent successes in reducing the shipment of supplies to the Vietcong from North Vietnam, rebel forces behead a provincial leader in Phuoc Vinh, just 55 miles from Saigon.

19 UN Secretary General Dag Hammarskjold and 12 others die when their plane crashes in Northern Rhodesia, cutting short a mission to end fighting between UN and Katanga troops. There are conflicting reports about whether or not the crash was an accident.

Sept 9 U.S. SENDS 40,000 TROOPS TO EUROPE

WASHINGTON—Due to the Berlin crisis, the United States is sending 40,000 regular Army troops to Europe, increasing the American force on the continent to 290,000. Most of the reinforcements will go to Germany. Secretary of Defense Robert McNamara, with the approval of President Kennedy, made the announcement today.

The announcement stated that the new troops will bring "United States units committed to the North Atlantic Treaty Organizations to full strength."

The domestic duties of the 40,000 troops will be taken over by National Guardsmen and Army, Navy, and Air Force Reserves. The Pentagon had called up 76,500 Guardsmen and Reservists two weeks ago.

Sept 16 U.S. AND SOVIET UNION EXPLODE NUCLEAR BOMBS

WASHINGTON—Both the United States and Soviet Union flexed their nuclear muscles today, as each test-detonated a nuclear bomb. For the 11th time this month, the Soviets exploded a nuclear weapon in the atmosphere, producing potentially harmful radioactive fallout. For the second day in a row, the U.S. detonated a bomb underground at the Atomic Energy Commission's test site in Nevada, with reportedly no harmful effects.

U.S. officials described the Soviets' weapon as approximately one megaton, meaning the equivalent of one million tons of TNT. The U.S. bomb was "low yield"—no more than 20,000 tons of TNT.

Paradoxically, both President Kennedy and Soviet leaders are expected to propose a ban on nuclear testing in addresses to the United Nations next week.

Sept 16 IKE ATTACKS KENNEDY'S POLICIES

CHICAGO—In a speech honoring Senator Everett Dirksen, former President Eisenhower offered his strongest criticism to date of the current administration.

Eisenhower said we should not "fail to be sorely distressed over Laos, and more especially over Cuba, and the seeming indecision and uncertainty that characterized governmental action there." The former president, pointing to criticisms of the Joint Chiefs of Staff and the CIA, expressed his determination that the bad press not impact America's men in uniform.

Eisenhower pointed to spiritual and material strength as the source of American national power. He seemed to question the wisdom of Kennedy's pet space program, suggesting that we should "defer buying tickets for a trip to the moon until we can pay cash for the ride."

Call him old-fashioned, but Eisenhower doesn't believe in spending money you don't have.

> *"[We should] defer buying tickets for a trip to the moon until we can pay cash for the ride."* — PRESIDENT DWIGHT EISENHOWER

Cutting to the heart of what many see as Kennedy's free-spending policies, Eisenhower suggested that the idea that federal money is a panacea for all of society's problems is a "soft-headed philosophy" that could ultimately lead to centralized government and undermine the foundations of American society. Finally, the former president pointed out Kennedy's unfulfilled campaign promises, citing "the total lack of any administration recommendation to the Congress for balancing the federal budget, and for civil rights legislation, both solemnly pledged in platform and campaign only a few months ago."

A STARK CONTRAST TO EISENHOWER

In 1960, John F. Kennedy campaigned for president as the nation's antidote to Dwight Eisenhower. While the two-term president and war hero remained popular and respected after eight years in the White House, Kennedy believed the country yearned for more youthful, more vigorous leadership.

Historians have been kinder to Eisenhower's presidency than Kennedy was in 1960. But there is no denying that the two men offered a striking contrast in demeanor, appearance, and style. Eisenhower, at age 70, was the nation's oldest president. Kennedy, at 43, was the youngest person elected to the presidency. Eisenhower was the last president born in the 19th century. Kennedy was the first to be born in the 20th century. As president, Eisenhower was more of a detached chairman of the board than a hands-on chief executive officer. He delegated responsibilities, especially after suffering two heart attacks during his second term. He often rambled during press conferences, furthering his image as a slightly out-of-touch grand-father.

Kennedy was an impatient young man who saw the Eisenhower years as dull and static, a reflection of the President's age and personality. In one of his first campaign speeches, he said he planned to be an activist president, explicitly criticizing Eisenhower's hands-off style.

The new president and his young wife, Jacqueline, brought glamour and charisma to what had been a gray-flannel, corporate White House. Jacqueline Kennedy was just 31, as beautiful as Kennedy was handsome. Their children, their sense of style, their engagement with the public made the White House seem exciting again.

Katanga and UN officials reach an agreement to cease fire and exchange prisoners.

The White House proposes legislation to provide $55 million in hurricane-damage relief for Louisiana and Texas. Carla, a Category 5 hurricane, devastated portions of the Gulf Coast and killed more than 40 people.

The Interstate Commerce Commission bans segregated seating aboard buses on interstate routes in the United States. Meanwhile, the President signs a bill making the Peace Corps permanent.

Kennedy appoints NAACP attorney Thurgood Marshall to the U.S. Court of Appeals for the Second Circuit. Six years later, Marshall will become the first black justice of the U.S. Supreme Court.

Secretary of State Rusk says he believes a peaceful solution to the Berlin crisis is possible. Attorney General Robert Kennedy, however, says that if necessary the President is prepared to use nuclear weapons to protect West Berlin.

In a highly anticipated speech to the UN General Assembly, President Kennedy challenges the Soviets to a "peace race," including general disarmament, but says he and his allies will remain firm on Berlin.

The President follows his UN speech with the signing of a bill that creates the U.S. Arms Control and Disarmament Agency, headed by William C. Foster

Sept 19 MILITARY CALLS UP RESERVES

WASHINGTON—The Pentagon today ordered to active duty approximately 73,000 members of the Army Reserve and National Guard. The troops are to be mobilized by October 15.

In the last four weeks, some 150,000 reservists have been called to active duty due to the brewing crisis in Berlin, Germany. In announcing the call-ups today, Secretary of Defense Robert McNamara insisted that the crisis is not escalating. The United States, he said, wants to be as prepared as possible.

Ten days ago, McNamara announced that the U.S. was sending 40,000 regular Army troops to Europe. Today, the Secretary said that the U.S. is not planning to send more than the 40,000 troops overseas.

The 150,000 reservists, many of whom have families and careers, will serve no more than 12 months, as mandated by federal law.

Sept 22 PEACE CORPS NOW OFFICIAL

WASHINGTON—The Peace Corps, a pet project of President Kennedy, became official today. The President signed a law that gave that agency permanent status and authorized $40 million for its first year of operation.

The Peace Corps, which faced little opposition in Congress, has already attracted more than 13,000 volunteers. Kennedy said that by next July, he hopes to have 2,700 Peace Corps workers in training or working abroad. "They will be farmers and teachers, craftsmen and nurses, doctors and technicians of all kinds," he said. "They will be a cross-section of the finest men and women that this nation has to offer."

The President signed other bills today as well. A juvenile delinquency bill authorizes $10 million a year to help communities establish programs aimed at reducing criminal behavior among youth. Another bill calls for five new plants that will turn seawater and brackish water into fresh water.

After signing 22 bills in all, Kennedy flew to his home in Hyannisport for the weekend.

With a stroke of the pen on the morning of September 22, JFK makes his Peace Corps dream a reality.

"They will be farmers and teachers, craftsmen and nurses, doctors and technicians of all kinds."

—KENNEDY, REFERRING TO PEACE CORPS VOLUNTEERS

Sept 22 ICC BANS SEGREGATION IN INTERSTATE TRAVEL

WASHINGTON—The U.S. Interstate Commerce Commission today ordered an end to segregation in interstate bus travel. The ICC ruled that, beginning November 1, segregation in interstate buses and at interstate bus terminal facilities will be deemed illegal.

On December 5, 1960, the U.S. Supreme Court ruled that segregation in interstate bus terminal restaurants was unconstitutional. Testing the ruling, interracial groups of Freedom Riders rode Greyhound and Trailways buses through the South this spring. The Riders were assaulted by segregationists at several locations, prompting the involvement of the U.S. Justice Department. Freedom Rides continued throughout the summer. Attorney General Robert Kennedy urged the ICC to ban segregation in interstate facilities, resulting in today's ruling.

President Kennedy has quietly supported his brother on this issue. He told the press on July 19: "In my judgment, there's no question of the legal rights of the freedom travelers, Freedom Riders, to move in interstate commerce."

Sept 23 MARSHALL NOMINATED AS FEDERAL JUDGE

WASHINGTON—The most renowned Negro attorney in America may soon be working for the United States government. Today, President Kennedy nominated Thurgood Marshall as a federal judge for the Second Circuit Court of Appeals. Marshall will await confirmation from Congress, which will not come until next year.

Since 1938, Marshall has served as special counsel for the NAACP. Known for his work ethic, he has fought hard to desegregate public schools. He represented the plaintiffs in the 1954 landmark case *Brown v. Board of Education*, in which the U.S. Supreme Court ruled that segregation in public schools was unconstitutional.

Marshall was the driving force behind the landmark *Brown* v. *Board of Education* ruling.

27 Less than six months after the Bay of Pigs fiasco, Kennedy names John McCone to direct the CIA. McCone replaces Allen Dulles, who had been instrumental in the agency's founding and became its first civilian director under Eisenhower.

28 Former Vice President Richard Nixon announces that he will run for governor of California in 1962 and has no plans to run for president in 1964.

29 Before the Senate adjourns, the White House will achieve confirmation of 60 new circuit and district court judges, and Kennedy will soon use recess appointments for 17 others. It is the largest expansion of the federal court system in U.S. history.

30 The President signs into law a compromise foreign aid bill, including $3.9 billion in appropriations.

October

1 South Vietnamese President Diem proposes a defense treaty with the United States, arguing that the battle against Communists in his country has become a war, not merely a guerrilla action.

2 East German crews fortify the Berlin Wall with a network of trenches and bunkers, reinforcing many sections that previously had consisted of only barbed-wire fences.

3 U.S. officials block a Soviet proposal to reorganize the leadership of the United Nations into an acting secretary general and three deputies. The American officials say the change will divide the international body into three clear factions.

Speaking at the UN, Kennedy proposes restrictions on nuclear proliferation, including a ban on space nukes.

"Every man, woman, and child lives under a nuclear sword of Damocles, hanging by the slenderest of threads...." —KENNEDY

Sept 25

JFK PREACHES PEACE AT UN

The President Outlines His Plan for Complete Nuclear Disarmament

NEW YORK—In a dramatic speech at the United Nations today, President Kennedy challenged the Soviet Union to a "peace race." Kennedy outlined a multi-step plan that would lead to complete nuclear disarmament throughout the world.

Though both the United States and USSR have tested nuclear weapons this month, Kennedy told the General Assembly that all nations should sign a nuclear test-ban treaty. "This can be done now," he said. "Test-ban negotiations need not and should not await general disarmament."

Continuing with what he called "our new Disarmament Program," Kennedy proposed that nations stop the production of fissionable materials for use in weapons. He added that nations should not be allowed to transfer these materials, or completed nuclear weapons, to nations currently lacking them. Kennedy also called for a ban of nuclear weapons in outer space.

Gradually, Kennedy urged, nations should destroy existing nuclear weapons and convert their materials to peaceful uses. They also should halt the unlimited testing and production of strategic nuclear delivery vehicles, and gradually destroy those devices.

Of all the proposals, only the test-ban treaty seems realistic in the near future. Nevertheless, the President offered a sobering assessment of the situation.

"Today, every inhabitant of this planet must contemplate the day when this planet may no longer be habitable," he said. "Every man, woman, and child lives under a nuclear sword of Damocles, hanging by the slenderest of threads, capable of being cut at any moment by accident or miscalculation or by madness. The weapons of war must be abolished before they abolish us."

JFK shows his commitment to nuclear disarmament by establishing the ACDA just one day after his UN speech.

Sept 26
PRESIDENT SIGNS "DISARMAMENT" BILL

NEW YORK—President Kennedy today took a step to rid the world of nuclear weapons. The President signed a bill, passed three days ago by Congress, that creates the Arms Control and Disarmament Agency (ACDA).

"Our ultimate goal, as the act points out, is a world free from war and free from the dangers and burdens of armaments," Kennedy said. "The new agency brings renewed hope for agreement and progress in the critical battle for the survival of mankind."

The new agency will work to establish a disarmament program that it could present to the rest of the world. William C. Foster, 64, undersecretary of commerce and former deputy secretary of defense under President Harry Truman, will head the new agency.

The Soviet Union is not likely to agree to a U.S. disarmament program anytime soon. In Moscow today, the press reported that the Kremlin has rejected the disarmament proposals that Kennedy made at the United Nations yesterday.

Oct 4
JFK: THE PRESIDENCY WILL NOT BE FOR SALE

WASHINGTON—President Kennedy doesn't believe in "buying" an election, particularly when it involves the presidency of the United States. Today, Kennedy appointed a bipartisan commission to address presidential election reforms. He wants the nine-member group to recommend ways to make presidential candidates less reliant on private donations.

The President said he does not want elections decided by special interests. Currently, wealthy corporations and individuals can influence the outcome of an election with their donations.

"Traditionally, the funds for national campaigns have been supplied entirely by private contributions," Kennedy said, "with the candidates forced to depend in the main on large sums from a relatively small number of contributors. It is not healthy for the democratic process—or for ethical standards in our government—to keep our national candidates in this condition of dependence. I have long thought that we must either provide a federal share in campaign costs, or reduce the cost of campaign services, or both."

Democrat Alexander Heard, a dean at the University of North Carolina, will head the commission, which will be comprised of four Democrats, four Republicans, and an independent.

4 The President signs an order that allows U.S. technicians to train the French military on how to use and defend against nuclear weapons.

5 On the 50th anniversary of the Chinese revolution, Kennedy sends a congratulatory message to Taiwanese President Chiang Kai-shek.

6 On the same day that he and Soviet Foreign Minister Gromyko fail to restart negotiations on the Berlin situation, President Kennedy sets a goal of providing nuclear fallout protection for every American.

7 The Atomic Energy Commission reports the 18th Soviet nuclear test since the USSR resumed testing in September.

8 A presidential study finds that black Americans have roughly proportional representation in federal jobs, but earn considerably less than white federal workers.

9 Despite the recent extension of the Civil Rights Commission, the administration faces calls to do more in the next session of Congress to enact a new program of civil rights measures.

10 The U.S. military detonates another underground nuclear device at the Nevada Test Site. It is the third test in Operation Nougat, which will include more than 30 test explosions over two years.

11 JKF underscores American commitment to the defense of South Vietnam. In a news conference, the President says that General Maxwell Taylor will travel to Saigon to assess South Vietnam's needs.

Oct 6   JFK Urges Fallout Shelters for Everyone

Washington—Should an enemy nation fire a nuclear weapon at the United States, President Kennedy wants to make sure that the American citizenry is prepared. Nothing can be done for those caught in the midst of the explosion. However, citizens can prepare for nuclear fallout—the residual radiation hazard from a nuclear explosion. Such radiation can be lethal if humans are exposed to too much of it.

Today, a letter from the President was read at a meeting of state Civil Defense directors in Washington. Kennedy urged that the federal government, the state governments, industry, and other institutions should aim to create "fallout protection for every American as rapidly as possible."

Kennedy wrote: "Radioactive fallout, extending downwind for as much as several hundred miles, could account for the major part of the casualties which might result from a thermonuclear attack on an unprotected population. Protection against this threat is within reach of an informed America willing to face the facts and act."

The President stated that the federal government is working to provide shelter space for large groups of people in communities across the country. But he added that many "homeowners, communities, and business firms can and will provide more adequate and better located shelter space for their own needs. The federal government is backing this effort with a massive dissemination of technical information."

Kennedy urged state and local governments to provide shelter for its citizens and to create laws that would "encourage private initiative in this effort."

Critics charge that shelters cannot completely protect citizens from fallout, even if they remain in the shelters for many days. Potential post-blast problems could include cancer, radioactive topsoil, and ensuing epidemics.

Oct 11   Kennedy: No Progress Made in Berlin Talks

Washington—In his first televised news conference since March, President Kennedy was in a downbeat mood today as he discussed international affairs. The central theme was communism and the Soviets' unwillingness to bend on vital issues.

The President said that he and Secretary of State Dean Rusk have had extensive conversations with Soviet Foreign Minister

At his televised press conference, Kennedy speaks glumly about Berlin and nuclear war.

Andrei Gromyko about the Berlin crisis, but that no progress has been made. Kennedy showed concern that the Soviets will continue to try to gain more power in Berlin and Germany. "Western Europe is an area of great resources, and the Soviet Union has long had policy ambitions in this area," he said, "so that this is a very, very serious matter unless we can reach a peaceful accommodation."

Kennedy said that the Allied nations will continue to discuss strategy regarding the Berlin crisis. Meanwhile, U.S. Ambassador to the Soviet Union Llewellyn Thompson will talk further with the Russians.

Regarding the situation in Vietnam, the President said he is sending a commission headed by General Maxwell Taylor to Saigon. Taylor will talk to Ngo Dinh Diem, the president of the Republic of South Vietnam, and the commission will address the needs of the republic, which is battling Communist guerrilla forces (the Vietcong).

The grim subject of nuclear war was also discussed. Kennedy said that next month the administration will suggest steps that families can take to protect themselves in case the unthinkable happens. "We're going to live through a long period of constant tension with these dangerous weapons…" Kennedy said, "therefore, anything we can do to increase the chances of protection for our families ought to be done."

Oct 11 NEW PANEL TO EXAMINE MENTAL RETARDATION

WASHINGTON—At his press conference today, President Kennedy announced that he will appoint a panel of doctors, scientists, and others "to prescribe a program of action in the field of mental retardation."

The President stressed the importance of helping such individuals and their families. He pointed out that it "is a serious personal matter to at least one out of every 12 persons" in this country and "disables 10 times as many as diabetes."

Kennedy said that at one time, most mentally retarded children were confined to institutions. The situation is better today, he said, but "the central problems of cause and prevention remain unsolved. I believe that we as a country, in association with scientists all over the world, should make a comprehensive attack."

Kennedy's sister Rosemary, just one year younger than him, was born with moderate mental retardation. Her mental condition has been much worse since undergoing a lobotomy at the age of 23.

The President said that mental retardation "is a matter of the greatest possible interest to me, and I am going to meet with the panel next week."

12 The U.S. Public Health Service detects elevated levels of radioactive iodine-131 in some regions' food supplies due to fallout from Soviet weapon tests in Asia.

13 U.S. officials at the United Nations repeat a challenge to the Soviets to sign a treaty ending nuclear weapon tests. Kennedy has warned that the U.S. may resume atmospheric tests otherwise.

14 The Civil Rights Commission calls for federal action to stop racial discrimination by labor unions and by National Guard units.

15 As part of Sky Shield II, a massive air-defense maneuver, the military halts all civilian flights in the U.S. and Canada for 12 hours.

16 After returning from a weekend at Cape Cod, the President meets at the White House with Martin Luther King, Jr., who urges the President to take stronger measures to end segregation.

17 In a speech at the Kremlin, Khrushchev hints at dropping his year-end deadline for a German peace treaty, but he also announces that the USSR will test a 50-megaton device later in the month. Washington immediately protests the weapons-testing plan.

18 South Vietnam declares a state of emergency just as General Taylor, the President's special representative, arrives to study whether the U.S. should deploy combat troops.

19 The national space agency successfully tests a multi-stage rocket. Agency head James E. Webb says that Kennedy's support has noticeably accelerated the country's progress toward its space goals.

Oct 16 JFK, MLK Meet at White House

Washington—President Kennedy met with civil rights leader Dr. Martin Luther King at the White House today to discuss ongoing civil rights initiatives.

Despite White House support for voting rights, those in the civil rights movement have perceived that the Kennedy administration has been less supportive in other areas. Ending housing discrimination is a campaign promise of Kennedy's that King and his colleagues seem to feel has not been adequately addressed.

In their meeting today, King directly asked the President for more affirmative action on housing rights. King also requested that Kennedy issue a "second emancipation," declaring segregation illegal in all its forms.

For his part, Kennedy is said to have blamed his administration's inaction on civil rights issues on congressional stonewalling. Overall, it is unlikely that Dr. King left the meeting satisfied that his movement is enjoying the full support of the White House.

Republic of South Vietnam President Ngo Dinh Diem will welcome General Taylor and his colleagues.

Oct 18 U.S. Contingent Arrives in Troubled South Vietnam

Saigon—Ngo Dinh Diem, president of the Republic of South Vietnam, today announced that he has placed his country in a state of emergency after the murder of a South Vietnamese official. The announcement came on the same day that an American contingent arrived in Saigon to assist Diem's government.

Colonel Hoang Thuy Nam, the top liaison officer to the International Control Commission, was tortured and killed by guerrillas of the Vietcong (Vietnamese Communists). Diem declared that the unstable military situation as well as a recent flood in the southern region of the country were the reasons he declared the state of emergency.

This morning, an 11-member American contingent, headed by General Maxwell Taylor, arrived in Saigon.

The team of diplomats, economic advisers, and military men will spend about a week in South Vietnam examining the republic's problems. The U.S. is committed to helping South Vietnam fend off the Communist threat. Today, Taylor spoke at length with President Diem.

A spokesman for President Kennedy said that the President will await the group's report before making any decisions. There is no indication that the United States is planning to send combat troops to Vietnam.

VIETNAM, BEFORE THE QUAGMIRE

As a senator, John Kennedy described Vietnam as the key to keeping Southeast Asia out of Communist hands. His opinion of the country's strategic importance did not change once he became president. In the fall of 1961, Kennedy sent military adviser General Maxwell Taylor to South Vietnam to assess the country's battle against the Vietcong, a Communist insurgency force supported by North Vietnam. Taylor recommended that JFK send thousands of combat troops to support Saigon's pro-Western regime.

Several Kennedy advisers, most prominently George Ball at the State Department, were against sending troops. But Kennedy saw Vietnam not only as a skirmish in the Cold War, but a potential problem at home. Former president Dwight Eisenhower publicly criticized him for failing to act swiftly to aid Saigon. Ike's criticism led to charges that Kennedy was soft on the Communist threat in Southeast Asia.

Meanwhile, JFK was getting signals that the Soviets, the Chinese, and perhaps even the North Vietnamese were looking to stabilize the region rather than risk direct U.S. involvement in the conflict. Kennedy decided, in essence, to split the middle and hope for stability. He dispatched more than 2,000 U.S. troops to South Vietnam by the end of 1961, but they were to act as "advisers" to the South Vietnamese regime. Still, they were in harm's way.

Although ambivalent about deploying combat troops, Kennedy was haunted by the prospect of a Communist victory in South Vietnam in 1961, especially after the Bay of Pigs fiasco.

Oct 23 SOVIETS DETONATE LARGEST BOMB EVER

WASHINGTON—The Soviet Union literally sent shock waves through much of the world today with the most powerful man-made explosion in history.

The Atomic Energy Commission announced that the Soviets set off two nuclear bombs at the Soviets Arctic testing area. The force of the first bomb was probably around 30 megatons, but possibly as high as 50 megatons. Previously, the most powerful bomb ever detonated was 15 megatons. Today, stations in Sweden and Japan detected the shock waves of the blast.

The Soviets also set off a smaller nuclear bomb underwater—an apparent first for that nation. Since September 1, the Soviets have test-detonated 23 nuclear bombs.

Kennedy's administration has not yet issued a response to today's events. However, when the Soviets announced last week they would explode a 50-megaton bomb, the White House said the explosion would accomplish nothing except to add more radioactivity to the atmosphere.

20 Apprehensive about likely fallout in their territories from a planned 50-megaton Soviet nuclear test, Denmark, Iceland, Norway, Sweden, Canada, and Japan ask the UN General Assembly to intercede.

21 Kennedy is reportedly exercising every day to strengthen his back. Decades later, medical records will reveal that the President was also receiving extensive painkiller injections throughout much of his time in the White House.

22 Tensions rise after East German border guards detain an American diplomat. Armed U.S. military policemen walk into East Berlin to enforce the diplomat's right to travel, and he is allowed to continue.

23 The Soviet Union detonates an estimated 30-megaton device in Siberia. It will be revealed later that the test was timed to mask the test of a nuclear torpedo, fired by the Soviet submarine B-130.

24 As the situation in Vietnam continues to deteriorate, Kennedy pledges more resources and tells Diem that the U.S. will "help Vietnam preserve its independence."

25 The American delegation to the UN condemns apartheid in South Africa. The republic's race policies have become increasingly controversial since it became a republic and left the British Commonwealth earlier in the year.

26 Facing a federal deficit for the year of nearly $7 billion, Kennedy directs all federal agencies to trim their budgets and says he will submit a balanced budget for fiscal year 1963.

American and Soviet tanks face each other at Berlin's Friedrichstrasse border.

Oct 28 SHOWDOWN AT BERLIN BORDER

WEST BERLIN—Last night, for the first time during the Cold War, American and Soviet tanks confronted each other. At the Friedrichstrasse border crossing between West Berlin and East Berlin, enemy tanks pointed their guns at each other. The tanks were less than 100 yards apart. The tense showdown lasted 16 hours before the Russian tanks backed away.

Over the previous three days, the U.S. Army had escorted officials over the Friedrichstrasse border and into East Berlin, defying the Communists' efforts to restrict border passings. In response, the Soviets ordered more than 30 tanks into East Berlin, with some of them rolling up to the Friedrichstrasse crossing. Meanwhile, four American tanks had already been posted at the border.

General Clay, a personal representative of President Kennedy, headed the American troops. He reported not to military superiors but directly to the President. During the showdown, the 6,000-plus U.S. garrison in Berlin was put on alert.

During the crisis, U.S. and Soviet military men crossed the border to inspect the other side's tanks. Finally, by midmorning today, the Soviet tanks retreated, driving about a mile away from the border. Soon afterward, the American tanks left the border area.

Ironically, American troops protected Soviet soldiers who ventured into West Berlin. On two occasions, U.S. military police shielded the Soviets from an angry West German mob, which numbered in the hundreds.

Oct 30 WHITE HOUSE DENOUNCES SOVIETS' 50-MEGATON BLAST

WASHINGTON—The Soviet Union exploded the most powerful bomb in history today, a reported 50 megatons, thus eclipsing their record of a week ago. The blast took place at the Soviets' Arctic testing area. Condemnations of the act are being heard throughout the world, including Washington. The White House today issued a statement denouncing the test.

"The Soviet explosion was a political rather than a military act," the statement read. "Any such weapon would be primarily a mass killer of people in war—and the testing of this device primarily an incitement to fright and panic in the cold war."

"Fear is the oldest weapon in history," the statement continued. "Throughout the life of mankind, it has been the resort of those who could not hope to prevail by reason and persuasion."

The statement concluded: "We have no wish ever to use this military power. We are ready, now as ever, to sign the test-ban treaty proposed at Geneva. We are ready, now as ever, to negotiate a treaty for general and complete disarmament. In the meantime, we will continue to take whatever measures are necessary to preserve the security of our country and of others who count on us."

"The Soviet Union has shown its complete disregard for the welfare of mankind…." —KENNEDY

Nov 1   U.S. TO PREPARE FOR ATMOSPHERIC TESTING

WASHINGTON—President Kennedy today ordered that preparations be made to resume atmospheric nuclear testing. The decision is in response to the approximately two dozen atmospheric nuclear detonations the Soviets have made over the last two months.

The President said he does not plan to conduct atmospheric tests. But, he said, "as a matter of prudence, we shall make necessary preparations for such tests so as to be ready in case it becomes necessary to conduct them."

Kennedy again condemned the Soviets' atmospheric tests. "I do not have to dwell on the irresponsible nature of these Soviet actions," he said. "The Soviet Union has shown its complete disregard for the welfare of mankind…."

The President said that the United States is ready to sign a nuclear test treaty. But, he added, in "view of the Soviet action, it will be the policy of the United States to proceed in developing nuclear weapons to maintain this superior capability for the defense of the Free World against any aggressor." He said that any atmospheric tests that the U.S. would conduct would be "only within limits that restrict the fall-out from such tests to an absolute minimum."

27 The administration announces financing programs designed to help American exporters compete with foreign companies for overseas business.

28 A confrontation ends in Berlin between Soviet and American tanks. The previous day, Soviet tanks had advanced near the Friedrichstrasse crossing in response to an October 22 border enforcement action by U.S. military police.

29 The American delegation to a Rome conference of the Food and Agriculture Organization will propose funding a $100 million world food bank to improve childhood nutrition worldwide.

30 True to its word, the Soviet Union detonates a 50-megaton nuclear device. "Big Ivan," as the Soviets call it, was designed and managed by Andrei Sakharov, who later will become a noted anti-nuclear dissident.

31 Reaction to the Soviet test ripples around the world. Vatican radio calls it an "insane decision." U.S. Senator Henry Jackson, head of a congressional atomic weapons subcommittee, says the U.S. will be forced to resume above-ground testing.

WSP members deliver a written plea for peace to the Russian mission to the UN in New York on November 1.

Nov 1 WOMEN MARCH TO "END ARMS RACE"

WASHINGTON—In Washington and in cities across the nation today, some 50,000 women participated in anti-nuclear marches. Some pushed baby carriages or walked beside their children. Others held signs that read, "Testing Damages the Unborn," "Save the Children," and "Let's Live in Peace, Not Pieces."

On September 22, while the Soviet Union was in the midst of a series of nuclear atmospheric tests, the organization Women Strike for Peace (WSP) called for this day of protest. WSP leaders called for an "appeal to all governments to end the arms race—not the human race."

The women urged citizens to ask their government leaders to pressure President Kennedy to begin negotiations for nuclear disarmament. Women marched in front of the White House, and they sent letters on behalf of their cause to First Lady Jacqueline Kennedy and to Nina Khrushchev, wife of Soviet Premier Nikita Khrushchev.

Numerous mass anti-nuclear protests have been staged in recent weeks, particularly in Europe.

Nov 3 TAYLOR, PRESIDENT OPPOSE COMBAT TROOPS IN VIETNAM

WASHINGTON—The United States will not be sending combat troops to Vietnam any time in the foreseeable future. So say officials close to President Kennedy and General Maxwell Taylor, who met with the President about the situation in Vietnam today.

After a three-week assessment visit to Vietnam, Taylor and his team submitted a report to President Kennedy. Today, the Commander-in-Chief met for two hours with Taylor and Deputy Assistant for National Security Affairs Walt Rostow. Neither of the three men revealed their discussions to the press. However, Taylor said that Republic of Vietnam President Ngo Dinh Diem had the "assets" to fend off the Communist threat. When asked if he was referring to manpower, Taylor said, "That is correct."

Officials confirmed that both the President and Taylor were against sending troops. However, it appears likely that the U.S. will send more military "advisers" to train Vietnamese soldiers in anti-guerrilla tactics. Specialists in transport and communications may also be sent to the Southeast Asian country, as might certain materiel, such as boats and helicopters. President Kennedy wants to discuss the Vietnam situation with Secretary of State Dean Rusk before making his decisions.

Nov 8 JFK Discusses Soviet Strength, Berlin, Cuba

WASHINGTON—President Kennedy held a news conference at the State Department this afternoon, fielding questions on foreign policy and assorted other issues. Several questions focused on the Soviets' military strength, and their strength relative to that of the United States. Reporters seemed especially keen to discuss what impact the Soviet resumption of nuclear testing might have. Kennedy reassured the press that the United States is well positioned and gaining ground under his administration, and "would not trade places with anyone."

On the matter of Berlin, the President is looking forward to a state visit by German Chancellor Adenauer. They presumably will have many hours to discuss Berlin, exchange information, and strategize on policy.

Asked why a threatened Cuban embargo has not yet been enacted, the President cited resistance to embargoing essential food and drug items. He claimed that "we are not anxious to be in the position of declaring war on the Cuban people…. Our dispute is not with the Cuban people but with the Communist control of Cuba."

Responding to critics who say that his administration is anti-business, Kennedy objected to the idea that there is hostility between government and business. Still, he said "that doesn't mean that we should not meet our responsibilities under antitrust."

Looking back at his record since assuming the Presidency in January, Kennedy pointed with pride at the increase in the minimum wage, the new housing bill, the decline in the number of unemployed Americans, and the steadily rising Gross Domestic Product. Areas in which the administration is directing its attention, but remain unfinished, include medical care for the elderly, civil rights, and education. According to Kennedy, "we are making substantial progress…and we'll meet our commitments before we're finished."

Despite his frustrations with the Soviet Union, the President pointed with pride to his domestic accomplishments.

Nov 11 — PRESIDENT PAYS TRIBUTE TO VETS AT ARLINGTON CEREMONY

ARLINGTON, VA.—President Kennedy laid a wreath at the Tomb of the Unknown Soldier in today's annual observance of Veteran's Day at Arlington National Cemetery. In words appropriate to the somber surroundings, Kennedy recalled the end of the First World War, Armistice Day, 43 years ago to the day, and the congressional resolution that implied that humankind's bloodiest war was behind us.

That, of course, was not to be. Indeed, said Kennedy, "wars still more destructive and still more sanguinary followed…. Man's capacity to devise new ways of killing his fellow men have far outstripped his capacity to live in peace with his fellow men."

And yet, Kennedy pointed out that from the ashes of the world wars have come ever-increasing efforts at international cooperation, a process that continues today. On this day that we honor all veterans, and especially those who made the greatest sacrifice of all, the President eloquently credited war with peace. He said that "the only way to maintain the peace is to be prepared in the final extreme to fight for our country—and to mean it."

Cellist Pablo Casals, nearing his 85th birthday, plays in the White House for the first time since 1904.

Nov 13 — CASALS PLAYS AT WHITE HOUSE

WASHINGTON—As a guest of the White House tonight, Alice Longworth enjoyed the soothing music of internationally renowned cellist Pablo Casals. The last time Longworth heard chamber music in the White House was when Casals played for her father, Theodore Roosevelt.

Casals, 84, left Spain for good during the Spanish Civil War in the 1930s, and he since has made Puerto Rico his home. Because the United States has officially recognized Spanish leader Francisco Franco, Casals has refused to play in America. However, Casals expressed his respect for John F. Kennedy, and the President responded by inviting Casals for a performance at the White House. Tonight was the perfect occasion, as Puerto Rican Governor Luis Munoz Marin was in town for a state dinner.

Casals, violinist Alexander Schneider, and pianist Mieczyslaw Horszowski entertained more than 150 guests, including President Kennedy, First Lady Jacqueline Kennedy, and Longworth, who was 20 when her father asked Casals to play in 1904.

Nov 15 COMMISSION WILL DEAL WITH JOBLESS YOUTH

WASHINGTON—The Baby Boomers—the millions of Americans who were born after World War II—are growing up, and now they need jobs. In a press statement today, President Kennedy announced the formation of a commission to address the issue.

The statement opened with great news: Overall unemployment in the United States dropped from 5.7 million in January 1961 to 3.9 million in October. However, Kennedy said, "I am particularly disturbed over the serious plight of the nearly one million out-of-school and out-of-work youth." The situation could become significantly worse in upcoming years, as more and more Baby Boomers come of age.

Today, Kennedy announced the establishment of the President's Committee on Youth Employment. The 23-member group, headed by Secretary of Labor Arthur Goldberg, will research the matter and offer solutions.

A TOP-DOWN LEADER

John Kennedy modeled his leadership style after activist presidents who eagerly grasped the levers of power. He quoted Woodrow Wilson, who once said that the president "is at liberty, both in law and conscience, to be as big a man as he can." Wilson, Abraham Lincoln, Theodore Roosevelt, and Franklin Roosevelt were, he said, models of leadership because they were strong, active leaders in command of events.

Once installed in the White House, Kennedy quickly made it clear that he intended to follow in the footsteps of his role models. He dispensed with Eisenhower's bureaucratic, layered approach to decision-making. He preferred a more intuitive approach, with all power radiating from the Oval Office. Kennedy was not fond of formal meetings, whether with his Cabinet or even his National Security Council.

Cabinet secretaries and other aides found that he was more attentive in one-on-one interviews, and the most successful of them knew to keep their presentations crisp and to the point. A door was always open for a small group of trusted insiders, including his brother Robert, speechwriter Theodore Sorensen, and political advisers Dave Powers and Kenneth O'Donnell.

His advisers found him to be a quick study. He peppered policy experts with questions, especially on foreign policy issues, and took an active leadership role in Cabinet meetings. Transcripts made during the Cuban missile crisis showed him in command of tense meetings, quick to question and probe various proposals for action.

9 Kennedy and Indian Prime Minister Jawaharlal Nehru issue a statement after four days of discussion. They agree on the neutrality of Laos, free access rights to Berlin, and the urgent need for a test-ban treaty.

10 Amid public skepticism over federal unemployment statistics, Kennedy appoints a new panel to review Labor Department methods of gathering and reporting data.

11 During a Veterans Day ceremony, the President places a wreath at the Tomb of the Unknown Soldier and says, "The only way to maintain the peace is to be prepared in the final extreme to fight for our country—and to mean it."

12 Three days after a chartered airliner crash kills more than 75 people near Richmond, Virginia, President Kennedy orders immediate steps to modernize the U.S. air traffic control system.

13 President and Mrs. Kennedy host a state dinner for Puerto Rican Governor Luis Munoz Marin. Cellist Pablo Casals performs at the White House event.

14 Kennedy and South Korean President Park Chung-hee meet at the White House. They issue a joint statement affirming the U.S. commitment to defend Seoul with armed force if necessary.

15 As weary Berliners begin to accept that their ordeal will not be short, East German workers continue to reinforce weak spots in the Berlin Wall. Escape attempts have become increasingly desperate and rarely successful.

Nov 23 SOVIETS DETAIN U.S. ARMY TRAIN

WEST BERLIN—A U.S. Army train, carrying 74 American troops and family members (including 11 children), was detained last night by Soviet border guards. The incident, which took more than 14 hours to resolve, occurred at the Marienborn checkpoint as the train attempted to pass into West Germany.

Following established protocol, the Soviets were denied permission to board and search the train despite claims that there was an East German stowaway on board. After a protracted deadlock, the train was allowed to pass once an East German citizen was turned over to the Soviets. The investigation is ongoing, and the Army has sent an officer from West Berlin to launch an inquiry.

Despite the apparent presence of a stowaway, as the Soviets claimed, American officials suspect that the detention was a Soviet attempt to set a precedent for searching Allied transports through the East-West checkpoints.

President Kennedy was briefed on the situation while enjoying his Thanksgiving holiday at the family compound in Hyannisport, Massachusetts. The Kennedys celebrated the holiday with a roast turkey dinner for 33. Most of the assembled guests were members of the President's large extended family.

Nov 28 KENNEDY EXPRESSES HIS VIEWS TO THE SOVIET PEOPLE

Moscow—Residents of Moscow flocked to newsstands today to read what President Kennedy had to say about their nation. On Saturday, Kennedy granted an in-depth interview with the editor of *Izvestia*, Alexei I. Adzhubei, Premier Khrushchev's son-in-law. Kennedy's words were reprinted as is, allowing him to direct an unfiltered message to the Soviet people.

The theme of Kennedy's plea was self-determination. The President said he wants the Soviets to stop spreading communism to other nations. If other countries decide on their own to adopt communism, so be it. But he urged that the Kremlin devote its attention solely to the welfare and security of its own people.

Kennedy expressed his discouragement regarding the crises of recent months—nuclear testing and Berlin. However, the tone of his comments was generally conciliatory and optimistic. It was best summarized in a statement he made halfway through the interview:

"We believe that if the Soviet Union—without attempting to impose the Communist system—will permit the people of the world to live as they wish to live, relations between the Soviet Union and the United States will then be very satisfactory, and our two peoples, which now live in danger, will be able to live in peace and with a greatly increased standard of living. And I believe we have such vast economic opportunities now in both of our countries that we should consider how we can get along, and not attempt to impose our views, one on the other or on anyone else."

"We believe that if the Soviet Union—without attempting to impose the Communist system—will permit the people of the world to live as they wish to live, relations between the Soviet Union and the United States will then be very satisfactory...." —KENNEDY

Dec 2 KENNEDY SALUTES PLAYERS AT ARMY-NAVY GAME

PHILADELPHIA—The Midshipmen emerged victorious from the annual Army-Navy football game, played today at Philadelphia Municipal Stadium. President Kennedy, a Navy veteran, was in attendance, though officially impartial in his role as commander-in-chief.

The President performed the pregame coin toss and then settled back in the stands to enjoy the game as a spectator.

In a public letter to the cadets and midshipmen, reproduced in the official program, the President praised the skill and spirit of the young men, both off and on the field. Claiming that the American people are the true winners of the game, he lauded the "skill and perfection with which the players of both teams perform, all of which bring to the Officer Corps of our Armed Forces lasting benefit in terms of leadership.... [O]ur nation is stronger, and the cause of freedom in the world is safer from encroachment."

Kennedy shakes hands with New York Mayor Robert F. Wagner at the Army-Navy game.

November

16 JFK arrives in Seattle at the start of a three-day trip through the West. He tells an audience at the University of Washington that "diplomacy and defense are not substitutes for one another. Either alone would fall."

17 In the first of several trips into politically conservative states, President Kennedy attends an Arizona event honoring the career of Senator Carl Hayden, age 84.

18 The President detours to Bonham, Texas, where he attends the funeral of Representative Sam Rayburn, who had served as speaker of the House for 17 years until his death.

19 Resuming his western tour, Kennedy has lunch at the California home of brother-in-law Peter Lawford before speaking at a Democratic Party dinner in Hollywood.

20 U.S. warships wait in waters near the Dominican Republic. Yesterday, their show of force reportedly convinced two brothers of the late Generalissimo Trujillo to leave the country and abandon plans to restore his dictatorship.

21 As West Berlin police struggle to contain protesting students near the Berlin Wall, Kennedy hosts a state visit and planning discussions with German Chancellor Konrad Adenauer at the White House.

22 Kennedy approves 15,000 additional military advisers for South Vietnam. Meanwhile, Diem's government is said to be reeling from internal corruption and a series of attacks by the Vietcong.

Congolese troops guard soldiers of a Sudanese contingent of UN forces in Matadi, Congo, in March 1961.

Dec 6 U.S. Not with "Doves" on Congo

WASHINGTON—With United Nations peacekeeping forces under attack in the Republic of the Congo, the United States is taking a more militant approach to the situation than France and Great Britain are.

Secessionists of the Katanga Province are fighting to gain their independence from the Congo. UN forces are working with the Congolese government to keep the country (all six provinces) together. The U.S. is responding to the secessionists' recent attacks at Elisabethville with an offer of 21 transport planes to the UN. Moreover, U.S. State Department spokesman Lincoln White supported the directive of UN Secretary General U Thant, which is for UN forces "to take such action as is necessary to defend themselves and carry on their operations in the Congo."

Britain and France, however, do not like the tone of Thant's order. They fear that the UN troops will use their military might to force the Katanga secessionists into submission. Such action, they claim, is not the role of the United Nations.

U.S. officials are concerned that if the Congo falls into further crisis, the Soviet Union will try to gain influence in that country. They fear that communism will spread in Africa just like it has in Southeast Asia.

Dec 6 JFK Talks Fitness at Banquet

NEW YORK—President Kennedy was awarded the National Football Foundation's Gold Medal at New York's Waldorf-Astoria Hotel last night. In his acceptance speech, he encouraged universal participation in athletics while decrying the decline in Americans' fitness levels in recent years. According to Kennedy, the "sad fact is that it looks more and more as if our national sport is not playing at all—but watching. We have become more and more not a nation of athletes but a nation of spectators."

The President pointed out that all this spectating is having a real impact on Americans' health. The Selective Service is an excellent barometer of our physical fitness as a nation. The number of young men classified as physically unfit for military service continues to rise, and it now requires a call-up of seven men to find two who are both physically and mentally able to serve.

Kennedy seeks to remedy this problem in several ways. He suggests a cultural shift that would encourage mass participation in sports and offer broad support for the U.S. Olympic development program. The new President's Council on Youth Fitness, which has devised basic fitness programs to be implemented in the nation's elementary and secondary schools, is certainly one step in the right direction. Kennedy encouraged parents to support their children in this new initiative, as "physical health and vitality constitute an essential element of a vigorous American community."

Citing Thomas Jefferson's own dedication to two hours of daily exercise, the President pointed out that if a "man who wrote the Declaration of Independence, was Secretary of State, and twice President could give it two hours, our children can give it 10 or 15 minutes."

Dec 11 | U.S. COPTER CREWS WILL FIGHT IN VIETNAM

SAIGON—Thirty-three U.S. Army helicopters, along with their pilots and crews, arrived in Saigon today. Thus, for the first time, the United States will be providing direct military assistance to South Vietnam in its fight against Communist guerrillas.

Two U.S. Army helicopter companies, totaling some 400 men, traversed the Saigon River aboard the aircraft ferry USS *Core.* Thousands of South Vietnamese lined the river to view the massive vessel.

General Maxwell Taylor, and even President Kennedy himself, have had extensive conversations with the South Vietnamese government about what can be done to help that country fend off the Communist threat. The most pressing need, President Ngo Dinh Diem has insisted, is helicopters. These aircraft are able to transport soldiers to the country's jungles and mountainous terrain, where many of the Vietcong (Communist) troops are gathered.

The U.S. previously sent military "advisers" to train and aid South Vietnamese soldiers. But this is the first time that American soldiers will be directly involved in the military operations. The U.S. has also provided Laos with helicopters, but not pilots and crew.

23 As the Kennedys spend Thanksgiving Day with more than 30 extended family members on Cape Cod, Soviet troops along the East German border detain a U.S. Army train for 15 hours.

24 The White House announces that a dozen more military contractors have agreed to give equal employment rights to minorities.

25 At Newport News, Virginia, the U.S. Navy commissions the USS *Enterprise,* the world's first nuclear-powered aircraft carrier.

26 In a shake-up that some call the "Thanksgiving Day Massacre," Kennedy reorganizes the leadership of the State Department. He replaces Chester Bowles with George Ball as undersecretary of state and appoints Averell Harriman assistant undersecretary for Far Eastern Affairs.

27 The State Department instructs U.S. Ambassador to South Vietnam Frederick Nolting to relax American insistence on participating in decisions by the Diem regime.

28 Moscow's *Izvestia* publishes an unabridged interview conducted with President Kennedy by editor Alexei Adzhubei, who is Premier Khrushchev's son-in-law. JFK seizes the chance to speak directly to Russians about his views on nuclear testing and Berlin.

29 The U.S. space program takes a key step toward manned orbital flight when it successfully launches and recovers Enos, a chimpanzee, after a nearly four-hour flight in Mercury 5.

30 By executive order, Kennedy approves the selective military use of jungle defoliant operations in Vietnam.

Negroes are arrested on December 12 for marching outside City Hall. Police Chief Laurie Pritchett has orchestrated the mass arrests.

Dec 13 NEGROES ARRESTED IN ALBANY

ALBANY, GA.—More than 200 Negroes were arrested here today, marking the second straight day of mass arrests in this southwest Georgia city.

Yesterday, 267 Negro students, prompted by the Student Nonviolent Coordinating Committee (SNCC), marched to Albany's Union Railway Terminal to protest segregation. They were arrested for trespassing. Today, 200 protesters knelt at the courthouse, praying for those who had been arrested. These protesters were also arrested. Police Chief Laurie Pritchett said he would not tolerate mass demonstrations by any "nigger organization."

The events here are becoming the biggest civil rights story since the springtime Freedom Rides. The leaders of the Albany movement are demanding an end to segregation, harassment, and reprisals for trying to vote. After today's events, hundreds of Negroes gathered and called for a downtown protest tomorrow.

The White House has yet to get involved in the Albany crisis.

Dec 14 JFK RAILS FOR WOMEN'S RIGHTS

WASHINGTON—Throughout his first year in office, President Kennedy has tried to ensure that all members of society are getting a fair slice of the pie. Today he showed his support for America's working women. By signing Executive Order 10980, Kennedy established the President's Commission on the Status of Women.

Former First Lady Eleanor Roosevelt will head the 26-member group, which will consist of 15 women and 11 men. The commission, the President stated, will review progress and make recommendations in the following areas:

• Employment policies and practices, including those on wages, under federal contracts.

• Federal social insurance and tax laws as they affect the net earnings and other income of women.

• Federal and state labor laws dealing with such matters as hours, night work, and wages, to determine whether they are accomplishing the purposes for which they were established and whether they should be adapted to changing technological, economic, and social conditions.

• Differences in legal treatment of men and women in regard to political and civil rights, property rights, and family relations.

• New and expanded services that may be required for women as wives, mothers, and workers, including education, counseling, training, home services, and arrangements for care of children during the working day.

• The employment policies and practices of the government of the United States, with reference to additional affirmative steps that should be taken through legislation, executive or administrative action to assure nondiscrimination on the basis of sex and to enhance constructive employment opportunities for women.

> *"…if we lose this war, our people will be swallowed by the Communist bloc."*
> *— SOUTH VIETNAMESE PRESIDENT NGO DINH DIEM*

Dec 15 KENNEDY EXPRESSES HIS COMMITMENT TO VIETNAM

WASHINGTON—Letters released by the White House today indicate America's strong commitment to South Vietnam in its fight against communism. The letters, the dates of which were not disclosed, were penned by President Kennedy and President Ngo Dinh Diem.

Regarding South Vietnam's war with Vietcong guerrillas, Diem wrote to Kennedy that "if we lose this war, our people will be swallowed by the Communist bloc."

Kennedy offered his sympathies, writing: "We have been deeply disturbed by the assault on your country. Our indignation has mounted as the deliberate savagery of the Communist program of assassination, kidnapping and wanton violence became clear…. We shall seek to persuade the Communists to give up their attempts of force and subversion."

The President also offered help to Diem, including military aid, writing: "We shall promptly increase our assistance to your defense effort…. I have already given orders to get these programs under way."

U.S. Army helicopter crews arrived in Saigon just four days ago.

The U.S. will help South Vietnam repel the Vietcong (pictured).

1 The White House announces that Abraham Ribicoff, secretary of Health, Education and Welfare, will chair a commission to study possible federal action on mental health issues.

2 President Kennedy attends the annual Army-Navy football game in Philadelphia. Officially impartial as commander-in-chief, the former *PT-109* commander nevertheless has to be pleased that Navy wins, 13-7.

3 This month, the Defense Department is working to protect the employment and housing rights of National Guardsmen and other reservists who are called to active duty or sudden mobilization.

4 The President extends until at least mid-1962 the existing ban on importing sugar from Cuba.

5 At the NFL Hall of Fame banquet, President Kennedy tells guests that Americans are becoming a "nation of spectators," and that school systems should embrace the standards of the national Council on Youth Fitness.

6 In New York, JFK asks leaders of the National Association of Manufacturers to support his negotiations with Europe on tariff cuts. He then flies to Florida to make the same appeal to the AFL-CIO.

7 In response to a deepening crisis in secessionist Katanga, the United States provides more than 20 troop transport planes to ferry UN ground troops to the Congo.

8 The President congratulates the people of Tanganyika upon the eve of their independence from Britain.

Dec 16 VENEZUELANS CHEER KENNEDYS

CARACAS—When Vice President Richard Nixon visited Venezuela three years ago, angry protesters pounded his car with clubs and pipes. Today, President Kennedy received a much more gracious reception. An estimated 300,000 people crowded the streets of Caracas to cheer the President and First Lady. Officials said there were no violent incidents and no arrests.

As evidenced by their trip to Europe in June, the attractive First Couple has attained international celebrity status. Today, Jacqueline Kennedy earned raves for her fashion sense (an apricot-colored coat) and her use of the Spanish language.

President Kennedy's Alliance for Progress also seems to be a hit among Venezuelans. The United States is supplying Venezuela and other Central American countries with loans and credits for road construction and agricultural and medical initiatives. The administration's generosity is part of its master plan of spreading democracy throughout Central America.

Addressing the people, Kennedy declared: "One of the first goals of the new inter-Americanism must be the elimination of all such tyranny, of whatever source or breed, until this is a hemisphere of democratic and independent nations from Cape Horn to the Arctic Circle." The crowd erupted in applause.

The Kennedys, who visited Puerto Rico yesterday, now move on to Columbia.

President Kennedy is warmly welcomed by the citizens of Caracas, who have embraced his message of democracy and freedom.

9 In a portent of things to come, the first two companies of U.S. Army helicopters deploy to Saigon.

10 In New Mexico, an attempt to demonstrate peaceful uses for nuclear detonation goes awry. Some 400 observers from more than a dozen nations are jolted by the unexpected strength of a blast.

11 On the heels of the helicopter arrivals, South Vietnam welcomes the arrival of a task force led by the aircraft carrier USS *Core*. On board are some 400 men, including helicopter pilots and support crew.

12 Hundreds of civil rights demonstrators are arrested during marches in Montgomery, Alabama, and Albany, Georgia.

13 As the Kennedys prepare for their first holiday season in the White House, President and Mrs. Kennedy host a party in the East Room for White House employees.

14 Kennedy establishes the President's Commission on the Status of Women, a compromise that fulfills a campaign promise to Eleanor Roosevelt but avoids mention of the controversial Equal Rights Amendment, which Kennedy's labor supporters oppose.

15 The Kennedys arrive in San Juan, Puerto Rico, to an enthusiastic welcome on their way to Venezuela and Colombia.

16 Martin Luther King, Jr., and more than 150 others are arrested in Albany, Georgia, as they hold a prayer vigil for previously arrested civil rights marchers.

More than 60 Negro demonstrators kneel in prayer outside Albany's City Hall on December 13.

Dec 18 CITY, NEGROES REACH AGREEMENT IN ALBANY

ALBANY, GA.—After month-long protests, the Albany movement came to an end today. City representatives agreed to desegregate Albany's bus and train facilities, release all jailed demonstrators, and arrange a meeting to listen to the concerns of local Negro citizens.

Hundreds of protesters were arrested in Albany during the last week, including 265 people two days ago. But unlike with the Freedom Rides, local whites refrained from violence, thus avoiding northern indignation. On December 15, Reverend Martin Luther King, Jr., had urged Negroes to continue protesting for the rights. "Don't get weary," he said. "We will wear them down with our capacity to suffer." King was arrested the next day but then released.

Some critics are calling the Albany movement a failure. The movement failed to elicit intervention by the federal government or spark national outrage, both of which happened with this spring's Freedom Rides.

Dec 20 JFK Visits Ailing Joe Sr.

West Palm Beach, Fla.—Joseph Kennedy, Sr., rested comfortably this morning after suffering a stroke yesterday afternoon. However, the stroke caused partial paralysis of his left side, and doctors are unsure about his fate. The Kennedy patriarch fell ill while playing golf yesterday.

President Kennedy and his wife, Jacqueline, arrived at the hospital this morning at 10:30. They stayed for 45 minutes, conferring with doctors and family. Joseph Kennedy was asleep throughout the visit. President Kennedy still plans to meet with British Prime Minister Harold Macmillan today, although the conference might be in Palm Beach instead of Bermuda, as planned.

Joseph Kennedy, 73, an Irish Catholic from Boston, was a successful businessman when he befriended Franklin D. Roosevelt during World War I. As president, FDR appointed Kennedy chairman of the U.S. Securities and Exchange Commission, and Kennedy later directed the Maritime Commission. He served as the U.S. ambassador to the United Kingdom at the beginning of World War II.

Caroline Kennedy marvels at the White House Christmas tree days before the trip to Florida.

Dec 25
A Subdued Christmas for Kennedy Family

West Palm Beach, Fla.—Christmas day for America's "ideal" family was anything but traditional today. The Kennedys spent the day in West Palm Beach, home of President Kennedy's father, who remains hospitalized.

Caroline Kennedy, four, and John Jr., one, found presents under the tree this morning. But a short time later, the family drove to St. Mary's Hospital, where they visited Joe Sr., gathered with family members, and attended mass at the hospital chapel.

The Kennedy patriarch has not recovered well since suffering a stroke six days ago. Not only is he partially paralyzed, but he developed symptoms of pneumonia. Dr. Walter Newborn performed surgery to relieve congestion in the chest and throat.

THE FIRST FATHER

Joseph P. Kennedy, John F. Kennedy's father, was an ambitious, highly successful business leader and political insider who carefully plotted his family's rise to the top of America's power structure. He was a graduate of Harvard, a bank president by the time he was 25, the first chairman of the Securities and Exchange Commission, and the U.S. ambassador to the Court of St. James in London in the early years of World War II.

Joseph Kennedy was at times a demanding father who often expressed impatience with young Jack's health problems. But once his son began his political career, Joe put the family's fortune and influence at his disposal. The President often noted that his father made the family's success possible.

John Kennedy respected his father's political acumen, although on occasion he acknowledged the pressure of having a hard-charging parent. JFK thought it would be a bad idea to give his brother Robert a high-profile presidential appointment, but he wound up offering him the post of attorney general because his father insisted.

In December 1961, Joseph Kennedy suffered a massive stroke while playing golf in Florida. JFK was in Washington at the time; he immediately flew to Florida to be at his father's side. Joseph, who was 73 when he fell ill, never spoke another word for the rest of his life. The stroke rendered him mute.

The President visited his father frequently in the months to come. During one such visit, a photographer took a picture of Kennedy kissing his father on the head. The bond between father and son was evident.

December

17 Kennedy tells an audience in Venezuela that the "new spirit of this hemisphere requires the elimination of all tyranny, until this is a continent from north to south of free men living under a system of liberty."

18 Albany, Georgia, officials release jailed civil rights protesters. The city promises, but later fails, to desegregate city transportation and address other grievances.

19 Joseph P. Kennedy, the President's father, suffers a stroke that will limit his ability to speak for the last eight years of his life.

20 According to *The New York Times*, approximately 2,000 American soldiers and advisers are on the ground in Vietnam.

21 The U.S. Army releases photographs that it says show an American Nike-Zeus anti-missile missile intercepting another missile in flight.

22 American forces suffer their first battlefield death in Vietnam when U.S. Army Specialist James T. Davis is killed.

23 President and Mrs. Kennedy travel to Palm Beach, Florida, where they visit Joseph Kennedy at St. Mary's Hospital.

24 After visiting his stricken father in Palm Beach, President Kennedy meets President Arturo Frondizi of Argentina to urge support for a meeting of the hemisphere's foreign ministers on Cuban-Soviet ties.

25 In a recorded television message to residents of Berlin, the President affirms his support for their freedom, saying "we are at your side now, as before."

Dec 27 KENNEDY "BACK" IN THE GROOVE

WEST PALM BEACH, FLA.—President Kennedy's back problem, which plagued him throughout the spring and into the summer, seems to be much improved. Dr. Preston Wade, a specialist from New York, examined the President today and declared that he had made much progress.

Earlier this year, Kennedy took shots of novocaine for his back and hopped along on crutches. Kennedy, who underwent back surgeries in the 1940s and '50s, has worn a corset as well as a lift in one of his shoes, and he often sits in a rocking chair. But Dr. Wade said that after two and half months of diligent exercise, the President's back is much stronger.

Said Press Secretary Pierre Salinger: "It will be several more months, however, before the President can resume vigorous physical activity, and he must expect to experience, as do all people with similar back troubles, ups and downs and occasional setbacks."

Dec 31 JFK ASSESSES HIS YEAR IN OFFICE

WEST PALM BEACH, FLA.—Newspapers nationwide today published President Kennedy's frank assessment of the first year of his term. Written for the United Press International by veteran journalist Merriman Smith, the article portrays a president cautiously confident that, after a year of escalating Cold War tensions, the Western alliance has come out ahead. From the Soviets' inability to add any Middle Eastern or African nations to their bloc, to what is looking more and more like societal failure in East Germany, it has been a tough year for communism.

Berlin and Southeast Asia remain trouble spots. And though Kennedy does not feel that the threat of war has materially diminished in the past year, the situation in Laos is not as immediately critical as it was. Moving forward, negotiations with the Soviets over Berlin will likely serve as a barometer of East-West relations for years to come.

Another source of concern is the Soviet resumption of atmospheric nuclear testing, something Kennedy is now saying he will not rule out for the United States, given the limitations of underground testing. Not surprisingly, the President does not expect the new year to hold much improvement with regard to relations between the United States and the Soviet Union.

Kennedy asserts that U.S. foreign policy under his administration is essentially staying the course of U.S. policy since the end of World War II. Like his predecessors, he believes that communism is best contained by the United States supporting the success of independent, free states worldwide.

THE PEACE CORPS

December

26 Second thoughts surround a yearlong plan to establish a highly profitable American network of communication satellites, which officials now believe is unlikely anytime soon.

27 While extending his visit to his father's side in Palm Beach, the President receives his own physical examination. The official report deems Kennedy "in excellent general health except for his back."

28 In response to a financial crisis facing the United Nations, the White House will seek approval from Congress to buy half of a $200 million UN bond issue.

29 The Kennedys cruise with family members on the presidential yacht that he has dubbed *Honey Fitz,* in honor of his grandfather.

30 Due to the illness of the President's father, the White House delays until March the First Lady's planned goodwill trip to India and Pakistan.

31 U.S. newspapers publish the President's own account of his first year in office; despite a lack of progress in East-West relations, he says, a third world war is less likely.

Decades after John F. Kennedy's untimely death, the Peace Corps remains one of his administration's best-known legacies. Ironically, JFK did not originate this vibrant symbol of his New Frontier. Minnesota Senator Hubert Humphrey proposed sending young American volunteers to the world's underdeveloped nations.

Humphrey's vision of young Americans helping poverty-stricken villagers in Africa, Asia, and the Indian subcontinent appealed to Kennedy's idealistic streak. He made the issue his own during a campaign stop at the University of Michigan in October, when he challenged students to consider careers in the Foreign Service or in other kinds of work in developing nations. He returned to the theme on November 2, using the phrase "peace corps" to describe a new organization devoted to alleviating poverty and disease across the globe.

Kennedy moved quickly to make this borrowed vision reality. On March 1, 1961, he created the Peace Corps with an executive order, and named his brother-in-law, Sargent Shriver, to head the effort. In describing the new organization, Kennedy said he wanted young Americans to experience first-hand conditions in the developing world. A member of the Peace Corps, he said, would eat local food, speak local languages, and otherwise live as local residents lived.

Kennedy described the Peace Corps as a vehicle for youthful idealism, but the initiative had a political edge as well. Kennedy believed the U.S. was losing support in developing countries because American diplomats were too far removed from daily life to make a difference.

More than 160,000 Americans have served in the Peace Corps since 1961.

PROFOUND CHALLENGES

Kennedy faces crises at home and abroad in 1962, including a showdown with the Soviets that puts the U.S. on the brink of nuclear war.

In his famous inaugural address, John Kennedy told the country and the world that he welcomed the many challenges his generation faced. In 1962, he had no shortage of challenges to welcome, no lack of crises to manage. By the end of that momentous year, he was as popular as he had ever been or would be.

Some of the issues he faced were variations on a theme: Cuba, Berlin, and Communist aggression in Southeast Asia. Others were just beginning to develop: the burgeoning civil rights movement in the South, nuclear proliferation, and a less-than-robust economy.

Vietnam loomed large during the opening weeks of the year, as the pro-American government of South Vietnam showed signs of collapse in the face of a Communist insurgency. Kennedy, though skeptical of committing the U.S. to a land war in Asia, nevertheless dispatched more military advisers to assist the beleaguered regime in Saigon.

His hand was forced again when he decided to resume nuclear testing after the Soviet Union unilaterally ended an informal boycott of such tests in late 1961. Kennedy loathed the idea of testing nuclear weapons because of the environmental damage they caused and because renewed testing seemed to foreshadow a new and very expensive arms race. JFK reminded the country in April that the world's nuclear powers held "the power of self-extinction."

That warning seemed to foreshadow the most significant event of 1962, the Cuban missile crisis. Kennedy learned in October that the Soviets were building missile sites in Cuba, sites that could be used to launch nuclear weapons against the U.S. Kennedy's advisers were divided about the nation's proper response. Some military aides, most prominently Air Force General Curtis LeMay, advocated an immediate strike against the sites. Others urged a more cautious approach.

JFK chose a middle ground, telling the world on October 22 that the U.S. would set up a blockade around Cuba to prevent the landing of any more missiles. He used back-channel talks to communicate with Soviet leader Nikita Khrushchev. And, perhaps most importantly, he made it clear to Moscow that he would not back down. Instead, the Soviets did, agreeing to remove the missiles after the U.S. privately assured Moscow that it would dismantle its own missiles in Turkey.

The Cuban missile crisis put the U.S. and Soviet Union near the brink of nuclear war. It was the most difficult episode of JFK's presidency, but it was not his only crisis that fall.

James Meredith was a young African-American who wished to enroll at the segregated University of Mississippi. When Meredith won a lawsuit allowing him to enroll, the town of Oxford, Mississippi, exploded in violence. Kennedy, was forced to send in federal troops on October 1.

Kennedy called the violence in Mississippi "the worst thing I've seen in forty-five years." That was just a few days before he learned that the Soviets had missiles in Cuba.

Robert and John Kennedy confer during the missile crisis.

MAN of the YEAR

TIME
THE WEE AZINE

Time stated that JFK took office with a "youth-can-do-anything sort of self-confidence."

"This job is interesting…but the possibilities for trouble are unlimited." —KENNEDY

Jan 5 JFK NAMED "MAN OF THE YEAR"

NEW YORK—*Time* has named President John F. Kennedy its "Man of the Year" for 1961. Kennedy becomes the fourth president so honored by the weekly newsmagazine, following Franklin Roosevelt, Harry Truman, and Dwight Eisenhower. It is the 35th year that *Time* has bestowed the title.

The cover portrait, which shows the 35th president looking solemn and reflective, is accompanied by an article that takes stock of the young chief executive's first year in office. The story reveals a president whose confidence, while still high, is somewhat subdued compared to that of President-Elect Kennedy a year earlier. As the President said, "This job is interesting…but the possibilities for trouble are unlimited. It represents a chance to exercise your judgment on matters of importance. It takes a lot of thought and effort. It's been a tough first year, but then they're all going to be tough."

In the final analysis, *Time* commends Kennedy for a job well done. The magazine notes that as Kennedy continues to develop the leadership qualities he has shown thus far in the battle against the forces of communism, he will certainly be remembered as a great president.

Jan 10 USSR, Cuba Broker Deal

Moscow—The Soviet Union and Cuba have reached accord on a new trade agreement. The deal, signed yesterday in Havana, calls for the Soviet Union to provide Cuba with such goods as oil, metals, chemicals, fertilizers, wheat, and machinery. Cuba will export sugar, alcohol, tobacco, and fruit to the Soviet Union.

The agreement was born out of the bad relations between the United States and Cuba in recent years. Economic sanctions launched by the Eisenhower administration in 1960 severely curtailed Cuba's access to oil—as well as its main market for sugar exports. Less than three months later, the United States broke off diplomatic relations with the Caribbean island.

JFK AND LBJ

Lyndon Johnson was a legendary figure on Capitol Hill during the Eisenhower years. As majority leader of the U.S. Senate, he was a shrewd, tough, and highly effective lawmaker.

As John Kennedy's vice president, the proud Texan found himself in the shadow of both Kennedy brothers and their high-profile advisers. The vice president resented the Ivy League types who populated the White House—particularly Robert Kennedy. The attorney general returned LBJ's contempt.

But Johnson had the President's respect and trust. Kennedy knew that Johnson helped him win Texas—and without the Lone Star State, JFK would have been a loser in 1960. Kennedy biographer Richard Reeves wrote that Kennedy often chastised friends and allies who poked fun at the earthy, unpolished vice president.

Kennedy sent Johnson to South Vietnam on an important fact-finding mission in 1961, and he asked him to chair a presidential Committee on Equal Employment Opportunity—a task force designed to eliminate racial discrimination in the workplace. In 1963, Johnson used his influence on Capitol Hill to rally support for JFK's civil rights program.

Johnson argued that developing countries would judge the U.S. by its leadership, or lack thereof, in the space race. That argument helped inspire JFK's pledge to land a man on the moon by the end of the 1960s.

Johnson and Kennedy may not have liked each other, but they often worked well together.

January

1 The administration is formulating proposals for key defense budget items for the next fiscal year, which starts July 1; $4.1 billion will be sought for Minuteman missiles and Polaris submarines.

2 While continuing with plans to airlift 4,000 more troops to West Germany, the White House uses several diplomatic channels to test Soviet flexibility on Berlin.

3 Kennedy increases regular U.S. Army troop strength by two divisions, paving the way to release an equal number of National Guard reservists on active duty later in 1962.

4 The President congratulates Syrian President Nazim al-Kudsi on his inauguration. Syria has been plagued by instability since seceding from the United Arab Republic in September 1961.

5 *Time* magazine names JFK its 35th "Man of the Year." He becomes the fourth consecutive U.S. president to receive the label.

6 Following the previous day's lifting of sanctions against the Dominican Republic by the Organization of American States, Washington restores diplomatic relations with that nation.

7 After arguments between General Lucius Clay and the State Department over how to handle military operations in Berlin, Kennedy meets with Clay and announces full unity on future tactics in the troubled city.

8 As the White House digests a confidential study urging drastic tariff cuts, the President meets with West German Economic Minister Ludwig Erhard to discuss European policies and the U.S. balance-of-payments deficit.

Kennedy earned bipartisan support for his foreign agenda, but not necessarily for his costly domestic plans.

Jan 11 KENNEDY'S WANT LIST

President's State of the Union Address Loaded with Requests

WASHINGTON—Democratic congressmen applauded while conservative Republicans squirmed in their seats today as President Kennedy made more than 30 requests in his State of the Union address.

After a year of stresses—including a back problem, his father's illness, and Cold War crises—the President appeared healthy and full of vigor today. He also plans to keep Congress quite busy throughout the year. His many proposals included:

"At year's end, the economy which Mr. Khrushchev once called a 'stumbling horse' was racing to new records in consumer spending, labor income, and industrial production." —KENNEDY

• Passage of the Manpower Training and Development Act, which would provide training to those "whose only skill has been replaced by a machine, or moved with a mill, or shut down with a mine."

• Passage of the Youth Employment Opportunities Act, to train and place young workers.

• A five-year tariff plan that would gradually eliminate all tariffs in the U.S. and European Common Market countries on all items that are produced mostly in the U.S. and those countries.

• A $3 billion commitment to the Alliance for Progress program.

• Funding for an international communications satellite system.

• The passage of a 1961 bill that would provide federal money for public school construction and an increase in teacher salaries.

• Funding for colleges, specifically scholarship money and classroom construction.

• Funding for medical and dental schools due to the shortage of doctors and dentists.

• Federal incentives for the building of public fallout shelters.

• Executive powers to adjust income tax rates during a recession.

• Tax credits to encourage modernization and expansion of industrial plants.

• Welfare reform, with an emphasis on helping people help themselves.

• Reform of the food and drug laws so that consumers are better protected.

• Improved unemployment insurance benefits.

• Salary increases for federal workers.

On issues of foreign policy, the President stressed that the U.S. has greatly improved its military preparedness over the past year. During this time of heightened Cold War tensions, he reiterated his commitment to a nuclear disarmament agreement.

"A year ago," he concluded, "in assuming the tasks of the presidency, I said that few generations, in all history, had been granted the role of being the great defender of freedom in its hour of maximum danger.... And while no nation has ever faced such a challenge, no nation has ever been so ready to seize the burden and the glory of freedom."

9 In the Rose Garden, Kennedy welcomes members of the Vienna Boys Choir, who perform a brief concert for guests.

10 As the Cuban economy reels under the U.S. embargo, Havana and Moscow agree on a new, $700 million trade agreement that will swap Cuban sugar and other goods for Soviet oil supplies.

11 In his first true State of the Union address, Kennedy asks Congress for the authority to cut income taxes and reduce tariffs.

12 The boards of the two largest U.S. railroad companies, the Pennsylvania and New York Central, agree to merge, subject to regulatory approval.

13 After months of instability in the Congo, fighting erupts in Stanleyville. Four rival regimes in the African country count on varying support from American, European, Soviet, and other interested foreign governments.

14 Underscoring Kennedy's ambitious goal of a manned flight to the moon, the administration plans to devote $5.5 billion of the next year's budget to military and civilian space exploration.

15 At his first news conference of 1962, the President says that no Americans in Vietnam are involved in combat operations.

16 U.S. and European Common Market negotiators reach partial agreement on lowering tariffs on agricultural products.

17 American tanks withdraw from the tense East Berlin border. On the same day in Geneva, Western and Soviet negotiators make progress toward restarting stalled nuclear test-ban talks.

JFK opened the conference by saying the U.S. needed to stress education in science and technology.

"We are taking a chance in all of Southeast Asia."
—KENNEDY

Jan 15 KENNEDY SUMS UP FIRST YEAR IN OFFICE, TOUCHES ON VIETNAM

WASHINGTON—President Kennedy briefly analyzed his first year in office during his news conference today. His biggest disappointment, he said, was the failure to reach an agreement on cessation of nuclear testing. Conversely, he said that the "great surge for unity in the Western nations and in our relations with Latin America" was "most heartening."

The President touched on some two dozen topics in his first press conference of the year. His only brief answer concerned Vietnam. When asked if U.S. troops were now in combat in Vietnam, he said "no" and then moved on to the next question.

Kennedy said that America's willingness to confront Communist aggression is a calculated risk. "We are taking a chance in all of Southeast Asia," he said. "We are taking a chance in other areas also."

Regarding civil rights, a reporter told the President that he had not made good on his promise to issue an order to prohibit racial discrimination in federally assisted housing. Kennedy said he will do so when he "considers it to be in the public interest." Perhaps feeling defensive about the matter, he asserted that his administration has made more progress in civil rights than had been made in the previous eight years.

Jan 16 — U.S. AND EUROPE AGREE ON TARIFF REDUCTIONS

BRUSSELS—The United States and the European Common Market have agreed on broad tariff reductions. The intent is to facilitate more trade across the Atlantic.

The Common Market will reduce tariffs on certain American agricultural products, which last year were valued at more than $600 million. Reciprocally, the U.S. will reduce tariffs on a variety of manufactured goods from Europe.

The Common Market agreed to tariff reductions on most fruits and vegetables, cotton, tallow, soybeans, hides, and skins. It did not agree to tariff concessions on many other agricultural products, including wheat, rice, tobacco, and livestock.

President Kennedy had called for the tariff reductions in his State of the Union address. Though he would have preferred greater reductions, he called the agreement "on the whole satisfactory."

Jan 21 — POLITICAL MOTIVES KILL PRESIDENT'S URBAN BILL

WASHINGTON—President Kennedy's goal of improving conditions in America's cities ran into a political roadblock today. His bill for creating the Department for Urban Affairs was rejected by the House Rules Committee. By a vote of 9-6, the committee decided not to send the bill to the House of Representatives for consideration.

The President was displeased with the committee's decision-making. He said he was "somewhat astonished" that all five Republicans on the committee voted against the bill. "I had gotten the impression two weeks ago…that they shared our concern for some effective management and responsibility of the problems of two-thirds of our population who live in cities," he said.

Race may have had something to do with the bill's defeat. Kennedy had said that he would appoint Robert C. Weaver, a Negro, as head of the department. Perhaps as a response to that decision, four Southern Democrats voted against the bill.

President Kennedy now plans to send not a bill but a "plan" to Congress to form the Department for Urban Affairs. If neither house votes to reject the plan, then the President will have the authority to create the department.

18 The White House submits a balanced budget proposal to Congress for fiscal year 1963 that includes nearly $93 billion each in revenue and expenses.

19 Two days after a similar U.S. gesture, the Soviets withdraw tanks from the center of East Berlin. In New York, Kennedy meets for the first time with UN Secretary General U Thant.

20 After a brief military coup in Santo Domingo followed by American threats to ban sugar imports from the country, civilian government is restored in the Dominican Republic.

21 The First Couple spend the day with Polish Princess Lee Radziwill, Jackie's sister.

22 To bolster the government in the Dominican Republic, President Kennedy announces emergency credit ($25 million) for the country.

23 A hearing on alleged military "muzzling" opens in a subcommittee of the Senate Armed Services Committee, as the administration prepares to defend its policy of censoring speeches and writings by military officers.

24 Kennedy announces that he supports the Pentagon's right to censor speeches made by members of the military.

25 Kennedy's first civil rights legislation, a voting rights bill, is introduced in Congress.

26 Less than two weeks after endorsing an 18-nation disarmament conference, the Soviet delegation in Geneva changes course and insists on returning to stalled three-party talks. U.S. and British negotiators decide to abandon treaty talks until further notice.

(41)
"B"

1. Can the president of the United States be removed from office for conviction of bribery? Yes

2. Check the applicable definition for "treaty":

    ___X___ agreement between nations

    _____ a tax

    _____ a written oration

3. Name the man who is nationally known for heading the Federal Bureau of Investigation for many years. Hoover

4. What officer is designated by the Constitution to be president of the Senate of the United States? Vice President

----

"C"

1. Can the state coin money with the consent of Congress? No

2. Name one area of authority over state militia reserved exclusively to the states. The appointment of officers

3. The power of granting patents, that is, of securing to inventors the exclusive right to their discoveries, is given to the Congress for the purpose of promoting progress.

4. The only legal tender which may be authorized by states for payment of debts is U. S. Currency.

Congressmen want to eliminate "impossible" tests (like this one) that many southern blacks must pass to be eligible to vote.

Jan 25 Dems Offer Voting Rights Bill

WASHINGTON—Unexpectedly, the Kennedy administration will push for voting rights legislation during this session of Congress. Political pundits have long stated that President Kennedy is apprehensive about civil rights issues for fear of alienating southern politicians. However, it appears that he is willing to put the rights of the people ahead of politics.

Today, Senator Mike Mansfield (D-MT) introduced a bill—supported by the President—to curb literacy tests and eliminate poll taxes in federal elections. In many southern states, citizens have to pass "literacy" tests that actually include complex questions about government. Whether or not the applicant passes is up to the subjective discretion of the registrar. This corrupt system allows registrars to accept white applicants and reject Negroes. Five states, all in the South, also have a poll tax, in which voters have to pay to vote—a fee that many impoverished Negroes consider unaffordable.

Mansfield's bill states that in presidential and congressional elections, registrants only have to prove that they were educated through the sixth grade. It also states that their education does not have to be in English.

Southern congressmen are expected to vehemently oppose the bill.

Kennedy gets 100 percent approval from a group of Democratic Party supporters.

Jan 25 KENNEDY'S APPROVAL RATING AT 77 PERCENT

PRINCETON, N.J.—John F. Kennedy is proving to be the most popular president of modern times. After his first year in office, according to the latest Gallup Poll, his approval rating stands at 77 percent.

In comparison, President Franklin Roosevelt's approval rating after one year was 69 percent. Dwight Eisenhower's one-year rating was 71 percent, and Harry Truman's was just 50 percent.

Kennedy, it seems, has won over the public since his inauguration. After all, only 49.7 of voters selected his name in the presidential election, and at the beginning of his presidency his approval rating was 69 percent. It went up from there, and it has not dipped below 70 ever since. Ironically, Kennedy's highest rating of the year, 83 percent, came after the Bay of Pigs fiasco last spring.

Only 11 percent of recent respondents disapprove of JFK's performance, and 12 percent have no opinion. His approval rating stands at 87 percent among Democrats and a healthy 58 percent among Republicans. Despite his commitment to civil rights for Negroes, Southerners give him a 70 percent approval rating. Young voters, those in their 20s, approve of him the most (80 percent).

Finally, despite Kennedy's "sex appeal" with many women, male citizens actually gave him a higher approval rating than female voters—78 percent to 75 percent.

January

27 Technical failures keep *Ranger 3,* an unmanned U.S. spacecraft, from shooting close-up images of the moon before a planned crash-landing of its scientific instruments on the lunar surface. *Ranger 3* misses the moon by 22,000 miles.

28 A story in the *New York Times* Sunday magazine portrays the Kennedys' interest in hosting cultural events at the White House. The story features photos of the First Couple with poets Robert Frost and Carl Sandburg, musician Pablo Casals, and composer Igor Stravinsky.

29 After three years of ebb and flow, the nuclear test-ban conference adjourns in Geneva. American, Soviet, and British delegates appear far from agreement on a framework for international arms control.

30 Failing to create a new urban affairs department through congressional action, the White House seizes on a new tactic: reorganizing the Housing and Home Finance Agency as a Department of Urban Affairs and Housing. The current agency's head, Robert Weaver, will become the first black Cabinet member.

31 White House Press Secretary Pierre Salinger agrees to visit Moscow later in the year for talks on better exchange of information between East and West.

February

1 Kennedy calls on Congress to reform federal social welfare programs. He states that "to demonstrate the compassion of free men—and in the light of our own constructive self-interest—we must bring our welfare programs up to date."

"Merely responding with a relief check to complicated social or personal problems… is not likely to provide a lasting solution."

—KENNEDY

Jan 29 SOVIETS: NUKE BAN TALKS ARE OVER

GENEVA—The nuclear test-ban talks, which had been ongoing since 1958, ended abruptly today. Officials from the United States, Great Britain, and the Soviet Union all agreed that they couldn't agree on the proper terms. But while the American and British delegates wanted to continue to keep the door open for future talks, Soviet delegate Semyon K. Tsarapkin insisted that negotiations were over. He blamed the U.S. and Britain. "The general conference on the discontinuance of nuclear weapons tests has been wrecked by the Western powers," he declared.

Throughout the long and seemingly endless talks, the three nations could not agree on how the test ban would be enforced. The U.S. and Britain wanted a neutral administrator to head the control system. The Soviets disagreed, claiming they would not be able to trust such an overseer. They also claimed that the Western powers wanted to use the "neutral" overseer to spy on the Soviets.

Meanwhile, the U.S. and Britain rejected the Soviets' proposal of a triumvirate overseer committee, which would include representatives of Communist bloc, Western, and neutral nations.

Feb 1 KENNEDY URGES WELFARE REFORM

WASHINGTON—President Kennedy today asked Congress to pass welfare-reform legislation while offering an array of proposals on the matter. Kennedy's suggestions centered on rehabilitation and prevention services.

"Merely responding with a relief check to complicated social or personal problems—such as ill health, faulty education, domestic discord, racial discrimination, or inadequate skills—is not likely to provide a lasting solution," Kennedy said. "Sounder public welfare policies will benefit the nation, its economy, its morale, and most importantly its people."

Kennedy's reform proposals include, among other things, training centers to teach skills to illiterate welfare recipients, day-care facilities for mothers who need to work, and counseling for unwed mothers and troubled families.

The President's proposals are expected to cost close to $200 million—roughly 10 percent of the $2 billion that the federal government devotes to welfare. Kennedy insisted that rehabilitation and prevention will actually save taxpayer money in the long run.

Feb 3 JFK Bans Trade with Cuba

WASHINGTON—President Kennedy today ordered a ban on virtually all trade with Cuba. No longer will the United States import tobacco, vegetables, and other products from Fidel Castro's Communist nation, nor will American companies be allowed to export goods to the island.

The ban on imports is expected to cost Cuba approximately $35 million a year—or roughly one-third of its annual revenue for food exports. For humanitarian reasons, the President will allow some food and medicine to be sent to Cuba. Nevertheless, the drastic loss of revenue will severely hurt the Cuban economy. Florida workers also will take a hit. Several thousand Floridians work in the cigar-making industry, which relies on tobacco from Cuba.

In 1960, before Kennedy took office, the U.S. stopped importing sugar and other goods from Cuba. It allowed the import of only food, tobacco, and medicine—until today. The decision reflects Kennedy's determination to rid the hemisphere of any and all Communist influence.

Feb 5 Castro Denounces U.S. Before Enormous Crowd

HAVANA—Some one million Cubans came out last evening to hear Premier Fidel Castro speak about the recent economic embargo imposed on Cuba by the Kennedy administration. In a message of defiance, Castro labeled the embargo a "felony" and vowed that he would not be intimidated by the U.S.

The capacity crowd listened attentively to the Communist revolutionary for more than two hours, except when they were cheering enthusiastically or offering the clenched-fist salute that is popular among Communists.

Castro also decried what he claimed to be an American effort to deny humanitarian items to the Cuban people, asserting that the embargo will leave Cubans unable to buy medicine.

Premier Castro saved some of his venom for the Organization of American States (OAS). He responded harshly to their decision to exclude Castro's regime from the powerful Latin American organization. According to Castro, the OAS ministers took action at the behest of the United States, which he claims is acting out of fear of a Latin American revolution.

2 The White House proposes legislation to authorize loans to the International Monetary Fund in order to "strengthen the position of the dollar as the world's major reserve currency."

3 By executive order, Kennedy bans all U.S. trade with Cuba, with limited humanitarian exceptions for certain food and medical supplies.

4 On the eve of the Vietnamese New Year, JFK prepares a recorded message to the Vietnamese people. Their "struggle against the aggressive forces of communism," he says, has been "a source of inspiration to people all over the world."

5 Crowds in Havana cheer as Premier Fidel Castro calls Kennedy a "shameless person." He vows that Cuba will not yield under the new American trade embargo.

6 Congress receives an appeal from the White House to authorize more than $5.7 billion over five years for education programs.

7 Frustrated by recent reports on the feasibility of a government-run satellite communication network, the President asks Congress to create a privately owned entity to operate the system.

8 The President claims an executive privilege right to refuse information requested by a Senate subcommittee investigating administration policy on military censorship. Committee chairman Senator John Stennis (D-MS) rules in favor of the President.

Feb 6 JFK: Money Needed for Education

WASHINGTON—President Kennedy today forwarded his Special Message to the Congress on Education, mapping out his vision for the future of education in the United States under his administration.

Underscoring the importance of education, Kennedy stressed how much is being lost when we do not see that all Americans are educated to their maximum capacity. Failure to do so means that young people are unable to make "the maximum contribution of which they are capable to themselves, their families, their communities and the Nation."

Despite acknowledging that American workers are some of the best trained in the world, Kennedy enumerated several failings of our educational system: One million students drop out of high school every year. Hundreds of thousands of qualified students fail to attend college, and of those who do, some 40 percent fail to complete their course of study. Moreover, postwar population growth means that the numbers of students entering the system is growing by leaps and bounds. In less than a decade, elementary school enrollment is expected to increase by 30 percent and college enrollment to double.

Kennedy delivered a similar message to Congress last year. Again, he is asking for funds—some $5.7 billion—to cover improved infrastructure and classroom construction; increased teacher salaries, training, and certification; and financing for grants, loans, and scholarships. In addition, he is asking for funding for special programs, including medical and dental education, science and engineering programs, adult illiteracy, educational television, and aid to handicapped children.

In concluding that it is the responsibility of the federal government to ensure access to education for all Americans, Kennedy pointed out that the "education of our people is a national investment." It is one that yields "tangible returns," he said, and is, in fact, "a basic benefit of a free and democratic civilization."

Kennedy said that the U.S. has increased its aid to South Vietnam as the guerrilla war against the Vietcong has escalated.

Feb 7 President Says Conflict Is Worsening in Vietnam

WASHINGTON—The war in Vietnam is escalating, and the United States continues to aid the South Vietnamese. President Kennedy discussed the conflict during his news conference yesterday, but only after a reporter urged him to address the issue.

"There is a war going on in South Vietnam, and I think that last week there were over 500 killings and assassinations and bombings, and the casualties are high," Kennedy stated. "As I said last week, it is a subterranean war, a guerrilla war of increasing ferocity. The United States, since the end of the Geneva Accord, setting up the South Vietnamese government as an independent government, has been assisting Vietnam economically to maintain its independence, viability, and also sent training groups out there, which have been expanded in recent weeks, as the attacks on the government and the people of South Vietnam have increased."

Currently, more than 3,000 U.S. service personnel are assisting the South Vietnamese against the Vietcong (Communist) guerillas. A small percentage of that total is engaged in combat operations.

"We are out there on training and on transportation," Kennedy said, "and we are assisting in every way we properly can the people of South Vietnam, who with the greatest courage and under danger are attempting to maintain their freedom."

General Paul D. Harkins (right) will head the U.S. Military Assistance Command, Vietnam.

"This is a war we can't afford to lose."
— PENTAGON SPOKESMAN

Feb 8

U.S. MILITARY PLANTS ROOTS IN SAIGON

WASHINGTON—The Pentagon today established the "United States Military Assistance Command, Vietnam" in Saigon. The action indicates that the U.S. is determined to stay in South Vietnam for a considerable period of time in order to help the Republic fight off the Communist Vietcong guerrillas.

General Paul Donal Harkins will head the command. A former lieutenant general, Harkins has been promoted to four-star general in order to illustrate the importance of his new position. President Kennedy was involved in his promotion.

With the word "Assistance" in the title, American officials want the world to know that the United States is not engaged in all-out war. However, U.S. forces are manning transport planes, helicopters, and watercraft in efforts to help the Republic Army in its battles against the Vietcong.

So far, only one American soldier has lost his life during the Vietnam conflict. However, the words of a Pentagon spokesman today indicate the seriousness of the situation. "We're drawing a line here…," he said. "This is a war we can't afford to lose."

9 Following the President's call for a national fallout shelter program, Defense Secretary Robert McNamara submits legislation that would spend $450 million and build shelters for 20 million people within a year.

10 The Russians free American U-2 pilot Francis Gary Powers in Berlin in exchange for Rudolf Abel, a convicted spy who ran a complex Soviet spy operation from a photography studio in New York.

11 Six U.S. Air Force and two South Vietnamese crewmembers are killed when their C-47 crashes during a psychological warfare mission. It is only the second U.S. aircraft to be lost in the conflict.

12 President Kennedy commutes to life in prison the death sentence of Jimmie Henderson, a Navy seaman convicted of murder.

13 At the White House, JFK holds talks with King Saud of Saudi Arabia on a wide range of Middle East issues.

14 Millions watch as CBS and NBC air a tour of the White House with Jacqueline Kennedy, who shows the results of her work to redecorate the residence.

15 News accounts quote President Kennedy confirming that American troops in Vietnam have orders to use weapons for defensive purposes.

16 When citizens protest outside the White House against nuclear weapons testing, JFK sends coffee and hot cocoa to the demonstrators.

17 Kennedy orders federal agencies to develop contingency plans for recovering from a nuclear war.

Feb 12 PRESIDENT COMMUTES SEAMAN'S DEATH SENTENCE

WASHINGTON—President Kennedy today commuted the death sentence of Navy seaman Jimmie Henderson. Convicted murderer Henderson will now spend his life in a federal prison.

Under the Uniform Code of Military Justice, enacted in 1951, only the President, as commander-in-chief, has the authority to approve the execution of a member of the United States Armed Forces.

Ten military men have been executed with presidential approval since 1951, most recently when President Eisenhower approved the execution of John Bennett in 1957. Bennett, who was convicted of the rape and attempted murder of an 11-year-old Austrian girl, went to the gallows just last year.

Feb 13 JFK HOSTS KING OF SAUDI ARABIA

WASHINGTON—President Kennedy and Saudi Arabia's King Saud met at the White House today. Their conference came two weeks after the U.S. leader paid a courtesy call on the King, who was recuperating in Palm Beach after a hospitalization in Boston.

The President and the King's conversation focused on several areas of agreement, such as the importance of deterring an Iraqi attack on Kuwait as well as economic assistance to the new Syrian regime. The two leaders also touched on issues for which they have yet to reach understanding.

King Saud expressed dissatisfaction with American aid to "leftists," though he was unable to produce any clear-cut examples. The King was also keen to discuss U.S. aid to Saudi development projects, as well as credit terms for Saudi Arabia's recent request to purchase some $16 million in American weapons.

Kennedy told the King that, while he disliked bothering him with administrative difficulties, the U.S. Consulate in Dhahran was unable to clear supplies and equipment through Saudi Customs. Another source of irritation in U.S.-Saudi relations is the fact that the Saudis continue to deny transit visas to Jewish Americans, including members of the United States Congress. The King promised to consider amending his policy.

Kennedy welcomed King Saud at Andrews Air Force Base and hosted a state dinner for the King at the White House.

Kennedy said that the U.S. has not sent *combat* troops "in the generally understood sense of the word."

Feb 14 KENNEDY OPENS UP ABOUT VIETNAM, LAOS

WASHINGTON—Responding to Republican criticism that he has been concealing information about the Vietnam conflict, President Kennedy spoke at length about the issue at today's press conference.

Stating that he was being as frank as possible, the President said: "We have increased our training mission. We've increased our logistic support. We are attempting to prevent a Communist takeover of Vietnam, which is in accordance with a policy which our government has followed…since 1954—and even before then, as I've indicated."

Although some 4,000 American troops are serving in Vietnam, Kennedy said, "We have not sent combat troops there, though the training missions that we have there have been instructed if they are fired upon to… of course, fire back to protect themselves. But we have not sent combat troops in the generally understood sense of the word."

Later in the news conference, the President expressed his concern about another Southeast Asian country, Laos. Both the U.S. and Soviet Union have pledged their commitment to neutrality in Laos. However, the country's neutral government is being pressured by right-wing royalists and Communist rebels. The cease-fire is Laos, Kennedy said, "is becoming increasingly frayed."

Kennedy was particularly concerned that recent conflict has occurred near China's border. "It's a very dangerous situation," he said. "If the cease-fire should break down, we would be faced with the most serious decision."

18 During a stopover in Saigon en route from Indonesia to Thailand, Attorney General Robert Kennedy says the United States will stay in Vietnam as long as necessary "to help a country that is trying to repel aggression with its own blood, sweat, and tears."

19 Secretary of Defense McNamara echoes the previous day's statement on Vietnam by RFK, saying that he is "very optimistic" about progress being made against the Vietcong.

20 Mercury capsule *Friendship 7* carries astronaut John Glenn through three orbits of the Earth and a safe landing in the Atlantic Ocean. Glenn is the first American to orbit the planet.

21 The day after John Glenn's history-making space flight, Khrushchev and Kennedy exchange greetings. JFK suggests that the two countries arrange for discussions on joint space projects.

22 With another airline industry labor dispute brewing between Eastern Airlines and its flight engineers, the President orders a federal board to investigate.

23 President Kennedy accompanies the family of astronaut John Glenn to their reunion with him at Cape Canaveral, Florida. The President presents NASA's Distinguished Service Award to Glenn and to Project Mercury Director Robert Gilruth.

24 According to sources in London, British Prime Minister Harold Macmillan called President Kennedy on their dedicated private telephone link to encourage American flexibility on Khrushchev's disarmament negotiations demands.

The First Lady and CBS reporter Charles Collingwood display some of the White House's treasured artwork.

Feb 14 JACKIE OFFERS TELEVISED TOUR OF THE WHITE HOUSE

WASHINGTON—TV viewers across America enjoyed an unprecedented treat this Valentine's Day. First Lady Jacqueline Kennedy took viewers on a tour of the redecorated White House in a taped, one-hour special on CBS and NBC. Never before had the White House been shown so extensively on television, nor had Americans spent so much time with Mrs. Kennedy.

Accompanied by CBS reporter Charles Collingwood, Kennedy showed off the redecorated rooms and precious artifacts of the White House, which 34 First Families have called home. Kennedy has been working on redecorating and restoring the White House since her husband took office. She has concentrated on adding authentic furnishings and period pieces so as to best reflect the great history of the magnificent residence.

In her soft, deliberate voice, Kennedy opened the program with a narration of the history of the White House. Dressed in a wool suit and pearls, she then gave a tour of the rooms. She often stopped to discuss a particular painting or antique, such as a chair from President Lincoln's administration.

President Kennedy made a cameo appearance during the program, but Mrs. Kennedy was obviously the star of the show. Ratings for the program, which will be released soon, are expected to be among the highest in television history.

Feb 16 — PRESIDENT OKAY WITH NUCLEAR PROTESTERS

WASHINGTON—More than 1,000 college students, protesting nuclear weapons, marched in front of the White House today. The demonstrators, sponsored in part by the Committee for a SANE Nuclear Policy, came from all across America, as far away as the West Coast.

The students were lawful as they marched in front of the iron fence that encircles the White House. Many carried signs with such proclamations as "Shelters Will Not Save Us," "Give Our Children a Chance," and "Peace Will Save 100%." The sign that stated "We Challenge the Soviet Union to Join a Peace Race" seemed to sum up the protesters' intent. They wanted *both* sides to lay down their nuclear weapons.

Their intentions were in line with those of the administration. In fact, President Kennedy asked White House staffers to serve coffee to the students. Two staffers brought out a large container of coffee as well as cups, spoons, milk, and sugar. On Capitol Hill, dozens of Congressmen welcomed the students and discussed relevant issues.

Some students tried to picket in front of the Soviet Embassy, but police turned them away. It is against the law to hold a demonstration within 500 feet of an embassy.

Feb 18 — RFK: "WE ARE GOING TO WIN IN VIETNAM"

SAIGON—While Republicans recently have criticized President Kennedy for concealing information about the conflict in Vietnam, Attorney General Robert Kennedy spoke openly today. Kennedy addressed reporters in Saigon, where he stayed for only two hours during his trip through Southeast Asia.

"We are going to win in Vietnam," Kennedy said. "We will remain here until we do win."

When asked if the United States was embroiled in a "war," Kennedy said, "We are involved in a struggle.... It is a struggle short of war."

But Kennedy also said, "This is a new kind of war, but war it is in a very new sense of the word." Referring to the Communist Vietcong, he said, "It is a war fought not by massive divisions, but secretly by terror, assassination, ambush, and infiltration."

Kennedy said that the "American people understand and fully support this struggle. Americans have great affection for the people of Vietnam. I think the United States will do what is necessary to help a country that is trying to repel aggression with its own blood, tears, and sweat."

February

25 For the second time this year, Kennedy refuses Khrushchev's proposal for a summit meeting between the two during a planned March disarmament conference in Geneva.

26 In *Bailey* v. *Patterson,* the U.S. Supreme Court upholds its previous ruling that "no state may require racial segregation of interstate or intrastate transportation facilities."

27 In a statement published in *Pravda,* the Soviet Union warns that American military action in Vietnam risks "alarming consequences" for world peace. Moscow says it will consider North Vietnam's request for support.

28 In a message to Congress, Kennedy repeats his earlier request for the creation of a new system of health insurance for the elderly as part of Social Security.

March

1 JFK urges Congress to establish a National Wilderness preservation system and enact the Water Resources Planning Act.

2 In a live television address, the President tells Americans that he plans to order resumption of atmospheric nuclear tests unless the Soviet leadership agrees to an effective test-ban treaty.

3 In a first-of-its-kind pact, the Federal Housing Administration and the state of Pennsylvania agree to ban government contracts with anyone who violates housing discrimination laws.

4 Soviet officials in Moscow reject Kennedy's appeal for a summit meeting on nuclear testing.

Astronaut John Glenn became the fifth person in space and the first American to travel completely around the Earth.

Feb 20 GLENN ORBITS THE EARTH!

CAPE CANAVERAL, FLA.—Astronaut John H. Glenn, Jr., today became the first American to orbit the Earth, equaling the April 1961 feat of Russian Yuri Gagarin. In his *Friendship 7* spacecraft, Glenn traveled around the planet three times over a period of four hours and 55 minutes before his capsule landed in the Atlantic Ocean. Glenn was safely recovered, and he suffered no apparent effects from his journey into space.

The only glitch was that for more than three hours, the automatic system was not functioning properly. However, Glenn had no trouble flying the spacecraft manually. A decorated Marine pilot in World War II and the Korean War, Glenn later set the transcontinental speed record from Los Angeles to New York.

Glenn described his view of Earth as a "tremendous, beautiful sight."

Today's breakthrough accomplishment was only a small step in the ultimate plan of putting a man on the moon. NASA officials plan to launch five more orbital missions this year. In the last of the five, they hope, the astronaut will orbit the Earth 18 times. NASA is anxious to determine how astronauts perform during a long period of time in space.

NASA is trying to achieve President Kennedy's goal of reaching the moon before the decade is out. The President watched the morning launch today on his bedroom television.

Feb 23 JFK Honors Astronaut

CAPE CANAVERAL, FLA.—President Kennedy traveled to Cape Canaveral, Florida, today with the family of triumphant astronaut John Glenn.

Three days ago, Glenn became the first American to orbit the Earth, with the successful completion of the nearly five-hour *Friendship 7* NASA mission. Glenn orbited Earth three times during the course of the 81,000-mile space flight. Glenn can also lay claim to a number of other "firsts," including being the first American astronaut to eat in space when he consumed a tube of applesauce. He is also the first astronaut to take photographs in space, though he was armed not with sophisticated NASA equipment but rather an inexpensive 35mm camera that he had purchased at a Cocoa Beach drugstore.

Kennedy's visit included a close presidential inspection of the heroic spacecraft as well as the presentation to Glenn of NASA's Distinguished Service Award. Today also marked Glenn's reunion with his family following his official debriefing on this historic mission.

Mar 1 JFK Urges Funding for Conservation Projects

WASHINGTON—President Kennedy today sent a message to Capitol Hill outlining his administration's plan to manage and conserve America's natural resources. The President proclaimed that the "standard of living we enjoy—greater than any other nation in history—is attributable in large measure to the wide variety and rich abundance of this country's physical resources."

Kennedy's message outlines several calls to action. Noting that the more than 340 million visits to outdoor recreation areas in 1960 are expected to double by 1970, Kennedy's plan prioritizes recreational development. He specifically asks Congress to allocate up to $500 million for land acquisition. He also directed Congress to establish a National Wilderness preservation system.

Emphasizing the importance of water as both a bare necessity and a force to be controlled, Kennedy is urging Congress to enact the Water Resources Planning Act. He also wants Congress to move forward on existing hydrological projects that are awaiting congressional approval.

Additional items on the President's action list include public lands, soil and range resources, timber, minerals, power, and research and technology. In closing, Kennedy expressed his hope that Congress will move forward with his agenda without delay. He noted that action will enable us to "repay our debt to the past and meet our obligations to the future."

5 South Vietnamese President Ngo Dinh Diem and U.S. planners decide to bomb villages that have been infiltrated by Vietcong in recent months.

6 Leaders of major U.S. railroads call for negotiations with key unions after a Presidential Railroad Commission report proposes changes to pay and working conditions.

7 To avoid the collapse of trade negotiations with Europe and other nations, the administration says it has reduced several import duties.

8 Mrs. Kennedy leaves Washington to begin a two-week goodwill trip to India and Pakistan.

9 Following fierce storms along the East Coast, Kennedy declares portions of Delaware, New Jersey, Maryland, and Virginia disaster areas, making them eligible for federal assistance.

10 Kennedy appoints Major General Marshall Carter deputy director of the CIA, replacing General Charles Cabell, who was forced out by the White House for his role in the Bay of Pigs disaster.

11 On her way to India and Pakistan, the First Lady stops in Rome and receives a private audience with Pope John XXIII.

12 Jacqueline Kennedy arrives in New Delhi, India, accompanied by her sister Lee Radziwill. The First Lady's successful trip will be featured in a U.S. Information Agency documentary film distributed overseas.

13 The White House sends Congress a request for nearly $4.9 billion in foreign aid for the next fiscal year, nearly 70 percent of which is for economic development.

"…no American president, responsible for the freedom of so many people, could in good faith make any other decision."

—*KENNEDY, ON U.S. RESUMPTION OF ATMOSPHERIC NUCLEAR TESTS*

Mar 2 KENNEDY ISSUES TEST-BAN THREAT

WASHINGTON—President Kennedy tonight gave Soviet Premier Khrushchev an ultimatum: agree to a treaty banning nuclear tests or else the U.S. will resume atmospheric testing.

Addressing the nation on television, the President said that the U.S. will offer a satisfactory treaty at the 18-nation Geneva conference on March 14. Considering that the Cold War rivals have not agreed on the terms of a ban in their three-plus years of talks, it seems unlikely that the Soviets will consider the treaty "satisfactory" to them. Kennedy, apparently, hoped to force the issue with today's threat.

The sticking point regarding the test-ban theory has been inspections. Kennedy insists that the language of the test-ban treaty call for inspections that the United States and Britain are comfortable with.

The President expressed his displeasure about the Soviets' decision to, last September, end the moratorium on nuclear testing, which the two nations had agreed to in 1958. "We know enough about broken negotiations, secret preparations, and the advantages gained from a long test series never to offer again an uninspected moratorium," he said tonight.

Though Kennedy has long acknowledged the harmful fallout effects of atmospheric nuclear tests, he said tonight that the Soviets gained a military advantage by being able to test their weapons. Thus, he said: "In the absence of any major shift in Soviet policies, no American president, responsible for the freedom of so many people, could in good faith make any other decision" but to resume testing.

Mar 9 ARE U.S. TROOPS ENGAGED IN COMBAT IN VIETNAM?

WASHINGTON—U.S. officials confirmed today that American pilots are accompanying South Vietnamese pilots on combat missions against the Vietcong. However, the official word from President Kennedy and the State Department is that U.S. personnel are engaged in training, not combat.

Washington's definition of "combat" is getting more and more ambiguous. Recently, reports have circulated claiming that the South Vietnamese are carrying out bombing raids and strafing attacks against the enemy. Yet U.S. officials state that although American pilots accompany the South Vietnamese on combat missions, their role is only to train them. President Kennedy stated on February 14 that American troops are not engaged in combat but that they have been instructed to fire back at the enemy if shot at.

South Vietnamese troops are taught how to use an American-made machine gun.

As with John and Bobby, the Kennedy family has used its clout to put Ted in position to hold a major public office.

Mar 14 TED KENNEDY WILL RUN FOR U.S. SENATE

BOSTON—Just three weeks after his 30th birthday, Edward "Ted" Kennedy today announced his candidacy for the U.S. Senate. He hopes to win the seat that his brother, John Kennedy, vacated when he became president.

The position will be a big step up for Kennedy, who is resigning his position as assistant district attorney in Suffolk County, Massachusetts. However, few are surprised by the announcement. President Kennedy has called Ted the best politician in the family, and plans allegedly were made for him to assume the Senate seat.

When he was president-elect, John Kennedy advised Massachusetts Governor Foster Furcolo to appoint Benjamin A. Smith II—JFK's college roommate—to fill John's Senate seat. Reportedly, the deal was that after Ted turned 30 (the minimum age to be senator), Smith would plan to leave the Senate and Ted would run in a special election. That election will be held this November.

Ted Kennedy is a graduate of Harvard and a U.S. Army veteran. He is the youngest of the Kennedy brothers.

14 Amid widespread pessimism over recent Soviet and American announcements on nuclear testing, the UN disarmament conference begins in Geneva.

15 Secretary of Defense Robert McNamara confirms that U.S. advisers in Vietnam, operating under defensive-fire rules of engagement, have exchanged fire with Vietcong forces.

16 Congress considers a White House proposal to develop federal consumer-protection laws for food, drugs, and other goods.

17 A successful Air Force test sends a Titan 2 intercontinental missile 5,000 miles from launch at Cape Canaveral to its target in the Atlantic Ocean.

18 The White House reveals a recent letter sent by President Kennedy to Soviet Premier Khrushchev. In the message, JFK proposed cooperation in space, including weather satellites, tracking stations, communications, and other projects.

19 Educator and activist Michael Harrington publishes *The Other America: Poverty in the United States*, a book that will influence President Kennedy's views on federal anti-poverty strategy.

20 Kennedy signs legislation that will more closely regulate pension and welfare benefit plans offered by U.S. companies.

21 After more than a week in India, Mrs. Kennedy arrives in Lahore, Pakistan.

22 U.S. support begins for the Vietnam Strategic Hamlet program, which is designed to cut Communist supply lines and give peasants weapons to defend themselves against the Vietcong.

Jackie Kennedy rides an elephant with her sister, Polish Princess Lee Radziwill, in Jaipur, India.

Mar 15 FIRST LADY TREATED LIKE A QUEEN ON VISIT TO INDIA

AGRA, INDIA—Continuing on her goodwill tour of India, First Lady Jacqueline Kennedy visited the Taj Mahal twice today—once during the day and then again at night, because, she said, she wanted to experience its beauty in the dark.

During her travels through India, Mrs. Kennedy has charmed her visitors with her style, sophistication, and graciousness. All the while, she has been treated like a queen. Yesterday, she was a guest of Prime Minister Jawaharlal Nehru. She visited his garden, rode a horse name Shahzadl (Princess), was entertained by a snake charmer, petted an elephant, and dined with the Prime Minister.

Mrs. Kennedy also visited an institution for vagrant boys—an experience she found quite moving. She said that "children are the same all over the world, and our feelings are the same toward them. It seems to me in a world where quite enough divides people, it is good to cherish a feeling and emotion that unites us all."

Mar 15 NEW LAW PROVIDES FOR TRAINING OF UNEMPLOYED

WASHINGTON—With President Kennedy's signature today, thousands of unemployed workers had reason for optimism. The new law calls for the training of large numbers of unemployed citizens from now until 1965.

The President had urged Congress to create and pass such legislation, and he received bipartisan support. Kennedy said that the new legislation will make possible "the training of hundreds of thousands of workers who are denied employment because they do not possess the skills required by our constantly changing economy."

The goal is to train 160,000 people next year, 285,000 in 1964, and 570,000 in 1965. The projected cost of the training program is $435 million.

THE CATHOLIC PRESIDENT

Jackie Kennedy once said that it was a shame that some Americans might hold her husband's religion against him. After all, she noted, "he's such a poor Catholic." Obviously, JFK was nobody's idea of a model Catholic family man.

Some historians, however, argue that he took the rituals of Catholicism seriously, perhaps influenced by his mother's strong faith. He attended mass regularly, even as president, and was friendly with Cardinal Richard Cushing of Boston.

Although Kennedy enjoyed Catholic political support, he certainly did not wear his religion on his sleeve. During his presidential campaign, he delivered a well-received speech in which he called for religious tolerance in the public sphere. However, he rarely if ever returned to the theme once elected. In Congress and as

Kennedy with Cardinal Richard Cushing

president, he tried hard to separate himself from issues closely identified with the Catholic Church, such as public aid for parochial schools. He had no wish to be seen as the Catholic Church's spokesman on American political issues.

Kennedy once told a hostile critic, "There is an old saying in Boston that we get our religion from Rome and our politics from home."

Mar 15 — U.S. TROOPS RETURNING FIRE IN SOUTH VIETNAM

WASHINGTON—U.S. military personnel are firing weapons at the enemy in South Vietnam, Defense Secretary Robert McNamara stated today. But they are instructed to do so, he said, only in self-defense.

"I think our mission in South Vietnam is very clear," McNamara said at a news conference. "We are there at the request of the South Vietnamese government to provide training." He added that "there has been sporadic fire aimed at United States personnel, and in some instances they've had to return that fire."

Although some U.S. troops have, according to McNamara, participated in "combat-type training missions," President Kennedy said yesterday that they are not combat troops. Asked if he would go to Congress for approval for sending combat troops to Vietnam, the President said, "If there is a basic change in that situation in Vietnam which calls for a Constitutional decision, I, of course, would go to the Congress."

23 The Kennedy administration extends its embargo on Cuban trade by banning all goods made from Cuban materials, regardless of where they were manufactured.

24 President Kennedy meets with former President Eisenhower in Palm Springs, California.

25 The administration encourages American companies to start or expand businesses in beleaguered West Berlin.

26 In a landmark voting rights case, the U.S. Supreme Court rules in *Baker* v. *Carr* that federal courts can determine whether state legislative reapportionment plans are constitutional.

27 Kennedy administration officials tell reporters that, although they will not rule out a first-strike use of nuclear weapons in response to a conventional Soviet attack, the chief U.S. strategy would be to use the bomb only in response to a nuclear attack.

28 The President meets with his National Security Council in Washington to receive a report on the disarmament talks in Geneva.

29 Continuing his efforts to expand federal involvement in scientific research, Kennedy sends Congress a proposal to establish an executive Office of Science and Technology.

30 Kennedy nominates Byron White to become a U.S. Supreme Court justice, to fill the seat of retiring justice Charles Whittaker.

31 Labor tension in the steel industry eases somewhat as the United Steelworkers Union and U.S. Steel ratify a 10-cents-an-hour pay increase, the smallest contract increase in 20 years.

Mar 18 KENNEDY TO KHRUSHCHEV: LET'S WORK TOGETHER IN SPACE

WASHINGTON—Just five days after issuing an ultimatum to Khrushchev regarding nuclear testing, President Kennedy wrote a letter to the Soviet premier on March 7 asking for cooperation in space exploration. In the letter, which the White House revealed to reporters today, Kennedy asked for cooperation in five areas:

- The establishment of an early operational weather satellite system.
- The establishment and operation of a radio tracking station to provide tracking services to each nation.
- The launch of one satellite apiece so that the two nations could map the Earth's magnetic field in space.
- The two superpowers work with other nations in the field of satellite communications.
- The two nations pool their efforts and exchange their knowledge in the field of space medicine.

Wrote Kennedy to Khrushchev: "The tasks [of space initiatives] are so challenging, the costs so great, and the risks to the brave men who engage in space exploration so grave, that we must in all good conscience try every possibility of sharing these tasks and costs and of minimizing these risks."

Mar 23 PAKISTANIS WELCOME JACKIE

RAWALPINDI, PAKISTAN—India and Pakistan, neighbors and rivals, have gone all out to welcome and impress First Lady Jacqueline Kennedy. During her goodwill tour of India, Mrs. Kennedy was showered with gifts, including a horse and a pair of tiger cubs. "We have been delighted with her visit," said Prime Minister Nehru. "She has been liked wherever she has gone."

The First Lady arrived two days ago in Pakistan, where more than 100,000 people lined the roads between the airport and the home of the governor of West Pakistan, where she is staying. Today, she was the guest of Pakistani President Mohammad Ayub Khan, who also gave her a horse.

Yesterday, Mrs. Kennedy joined 80,000 spectators at the 320-year-old Shalamar Garden for the Pakistani National Horse and Cattle Show. After the sun went down, with spotlights upon her, she spoke to the crowd. "All my life I've dreamed of coming to the Shalamar Garden…," she said. "I only wish my husband could be with me and that we had something as romantic to show to President Ayub when he came to our country."

Jackie attended a horse and cattle show and received a horse as a gift.

Mar 27 PRESIDENT DISCUSSES NUCLEAR WAR STRATEGY

WASHINGTON—In a series of press briefings, Kennedy administration officials have assured the public that the United States' nuclear program is structured to act as a deterrent, in the event of a nuclear attack against the U.S., and that the administration has no intention of firing the first shot.

Nonetheless, government officials also made it clear that they are not going to take the nuclear option off the table, if faced with a powerful Soviet conventional-weapon offensive.

The briefings were in response to a recent *Saturday Evening Post* article by Stewart Alsop, in which Kennedy's position on the first-strike option was cast as somewhat more fluid. According to Alsop, Kennedy said that the United States "must maintain a sufficient margin of superiority in nuclear striking power so that Khrushchev will be certain that, if he strikes first, he will receive a devastating counterblow. But Khrushchev must not be certain that, where its vital interests are threatened, the United States will never strike first."

KENNEDY AND CAPITOL HILL

John Kennedy moved directly from the U.S. Senate to the presidency in 1961, making him the first senator in 40 years to do so. Kennedy's experience as a U.S. representative and senator figured to help him in his dealings with Congress. In addition, his fellow Democrats enjoyed huge advantages in both houses. During Kennedy's first two years, Democrats had a 263-174 advantage in the House of Representatives and a 64-36 advantage in the Senate.

Controlling Congress, however, was more easily said than done. Kennedy's relations with his former colleagues were not especially warm. Many southern Democrats were suspicious of a northeastern Catholic, especially when civil rights began to take center stage in 1962 and '63. Republicans were more than happy to welcome southern Democrats' support to block or stall the President's agenda.

The House Rules Committee, which controlled all legislation in the House, was stacked against JFK in 1961. To pacify recalcitrant Democrats, he promised to balance the federal budget to help win control of the committee's key conservatives. He did not keep that promise.

The President complained that congressional Democrats were not supportive enough of his agenda. In fact, it took Kennedy's death in 1963 to rally Democrats to fall in line behind his policies.

1 The President sends a message to Asian education ministers meeting in Tokyo. He tells them that Americans "share with you the vision of the revolutionary role which education can play in building strong, free, and independent nations."

2 Kennedy announces that Edward Crafts will head a newly created Bureau of Outdoor Recreation, which will be part of the Department of the Interior.

3 The Department of Defense orders the completion of racial integration of all military reserves other than the National Guard. Although the desegregation had been ordered under President Truman, six all-black reserve units still exist in 1962.

4 Some American observers interpret comments in a recent speech by Fidel Castro as an indication that Cuba is beginning to move away from its alliance with the Soviet bloc.

5 The Kennedy administration signals support for a new approach to federal transportation policy, with an emphasis on competition instead of regulation. President Kennedy urges Congress to support urban mass transportation programs.

6 JFK asks Congress to give residents of the Virgin Islands, who became U.S. citizens in 1927, the right to elect their own governor.

7 American and British delegations support a censure resolution against Israel by the UN Security Council in response to Israel's brief military incursion into Syria in March.

The Soviets, Kennedy said, won't budge on the issue of inspections.

Mar 29
KENNEDY: NO HOPE FOR A TEST-BAN TREATY

WASHINGTON—The Conference of the Eighteen Nation Disarmament Committee, which convened in Geneva more than two weeks ago, seems to be headed for failure. Any flicker of hope for a nuclear test-ban treaty seems to have died out. President Kennedy admitted as much today at his news conference.

"I am convinced that the problem of inspection has now emerged clearly as the central obstacle to an effective test-ban treaty," Kennedy said. "We cannot accept any agreement that does not provide for an effective international process that will tell the world whether the treaty is being observed. The Soviet government so far flatly rejects any such inspection of any shape or kind. This is the issue that has been made clear in Geneva."

On March 2, Kennedy had issued an ultimatum to the Soviets: agree to a test-ban treaty or else the U.S. would resume atmospheric testing. When questioned today whether the U.S. would indeed resume testing, Kennedy responded ambiguously, saying: "No, we are going to continue to work—the position remains the same as it did in our speech of March 2."

Mar 29
PRESIDENT PROPOSES OFFICE OF SCIENCE AND TECHNOLOGY

WASHINGTON—President Kennedy today, in a special message to Congress, requested the creation of the Office of Science and Technology. Currently, a special assistant for science and technology, Dr. Jerome B. Weisner, reports to the President. That position was created in 1957 following the Soviets' launch of the Sputnik satellite. But under Kennedy's proposal, a whole office would be created, with Weisner as its director.

With the new arrangement, Kennedy stated, "the President will have permanent staff resources capable of advising and assisting him on matters of national policy affected by or pertaining to science and technology." He added, "Considering the rapid growth and far-reaching scope of federal activities in science and technology, it is imperative that the President have adequate staff support in developing policies and evaluating programs in order to assure that science and technology are used most effectively in the interests of national security and general welfare."

Mar 30

WHITE APPOINTED TO SUPREME COURT

WASHINGTON—President Kennedy has named former corporate lawyer and U.S. Deputy Attorney General Byron "Whizzer" White as the newest associate on the Supreme Court of the United States.

White's standout career began at the University of Colorado, where he was a star football, baseball, and basketball player. He was named a Rhodes Scholar and was a member of Phi Beta Kappa.

After graduation, he starred as a running back with the Pittsburgh Pirates (now Steelers) and Detroit Lions, leading the National Football League in rushing in 1938 and 1940. He completed some graduate studies at Oxford University, then enrolled in Yale Law School. Joining the U.S. Navy during World War II, White served as an intelligence officer, earning a Bronze Star. He returned to Yale after the end of the war and graduated first in his class.

White's appointment comes after many years as a successful litigator and political appointee. At the age of 44, he is the youngest justice ever appointed to the nation's highest court.

Byron "Whizzer" White once starred as an NFL running back.

Mar 31 — JFK THRILLED WITH STEEL, UNION AGREEMENT

PITTSBURGH—With the help of the Kennedy administration, the steel industry and the United Steelworkers of America reached agreement on a new contract today. Kennedy had urged both sides to avoid a repeat of the 1959-60 steelworkers strike, which hurt the U.S. economy.

Thrilled with the agreement, Kennedy phoned leaders of both sides to offer his congratulations. The new contract will provide better job and income security for the union's 450,000 members. While workers will receive a pay raise, the average increase (less than 3 percent) should not have much of an inflationary impact on the economy, which the President was concerned about.

"I am sure that the nation will agree with me," Kennedy said, "that the most notable aspect of this settlement is that it demonstrates that the national interest can be protected and the interests of the industry and of the employees forwarded through free and responsible collective bargaining."

April

8 A Cuban military court sentences more than 1,100 prisoners captured during the Bay of Pigs invasion to 30 years in prison. Castro offers to free the men in exchange for $62 million.

9 A day after more than 90 percent of French voters approve a referendum designed to end French rule in Algeria, a large number of French colonists plan to leave the North African colony in advance of its independence.

10 Only a few weeks after Kennedy urged steelworkers to accept a modest pay increase, U.S. Steel and other steel companies raise prices by $6 per ton.

11 Angered by the timing of the 3.5 percent increase in steel prices, President Kennedy pressures companies to reverse it.

12 At a news conference, JFK says that he hopes military reservists who were called up during the Berlin crisis will be released from active duty in August.

13 In the face of pressure from the White House and Congress, steel companies rescind their recent price increase.

14 In exchange for a $2.5 million ransom paid by Cuban exiles, Castro releases 60 wounded or ill Bay of Pigs prisoners.

15 The First Family spends Sunday on the Kennedy estate in Glen Ora, Virginia.

16 At the Supreme Court, Byron White is sworn in five days after being confirmed by the Senate.

17 The Justice Department is reportedly planning to sue segregated public school districts that have received federal education money.

Apr 5 PRESIDENT OFFERS A NEW TRANSPORTATION POLICY

WASHINGTON—America's national transportation policy, President Kennedy said today, is a "chaotic patchwork of inconsistent and often obsolete legislation." Today the President offered a way to fix the problems. He asked Congress for a national policy that would emphasize less regulation of transportation systems as well as federal aid for cities' mass transit systems.

Under the President's proposal, railroads and trucks could cut freight rates on bulk commodities (including coal and ore) without government approval. Also, railroads, airlines, and bus companies could lower passenger fares without the government's okay.

In the new plan, cities whose mass transit systems are in trouble could apply for emergency federal aid. Moreover, the federal government would give grants to cities that make long-range mass transit plans. The federal government also would provide funds to states for research and planning of highway systems. The costs of these upgrades will be expensive. But, Kennedy insisted, "we must begin to make the painful decisions necessary to providing the transportation system required by the United States of today and tomorrow."

GETTING TOUGH WITH BIG STEEL

The steel industry was one of America's largest in the 1960s. The United States and the Soviet Union measured their progress and prosperity by comparing and contrasting steel output. More than a half-million Americans worked for the nation's steel companies, the largest of which was U.S. Steel.

In spring 1962, the Kennedy administration mediated a dispute between the large steel companies, including U.S. Steel, and the steelworkers union. The White House persuaded labor to accept a new contract with a pay freeze while accepting management's offer to boost contributions to the workers' pensions. Kennedy feared that wage hikes would lead to price hikes, which would damage the economy.

Just days after the unions signed a new contract, U.S. Steel announced that it would increase prices by 3.5 percent. Kennedy was outraged. "You double-crossed me!" he told the head of U.S. Steel, Roger Blough.

The President vented his anger in public on April 11, 1962, during a press conference. He praised workers for their willingness to sacrifice, but then condemned management in bitter tones. He said that all Americans would suffer because of the companies' greed. Privately, he was even harsher. The Justice Department, headed by his brother, began investigating the expense accounts of steel executives and opened antitrust probes. Small steel companies that did not raise prices were awarded lucrative defense contracts.

The intense pressure was too much to bear. U.S. Steel and other big companies announced that they would roll back prices, handing John Kennedy an enormous and very popular victory.

Apr 11 | KENNEDY CHASTISES U.S. STEEL COMPANIES

WASHINGTON—Usually calm and composed, President Kennedy today erupted in anger. During his news conference, he unleashed his wrath on America's major steel corporations, which recently raised steel prices by $6 a ton. Kennedy called the action "a wholly unjustifiable and irresponsible defiance of the public interest."

For months, the administration has negotiated with the steel companies and the United Steelworkers Union to minimize increases in prices and wages. The administration is satisfied with its recently agreed-upon work contract. However, Kennedy was furious with the subsequent spike in steel prices—especially since the steel industry is profitable.

The President said that the increased prices will have a negative effect on the economy. The cost of everything from houses and cars to appliances and tools, he said, will go up. He added that the U.S. will have a harder time selling its products overseas.

In one fury-ridden sentence, he declared: "In this serious hour in our nation's history, when we are confronted with grave crises in Berlin and Southeast Asia, when we are devoting our energies to economic recovery and stability, when we are asking reservists to leave their homes and families for months on end, and servicemen to risk their lives—and four were killed in the last two days in Vietnam—and asking union members to hold down their wage requests, at a time when restraint and sacrifice are being asked of every citizen, the American people will find it hard, as I do, to accept a situation in which a tiny handful of steel executives whose pursuit of private power and profit exceeds their sense of public responsibility can show such utter contempt for the interests of 185 million Americans."

The President acknowledged the companies' freedom to raise prices. But he added that members of Congress are planning "appropriate inquiries into how these price decisions are so quickly made, and reached, and what legislative safeguards may be needed to protect the public interest."

Kennedy felt betrayed by the steel companies, whose price increases could affect the economy.

Apr 14 CASTRO RELEASES 60 REBELS

HAVANA—A crowd of several thousand Cuban exiles gathered at the Miami International Airport today to welcome home 60 ill or wounded Cuban prisoners. Each of the men had been sentenced to 30 years in prison for treason—specifically, for the invasion of Cuba last April.

Last week, Cuban Premier Fidel Castro put the 1,179 prisoners up for ransom ($62 million). He released these 60 ailing men because the organization Cuban Families Committee for the Liberation of Prisoners of War is willing to negotiate. The organization stated that it has received, from American corporations and individuals, pledges of food and equipment worth at least $26 million. An organization spokesman said they would try to convert the goods to cash to help pay the ransom.

The U.S. government refuses to meet any of Castro's demands. Back in February, President Kennedy banned virtually all trade with the Communist-backed country.

Apr 21 KENNEDY OPENS WORLD'S FAIR WITH TURN OF A KEY

PALM BEACH, FLA.—President Kennedy today launched the Seattle World's Fair from Palm Beach, Florida. Declaring "let the fair begin," Kennedy closed a telegraphic key. The impulse traveled through telephone lines to a computer in Maine, which commanded a giant antenna to pick up a sound signal that was then transmitted to the grounds of Seattle's Century 21 Exhibition. The signal activated a stand of lights and hundreds of bells, eliciting cheers from the 12,000 fairgoers.

"This manner of opening the fair is in keeping with the exposition's space age theme," Kennedy declared. "Literally, we are reaching out through space on the new ocean to a star which we have never seen, to intercept sound in the form of radio waves…."

The Space Needle, 605 feet tall, represents the theme of the fair. Fairgoers from around the world will be treated to numerous space-oriented and futuristic displays. Said Kennedy: "I am confident that as this sound from outer space is utilized to open the fair, the fair in turn will open the doors to further scientific gains by letting all see what has been accomplished today. By closing this key may we open not only a great world's fair, may we open an era of peace and understanding among all mankind."

The Space Needle is the centerpiece of the Seattle World's Fair.

"Literally, we are reaching out through space on the new ocean to a star which we have never seen, to intercept sound in the form of radio waves…." —KENNEDY

Apr 25 U.S. ATMOSPHERIC TESTING RESUMED

WASHINGTON—Earlier today, the United States detonated a warhead over Christmas Island in the Pacific Ocean. The explosion occurred just one day after the Atomic Energy Commission released a statement saying that the Kennedy administration had authorized the resumption of atmospheric nuclear testing.

Despite President Kennedy's stated goal of a permanent ban on atmospheric tests, and an 11th-hour appeal from UN Secretary General U Thant, the detonation went off as scheduled. It was the first aboveground U.S. nuclear test since October 1958.

An agreement between the Eisenhower administration and the Soviet Union had halted all tests, effective November 1, 1958. That agreement held until the Soviets announced, on August 31, 1961, that they intended to violate the agreement. They proceeded to launch a series of 45 tests over the course of two months. Not wanting to leave the United States at a disadvantage, Kennedy ordered an underground test at the Nevada proving grounds. That test was held on September 1 of last year, and was followed up seven months later with today's blast at altitude.

JFK AND THE MOB

As a U.S. senator, John F. Kennedy sought to limit organized crime's influence over labor unions, targeting in particular the Teamsters union and its president, Jimmy Hoffa.

Once the presidential campaign got underway, JFK's relationship with organized crime became much murkier. Three figures loom large in any discussion of Kennedy and the mob: Sam Giancana, head of the mob in Chicago; Frank Sinatra, the legendary singer who was friendly with both JFK and Giancana; and Judith Campbell, one of Sinatra's former lovers who became involved with JFK and Giancana at the same time in 1962.

Campbell, many years later, said she served as a messenger between Giancana and Kennedy when the White House considered a mob rubout of Cuban leader Fidel Castro. Historians believe that Kennedy ended the relationship with Campbell after FBI Director J. Edgar Hoover showed him evidence of the woman's connection to the mobster.

Giancana and the Chicago mob also figure in stories about the close vote in Illinois during the 1960 presidential election. According to some accounts, Joseph Kennedy sent a message to Giancana through Sinatra, asking for his help in the campaign. Critics suggest that the mob influenced the outcome in Illinois and thus gave Kennedy the presidency. However, JFK would have won even if Richard Nixon had taken the state.

25 Wasting no time after getting the go-ahead from the White House, engineers detonate a nuclear device near Christmas Island in the Indian Ocean.

26 Just three months after the American spacecraft *Ranger 3* failed to reach the moon, *Ranger 4* crashes as planned on the far side of the lunar surface.

27 A federal grand jury indicts U.S. Steel and Bethlehem Steel companies and executives on charges of conspiring to fix prices and rig bids for military contracts.

28 Kennedy signs into law a bill expanding the Peace Corps and providing funds to support nearly 10,000 volunteers by late 1963.

29 After concluding a two-day visit with British Prime Minister Macmillan, President Kennedy hosts a White House dinner in honor of 49 Nobel Prize winners from the Western Hemisphere.

30 During a speech to a skeptical audience in Washington, Kennedy tells the U.S. Chamber of Commerce that he does not intend to assume a price-setting role.

May

1 During traditional May Day parades, Russian weapons are shown on the streets of two Eastern bloc states. East Germans display the type of surface-to-air missiles that downed the U-2 flight of Francis Gary Powers; Yugoslavian forces display Soviet-made T-54 tanks.

2 The military detonates the fourth nuclear bomb since testing resumed in late April, creating a mushroom cloud that rises to a height of 62,000 feet.

Ranger 4 (pictured) was supposed to take photos of the moon and transmit them to Earth before crashing, but it failed to do so.

Apr 22 *RANGER 4* CRASHES ON THE MOON

GOLDSTONE, CALIF.—After nine failed attempts, NASA today achieved its goal of sending a spacecraft to the moon. At 4:49 A.M. Pacific time, *Ranger 4* crashed on the far side of the moon. It was only the second man-made object to land on the lunar surface; the Soviets achieved the feat in September 1959 with *Luna 2*.

Launched from Cape Canaveral, Florida, on Monday afternoon, *Ranger 4* traveled 231,486 miles in just under 64 hours. In California, scientists at the Goldstone Deep-Space Instrumentation Facility tracked the spacecraft over the final few hours. They reported that *Ranger 4* initially missed the moon by 900 miles, but it got caught in the moon's gravitational pull and plummeted to the surface. The craft's television cameras and other instruments went dead when it crash-landed.

Despite failing to meet all its aims, the mission marked a big step toward achieving President Kennedy's goal of putting a man on the moon by 1969.

Apr 24 KENNEDYS DINE WITH 49 NOBEL LAUREATES

WASHINGTON—In an unprecedented event, 49 Nobel Prize winners dined at the White House tonight. President Kennedy said that the gathering was "probably the greatest concentration of talent and genius in this house, except for those times when Thomas Jefferson dined alone."

Besides the 49 Nobel Laureates, the President invited 124 notable scientists, writers, and educators. Many of the guests dined with President Kennedy in the State Dining Room, while the others joined First Lady Jacqueline Kennedy in the Blue Room. After a dinner of French cuisine, actor Frederic March read an unpublished writing of the late Ernest Hemingway, himself a Nobel Prize winner.

Of the 49 Nobel Laureates in attendance, 46 were American. Dr. J. Robert Oppenheimer, known as the "father of the atomic bomb," and Dr. Linus Pauling, a

The Kennedys chat with writers Pearl Buck (Nobel Prize for Literature) and Robert Frost (four-time Pulitzer Prize winner).

3 A federal emergency board recommends a pay raise for a half-million non-operating employees of U.S. railroads. The board urges railroads and unions to negotiate more constructively.

4 Attending the ceremonial opening of a wharf in New Orleans, Kennedy campaigns for passage of the Trade Expansion bill by Congress. He says that when it comes to its economic future, the country must "trade or fade."

5 During a secret meeting of NATO ministers in Greece, the United States pledges all five of its Atlantic Polaris submarines to the defense of the alliance, creating a de facto NATO nuclear deterrent.

6 U.S. officials study the apparent success of the test firing and detonation of a nuclear warhead carried by a Polaris missile in the Pacific.

7 CIA officials brief Attorney General Robert Kennedy about an agency operation designed to pay mafia operatives to assassinate Fidel Castro.

8 Speaking at the United Auto Workers convention, the President urges restraint by labor in its bargaining demands. He adds that his administration will not use federal power to resolve every labor dispute.

9 Kennedy criticizes both sides in the burgeoning Laotian crisis. He condemns the Communist seizure of a provincial capital and the government of Laos for putting off negotiations on a national unity government.

10 Reacting to news of several nuclear tests by France, a Soviet delegate in Geneva says the USSR would not sign any test-ban treaty not signed by the French.

Nobel winner in chemistry and a peace activist, were among the distinguished guests. Just last month, Pauling wrote a letter to President Kennedy in which he criticized his decision to resume atmospheric nuclear testing. Tonight's dinner, however, was a joyous event filled with music, dancing, and plenty of stimulating conversation.

May 7 / WHITE'S "PRESIDENT" BOOK WINS PULITZER

NEW YORK—Theodore H. White won the Pulitzer Prize for General Nonfiction today for *The Making of the President, 1960,* his book about John F. Kennedy's run for president. A longtime reporter and novelist, White incorporated his exceptional talents in the groundbreaking book.

The narrative, which traces Kennedy's campaign run from the primaries to Election Day, reads like a compelling novel. Critics have complained that White's bias is evident: Kennedy comes across as the hero, with Republican candidate Richard Nixon the villain. However, White offers great insight into the strategies, feuds, and closed-door decisions that went into the presidential campaign.

An American soldier scans the Vietnamese landscape in spring 1962.

May 11 — McNamara Optimistic About the War in Vietnam

SAIGON—After a two-day visit to South Vietnam, U.S. Defense Secretary Robert McNamara beamed with optimism. "I found nothing but progress and hope for the future," he told reporters before returning to Washington.

McNamara said he does not see a reason to send more servicemen or material to Vietnam. He said that South Vietnam has all the American help it needs to battle the Vietcong insurgents. Currently, an estimated 6,000 Americans are assisting the Vietnamese as "advisers," "trainers," and support workers.

McNamara said that stories about Americans involved in combat situations (exchange of fire) have been overblown. He emphasized the effectiveness of the strategic hamlet program, in which villagers have been relocated to military zones that are well guarded.

Nevertheless, all is not well in South Vietnam. Many of the thousands of villagers had to be forcibly removed to the strategic hamlets, causing resentment and anger among the citizenry. Moreover, McNamara said that South Vietnam's war against the insurgents will last "not months but years."

May 14 — JFK's Executive Order Establishes Council on Aging

WASHINGTON—President Kennedy today issued Executive Order 11022, establishing the President's Council on Aging.

The Council is charged with several responsibilities with respect to serving America's elderly. Its foremost duty is to recommend policies and programs that will help the federal government meet the needs of aging Americans. Special attention will be paid to those needs that might fall under the purview of multiple agencies or departments.

The order calls for the council to be chaired by the secretary of Health, Education and Welfare. Other members are to include the secretaries of Agriculture, Commerce, Labor, and Treasury.

The establishment of this council abolishes the existing Federal Council on Aging, which was established on March 7, 1959, by a letter from President Eisenhower to the former Secretary of Health, Education and Welfare.

May 15 · U.S. Deploys 4,000 Troops to Thailand

WASHINGTON—With the civil war in Laos nearing the Thai border, President Kennedy today announced that 1,000 U.S. troops will be deployed to Thailand, joining the 1,000 U.S. Army troops that arrived there earlier this month. A battalion of 1,800 Marines will arrive on Thursday, and more troops will follow—including Air Force personnel.

According to the President, the action is in response to the recent attacks by the Communist Pathet Lao forces against Royal Laotian troops in northwest Laos. Kennedy said that the U.S. forces are going to Thailand to "help ensure the territorial integrity of this peaceful country."

"A threat to Thailand is of grave concern to the United States," Kennedy said. "I have, therefore, ordered certain additional American military forces into Thailand in order that we may be in a position to fulfill speedily our obligations under the Manila Pact of 1954, a defense agreement...."

The President said: "There is no change in our policy toward Laos, which continues to be the reestablishment of an effective cease-fire and prompt negotiations for a government of national union." According to a U.S. State Department spokesman, the Soviet Union feels the same way. Secretary of State Dean Rusk met today with Soviet Ambassador Anatoly Dobrynin. Both men, according to the spokesman, confirmed their commitment to a cease-fire in Laos and the establishment of a neutral coalition government.

General Paul D. Harkins (right) gets a briefing from Lieutenant Colonel J. B. Barrett in Udorn, Thailand.

11 As talks are set to resume on British membership in the European Common Market, it becomes clear that West Germany and France oppose full membership for Britain.

12 In response to the escalating conflict in Laos, Kennedy orders 1,800 Marines and naval and air support to Thailand to block any attempt by Communist forces to cross the border there.

13 An administration report calls for greater effort on the part of federal agencies to "develop a more favorable environment for science within the government."

14 By executive order, Kennedy creates the President's Council on Aging. Its mission is to study when and how government should act to respond to the needs of aged citizens.

15 Even as the U.S. increases its troop strength in Thailand near the Laotian border, U.S. and Soviet diplomats move to implement a year-old agreement between the two countries to set up a neutral government in Laos.

16 Despite a conciliatory message from Kennedy to West German Chancellor Konrad Adenauer over recent public disagreements between Washington and Bonn, Adenauer says an alliance should not be a muzzle.

17 During a news conference, JFK criticizes comments by French President Charles de Gaulle, who called for an independent nuclear deterrent for Europe.

18 Soviet Premier Khrushchev compares the deployment of American forces in Thailand to the Korean War, and predicts that U.S. troops will end up fighting in the region.

May 15 SENATE KILLS CIVIL RIGHTS BILL

WASHINGTON—A civil rights bill supported by President Kennedy died in the Senate today. The bill would have allowed any American citizen with a sixth-grade education to vote in federal elections. By a vote of 49 to 34, the bill was formally set aside.

The main purpose of the bill was to end the unfair practice of literacy tests in the South. In certain southern states, citizens have to pass "literacy" tests—which include difficult questions about government—in order to vote. In most cases, registrars give Negro applicants a failing grade. By denying suffrage to Negroes, whites are able to maintain their power structure.

Over the last three weeks, southern senators vocally opposed the bill, while support for the bill paled in comparison. However, the administration may call for new civil rights legislation later in the year. Attorney General Robert Kennedy, in particular, is determined to end voting injustice in the South.

May 20 MONROE TREATS JFK WITH SPECIAL "HAPPY BIRTHDAY"

NEW YORK—Fifteen thousand people attended President Kennedy's birthday celebration at Madison Square Garden last night—and 15,000 jaws dropped to the floor during a performance by Marilyn Monroe.

Monroe walked onto the stage and sang "Happy Birthday," turning the normally innocuous song into a something out of a burlesque show. Wearing a skintight, flesh-colored, rhinestone-studded dress, America's most popular sex symbol sang "Happy Birthday" with a breathy, sultry delivery, concluding, "Happy birthday, Mr. President, happy birthday to you."

Monroe then sang six lines of "Thanks for the Memories," with the words changed for Kennedy:

Thanks, Mr. President,
For all the things you've done,
The battles that you've won,
The way you deal with U.S. Steel
And our problems by the ton,
We thank you…so much.

Following the performance, two men carried a giant cake onto the stage. Kennedy then took the stage and addressed the crowd. "I can now retire from politics," he joked, "after having had 'Happy Birthday' sung to me in such a sweet, wholesome way." The crowd erupted in laughter.

SERIAL INFIDELITY

Historian Robert Dallek described John Kennedy's sex life in the White House as "almost madcap." He allegedly slept with high-class prostitutes, his wife's press secretary, White House staff members, a 19-year-old intern, and Hollywood celebrities, including Jayne Mansfield and Marilyn Monroe. Rumors linking the President to Monroe began to circulate in 1962, after she breathlessly serenaded him with a rendition of "Happy birthday, Mr. President" at a fundraiser. He instructed aides to tell editors that the stories were not true.

Many of his one-night conquests were complete strangers who were brought to the White House through a service entrance.

One of his mistresses was a woman named Judith Campbell, who also shared the bed of a prominent mobster named Sam Giancana. Kennedy stopped sleeping with her in 1962, when FBI Director J. Edgar Hoover met with JFK and showed him evidence of Campbell's mob connections.

Kennedy's reckless behavior nearly became a scandal in October 1963. The FBI discovered that one of his mistresses, Ellen Rometsch, a German woman married to a

Judith Campbell

U.S. Army sergeant, was a prostitute and a possible East German spy. She was expelled from the country, but her connections to a prominent Washington lobbyist, Bobby Baker, led to newspaper stories and talk of a congressional investigation. But the inquiry came to an abrupt end when Kennedy ordered Hoover to meet with two top senators. Hoover showed them the dirt he had on other senators, and talk of an investigation came to a quick end.

The public learned the truth about JFK's infidelity long after the President's death.

19 At a celebration in honor of the President's upcoming birthday, Marilyn Monroe sings "Happy Birthday" in a style that seems alternately sultry and disoriented. Monroe, who is rumored to be involved in a relationship with Kennedy, will live only three more months.

20 After Elvis Stahr resigns as secretary of the Army, Kennedy appoints Cyrus Vance to the position.

21 The American Medical Association sponsors a national television broadcast that attacks President Kennedy's proposal to provide medical care through the Social Security system.

22 The President orders the Department of Health, Education and Welfare to support a program to construct and staff surgical facilities in Vietnam.

23 Alarmed by the plight of refugees flooding into Hong Kong from China, the White House uses emergency powers to waive immigration restrictions. The U.S. will admit Chinese with desirable technical skills as well as several thousand Chinese who have family members in the U.S.

24 Astronaut Scott Carpenter becomes the second American to orbit Earth. He circles the planet three times in *Aurora 7* before enduring a harrowing, three-hour delay in recovery from his floating capsule.

25 Kennedy speaks to participants in the first White House conference on conservation since Teddy Roosevelt was president. The President focuses on preservation of green space along the East Coast and on the role of science in conservation.

Kennedy talks about improved senior health care, which he hopes to pay for by taxing Social Security.

May 22 — KENNEDY, AMA IN FIGHT OVER SENIOR HEALTH CARE

WASHINGTON—How should medical care for senior citizens be financed? President Kennedy's administration and the American Medical Association have vastly different opinions, and the two sides are appealing to the American people.

Two days ago, the President spoke about the issue at New York's Madison Square Garden in an address that was covered by all three networks. Kennedy is trying to push through the King-Anderson bill, which would finance elderly care by a one-half percent increase in Social Security payments (a quarter percent each for employer and employee). The new system would not cover doctor bills or drug costs, but it would pay for up to 90 days' worth of hospital bills, 180 days' worth of nursing-home services, and home services for up to 240 visits a year.

The AMA, though, strongly opposes the bill. The organization of doctors bought an hour of airtime last night on nearly 200 television stations. Speaking in a deliberately empty Madison Square Garden, Dr. Edward Annis told the American people that the President's plan was "a cruel hoax and a delusion," and would lead to wasteful use of taxpayer dollars. The doctor said that socialized medicine has failed in Great Britain, and that it would be a bad idea for Americans. He said it would destroy private voluntary health insurance programs, to which more than half of America's senior citizens belong.

Many seniors, however, support the King-Anderson bill. In fact, some 400,000 have pledged their support in letters to congressmen. Kennedy said: "This year, or certainly as inevitably as the tide comes in, next year, this bill is going to pass."

May 24 — CARPENTER FINALLY RETRIEVED AFTER ORBITING THE EARTH

WASHINGTON—Scott Carpenter successfully completed his three orbits around Earth today, but the landing turned into an ordeal. For approximately 45 minutes, no one knew where he had landed. Finally, his capsule was spotted in the Atlantic Ocean. Carpenter and his *Aurora VII* capsule landed 250 miles beyond its intended landing point in the Caribbean. Without communication, he had to wait three hours before a rescue helicopter arrived to retrieve him.

Carpenter became the second American astronaut to orbit Earth. He was also the first American to eat solid food in space. Despite Carpenter's ordeal in the ocean, doctors reported that he was in fine health.

President Kennedy was among the millions of Americans who worried about Carpenter's fate. "The American people will be gratified by the successful orbital flight of Lieutenant Commander Scott Carpenter," the President said in a press statement. "The skill and initiative of those who participated in the rescue, coupled with Commander Carpenter's courage, is heartwarming to all of us."

Scott Carpenter emerges from the water after his three-hour ordeal.

May 25 JFK HOSTS CONFERENCE ON CONSERVATION

WASHINGTON—Late this morning, President Kennedy addressed an assembled group of senators, congressmen, governors, and administration officials who gathered for the White House Conference on Conservation.

The President acknowledged that conservation is an issue that "involves not only all the people of this nation but in a very real sense all the people of the world." He emphasized the growing importance of focusing foreign aid on programs that encourage resource development and conservation on a global scale.

Moving forward, Kennedy said he would like to see science and conservation work in concert. He would specifically welcome scientific advances in desalinization technology, noting that the ability to turn saltwater into fresh water would have a remarkable impact on the American West and Southwest. Beyond our borders, Kennedy pointed out, "how extraordinary an accomplishment it will be when we can bring water to bear on the deserts surrounding the Mediterranean and the Indian Sea and all the rest."

In closing, the President stated that he wants his administration to be identified with the cause of natural resources conservation, much like that of Theodore Roosevelt, who was the last president to hold a White House Conference on Conservation. Kennedy's commitment to this cause was made clear when he said: "I can think of no more suitable effort for an administration which is concerned with progress than to be identified in a sense with past efforts and future efforts to preserve this land and maintain its beauty."

May

26 The President steps up his effort to fund medical care for the elderly. He sends weekend messages on the issue to both the National Council of Senior Citizens and the National Conference on Social Welfare.

27 U.S. helicopter pilots ferry Laotian government reinforcements in an unsuccessful counterattack against Communist Pathet Lao guerrillas and North Vietnamese regulars in northwest Laos.

28 The stock market suffers its biggest one-day loss since 1929. In heavy trading, New York Stock Exchange equities lose more than $20 billion in value.

29 The Wall Street roller coaster ride continues, as the NYSE rebounds to recover 60 percent of the previous day's big losses. Stock tickers run more than four hours after the close of trading to account for the heavy volume of trades.

30 A day after his birthday, the President and Mrs. Kennedy spend Memorial Day at Glen Ora in Middleburg, Virginia.

31 Convicted Nazi war criminal Adolf Eichmann is hanged in Israel for his role in sending millions of Jews to their deaths in Europe.

June

1 Pentagon officials announce plans to build a dozen fallout shelters in Forest Service buildings.

2 The White House reveals an ambitious plan for building new federal offices, including significant redevelopment along Pennsylvania Avenue.

A Laotian refugee holds her baby after arriving at the Thai border town of Xieng Khong.

May 27 FIGHTING BREAKS OUT IN LAOS

VIENTIANE, LAOS—Hopes for a peaceful solution in Laos are growing increasingly bleak. After a yearlong cease-fire, pro-Communist forces unleashed attacks in Laos three weeks ago, yesterday, and again today. The latest assault occurred in Northwest Laos near Houei Sai along the Thai border. President Kennedy sent several thousand troops to Thailand, near that border, following the May 6 attack.

U.S. military advisers said that several companies of pro-Communist rebels participated in today's attack. They believed, although they could not confirm, that the rebel troops were from North Vietnam. Yesterday, pro-Communist forces waged an offensive in southern Laos.

Both the United States and Soviet Union have announced their commitment for a neutralist government in Laos headed by Prince Phouma. The Prince wants to form a coalition government by June 15, but that goal seems in jeopardy.

May 27 AMERICAN AND VIETNAMESE FORCES LAUNCH NEW OPERATION

SAIGON—Scant details emerged yesterday about Operation Sunrise, a far-reaching joint South Vietnamese/American campaign to flush the Communists out of the areas around Saigon.

Secretly launched last week, the operation incorporates elements of the Strategic Hamlet program, in which a series of fortified villages are populated by well-armed villagers.

The multiphase process involves setting up these strategic hamlets in areas already cleared of Vietcong by troops. In some cases, far-flung villagers will need to be relocated to a strategic hamlet. Residents of each strategic hamlet will be given weapons and instruction in defense. Further, health, education, and social service programs will be established in each hamlet to assure a smooth transition for the new communities.

Though strategic hamlets have been utilized by the South Vietnamese for several months, and the plan has been successfully employed against Communist guerrillas in other parts of Asia, the Kennedy administration only recently began supporting the plan by offering equipment and technical assistance.

Jun 1 FEDERAL GOVERNMENT TO FUND FALLOUT SHELTERS

WASHINGTON—The Pentagon announced today a plan to install fallout shelters in buildings to be constructed for the U.S. Forest Service. The 12 buildings would be designed to hold 1,750 people in all, 50 in the smallest and 450 in the largest. The pilot project, a joint effort between the Department of Defense and the Department of Agriculture, is the first federal fallout shelter plan. The total cost of the program remains unclear.

The locations of the shelters will be as follows: Missoula, Montana; Kamiah, Idaho; Basalt, Colorado; Gunnison, Colorado; Mayhill, New Mexico; Prescott, Arizona; Boise, Idaho; Clarkesville, Georgia; Alexandria, Louisiana; Moscow, Idaho; Wenatchee, Washington; and Libby, Montana.

SKY-HIGH APPROVAL RATINGS

Through the first two years of his administration, President Kennedy could do nothing wrong—at least, that's what the polls showed. Even in the aftermath of the Bay of Pigs fiasco in the spring of 1961, he remained popular. According to a Gallup poll taken just after the botched invasion, 83 percent of respondents believed the President was doing a good job. Kennedy himself was amazed. "The worse you do, the better they like you," he said, half in jest.

Kennedy's job approval ratings fell in 1962, but only slightly. Early in the new year, the Gallup poll found that 77 percent of voters approved of JFK's job performance, and 56 percent believed that their standard of living had improved since Kennedy's inauguration.

During the summer, however, Kennedy's poll numbers declined as white supremacists confronted civil rights activists in the

South and the Soviet Union continued to challenge the U.S. presence in West Berlin. His approval ratings sank, and while they remained at a respectable level (around two-thirds of Americans still approved of his job performance), the numbers were sinking. Kennedy began to worry about his reelection prospects.

The Cuban missile crisis of October 1962 renewed the President's popularity. Before the crisis, his approval rating was stuck at 66 percent. Afterward, it rose to 77 percent. The Kennedy magic seemed to be back.

3 A New York-bound Air France flight crashes on takeoff in Paris, killing 130 people, most of them Americans returning from a European art tour. It's the fourth crash of a Boeing 707.

4 Technicians destroy a malfunctioning Thor rocket and its nuclear warhead during a failed test above Johnson Island in the Pacific.

5 Secretary of the Treasury C. Douglas Dillon says the next budget will include both income tax cuts in all brackets and offsetting revenue-raising items.

6 At West Point, JFK tells graduating cadets that they will be called on to be diplomats as well as soldiers. In an era of high-stakes nuclear weaponry, he says, officers have "a responsibility to deter war as well as to fight it."

7 The President tells reporters that he will seek "across-the-board" tax cuts for individuals and businesses in order to prevent the economic recovery from stalling.

8 President Kennedy names Dr. Jerome Wiesner, a key science adviser and disarmament expert, to lead the new federal Office of Science and Technology.

9 This month sees a continuation of what some investors call "the Kennedy Slide," a stock market decline since December 1961 that has seen the S&P 500 stock index drop by nearly a quarter.

10 Education officials in the South breathe a sigh of relief as they close the first school year free of significant desegregation-related unrest since 1954, the year of the U.S. Supreme Court's landmark *Brown v. Board of Education*.

West Point cadets stand at attention in honor of the nation's commander-in-chief.

Jun 6 JFK Speaks to West Point Grads

NEWBURGH, N.Y.—President Kennedy was the keynote speaker at the commencement exercises of the United States Military Academy at West Point today. Kennedy spoke at 10 A.M. in the Field House before an audience that included General William Westmoreland and both the secretary of the Army and the chairman of the Joint Chiefs of Staff.

Kennedy opened his remarks by lightheartedly exercising his right as commander-in-chief: He ordered all existing cadet punishments and restrictions to be rescinded! The President's words soon took on a more serious tone, as Kennedy told the cadets that once the celebration of graduation passed, "the demands that will be made upon you in the service of your country in the coming months and years will be really more pressing, and in many ways more burdensome, as well as more challenging, than ever before in our history."

Kennedy went on to enumerate the difficult and challenging leadership positions these young men will be expected to fill in the coming years—in Africa, Indochina, Latin America, and Europe. Their roles will not be limited to the military, but will extend to the political, diplomatic, and economic realms of international relations. That, said Kennedy, requires a "whole new kind of strategy, a wholly different kind of force, and therefore a new and wholly different kind of military training."

"Above all," Kennedy told the young officers, "you will have a responsibility to deter war as well as to fight it."

"...the demands that will be made upon you in the service of your country in the coming months and years will be really more pressing, and in many ways more burdensome, as well as more challenging, than ever before in our history."

—KENNEDY, TO WEST POINT GRADUATES

Jun 11 — JFK DEFENDS ECONOMIC POLICY IN YALE ADDRESS

NEW HAVEN, CONN.—President Kennedy this morning served as the keynote speaker at Yale University's 261st commencement on the Old Campus at the prestigious Connecticut university. Prior to taking his place at the dais, Kennedy was awarded an honorary degree, Doctor of Laws.

Kennedy, a Harvard man, began the address in a comical fashion, poking fun at the contentious Harvard-Yale relationship. He named all the Yale men—politicians, businessmen, journalists, and advisers—with whom he has had difficulty throughout the years.

From there, the President transitioned to current affairs—notably the economy, which became the central topic of his address. He attacked what he called the "myth" of big government. He noted that while the United States government has spent more under each successive president, the amount itself has grown at a slower rate than that of the economy as a whole. The President also debunked the ideas that a budget deficit invariably leads to inflation and that a budget surplus is always better for the economy than a budget deficit.

Kennedy also made a point of discussing consumer confidence, always an important economic driver and indicator and one that is always "a matter of myth and a matter of truth." The President is clearly stung by press accusations that the actions of his administration are having a negative impact on confidence, and thus the economy as a whole. Refuting these charges, Kennedy said that the "solid ground of mutual confidence is the necessary partnership of government, with all of the sectors of our society in the steady quest for economic progress."

11 In New Haven, Connecticut, the President delivers a commencement address at Yale University. He calls for cooperation between business and government, dismissing the notion that the stock market declines reflect lack of confidence in his policies.

12 Conservatives object to Kennedy's remarks at Yale in which he criticized the "mythology" of balanced budget thinking. Federal budget deficits and inflation, he argued, don't go hand-in-hand.

13 In Washington, Kennedy and Panamanian President Roberto Chiari hold inconclusive discussions on how to resolve Panama's objections to the 1903 Panama Canal treaty.

14 Indian Prime Minister Jawaharlal Nehru signals an interest in accepting a Soviet offer of MIG fighters for defensive purposes.

15 The President appeals to unionized flight engineers to submit to binding arbitration instead of striking against major U.S. airlines. Despite the government intervention, 1,700 members of the union appear ready to walk out.

16 Vietcong guerrillas ambush a military convoy north of Saigon and kill two U.S. Army officers.

17 Leaders of a far-right French movement in Algeria agree to suspend a bloody terror campaign in the colony. They agree to the suspension after receiving promises of amnesty from nationalist leaders who are expected to rule after Algerian independence.

Jun 16 Two Officers Killed in Vietnam

SAIGON—Two U.S. Army officers were killed today during an ambush by Communist insurgents some 30 miles north of Saigon. Approximately 20 South Vietnamese citizens, mostly soldiers, also were killed.

Captain Walter R. McCarthy of Columbia, South Carolina, and a lieutenant whose name has not yet been released died in the ambush. They had been serving as military "advisers."

Today's events proved just how dangerous South Vietnam has become. An armored convoy of seven vehicles was driving behind a civilian motorbus on Route 13. The bus drove over a land mine and exploded, with its occupants dying in the blaze. When the convoy slowed to a halt, Communist rebels emerged and attacked the South Vietnamese troops and the two American advisers. In addition to the land mine, the rebels employed rifles, machine guns, and a bazooka.

Jun 22 JFK Lauds Africa-Bound Group

WASHINGTON—President Kennedy addressed members of Operation Crossroads Africa on the White House South Lawn this morning. The student organization, 292 strong, is bound for a summer of volunteerism in Africa, where they will work in schools and hospitals and on infrastructure projects.

The President told the group's members that they were the progenitors of the Peace Corps, the American international volunteer organization that Kennedy established via executive order in March of last year.

Kennedy told the assembled students that he was glad to welcome them to the White House. He said that "in going to Africa you represent the best of our country, and I know they will welcome you. And I think that you will have the feeling of having served this country and, in a broader sense, the free community of people in a very crucial time."

Reverend James H. Robinson, director of Operation Crossroads Africa, and U.S. Senator Hubert H. Humphrey (D-MN) also addressed the student volunteers.

A big believer in volunteerism, JFK expresses his support to members of Operation Crossroads Africa.

Jun 22 JFK's Farm Bill Killed

WASHINGTON—The Kennedy administration is poised to send new farm legislation to Capitol Hill to replace the omnibus bill killed yesterday in the House of Representatives. The dead bill called for strict controls on the production of wheat and feed grains.

Opponents of the bill claim it could cost taxpayers a billion dollars annually while simultaneously harming farmers. Indeed, opposition to the bill was widespread, with only one Republican voting with the Democratic majority for passage, while 48 Democrats crossed the aisle to help kill the measure.

The White House claimed that defeat of the bill would "return the country to…ruinous deficit farm programs." House Republican Leader Charles Halleck countered that "it was a thoroughly bad bill."

Jun 25 Supreme Court Bans Prayer in Public School

WASHINGTON—The U.S. Supreme Court today ruled against prayer in public school. In *Engel* v. *Vitale,* the high court declared that a prayer recommended for classroom reading by the New York Board of Regents could not be read. By a vote of 6-1, the justices decided that requiring prayer in public school violates the First Amendment of the U.S. Constitution, which emphasizes free exercise of religion.

The prayer in question reads: "Almighty God, we acknowledge our dependence upon Thee, and we beg Thy blessing upon us, our parents, our teachers, and our country. Amen."

The American Jewish Committee, the Synagogue Council of America, and the American Ethical Union (a nontheistic organization) had opposed the prayer. The Supreme Court agreed, saying that because the prayer was created by government officials to promote a religious belief, it was impermissible.

The ruling was the latest controversial decision by the Supreme Court, which has been praised as progressive and derided as excessively liberal since Earl Warren was named chief justice in 1953. The decision also coincides with America's liberal swing in recent years, particularly since the rise to prominence of John F. Kennedy.

Second-graders say a prayer in Horace Mann Elementary School in Washington, D.C.

Jun 27 PRESIDENT SENDS WARNING TO CHINA

WASHINGTON—President Kennedy today made a clear warning to Communist China: Should that nation try to occupy the islands of Matsu and Quemoy, the United States would defend them.

At his press conference today, the President stated that large movements of Chinese Communist forces have recently occurred in the area of the Taiwan Strait. The purpose of the movements is unclear, he said, but he emphasized that the "United States will take the action necessary to assure the defense of Formosa and the Pescadores."

Formosa, also known as Taiwan, maintains its independence of Communist China and is an ally of the United States. The Formosa Resolution of 1955, a bill enacted by the U.S. Congress, established an American commitment to defend Formosa. "In the last crisis in the Taiwan area in 1958," Kennedy said today, "President Eisenhower made it clear that the United States would not remain inactive in the face of any aggressive action against the offshore islands which might threaten Formosa."

At today's news conference, the President said he stood by his statement of October 16, 1960, when he said: "The position of the [Eisenhower] administration has been that we would defend Quemoy and Matsu if there were an attack which was part of an attack on Formosa and the Pescadores. I don't want the Chinese Communists to be under any misapprehension. I support the administration's policy towards Quemoy and Matsu over the last five years."

The President asserted that the United States would engage in force only if necessary. He stated today: "As Secretary Dulles said in 1955, and I quote, 'The treaty arrangements which we have with the Republic of China make it quite clear that it is in our mutual contemplation that force shall not be used. The whole character of that treaty is defensive.' This continues to be the character of our whole policy in this area now."

Jun 28 KENNEDY SIGNS MIGRATION AND REFUGEE ASSISTANCE ACT

WASHINGTON—President Kennedy today signed the Migration and Refugee Assistance Act of 1962. The legislation is the result of a request Kennedy sent to Capitol Hill just over a year ago.

Created to provide for crisis assistance to displaced persons and refugees worldwide, the passage of the act was spearheaded by Senator J. William Fulbright (D-AR), chair of the Senate Foreign Relations Committee, and Representative Francis E. Walter (D-PA), chair of the House Judiciary Committee's Subcommittee Number One.

In his statement upon signing the legislation, the President congratulated Congress and assured the American people that "this government's leadership will be maintained in the great humanitarian endeavor of helping the world's stateless and homeless people…. In continuing this endeavor, we will be carrying forward a great American tradition which is as well-known as the generosity of our people in coming to the aid of those in need."

Jul 1 | MEXICO LOVES THE KENNEDYS

MEXICO CITY—After years of lukewarm relations with the United States, the Mexican government—and its people—proved extraordinarily gracious during President Kennedy's visit this weekend. On Friday, the President and First Lady Jacqueline Kennedy were overwhelmed by the throngs of people—estimated at 1.5 million—lining the roads from the airport to Mexico City. Today, some 5,000 people applauded when the couple entered the Basilica of Guadalupe for Sunday mass. In a surreal scene, some 200,000 Mexican citizens gathered in the area of the church.

While Kennedy had to "overcome" the fact that he was Catholic to get elected president, his faith is a definite asset in his relations with Mexico, a deeply devoted Catholic country. Even Mexican President Adolfo Lopez Mateos hugged Kennedy today after the two leaders concluded their three days of talks.

Mateos has fully embraced Kennedy's Alliance for Progress, in which the United States promotes economic development, social progress, and political freedom among Latin American countries. During the weekend's talks, Kennedy announced that the U.S. would grant a $20 million loan to Mexico to bolster its agricultural industry. He also promised to reduce trade barriers between the two nations. In return, he secured a strong relationship with his friends to the south.

An estimated 1.5 million people lined the streets for the Kennedys' seven-mile ride into Mexico City.

Jul 6 U.S. NUCLEAR TEST RESULTS IN MASSIVE CRATER, FALLOUT

LAS VEGAS—In a nuclear test conducted by the Lawrence Livermore National Laboratory, a thermonuclear bomb was detonated today at the Yucca Flat at the Nevada Test Site. The explosion resulted in the largest man-made crater in American history.

Although the Defense Department was minimally involved in today's test, scientists were more concerned with engineering and economics than military gains. They were trying to determine if nuclear explosions are practical for massive excavation projects, such as leveling mountainous terrain for the creation of highways.

Certainly, the nuclear bombs can blow big enough holes, but medical doctors are worried about the nuclear fallout. In today's test, two radioactive clouds rose two miles and three miles into the air, respectively. Winds blew them on a northeasterly path. Scientists have shown, and the Kennedy administration has acknowledged, that nuclear fallout can cause serious illness among people and animals.

A TAX CUTTER

Although the U.S. economy chugged along steadily if unspectacularly during President Kennedy's first 18 months in office, JFK was worried that the nation might fall into recession in late 1963 or early 1964—just in time to cast a shadow over his reelection campaign. Kennedy was more concerned with foreign affairs than domestic policy throughout his presidency, but he also understood that pocketbook issues, such as inflation and unemployment, were more immediate to most American voters.

Under the influence of economist Walter Heller, Kennedy launched a campaign to cut federal taxes in mid-1962. Heller, who served as JFK's chairman of the Council of Economic Advisors, was a disciple of English economist John Maynard Keynes, who had advocated government stimulus spending to boost flagging private economies. Beginning in early 1962, Heller urged Kennedy to cut personal income tax rates, which topped out at 91 percent, to stimulate consumer spending. The idea appealed to Kennedy, in part because the stimulus could forestall or even prevent a recession during his reelection campaign.

The President lobbied key political figures and businessmen in the fall of 1962, and he made a tax cut a centerpiece of his 1963 State of the Union speech. However, he faced stiff opposition from fellow Democrats. Some Dems preferred more federal spending rather than reduced revenues, while others believed that the rich would unduly benefit from the plan.

Kennedy still was trying to persuade Congress to go along with the tax cut when he was killed. Congress passed the plan, which reduced the top personal income tax rate to 70 percent.

Jul 11 — ADMINISTRATION GIVES BUSINESSES A BREAK

WASHINGTON—The Kennedy administration is giving businesses a tax break that is expected to bolster the American economy. The President today announced that federal tax depreciation schedules will be revised immediately. Businesses will be able to deduct the costs of equipment and machinery at a more rapid rate, thus saving money each year. Altogether, businesses are expected to save $1.5 billion in taxes in 1963.

The new plan will allow businesses, including self-employed businessmen, to write off their old machinery and equipment more rapidly and encourage them to invest in new and more efficient machinery and equipment. This would spur economic growth.

Said the President: "By encouraging American business to replace its machinery more rapidly, we hope to make American products more cost competitive, to step up our rate of recovery and growth, and to provide expanded job opportunities for all American workers."

Jul 12 — NASA DETAILS PLANS FOR APOLLO MOON MISSIONS

Houston—In a press conference yesterday, NASA officials outlined the space agency's $20 billion plan to land a man on the moon.

The main decision announced by NASA brass was that the mission will be designed as a lunar orbit rendezvous, as opposed to an Earth orbit rendezvous or a direct flight. That is, the primary spacecraft—the command module—will remain in lunar orbit, while an exploratory lunar module will land on the surface of the moon, then rejoin the command module for the return flight to Earth.

According to NASA administrator James Webb, "We are putting major emphasis on lunar orbit rendezvous because a year of intensive study indicates that it is most desirable, from the standpoint of time, cost, and mission accomplishment." The lunar orbit rendezvous mode is expected to cost as much as $1.5 billion less than the other modes, and be ready for launch several months sooner.

In addition, NASA has immediate plans to begin development of the lunar landing craft. Its purpose is to bring two of the three members of the mission crew to the surface of the moon while the third remains in the command module. The agency also will be utilizing Saturn rockets to test the lunar orbit in advance of the missions.

The Apollo missions, if accomplished, would be the fulfillment of the challenge President Kennedy set forth before a joint session of Congress in May 1961: landing a man on the moon and returning him to Earth before the end of the decade.

5 The administration asks Congress for $23 million to install devices on U.S. nuclear weapons that would help prevent their unauthorized use.

6 Nuclear technicians detonate a hydrogen bomb just under the surface of the Nevada desert. It is part of a series of tests to determine if nuclear weapons can be safely and effectively used in large-scale excavation projects.

7 Algeria's fledgling government deals with multiple security threats. It claims that Morocco has occupied the Algerian settlement at Safsaf, and it is cooperating with French troops to quell post-independence violence in Oran.

8 JFK laments results from a recent report by the Council on Youth Fitness, which showed, he says, "that at least 60 percent of our children do not participate in a daily program of physical activity."

9 An electromagnetic pulse from a high-altitude U.S. nuclear test knocks out streetlights and sets off burglar alarms 800 miles away in Hawaii.

10 President Kennedy signs a bill that requires new televisions to include UHF-channel reception capability.

11 Kennedy applauds the successful July 10 launch of the privately funded Telstar satellite, intended to transmit television signals across the Atlantic Ocean.

12 Concerned by the political tactics of Brazilian President Jango Goulart, the White House postpones a planned Kennedy trip to the South American nation until the fall.

Jul 18 KENNEDY PITCHES ELDERLY HEALTH CARE BILL TO AMERICANS

WASHINGTON—President Kennedy delivered terse remarks to the American people yesterday on the heels of the Senate defeat of his Medical Care for the Aged bill.

Speaking from the White House Fish Room, Kennedy called the bill's failure to pass the Senate by a two-vote margin "a serious defeat for every American family."

The President noted that the bill was designed to not only benefit elderly Americans but also all "who have parents who are liable to be ill, and who have children to educate at the same time…they have suffered a serious setback."

Kennedy then put the onus on the electorate to see the bill passed upon its planned reintroduction in January 1963. Noting that opposition was largely Republican, the President suggested that the American people make their own determination about this bill with their vote at the midterm elections. "I hope that we will return in November a Congress that will support a program like Medical Care for the Aged," Kennedy said. "I hope it will pass."

Jul 20 TAYLOR TAPPED TO HEAD JOINT CHIEFS OF STAFF

WASHINGTON—President Kennedy shook up the military high command today by naming General Maxwell Taylor as chairman of the Joint Chiefs of Staff. Maxwell will replace General Lyman Lemnitzer, whose two-year term expires on September 30. Lemnitzer will replace General Lauris Norstad as commander of U.S. and NATO forces in Europe. Norstad will retire on November 1.

Taylor, 60, graduated from the U.S. Military Academy in 1922 and was the first Allied general to land in France on D-Day. He served as Army chief of staff during the Eisenhower administration but resigned due to his disagreement with President Eisenhower's reliance on a nuclear deterrent as strategic policy. Taylor believes strongly in conventional forces.

After the Bay of Pigs fiasco in 1961, President Kennedy felt he had received poor advice from the Joint Chiefs of Staff. He appointed Taylor, whose "flexible response" philosophy resonates with Kennedy's, to investigate the failure of the Cuban invasion.

Over the last year, Taylor has served as the President's top military adviser—a role that formally belongs to the chairman of the Joint Chiefs of Staff. Kennedy, who has become good friends with Taylor, undoubtedly is looking forward to the transition.

Like Kennedy, General Maxwell Taylor often believes in nuanced strategies for military crises.

Jul 22 Kennedys Host the Glenns in Hyannisport

HYANNISPORT, MASS.—The President and Mrs. Kennedy passed an enjoyable weekend hosting celebrated astronaut Colonel John Glenn, Mrs. Glenn, and the couple's two children at the "summer White House" in Hyannisport, Massachusetts.

The eventful weekend included several trips on various Kennedy vessels, both motor and sail. Colonel Glenn and Mrs. Kennedy enjoyed tandem waterskiing while Ethel Kennedy, wife of Attorney General Robert Kennedy, drove the towboat.

The weekend's only low point occurred when the President ran his sloop *Victoria* aground near the family compound, then ran into more trouble when his mainsail collapsed as the boat was in the process of being relaunched. Nevertheless, it appeared to be a relaxing and enjoyable weekend for all involved

Jul 23 Telstar Sends TV Signal Across Atlantic Ocean

ANDOVER, MAINE—Scientists took communications technology to a new, exciting level today. For the first time, a communications satellite, Telstar 1, relayed a television signal across an ocean, from Andover, Maine, to southern England.

The English were supposed to watch a press conference by President Kennedy acknowledging the event. However, they received the transmission signal before Kennedy was ready. Their first glimpse of American TV was instead a baseball game between the Philadelphia Phillies and Chicago Cubs at Chicago's Wrigley Field.

Bell Labs constructed the satellite, which NASA launched into space on July 10 aboard a Delta rocket. With a helical antenna, Telstar received microwave signals from the ground station. These signals were amplified and rebroadcast to the receiving station in England.

"This is another indication of the extraordinary world in which we live," Kennedy said. "This satellite must be high enough to carry messages from both sides of the world, which is of course a very essential requirement for peace." The President added that "speedier communications…are bound to increase the security and well-being of all people."

The Telstar satellite can relay telephone calls and television signals from the U.S. to Europe.

13 The President signs a four-year extension of the Sugar Act, which among other things gives the administration power to restrict sugar trade with Cuba and other countries.

14 Kennedy calls on Soviet leaders to cooperate in a "creative search for ways to end the arms race." The 17-nation Geneva conference is set to resume two days from now.

15 As an alternative to a quick tax cut, the Kennedy administration is considering the possibilities of speeding federal spending to invigorate the economy.

16 As the disarmament conference reopens in Geneva, Western delegates express flexibility on allowing the Russians to complete a nuclear test series before any test ban takes effect.

17 After the Senate narrowly fails to pass a medical care program for the elderly, an angry Kennedy vows to a television audience that he will take the issue to voters in the fall midterm elections.

18 At the White House, the President honors four test pilots of the experimental X-15 rocket, which the previous day reached an altitude of nearly 60 miles and flew at nearly 3,800 mph.

19 A day after the Peruvian military seized power, Kennedy suspends diplomatic relations with Peru, declaring that the coup is a "serious setback" to democracy.

20 Kennedy shakes up his military leadership team, naming General Maxwell Taylor chairman of the Joint Chiefs of Staff. He succeeds General Lyman Lemnitzer, who becomes U.S. commander in Europe. General Earle Wheeler becomes U.S. army chief of staff.

Jul 23 U.S., Soviet Union Agree on Neutrality in Laos

GENEVA—The Soviet Union and Western nations showed today that diplomacy can work in Southeast Asia. Representatives of 14 countries signed an agreement that guarantees the neutrality and independence of Laos.

Secretary of State Dean Rusk signed on behalf of the United States. Most significantly, Soviet Foreign Minister Andrei Gromyko presided over the ceremony, which was held in the Palais des Nations, the European headquarters of the United Nations. The 14 nations agreed that the members of the International Control Commission will work to establish neutrality in Laos. The commission will oversee the withdrawal of foreign troops.

Pro-Communist Pathet Lao rebels have been waging guerrilla warfare against government forces. Today's agreement helps ease worries that Laos will become another Korea; i.e., the stage for a proxy war between Cold War powers. British Prime Minister Harold Macmillan said: "The conference has been able to show the world that difficult international problems can be solved by discussion and mutual compromise."

"I intend that the federal career service be maintained in every respect without discrimination and with equal opportunity for employment and advancement." —KENNEDY

Jul 24 President Calls for Equal Rights for Working Women

WASHINGTON—Equal rights has been a running theme of John F. Kennedy's presidency, and today he stood up for America's working women. The President instructed government agencies to take measures to ensure that gender discrimination in appointments and promotions be eliminated in their departments.

"I intend," Kennedy said, "that the federal career service be maintained in every respect without discrimination and with equal opportunity for employment and advancement."

Kennedy made his statement after conferring with the Commission on the Status of Women, which he launched with an executive order last December.

A White House statement said that today's announcement "hits in particular at any remaining outmoded practices and customs in the employment and advancement of women in the federal service."

Jul 26 WELFARE BILL GIVES HOPE TO THE NEEDY

WASHINGTON—President Kennedy signed a welfare-reform bill today that he believes will help the 7.4 million Americans currently on relief. "This measure embodies a new approach," Kennedy said, "stressing services in addition to support, rehabilitation instead of relief, and training for useful work instead of prolonged dependency."

The legislation calls for an increase of $300 million in federal contributions to the welfare system. However, supporters of the bill are banking that the new rules will help welfare recipients help themselves—and thus decrease the burden on American taxpayers.

The Public Welfare Amendments bill calls for:

• Funding for day-care centers so that mothers are able to leave the home and find employment—instead of relying on welfare.

• The restructuring of welfare-system rules to encourage the able-bodied to take part in on-the-job training and participate in community works projects.

• More federal money for rehabilitative and preventative services, such as counseling for troubled individuals and families.

• More federal aid to states for the training of welfare personnel.

• Welfare assistance to both unemployed parents instead of just one (which the current law calls for). The extra check is designed to help families stay together.

"Our objective," Kennedy said, "is to prevent or reduce dependency and to encourage self-care and self-support—to maintain family life where it is adequate and to restore it where it is deficient."

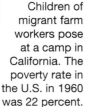

Children of migrant farm workers pose at a camp in California. The poverty rate in the U.S. in 1960 was 22 percent.

21 The President instructs Attorney General Robert Kennedy to look into a demonstration 11 days earlier in Albany, Georgia, which resulted in the jailing of civil rights leaders Martin Luther King, Jr., and Ralph Abernathy.

22 In Massachusetts, astronaut John Glenn and his wife wrap up a weekend waterskiing and sailing with President and Mrs. Kennedy and other members of the Kennedy family.

23 The U.S. and 13 other countries sign an agreement in Geneva that guarantees the neutrality of Laos.

24 A new executive order forbids federal departments and agencies from discriminating against women in employment matters.

25 On the 10th anniversary of the establishment of the Puerto Rican Commonwealth, President Kennedy agrees that residents of the island should be allowed self-determination on statehood, independence, or commonwealth status.

26 The President signs a bill that revises public welfare programs to emphasize training and other forms of support over relief payments.

27 General Electric agrees to pay a fine of nearly $7.5 million to the government for engaging in price-fixing.

28 The President and his arms control team agree to consider a simplified plan for an international inspection program as part of any nuclear test ban.

29 The White House regroups after a House committee blocks an extensive federal fallout shelter program.

Prince Phouma and Kennedy have achieved their goal in Laos: the Declaration of Neutrality.

Jul 31 LAOTIAN PRIME MINISTER CONCLUDES WASHINGTON VISIT

WASHINGTON—Prince Souvanna Phouma, the prime minister of Laos, left Washington yesterday at the conclusion of a productive visit. In four days of meetings with President Kennedy, Secretary of State Dean Rusk, and other U.S. leaders, the Prince affirmed his commitment to peace in Southeast Asia following his government's official Declaration of Neutrality, set forth earlier this month.

The Prime Minister and President Kennedy are both optimistic about the future in light of the conclusion of the new Geneva Settlement on Laos. The two leaders affirmed their nations' commitment to supporting the agreement and their respective obligations to ensuring its success.

The Prime Minister expressed his gratitude to the United States and the role it played in the execution of the settlement, while Kennedy confirmed America's support of peace in Laos, in both word and deed.

Aug 6 SOVIETS EXPLODE 30-MEGATON BOMB

WASHINGTON—The Soviet Union exploded a "super bomb" above the Arctic yesterday. With a force of approximately 30 megatons, it was one of the largest nuclear explosions ever recorded.

Today, the Atomic Energy Commission announced that the Soviets have been conducting atmospheric nuclear tests over the past week. Yesterday's explosion was, so far, the largest of the series.

Last fall, the Soviets broke the moratorium on atmospheric nuclear testing, which they and the United States had agreed to in 1958. The U.S. responded with its own atmospheric nuclear tests earlier this year.

Ominously, August 6 marked the 17th anniversary of the bombing of Hiroshima. To commemorate the event and to protest the resumption of nuclear testing, activists gathered in Hiroshima, Tokyo, London, and other cities throughout Europe.

Aug 18 — KENNEDY DEDICATES THE SAN LUIS DAM

Los Banos, Calif.—President Kennedy dedicated California's new San Luis Dam today, the cornerstone of the government's $500 million plan to increase the flow of water for irrigation in the region.

In his address during the dedication ceremony, Kennedy emphasized America's spirit of cooperation as well as the willingness of its people to recognize that local projects can have national benefits. Accordingly, Kennedy said, "the way to move ahead is to realize the we are citizens of one country…and if one state stands still, so do all the rest."

The President also noted that this project, like so many conservation projects, represented several decades of hard work and commitment by dedicated advocates—some of whom did not live to see the fruit of their labors.

Kennedy used the event as an opportunity to promote his conservation agenda. He said that both Point Reyes and Texas' Gulf Coast should be added to the park system as National Seashores. He also stressed the importance of a wilderness preservation bill, a Youth Unemployment Act with provisions for a Youth Conservation Corps, and the expansion of outdoor recreation facilities. The President mentioned, not for the first time, the need to apply scientific know-how to conservation efforts, with desalinization technology a high priority.

"Our task in the simplest terms," according to Kennedy, is "to strengthen the United States of America."

A day after dedicating the Oahe Dam in South Dakota, JFK oversaw the San Luis Dam dedication (pictured).

Aug 22 JFK: Soviet Technicians, Supplies Arrive in Cuba

WASHINGTON—At his news conference today, President Kennedy confirmed reports that Soviet men and supplies have arrived in Cuba in large numbers recently.

When questioned about this, the President responded, "Yes. New supplies definitely, in large quantities. Troops? We do not have information, but an increased number of technicians."

Asked about the significance of this, Kennedy said, "Well, we're examining it." He said there is no evidence of Soviets arriving in other Latin American countries (Cuba is the only one aligned with the Soviet Union). He added: "What we're talking about are supplies and technicians of a rather intensive quantity in recent weeks." The President then moved on to another question.

The situation undoubtedly will be carefully monitored. Keeping Soviet influence out of the Western Hemisphere has been a top priority of the Eisenhower and Kennedy administrations.

BROTHERS IN ARMS

Eight years younger than the President, Robert Kennedy seemed to relish his role as a behind-the-scenes operator. He earned his reputation as a superb political organizer when he managed his brother's 1952 campaign for the U.S. Senate, and he reprised that role in the 1960 presidential campaign.

Thin, intense, and completely committed to his brother's ambitions, Bobby Kennedy gained a reputation as a ruthless political operator during the 1950s. As attorney general, he served as the President's sounding board as well as his most trusted adviser. He also was willing to serve as John's enforcer. In early 1962, when the President was battling the steel industry over proposed price increases, Attorney General Kennedy issued subpoenas to obtain copies of expense accounts and other information from top executives. The steel companies eventually backed down.

The unfolding civil rights movement brought the two bothers even closer together, as they formulated a response to the demands of activities and the political sensitivities of southern Democrats. Historians agree that Robert Kennedy seemed to understand the issue in a way the President did not. In June 1963, Robert successfully urged John to deliver a national address on race relations while Governor George Wallace was trying desperately to keep the University of Alabama as a "whites-only" institution. The President agreed, and, in a speech the two brothers worked on, he declared civil rights to be a profoundly moral issue. Days later, President Kennedy introduced a new civil rights bill that would become law only after his assassination.

Aug 27 HOUSE VOTES TO BAN POLL TAXES

WASHINGTON—The House of Representatives today voted for a new constitutional amendment, one that would prohibit the poll tax as a requirement to vote in federal elections. If approved by the legislatures of three-quarters of the states, it will become the 24th Amendment to the U.S. Constitution.

Currently, five states require citizens to pay a poll tax in order to vote in federal elections: Texas, Alabama, Mississippi, Virginia, and Arkansas. Many southern states adopted the poll tax decades ago in order to disenfranchise Negro voters. State legislatures made every citizen pay the poll tax except those whose parents or grandparents had voted.

Although the House approved today's proposal 295 to 86, civil rights supporters say that it will have little effect in ending Negro disenfranchisement. Only in Alabama and Mississippi is the poll tax a significant problem. Southern whites employ other tools to keep Negroes from voting, including literacy tests, termination of employment, and physical threats.

The Kennedy administration had supported legislation that would outlaw literacy tests as well as poll taxes, but southern opposition killed the bill. The President announced his approval of today's measure, as insignificant as it may be.

"Today's action by the House of Representatives in approving the poll tax amendment culminates a legislative effort of many, many years to bring about the end of this artificial bar to the right to vote in some of our states," he stated. "This is a significant action which I am confident will be approved quickly by the required 38 state legislatures."

Aug 29 JFK TABS GOLDBERG TO REPLACE FRANKFURTER

WASHINGTON—A liberal-leaning U.S. Supreme Court likely tipped even more in that direction today. President Kennedy announced that Associate Justice Felix Frankfurter, a political independent, will retire, and that he will appoint left-of-center Democrat Arthur J. Goldberg to fill his seat. The word around Washington today is that Congress will confirm Goldberg's appointment. If so, the Court will seat six Democrats and three Republicans.

Goldberg, 54, is currently the U.S. secretary of labor. The son of Jewish immigrants, he was a close adviser of President Franklin Roosevelt and a prominent labor lawyer. Goldberg was a chief legal adviser in the merger of the American Federation of Labor (AFL) and the Congress of Industrial Organizations (CIO) in 1955, and he served as general counsel for the United Steelworkers of America.

7 President Kennedy gives Food and Drug Administration researcher Frances Kelsey the President's Award for Distinguished Federal Civilian Service. Kelsey's investigation blocked U.S. distribution of the sleeping drug thalidomide at a time when the drug's dangers were not yet known.

8 As the President meets with foreign affairs advisers to discuss issues in Asia, Africa, and Europe, news arrives that West German Chancellor Adenauer is warning nonaligned nations not to endorse or sign the proposed peace treaty between Moscow and East Germany.

9 JFK authorizes a mission to defoliate several mangrove swamps along Vietnam's Mekong River from which guerrilla forces are able to operate.

10 Despite disagreements with Britain and Belgium on Congo policy, the American delegation at the UN proposes trade sanctions if Congo's rebellious Katanga Province fails to accept a federal constitution.

11 The President names Charles Bohlen as the U.S. ambassador to France.

12 In another space first, the Soviets launch two separate, manned space capsules in two days on missions designed in part to test the effects of prolonged weightlessness.

13 JFK speaks live to a nationwide television audience on the state of the economy. He rejects calls for an immediate cut in personal income taxes, but says he will propose tax reform to Congress in 1963.

The President shares pens with those who contributed to the historic Communications Satellite Act.

Aug 31 | NEW BILL COULD LEAD TO WORLDWIDE TELEVISION

WASHINGTON—Working together, industry and government will attempt to create a satellite system that will allow television signals to be transmitted around the world. Today, President Kennedy signed the Communications Satellite Act, which calls for an industry-government corporation that will try to make the goal a reality.

Kennedy said that within a few years, the satellite system "should make possible...a vastly increased capacity to exchange information cheaply and reliably with all parts of the world by telephone, telegraph, radio, and television. The ultimate result will be to encourage and facilitate world trade, education, entertainment, and many kinds of professional, political, and personal discourse which are essential to healthy human relationships and international understanding."

The President said that "safeguards" are included in the bill to protect the public interest. "No single company or group will have the power to dominate the corporation," he said. Of the 15 members of the corporation's board of directors, commercial participants will elect six and public shareholders in the corporation will elect six. The President will appoint three government officials to the board.

"There is no evidence of any organized combat force in Cuba from any Soviet bloc country; of military bases provided [by] Russia...of the presence of offensive ground-to-ground missiles.... Were it to be otherwise, the gravest issues would arise." —KENNEDY

Sept 4 CUBA HAS SOVIET WEAPONS

WASHINGTON—The Soviet Union has provided Cuba with sophisticated weaponry and military technicians, President Kennedy announced today.

"Information has reached this government in the last four days from a variety of sources which establishes without doubt that the Soviets have provided the Cuban government with a number of anti-aircraft defense missiles with a slant range of 25 miles which are similar to early models of our Nike," the President announced in a White House statement. "Along with these missiles, the Soviets are apparently providing the extensive radar and other electronic equipment which is required for their operation.

"We can also confirm the presence of several Soviet-made motor torpedo boats carrying ship-to-ship guided missiles having a range of 15 miles. The number of Soviet military technicians now known to be in Cuba or en route—approximately 3,500—is consistent with assistance in setting up and learning to use this equipment. As I stated last week, we shall continue to make information available as fast as it is obtained and properly verified."

The President continued: "There is no evidence of any organized combat force in Cuba from any Soviet bloc country; of military bases provided [by] Russia; of a violation of the 1934 treaty relating to Guantanamo; of the presence of offensive ground-to-ground missiles; or of other significant offensive capability either in Cuban hands or under Soviet direction and guidance. Were it to be otherwise, the gravest issues would arise.

"It continues to be the policy of the United States that the Castro regime will not be allowed to export its aggressive purposes by force or the threat of force. It will be prevented by whatever means may be necessary from taking action against any part of the Western Hemisphere. The United States, in conjunction with other Hemisphere countries, will make sure that while increased Cuban armaments will be a heavy burden to the unhappy people of Cuba themselves, they will be nothing more."

14 For the first time in 35 years, the U.S. Senate invokes cloture, a procedural move that ends a liberal filibuster against Kennedy's legislation on a communications satellite system.

15 Latin American unrest continues to occupy White House attention. As Washington prepares to reluctantly recognize the military junta in Peru, clashes in Argentina cause fears of a coup there, too.

16 On the same day that General Douglas MacArthur, 82, is honored by Congress for his military service during three wars, President Kennedy sits down with MacArthur to discuss world issues.

17 Embarking on another tour of western states, JFK dedicates a dam in South Dakota before spending the night at Yosemite National Park.

18 Continuing the conservation theme of his tour, Kennedy dedicates the San Luis Dam in California, part of a $500 million project designed to irrigate southern portions of the state.

19 As controversy rages over the shooting of a young man during a Berlin escape attempt, the U.S. commander in the city appeals to his Soviet counterpart to prevent future "acts of terror" by East German border guards.

20 Administration officials are considering ways to speed economic aid to the fragile Algerian government, in order to prevent Communists from influencing the regime.

21 The U.S. is monitoring the arrival in Cuba of large quantities of supplies and several thousand Soviet technicians.

Sept 11 · SOVIETS ACCUSE THE U.S. OF AGGRESSION IN REGARDS TO CUBA

WASHINGTON—The political situation in Cuba has taken a bizarre and disturbing twist. The Soviet government today released a statement that accused the United States of escalating tensions—an accusation that the Kennedy administration denies.

For more than a week, the administration has been disturbed by the import of Soviet weaponry and military technicians to Cuba. Four days ago, President Kennedy asked Congress for authority to call up 150,000 reservists. Officials said that Kennedy did not intend to call up the reservists in the foreseeable future, and that his motivation for the request was to be better prepared to deal with the Berlin crisis. The President had been granted similar powers last year, but his time limit for call-ups expired on July 31, 1962.

But in their 4,700-word press release, the Soviets reacted with alarm to Kennedy's request from Congress. The theme is that the U.S. is gearing up for war against Cuba and the Soviet personnel on the island. "If the aggressors unleashed war," the statement warns, "our armed forces must be ready to strike a crushing retaliatory blow at the aggressor."

The statement said that the Soviets transported weapons to Cuba only for defensive purposes, and that they had no intention of taking aggressive action against the United States.

Kennedy's space dreams are becoming a reality in Huntsville, Alabama.

Sept 12 · ROCKET MAN TO JFK: "WE'LL DO IT!"

HOUSTON—President Kennedy's two-day tour of space installations has been packed with excitement. Yesterday morning, the President visited the George C. Marshall Space Flight Center in Huntsville, Alabama. Dr. Wernher von Braun, the director of the center, showed the President a model of a Saturn C-5 rocket.

"This is the vehicle designed to fulfill your promise to put a man on the moon in this decade," said von Braun. He then paused and declared. "And, by God, we'll do it!"

From Huntsville, Kennedy flew to Florida to visit the Launch Operation Center in Cape Canaveral. He then arrived, late yesterday, in Houston, where more than 100,000 people lined the motorcade route from the airport to the city. This morning, the President promoted the exploration of space during his address at Rice University Stadium.

Said Kennedy in front of 50,000 people: "This generation does not intend to flounder in the backwash of the coming age of space. We mean to be a part of it. We have vowed that we shall not see it governed by a hostile flag of conquest, but by a banner of freedom and peace…. We choose to go to the moon in this decade and do the other things not because they are easy, but because they are hard."

JFK stated that Castro is failing because of "his own monumental economic mismanagement."

22 U.S. nuclear submarines *Skate* and *Seadragon* achieve a dramatic first: an under-ice rendezvous at the North Pole.

23 In response to a growing Soviet threat in Cuba, the White House secretly orders an increase in covert anti-Castro activities. Kennedy requests contingency plans in the event the Soviets deploy nuclear weapons in Cuba.

24 By executive order, JFK extends eligibility for the Bronze Star to American soldiers serving in Vietnam and Laos, where U.S. forces are not technically at war.

25 UN Secretary General U Thant travels to Moscow, where he plans talks with Soviet Premier Khrushchev on Berlin, the Congo, and other issues.

26 The United States plans to propose in Geneva tomorrow a treaty to ban nuclear tests in the atmosphere, in space, and under water, but not underground.

27 The President praises Congress for passing a proposed 24th Amendment to the U.S. Constitution, which would prohibit states from requiring payment of poll taxes in order to vote in federal elections.

28 American and British delegations in Geneva unveil two nuclear test-ban options. The preferred total ban would include enforcement by international inspectors; the second option would halt all but underground tests pending further negotiations.

29 Kennedy nominates Labor Secretary Arthur Goldberg to replace retiring U.S. Supreme Court Associate Justice Felix Frankfurter.

Sept 13 JFK PRESS CONFERENCE FOCUSED ON CUBA

WASHINGTON—Concerns about Cuba took center stage this evening during President Kennedy's press conference in the State Department Auditorium. Noting that the Castro regime has stepped up its courtship of the Soviet Union in the face of the economic and political collapse of Cuba, Kennedy assured the press corps that the United States has the situation in Cuba "under our most careful surveillance."

Kennedy's opening statement was decisive, as he said that "if Cuba should ever attempt to export its aggressive purposes by force or the threat of force against any nation in this hemisphere," the United States "will do whatever must be done to protect its own security." The President also made a point of restating America's commitment to helping Cuban refugee leaders who are actively opposing Castro's hold on Cuba.

Kennedy fielded questions on other important issues of the day, including the increasing anti-Negro violence in the struggle for voting rights across the South. America's military space program, the strength of the United States' reserve forces, and the upcoming midterm elections were other issues touched on during Kennedy's 43rd presidential news conference.

The goal of the Public Works Acceleration Act is to provide work for the jobless and improve "economically distressed" communities.

Sept 14 KENNEDY SIGNS PUBLIC WORKS ACT

WASHINGTON—Lending a hand to the have-nots has been a hallmark of the Kennedy presidency. Today, the President again showed his compassion by signing the new Public Works Acceleration Act to provide $900 million for public works projects in economically depressed areas. Moreover, the federal government will provide financial assistance to local public works projects.

The purpose of the program, Kennedy stated today, is "to relieve unemployment and spur economic expansion in those areas of the country which have failed to share fully in the economic gains of the recovery from the 1960–61 recession."

Areas that are "economically distressed" (as designated in the Area Redevelopment Act of 1961), and those with high unemployment, are eligible for funding. Organizers hope to put unemployed citizens to work on development projects that will benefit their communities.

Kennedy called the new act "an important companion measure to other efforts already under way." According to the President, the Area Redevelopment Administration has begun to stimulate the economies of long-suffering communities. "Through the manpower development and training program," he said, "tens of thousands of jobless men and women will soon be learning the skills needed to improve their employment prospects and productivity."

Sept 17 NINE NEW ASTRONAUTS SELECTED

HOUSTON—Nine new American astronauts were introduced at a news conference at the University of Houston today. These men—all in their 30s, married, and parents—will join the seven veteran astronauts of Project Mercury in NASA's next great space adventure. NASA expects that a select number of them will fulfill President Kennedy's goal of landing on the moon.

Each of the 16 astronauts will train for Project Gemini, in which two manned capsules will rendezvous in space. Project Apollo, which calls for a moon landing before decade's end, will follow.

Three of the new astronauts are Air Force veterans: Major Frank Borman, 34; Captain Thomas Stafford, 32; and Captain James McDivitt, 33. Three hail from the Navy: Lieutenant Commander James Lovell, 34; Lieutenant Commander John Young, 32; and Lieutenant Charles Conrad, Jr., 32. Elliot See, Jr., 35, a test pilot for General Electric, and Neil Armstrong, 32, a test pilot with NASA, are the other new astronauts.

Sept 18 CONGRESS SAYS NO TO JFK'S FALLOUT SHELTERS

WASHINGTON—The Kennedy administration's request for $538 million for nuclear fallout shelters is being met with deaf ears in Congress.

The Senate approved only two of the parts of the total request. One was to provide $93 million to continue the federal program of selecting and stocking fallout shelters in government buildings throughout the United States. The Senate also approved funding for construction of fallout shelters in federal buildings. However, the House today voted down both proposals.

As part of his initial $538 million proposal, the President had also called for the construction of fallout shelters in other public buildings, including schools and hospitals.

Congressmen oppose the funding of shelters for multiple reasons, including cost as well as the dubious effectiveness of the structures. Moreover, American citizens have become increasingly angry that shelters have been posited as an "answer" to the nuclear problem. Last fall, *Newsweek* was appalled "that the talk of shelters and protection has…transmuted the unutterable horrors of thermonuclear war into a rather cozy affair."

Congress and the public are rejecting Kennedy's pitch for more fallout shelters.

August 1962

30 The President blasts legislators who are seeking to cut the foreign-aid program. Kennedy calls it ironic that his most fervent anti-Communist political opponents "are the ones who want to cut this program the hardest."

31 Kennedy signs the Communications Satellite Act, which creates a private, government-regulated corporation to operate communications satellites.

September

1 The White House announces that a U.S. Navy plane, flying a training mission 15 miles off the Cuban coast, was fired on by two Cuban naval vessels. Washington warns of a counterattack.

2 The Soviet Union announces an agreement to provide Cuba with arms and military advisers. Soviet economic and industrial aid was also included in the accord.

3 A State Department report to Kennedy concludes: "On the basis of existing intelligence, the Soviet military deliveries to Cuba do not constitute a substantial threat to U.S. security."

4 President Kennedy announces that "the Soviets have provided the Cuban government with a number of anti-aircraft defense missiles."

5 After a U-2 spy plane flies off course over Sakhalin Island, the President tells the Soviets that the intrusion was unintended and a "navigational error."

6 Kennedy asks Congress to end a federal pricing system under which foreign textile producers pay less for cotton than U.S. companies.

Sept 24 — CONGRESS GRANTS CALL-UP POWERS TO THE PRESIDENT

WASHINGTON—The House today granted President Kennedy's request to call up 150,000 ready reservists and extend the active-duty tours of servicemen. Representatives approved the bill 342–13. The Senate had okayed the bill unanimously, 76–0.

Last year, a mobilization bill allowed the President to call up 250,000 reservists. When the Berlin crisis intensified, he called up 148,000 men. Because that provision expired on July 31, 1962, Kennedy had to make his latest request.

The overwhelming votes in favor of the President's request sends a message to the world that Congress is standing by the commander-in-chief. Recently, many congressmen have expressed their dissatisfaction with the Soviet Union, which they feel has been pushing limits in Berlin and Cuba.

Sept 26 — LARGEST ATOMIC POWER PLANT TO OPEN IN HANFORD

WASHINGTON—Hanford, Washington, will be home to the world's largest nuclear power plant. President Kennedy today signed legislation approving the facility.

Currently, a reactor is being constructed in Hanford to produce plutonium for weapons. But now the reactor will serve a dual purpose. Washington Public Power will construct and operate a generating plant; it will use steam provided by the reactor to produce electricity for homes and factories in the Pacific Northwest. The generating plant will cost an estimated $130 million and produce close to a million kilowatts, making it, according to Kennedy, "four times larger than any other project in the world."

Kennedy said that the project "is for peacetime application…. [It] presents an opportunity, dearly in the public interest, to obtain the maximum benefits from the public investment already committed for this facility and to demonstrate national leadership in resources development while furthering national defense objectives."

Sept 26   U.S. TO SELL SUPERSONIC MISSILES TO ISRAEL

WASHINGTON—For many years, the United States has stuck to its policy of not selling weapons to Middle Eastern countries. Now the administration is changing its stance. The State Department admitted today that the U.S. will sell supersonic Hawk missiles to Israel.

Recently, other Middle Eastern countries—quiet enemies of Israel—have acquired weapons from the Soviet Union. The American objective is to keep a balance of power in the Middle East. If Arab countries feel they can overpower Israel, U.S. officials believe, they might attack that nation.

Israel, an ally of the United States, will purchase the short-range defensive missiles as well as supporting equipment. Moreover, Americans will train Israeli crews to use the weapons. The training will take place in the United States.

The Kennedy administration has informed Gamal Abdel Nasser, president of the United Arab Republic, of the decision. Administration officials expressed to Nasser that these are *defensive* weapons, and that America seeks peace in the Middle East and good relations with Arab countries.

Sept 28   McNAMARA SUPPORTS USE OF NUKES IN BERLIN

WASHINGTON—The United States, it seems, is prepared to use nuclear weapons to defend its interest in Berlin. Secretary of State Robert McNamara strongly implied that assertion today in his news conference.

McNamara, after returning from Berlin, said: "It is our policy to utilize whatever weapons are needed to preserve our vital interests. Quite clearly, we consider access to Berlin a vital interest."

McNamara did not specifically say that that the U.S. would use nuclear weapons against Soviet forces. However, he said he had visited nuclear storage sites on his visit to Berlin, and he mentioned specific weapons that can be armed with nuclear warheads. He added that he was impressed by the readiness of American troops.

Clearly, McNamara's "tough talk" was meant as a message to Nikita Khrushchev. The Soviet premier has pushed for a peace treaty concerning East Germany, but not Berlin. U.S. officials believe that after the treaty is signed, Khrushchev would try to restrict U.S. rights in Berlin. Nevertheless, McNamara's remarks conflict with the philosophy of President Kennedy, who opposes the use of nuclear weapons to settle international conflicts.

7 The White House proposes legislation that grants presidential authority to call up 150,000 reservists for one year if a crisis arises.

8 During a tour of six nations, Vice President Lyndon Johnson promotes U.S. foreign aid policies. In a private meeting with Pope John XXIII, Johnson talks with the pontiff about school desegregation and other issues.

9 Communist China announces it has shot down a U-2, owned and flown by Nationalist China, over the eastern portion of its mainland.

10 Two black churches near Sasser, Georgia, one associated with a voter registration campaign, are burned. During an arson investigation at the scene, FBI agents are attacked by a white resident.

11 A Soviet spokesman calls the U.S. move to activate 150,000 reservists an act of aggression, and warns that an American attack against Cuba or Russian ships could start a nuclear war.

12 Fresh from an encouraging meeting with Marshall Space Flight Center Director Dr. Wernher von Braun, President Kennedy tells a Houston audience that he is confident the United States will put a man on the moon "before the end of this decade."

13 During a news conference, Kennedy says he will act without hesitation against Cuba if necessary to protect American security, despite the presence of Soviet personnel and weapons.

14 The President signs a bill that provides $900 million for immediate-action public works projects in several economically depressed parts of the country.

With segregationists on edge in Mississippi, Kennedy was careful to avoid a civil rights "lecture."

Sept 30 — IN TV ADDRESS, KENNEDY CALLS FOR CALM IN MISSISSIPPI

WASHINGTON—After federalizing the Mississippi National Guard to confront white rioters at the University of Mississippi, President Kennedy addressed the nation tonight. In his thousand-word speech, the President explained his actions and reached out to the people of Mississippi to peacefully accept the admission of Negro James Meredith to the university.

Federal courts had ruled that Meredith had the constitutional right to enroll at Ole Miss. Kennedy said that he had the "obligation" to "implement the orders of the courts." Now, he said, citizens of Mississippi needed to accept the ruling and refrain from violence. "The eyes of the nation and all of the world are upon you and upon all of us," he said. "And the honor of your university—and state—are in the balance."

The President was careful not to lecture Mississippians on the issue of civil rights. Most likely, he felt that a scolding would only exacerbate conditions. Instead, he said: "You have a great tradition to uphold—a tradition of honor and courage, won on the field of battle and on the gridiron, as well as the university campus."

Civil rights activists likely were alarmed when the President said: "Neither Mississippi nor any other southern state deserves to be charged with all the accumulated wrongs of the last 100 years of race relations to the extent that there has been failure. The responsibility of that failure must be shared by us all, by every state, by every citizen."

The President likely chose those words only to calm tensions. In Mississippi, white legislators continue to defy Supreme Court orders to integrate public schools. Whites also employ extra-legal means to keep Negroes off the voting rolls. In 1960, only 6.7 percent of Mississippi's Negroes were registered to vote.

15 The administration is frustrated by its failure to convince allies to stop or reduce trading with Cuba.

16 Congress approves a U.S. loan of $100 million to the United Nations, whose membership of nations has reached 104, more than twice the original 51 members.

17 NASA presents a new astronaut class of nine, including Neil Armstrong.

18 In Massachusetts, the Kennedy political dynasty grows as President Kennedy's brother Edward wins the Democratic nomination for Senate.

19 Congress and the administration settle on language for a joint resolution that backs the use of military force if needed in response to Cuban or Soviet aggression.

20 Argentina slips closer toward chaos when an armored rebel column clashes with government forces near Buenos Aires.

21 The President commends Pan Am and its pilot union for avoiding a costly strike by submitting to voluntary arbitration.

22 Soviet Foreign Minister Andrei Gromyko bluntly warns the UN General Assembly that American intervention in Cuba will cause a nuclear war.

23 In a television interview on foreign affairs, Kennedy urges Congress to restore pending cuts to foreign aid legislation.

24 Mississippi Governor Ross Barnett defies federal desegregation orders for the University of Mississippi. He orders the arrest of any federal official who tries to arrest state officers who are themselves trying to prevent the enrollment of James Meredith.

"The eyes of the nation and all of the world are upon you and upon all of us. And the honor of your university— and state—are in the balance."

—KENNEDY, TO THE CITIZENS OF MISSISSIPPI

KENNEDY AND CIVIL RIGHTS

John Kennedy was wary about the civil rights movement in the South. The Democratic Party's white southern base opposed the efforts of northern Democrats to support the demands of African Americans. And the party's liberals resented the power of white segregationists on Capitol Hill and in the South's state capitals.

Kennedy knew the importance of the African American vote, but he also knew he needed white southern support as well. So in 1960, he steered a middle ground. He reached out to prominent African Americans during his campaign and gave several speeches about civil rights. But he was careful to avoid any direct challenge to the status quo in the segregated South.

Once in the White House, Kennedy regarded civil rights as a distraction from his intense focus on foreign affairs and the Cold War with the Soviet Union. He was determined to avoid a confrontation similar to that in Little Rock, Arkansas, in 1957, when President Eisenhower sent in federal troops to desegregate that city's public schools. He believed that news photographs of that ugly confrontation handed the Soviets a propaganda victory.

White reaction and black determination in the South forced Kennedy's hand and eventually led him to declare civil rights to be a moral issue. In a speech on June 11, 1963, JFK asked white Americans to support the cause of equal rights. It was by far his most impassioned speech on the subject.

The following day, a prominent civil rights leader, Medgar Evers, was shot to death in Mississippi. The President himself believed that his support for civil rights threatened his reelection in 1964.

One Negro soldier helps another black soldier, who was hit by flying glass during the race riot in Oxford.

Oct 1 KENNEDY SENDS TROOPS TO SUBDUE OLE MISS RIOTERS

OXFORD, MISS.—A race riot at the University of Mississippi, which erupted yesterday, continued through the night. Some 23,000 U.S. troops were called in to quell the violence. Two men have been killed and dozens have been injured during the mayhem.

Tensions had been brewing for weeks because of the efforts of James Meredith, a Negro, to enroll at the all-white university. On September 13, a federal district court ordered the university to admit Meredith. However, Governor Ross Barnett ordered state police to ignore the order. On September 26, state police turned away Meredith and the federal marshals who escorted him.

After Barnett was found guilty of contempt of court, Meredith arrived yesterday to register at the school. He was accompanied by several hundred federal marshals, U.S. border guards, and prison guards. But upon his arrival, rioting broke out in Oxford. Students and local whites threw bottles and rocks at federal marshals, who battled back with tear gas. Rioters set cars on fire, and shots were fired. One federal marshal was shot in the neck and critically wounded.

President Kennedy quickly issued an executive order, federalizing the Mississippi National Guard and authorizing the use of armed forces. Troops gained control of the situation by morning. At 8:30 A.M., Meredith registered at the school.

Oct 3 ASTRONAUT SCHIRRA ORBITS EARTH IN "SWEET LITTLE BIRD"

CAPE CANAVERAL, FLA.—American Astronaut Wally Schirra orbited Earth six times before splashing into the ocean today. The mission went off without a hitch, and Schirra landed just five miles from his target in the central Pacific. Crewmembers of the USS *Kearsarge* retrieved the latest NASA hero, who was physically unaffected by his 10-hour trip into space.

Minutes before landing, Shirra exclaimed, "I feel marvelous. This is a beautiful flight." And after hearing that he had landed just 9,000 yards from his target, he replied, "That's pretty close, isn't it? Boy, this is a sweet little bird. I just can't get over it."

Once on the carrier, Schirra experienced another thrill: a phone call from President Kennedy. The 39-year-old New Jerseyan was on Cloud 9 all evening, saying he was ready for another trip tomorrow.

"The spacecraft did everything I wanted it to do," Schirra said, "and I was able to accomplish everything I wanted to accomplish during the flight."

Oct 4 JFK Gets His Trade Bill

WASHINGTON—Congress today approved President Kennedy's foreign trade bill, which will give the President authority to negotiate tariff reductions. It also allows the government to authorize assistance to companies that are suffering due to import competition.

The bill will allow the government to negotiate for reductions up to 50 percent on tariffs. It also allows the government to negotiate with Europe's Common Market nations for the removal of tariffs on certain items. Kennedy has been championing tariff reductions all year, believing they will facilitate more foreign trade and thus bolster the American economy.

Reduced tariffs on imports will hurt American companies that produce the same goods. That is why Kennedy requested, and received, the authority to help these companies and its workers. The bill allows for such relief as tax credits, loans, and job training.

Oct 10 New Bill Should Lead to Safer Drugs

WASHINGTON—President Kennedy signed a bill today designed to provide safer and more effective drugs to the American consumer. "It will also insure," he said, "that our pharmaceutical industry will be even better equipped to provide us with the best possible drugs to be found anywhere."

With the new bill, consumers will be more aware of what they're taking. The drug's common name, and not just its trade name, will have to be on the bottle, and in readable print. In their advertising for a drug, the pharmaceutical companies will have to summarize its side effects.

In addition, the Food and Drug Administration will have expanded powers for factory inspection. No drugs will be marketed without the approval of the Secretary of Health, Education and Welfare. And if evidence exists that a drug is unsafe, the Secretary can order it off the market immediately.

25 Western allies send identical notes to Moscow condemning its refusal to discuss the future of the Berlin Wall.

26 A new law provides $250 million for the Atomic Energy Commission for the next fiscal year, including funding for the first-ever nuclear power plant, in Hanford, Washington.

27 The President signs a compromise Food and Agriculture Act, which gives him a portion of the authority he had sought earlier in the year to regulate crop production.

28 Secretary of Defense Robert McNamara reiterates America's willingness to defend Berlin with nuclear weapons. Earlier this week, the administration also set a precedent in the Middle East by agreeing to sell missile defense systems to Israel.

29 President Kennedy federalizes the Mississippi National Guard and orders U.S. marshals to the University of Mississippi in Oxford in order to protect James Meredith during his registration and entry to classes.

30 The President delivers a television address on the situation in Mississippi, appealing to students to show the "courage to accept those laws with which you disagree as well as those with which you agree."

Oct 18 U.S. TO PUT SQUEEZE ON CUBA

WASHINGTON—The Kennedy administration is working on ways to counter the Soviet delivery of arms to Cuba. Today, a Pentagon spokesman revealed that, earlier this month, the United States sent 12 jet fighters to southern Florida in response to the many MIG jets that the Soviets delivered to Cuba.

Meanwhile, the Kennedy administration is working on establishing a quarantine of the island. The plan would call for sanctions against foreign companies that try to trade with Cuba.

The International Longshoreman's Association is taking its own stance against Communist regimes. The union announced last week its longshoremen would not handle any Soviet or Cuban cargo.

Finally, the President today met with Soviet Ambassador Andrei Gromyko. However, the talks centered on the situation in Berlin, not Cuba.

Oct 21 CUBA CRISIS MAY BE BREWING

WASHINGTON—President Kennedy cut short his campaign tour yesterday and headed back to Washington. White House officials said that the President came back due to a cold, but the buzz in Washington is that he is needed in the U.S. capital due to a brewing crisis.

The administration has kept mum about the issue, but there has been a flurry of unusual activity at the White House lately, and those involved in national security have been at work this weekend. As for President Kennedy, he went to church this morning but showed no signs of a cold. Spokesmen said that the President will address the nation early this week.

The speculation is that the crisis centers on Cuba. The administration has been unnerved in recent weeks by the shipment of Soviet weapons to the island nation, even though those weapons are said to be defensive in nature (anti-aircraft missiles). The U.S. is currently planning a strict quarantine of Cuba. Moreover, the Navy and Marines are sending thousands of men to the island of Vieques, near Puerto Rico. Administration officials have tried to downplay the deployment.

More information about the secret crisis should emerge in the upcoming days, be it through official or unofficial channels.

CAROLINE AND JOHN-JOHN

Small children hadn't lived in the White House since Teddy Roosevelt's brood in the opening years of the 20th century. Naturally, the country was enthralled with the antics of Caroline, who was born on November 27, 1957, and John Jr., better known as John-John, who was just two months old when the family moved to the White House.

Caroline was introduced to political life at the age of two, when she accompanied her parents on the campaign trail in 1960. Candidate Kennedy often joked that his daughter's first words were "plane," "goodbye," and "New Hampshire." When Caroline was given a pet pony, which she named Macaroni, the White House was inundated with mail from children and horse lovers. Macaroni, Kennedy noted, stirred up more interest than a proposal to ban nuclear arms testing.

As John Jr. grew from infancy to the terrible twos, he delighted JFK's advisers with his unbearably cute vocabulary. He called his father "pooh-pooh head" one night as the President entertained guests for dinner. On another occasion, John-John was captured on film peeking out from under his father's desk in the Oval Office. It made for one of the most famous photos of an image-filled presidency.

The Kennedy children were far too young to appreciate their front-row seat to history. But they certainly were a part of the drama of those years. During the Cuban missile crisis, for example, the President took time from his tense deliberations to ask if Caroline had been eating candy. Caught red-handed, she refused to answer the President of the United States.

The President then went back to the business of preventing world war.

1 Rioting in Oxford results in two deaths and injuries to dozens of people, including 25 U.S. marshals.

2 Kennedy signs legislation that will help fund UN missions in Congo and other trouble spots. Also on this day, the federal government blocks entry to all U.S. ports by cargo ships bound for Cuba.

3 JFK seeks a Taft-Hartley injunction to prevent 75,000 union longshoremen around the country from striking. Meanwhile, NASA's latest astronaut, Wally Schirra, orbits Earth six times.

4 Congress agrees on legislation that authorizes the President to negotiate on foreign trade and provide support to American interests harmed by tariffs and other trade problems.

5 Congress sends the White House a bill to fund a pay raise for federal workers.

6 Another incident in Berlin: East German guards shoot a 21-year-old West Berlin man who was helping an elderly couple escape through a tunnel under the Berlin Wall. A British ambulance fails to gain entry to help the victim.

7 The United States withdraws military advisers from Laos despite indications that Communist forces are subverting an agreement to establish a neutral government.

8 Cuba asks the United Nations to condemn what it calls the American "naval blockade."

9 The U.S. Supreme Court agrees to hear a case on prayer and Bible readings in public schools. However, it refuses to reconsider the lower court order that admitted James Meredith to the University of Mississippi.

MRBM LAUNCH SITE 1
SAN CRISTOBAL, CUBA
23 OCTOBER 1962

MISSILE ERECTOR

CABLE

MISSILE SHELTER TENT

TRACKED PRIME MOVERS

FUEL TANK TRAILERS

OXIDIZER TANK TRAILERS

A reconnaissance photo of San Cristobal in western Cuba reveals missile erectors (top middle).

"I call upon [Soviet Premier] Khrushchev to halt and eliminate this clandestine, reckless, and provocative threat to world peace and to stable relations between our two nations." —KENNEDY

Oct 22 U.S.–SOVIET SHOWDOWN
USSR Has Constructed Nuclear Missile Sites in Cuba

WASHINGTON—America stands on the brink of perhaps the biggest crisis in the nation's history. Addressing the nation this evening, President Kennedy announced that the weapons that the Soviet Union shipped to Cuba are not simply limited-range defensive weapons, as the Soviets had indicated. Instead, the Soviets are constructing, throughout Cuba, offensive missiles that can carry nuclear warheads. Some missiles have ranges of 1,000 miles and others more than 2,000 miles, meaning they can reach most cities in the United States.

The President said that since last Tuesday (October 16), the U.S. has compiled "unmistakable evidence" that "a series of offensive missile sites is now in preparation on that imprisoned island. The purpose of these bases can be none other than to provide a nuclear strike capability against the Western Hemisphere."

Kennedy said the presence of these "clearly offensive weapons of sudden mass destruction" was a "deliberate defiance of the Rio Pact of 1947, the traditions of this Nation and hemisphere, the joint resolution of the 87th Congress, the Charter of the United Nations, and my own public warnings to the Soviets on September 4 and 13."

According to the President, Soviet Ambassador Andrei Gromyko had told him last Thursday that the weapons were not offensive. Kennedy quoted Gromyko as saying that "the Soviet government would never become involved in rendering such assistance [for offensive weapons]."

The President said that the U.S. will take the following steps immediately:

• A strict quarantine on all offensive military equipment shipped to Cuba. However, he said, the U.S. will not deny shipments of "necessities of life" to Cuba.

• Increased surveillance of Cuba and its military buildup. Kennedy said: "Should these offensive military preparations continue, thus increasing the threat to the hemisphere, further action will be justified. I have directed the Armed Forces to prepare for any eventualities."

• Kennedy: "It shall be the policy of this nation to regard any nuclear missile launched from Cuba against any nation in the Western Hemisphere as an attack by the Soviet Union on the United States, requiring a full retaliatory response upon the Soviet Union."

• An immediate meeting of the Organ of Consultation under the Organization of American States will convene. The meeting, Kennedy said, will be to "consider this threat to hemispheric security and to invoke articles 6 and 8 of the Rio Treaty in support of all necessary action."

• The U.S. will ask for an emergency meeting of the United Nations Security Council "to take action against this latest Soviet threat to world peace. Our resolution will call for the prompt dismantling and withdrawal of all offensive weapons in Cuba, under the supervision of UN observers, before the quarantine can be lifted."

• Finally, Kennedy said, "I call upon [Soviet Premier] Khrushchev to halt and eliminate this clandestine, reckless, and provocative threat to world peace and to stable relations between our two nations. I call upon him further to abandon this course of world domination, and to join in an historic effort to end the perilous arms race and to transform the history of man."

CRISIS IN CUBA

Historians believe that President Kennedy handled the Cuban missile crisis with a deft combination of power and flexibility, thanks in part to lessons he had learned during the failed Bay of Pigs invasion in 1961.

The crisis unfolded quietly during the summer. American aerial intelligence over Cuba photographed large crates as they were unloaded from Soviet ships. In late August, Kennedy was handed spy photos showing that the Soviets and Cubans were building sites for surface-to-air missiles. Soviet diplomats said the buildup was strictly defensive, but on October 16 JFK saw photos that proved that the Soviets were installing offensive missiles with nuclear capability.

Kennedy put together the equivalent of a war cabinet, which he called the Executive Committee, or ExComm. These top advisers played out various options, ranging from invasion to a blockade. Tape recordings of the ExComm meetings show Kennedy constantly probing for more information, asking questions, playing devil's advocate. Top military brass, especially Air Force General Curtis LeMay, demanded a surprised bombardment of the sites, even if it meant outright war with the Soviets.

The Cuban missile crisis taught Kennedy to be skeptical of advice from the military and from sources like the CIA. His measured decision to blockade Cuba led to a peaceful end to the crisis.

10 The President signs into law federal tax deductions for pension savings investments by self-employed business owners. He also signs legislation that contains strict rules on prescription drug testing and distribution.

11 Pope John XXIII convenes the Second Vatican Council, which will last more than three years and continue under Pope Paul VI. For many American Catholics, the council will liberalize their religious experience during an era of dramatic social change.

12 Another in a recent series of border skirmishes between Indian and Chinese troops results in 50 casualties and heightened tension between the two Asian giants.

13 Beginning on Columbus Day, the President makes a campaign swing through New York, New Jersey, Pennsylvania, and Kentucky. He supports Robert Morgenthau's gubernatorial bid in New York, as well as Democratic candidates for Congress.

14 U.S. officials gather intelligence photos that show that the USSR has placed missiles in Cuba.

15 As President Kennedy welcomes Algerian Premier Ahmed Ben Bella to Washington with a 21-gun salute, photo analysts discover that the weapons in Cuba are Soviet SS-4 nuclear missiles capable of reaching Washington and New York.

16 At breakfast, Kennedy is briefed on the Cuban missiles, which are not yet operational or armed. Later in the day, the President forms a crisis team, the Executive Committee of the U.S. National Security Council, or EX-COMM, comprised of 19 trusted advisers.

By signing the proclamation, Kennedy prohibited the Soviets from sending offensive weapons to Cuba.

Oct 23 PRESIDENT ORDERS NAVAL AND AIR QUARANTINE OF CUBA

WASHINGTON—President Kennedy today signed a proclamation stating that Cuba will be under naval and air quarantine. Beginning at 10 A.M. Eastern time tomorrow, Soviet ships will no longer be able to carry offensive weapons into Cuba.

The consequences could be severe. The President had authorized Secretary of Defense Robert McNamara to employ the United States military—as well as the might offered by members of the Organization of American States—to enforce the quarantine. According to the President's proclamation, military personnel will have the right to board and inspect a foreign vessel.

"In carrying out this order," the President's proclamation read, "force shall not be used except in case of failure or refusal to comply with directions, or with regulations or directives of the Secretary of Defense issued hereunder, after reasonable efforts have been made to communicate them to the vessel or craft, or in case of self-defense. In any case, force shall be used only to the extent necessary."

Kennedy did not sign the proclamation until it was approved by the Organ of Consultation of the Organization of American States. OAS members voted 19-0 in favor of the measure.

Oct 23 SOVIETS CLAIM THAT THE U.S. IS THE AGGRESSOR

WASHINGTON—In a written rebuttal to President Kennedy's Monday speech, the Soviet government painted the United States—and not the Soviet Union, as Kennedy had insisted—as the aggressor in the Cuban missile crisis.

The Soviet statement, handed to U.S. Ambassador Foy Kohler, said that the Soviet missiles in Cuba were defensive weapons, constructed only so that Cuban Premier Fidel Castro could protect his country.

The Soviets feel that the United States has overreacted to the situation—and overstepped its bounds. They particularly oppose the quarantine of Cuba that Kennedy has imposed. The Soviets said they have asked the United Nations Security Council to address America's "threat to peace."

The Soviets stated that their armed forces are making preparations to become combat ready. They added that the United States is risking thermonuclear war, although no explicit threat was made and, in fact, the statement's tone was cautious. Moscow radio declared that the Soviets would not use nuclear weapons against the U.S. "unless aggression is committed."

Oct 23 CASTRO: WE WILL NEVER BE AGGRESSORS, VICTIMS

HAVANA—Cuban Premier Fidel Castro is reacting defiantly to the United States' stance on the missile crisis. Echoing Soviet officials, Castro says that the missiles constructed in his country are for defensive purposes only.

"We will acquire the arms we deem necessary for our defense," Castro said. "And we don't have to give an accounting to anyone. None of our arms are offensive because we have never been aggressive. We will never be aggressors, but we will never be victims, either."

Castro rejected President Kennedy's demand that United Nations inspectors be allowed into his island nation. "We refuse to give permission to anyone to examine, to investigate our country—no matter who it is," he said. "Anyone who comes to inspect anything in Cuba had better come prepared for battle.

"If they impose a total blockade, we will resist it. We can resist. We will not starve to death. If there is a direct attack, we will repel it. I can't speak more plainly."

Castro, who compared Kennedy to Adolf Hitler, appears emboldened by his new weapons, which can reach most U.S. cities and can be armed with nuclear warheads.

"We are calmed by the knowledge that, if they attack us, the aggressor will be exterminated," Castro said. "[Kennedy] proposes that we disarm. We will never do so while the U.S. continues to be an aggressor."

Castro insists that the U.S., and not Cuba or the USSR, is the aggressor in this crisis.

Although engaged in continuous discussions on the crisis, Kennedy sticks to a planned political schedule to avoid tipping his hand to the Soviets—or alarming the American public. The same night, a U-2 mission discovers SS-5 missiles in Cuba, which are capable of reaching all of the continental U.S.

Kennedy meets as previously scheduled with Soviet Foreign Minister Gromyko, who says Soviet aid to Cuba is peaceful. In response, JFK reads his September 4 announcement that the U.S. will not allow offensive weapons in Cuba. There is no open discussion of the missiles, but U.S. planners are considering either a blockade or an overwhelming air strike.

Before leaving for another campaign trip, Kennedy and the Joint Chiefs discuss blockade and air strike options. The President asks his speechwriter to draft a television message for either decision.

The President cuts short his campaign trip, blaming it on a cold, and returns to Washington for a final decision about military options on Cuban.

The crisis builds to a fever pitch. U-2 photos show Soviet fighters, bombers, and cruise missile launchers being assembled in Cuba. Advised that air strikes may not destroy all of the missiles, JFK opts for a blockade. He calls editors at *The New York Times* and *Washington Post* and convinces them not to break the story before he speaks to the nation.

The *Enterprise,* a nuclear-powered aircraft carrier, is being used in the barricade.

Oct 24 UNITED STATES, SOVIETS CAUTIOUS DURING BLOCKADE

WASHINGTON—Both the United States and the Soviet Union monitored each other carefully and cautiously today, the first day of the American-imposed quarantine of Cuba.

The Defense Department reported that some Soviet ships had changed course to avoid the U.S. naval blockade. The U.S. is prohibiting shipments of weapons, not food or other goods, so execution of the blockade will be difficult.

Yesterday, President Kennedy received a message from Premier Khrushchev. The Soviet leader suggested that he and Kennedy should meet, but the message was vague and the administration was unclear about Khrushchev's stance on the crisis. No summit meeting has been planned. Kennedy's stance is clear: The missiles in Cuba must be removed, and inspectors must be allowed to verify their removal; until then, the blockade will continue.

U Thant, acting secretary general of the United Nations, has urged the U.S. and USSR to suspend their actions on Cuba for two to three weeks. Kennedy is expected to respectfully reject that request.

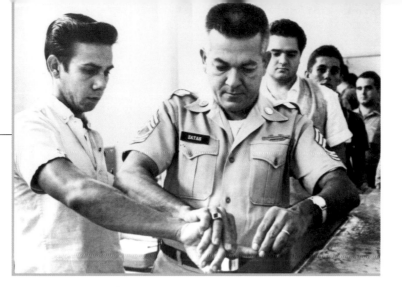

A U.S. Army sergeant processes an Army volunteer in Miami on October 23.

Oct 25 TENSIONS HIGH; MILITARY ACTION CONSIDERED

WASHINGTON—In Washington, Moscow, and all over the world, tensions remained high today due to the Cuban missile crisis.

Less than 24 hours after the American blockade of Cuba went into effect, the U.S. Navy this morning intercepted a Soviet oil tanker, *Bucharest,* that was bound for the island nation. The vessel was allowed to proceed after Navy personnel determined that it was carrying oil, not arms. At least a dozen other Soviet ships have steered away from the blockade, perhaps because they were carrying weapons.

Meanwhile, the U.S. was building up its military strength in Florida. U.S. officials would not comment on the activity. At the very least, the military is getting prepared in case a conflict arises in or around Cuba. However, some fear that the U.S. might take aggressive action; that is, try to destroy the missile sites in Cuba or attempt to invade the island. Such aggression would be extraordinarily risky. The Soviets have constructed antiaircraft missile bases on the island, and Cuba now has missiles that have nuclear capability.

President Kennedy has been conferring with advisers for days about the crisis. With the blockade, he is drawing a line in the sand. However, the question remains whether he will take bolder steps, meaning further military action. Some members of his Joint Chiefs of Staff are especially hawkish, particularly General Curtis LeMay, who commanded the infamous incendiary air attacks on Japanese cities during World War II.

In Moscow, Premier Khrushchev has agreed to UN leader U Thant's plea for a moratorium, in which the U.S. would suspend the blockade for two to three weeks and the Soviet Union would stop sending weapons to Cuba. President Kennedy has agreed to consider the moratorium, but he is not yet committed to it.

Left to right: Soviet Ambassador Valerian Zorin, Cuban Ambassador Mario Garcia Inchaustegui, and U.S. Ambassador Adlai Stevenson.

Oct 25 — STEVENSON CONFRONTS SOVIET AMBASSADOR AT UN

NEW YORK—U.S. Ambassador Adlai Stevenson captured the world's attention today with a dramatic oration at the United Nations about the Cuban missile crisis. As a result, he appeared to gain international support for the United States.

During Security Council deliberations, Soviet Ambassador Valerian Zorin insisted that the U.S. photographs that showed Soviet military bases in Cuba—the premise for the entire crisis—were fakes.

Stevenson strongly confronted his adversary, saying: "Do you, Ambassador Zorin, deny that the USSR has placed and is placing medium- and intermediate-range missiles and sites in Cuba?... Don't wait for the translation! Yes or no?"

Zorin responded: "I am not in an American courtroom, sir, and I do not wish to answer a question put to me in the manner in which a prosecutor does...."

Stevenson interrupted: "You are in the courtroom of world opinion right now, and you can answer yes or no. You have denied that they exist, and I want to know whether I have understood you correctly.... I am prepared to wait for my answer until hell freezes over, if that's your decision. And I am also prepared to present the evidence in this room."

Stevenson did present the evidence, showing reconnaissance photos of the missile sites. Seemingly no one doubted their authenticity.

Oct 26 — FALLOUT SHELTERS CAN FIT 60 MILLION AMERICANS

WASHINGTON—In the midst of the Cuban missile crisis, the Defense Department today issued a report about the U.S. Civil Defense program. The report stated that, so far, 112,000 structures in the United States are adequate for use as fallout shelters—places of protection in the event of a nuclear attack. Those structures could accommodate 60 million people, or about one-third of the U.S. population. The report stated that the 112,000 structures have a "protection factor" of 100. That means that the radiation out inside the shelter would be 100 times greater than the

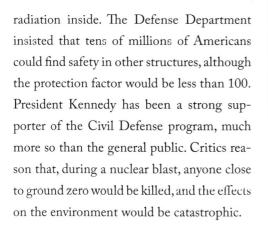

A third of Americans might find safety in a fallout shelter such as this one.

radiation inside. The Defense Department insisted that tens of millions of Americans could find safety in other structures, although the protection factor would be less than 100. President Kennedy has been a strong supporter of the Civil Defense program, much more so than the general public. Critics reason that, during a nuclear blast, anyone close to ground zero would be killed, and the effects on the environment would be catastrophic.

Oct 26 SOVIETS CONTINUE TO BUILD MISSILE SITES

WASHINGTON—The U.S. blockade of Cuba and President Kennedy's threats to the Soviet Union have not compelled the Soviets to dismantle their missiles in Cuba. In fact, just the opposite is apparently occurring.

According to a White House statement issued today, the "development of ballistic missile sites continues at a rapid pace."

The statement continued: "Through the process of continued surveillance, directed by the President, additional evidence has been acquired which clearly reflects that as of Thursday, October 25, defense build-ups in these offensive missile sites continued to be made." The statement added that "serious attempts are under way to camouflage their efforts."

U.S. officials have said that this activity must end before the U.S. would consider negotiations with Moscow to end the crisis.

For the Kennedy administration, time is of the essence. The Soviets are constructing sites for not just *medium*-range nuclear weapons—which can strike the southeastern United States—but intermediate-range weapons, which can reach most cities in the U.S.

The President is still weighing whether to use force to eliminate the threatening missile sites. He does believe that he has the support of the Organization of the American States (OAS) to do so. Jose Mora, secretary general of the OAS, today offered "multilateral support" for such an action.

Meanwhile, U Thant, the acting secretary general of the United Nations, has made progress in negotiations. Soviet Premier Khrushchev agreed to temporarily avoid the U.S. blockade, while U.S. representatives promised to try to avoid a direct confrontation over the next few days.

27 Hope turns to frustration as Premier Khrushchev makes more demands. He secretly worries that he has lost control of his commanders in Cuba, one of whom orders the downing of an American U-2 plane. President Kennedy and EX-COMM decide to respond to Khrushchev's first, more positive letter, but ignore the second.

28 Fearful that President Kennedy is preparing to invade Cuba, Premier Khrushchev orders the withdrawal of Soviet weapons and personnel. The crisis is over. In Havana, Castro is furious that he was not informed of Khrushchev's decision, which extracted no American concessions on other Cuban issues.

29 India urgently requests American assistance in its border dispute with China. Washington agrees to provide military supplies and other assistance.

30 The UN General Assembly votes to deny membership to Communist China.

31 In Havana, Castro tells visiting UN Secretary General U Thant that he will not allow inspection of installations in Cuba unless the U.S. abandons its naval base at Guantanamo Bay and meets other conditions.

Oct 27 KHRUSHCHEV LETTERS TO WHITE HOUSE RESULT IN DISMAY

WASHINGTON—U.S. leaders have ridden an emotional roller coaster these last two days after the writing of two letters from Premier Khrushchev—one filled with promise, the other disappointment.

Late on Friday evening, White House officials received the Soviet Premier's first letter. Khrushchev offered to remove the Soviet missiles in Cuba under United Nations inspection, and he promised not to send weapons to that nation in the future. President Kennedy was elated by this capitulation and prepared to agree to such terms, which would end the crisis.

This morning, however, Moscow broadcast a second message from Khrushchev to the White House, one that had not yet arrived in Washington. This Soviet proposal introduced new conditions for withdrawal, most significantly that the United States remove its offensive weapons from Turkey. Moreover, the Premier proposed a one-month deadline for the overall agreement to be reached, and he made no mention of halting the construction of missile bases in Cuba within that period.

President Kennedy did not find either of these proposals acceptable. After hearing the Moscow broadcast, the White House released a statement saying that "as an urgent prelim nary to consideration of any proposals... offensive weapons must be rendered inoperable and further shipment of offensive weapons to Cuba must cease—all under effective international verification."

The statement indirectly took the Turkey proposal off the table, saying "it is the Western Hemisphere countries and they alone that are subject to the threat that has produced the current crisis."

Khrushchev has yet to respond to the White House statement. Thus, the crisis continues.

Meanwhile, there were disturbing developments in and above Cuba today. A U-2 reconnaissance plane was reported missing after attempting to photograph missile sites in Cuba. It is feared that the plane was shot down. Another U.S. aircraft was fired upon today, reportedly by Cubans. The Pentagon responded that the United States would retaliate if U.S. planes were attacked.

Oct 27 GOVERNORS VOW TO SUPPORT FEDERAL CIVIL DEFENSE PLAN

WASHINGTON—President Kennedy today urged America's governors to help accelerate the federal Civil Defense program. A group of nine governors vowed that they and their states would fully cooperate. The President and the governors agree that American citizens should be prepared to take shelter should the Cuban missile crisis escalate into a nuclear attack on U.S. soil.

At the White House, Kennedy hosted nine governors, all members of the Committee on Civil Defense of the Governors' Conference. They pledged to cooperate in the accelerated plan and urge fellow governors to do the same.

Currently, 112,000 structures in the United States have been deemed adequate for use as fallout shelters—places of protection in case of a nuclear attack. Those structures can accommodate 60 million people. The new plan calls for an increase in the number of fallout shelters to accommodate 110 million to 120 million Americans. The plan is *not* calling for new construction of more shelters; instead, it calls for the marking of thousands of less-safe, but still protective, buildings.

The federal plan is for the government to stock the 112,000 buildings—but not the newly marked structures—with food and supplies. Congress approved only $75 million in funding for civil defense and fallout protection. Kennedy had requested nearly $700 million.

BEHIND THE SCENES OF THE MISSILE CRISIS

John Kennedy was a fan of Ian Fleming's spy novels, featuring a dashing hero named Bond, James Bond. During the Cuban Missile Crisis, there was enough behind-the-scenes intrigue to satisfy any James Bond reader.

Even before JFK announced the imposition of a blockade around Cuba beginning on October 22, 1962, there had been secret meetings between Soviet diplomats and administration officials about the impending crisis. Like many of James Bond's antagonists, the Soviet diplomats cheerfully misled Washington by insisting that the buildup was for defensive purposes only. Once JFK learned the truth and prepared to confront the Soviets, private diplomacy took on a new urgency.

Kennedy summoned the Soviet ambassador, Anatoly Dobrynin, to the White House and told him to tell Moscow that he was prepared to go to war over Cuba. Meanwhile, in the Kremlin, Soviet leader Nikita Khrushchev told a visiting group of American businessmen that he would retaliate if U.S. warships opened fire on Soviet ships off Cuba. As the standoff near Cuba continued, Soviet diplomat (and presumed KGB spy)

Alexander Formin and American reporter John Scali met secretly on October 26 in a quiet Washington restaurant.

Formin asked Scali to pass on a message to the State Department: The Soviets would dismantle the missiles if the U.S. promised it would not invade Cuba. Scali met with Kennedy, who expressed an interest in the proposal. The reporter passed the message to Formin.

The following evening, the President's brother, Robert Kennedy—acting outside of his role as attorney general—met with Soviet Ambassador Dobrynin in the White House and pleaded with him to persuade Khrushchev to remove the missiles from Cuba. Dobrynin was not optimistic. Robert, his eyes red and watery, said his brother was trying to avoid a conflict but was under intense pressure from the military. The Soviets were holding out for a U.S. plan to remove outdated nuclear missiles from Turkey. Robert said his brother would do so, but not until the crisis was resolved. That was good enough for the Soviets.

The resolution came on October 27. The world breathed a sigh of relief.

Kennedy leaves St. Stephen's Church shortly after the announcement that Khrushchev ordered Soviet missile bases in Cuba dismantled and rockets returned to Russia.

Oct 28 SOVIETS BACK DOWN!
Khrushchev Agrees to Remove Missiles in Cuba

WASHINGTON—The Cuban missile crisis, the two-week Cold War conflict that put the world on the brink of nuclear war, appears to be over. After a battle of wills between the United States and Soviet Union, the Soviets have backed down.

In a message broadcast in Moscow today (9 A.M. Eastern time), Premier Khrushchev announced that the Soviets would terminate construction of their military bases in Cuba and send the missiles back to the Soviet Union. He said that these actions would take place under United Nations supervision.

President Kennedy accepted these terms. In his message to Khrushchev, he stated: "I consider my letter to you of October 27 and your reply today as firm undertakings on the part of both governments which should promptly be carried out. I hope that the necessary measures can at once be taken through the United Nations, as your message says, so that the United States in turn will be able to remove the quarantine measures now in effect."

Yesterday, President Kennedy sent a message to Khrushchev offering to lift the naval blockade of Cuba and assuring that no Western Hemisphere country, including the United States, would invade Cuba. These two promises were good enough for Khrushchev, who has said all along that the missiles were installed in Cuba for defensive purposes only.

Early yesterday, Khrushchev had urged the U.S. to remove its missile sites in Turkey as part of the agreement to end the crisis. In today's agreement, Turkey was not mentioned.

Both leaders discussed other issues in their messages today. Khrushchev insisted that the United States end surveillance flights over Soviet territory and Cuba. He and Kennedy also discussed, in broad terms, the need for nuclear disarmament.

"I agree with you that we must devote urgent attention to the problem of disarmament, as it relates to the whole world and also to critical areas," Kennedy wrote. "Perhaps now, as we step back from danger, we can together make real progress in this vital field. I think that we should give priority to questions relating to the proliferation of nuclear weapons, on earth and in outer space, and to the great effort for a nuclear test ban. But we should also work hard to see if wider measures of disarmament can be agreed and put into operation at an early date."

Today's agreement is being hailed as a great victory for President Kennedy, who stood strong against the Soviets without being overly zealous. Some of his military advisers had urged the President to bomb the missile sites, but Kennedy took a more cool-headed approach. The botched invasion of Cuba in April 1961, which he later regretted, undoubtedly played a role in this month's decision-making.

The losers are the Soviet Union, which will be perceived as the weaker adversary in this power play, and Cuban Premier Fidel Castro. Castro has complained vociferously over the last few days about Cuba being treated as a pawn in this Cold War battle. Although the Cuban people will no longer worry about a U.S. bombardment or a nuclear war, Castro has lost his missile defenses—a blow to his considerable ego.

KENNEDY'S CHRONIC PAIN

On the day John Kennedy took office, tan from a Florida vacation and coatless on a cold January day, the new White House press office released a report about the President's physical well-being. Kennedy's two doctors, Eugene Cohen and Janet Travell, pronounced the President to be in excellent health. The press dutifully reported the story, with *The New York Times* mentioning the President's health in a headline on Page 1.

The medical report was beyond political spin—it was an utter fabrication. Poor health had been Kennedy's constant companion since childhood. His "minor" maladies ranged from poor digestion to allergies to partial deafness. Moreover, Kennedy suffered from crippling back pain and Addison's disease. He depended on cortisone to regulate his adrenal glands; he regularly injected himself with the drug,

usually in the thigh. He also relied on a cocktail of painkillers, including Demerol, and shots of novocaine to manage his back pain.

Beginning in 1960, Kennedy called on the services of German-born physician Max Jacobsen, known as "Dr. Feelgood" to his celebrity patients. He specialized in painkillers and amphetamines, and Kennedy grew so dependent on his concoctions that he flew Jacobsen to France—on a separate plane—during his visit in 1961.

Kennedy's medical regimen was complex and secretive. Doctors Cohen and Travell were unaware of Dr. Jacobsen's treatments. Robert Kennedy, however, knew, and he asked the FBI to analyze Jacobsen's concoctions to measure their addictive qualities. The President preferred not to know. "I don't care if it's horse piss," he said. "It works."

8 The White House basks in the glow of good results from the November 6 midterm elections. Democrats gain four Senate seats and lose six in the House. The administration grows optimistic about its chances for enacting education and health insurance reforms.

9 American flags fly at half-staff in honor of former First Lady Eleanor Roosevelt, who died earlier in the week. President Kennedy calls Mrs. Roosevelt "one of the great ladies" in U.S. history.

10 American naval ships continue to observe and photograph—but not board—cargo ships leaving Cuba, in order to verify the removal of Soviet missiles.

11 The Pentagon discloses that it counted 42 missiles on board Soviet cargo ships leaving Cuba, two more than Premier Khrushchev said had been deployed. The official cautioned that without ground inspection, the U.S. "never could be sure that 42 was the maximum number that the Soviets brought to Cuba."

12 As the Cuban situation cools, attention turns to this week's visit to Washington by West German Chancellor Adenauer. He and President Kennedy are expected to focus on a strategy for negotiating with Moscow over Berlin.

13 The Kennedy administration looks favorably on a request from India to send transport planes and weapons-manufacturing equipment for use against China.

14 The administration projects a nearly $8 billion budget deficit for the year, the second largest ever in peacetime. With the expected advent of new tax cuts, a deficit is projected for the following year.

Oct 29 India to Use American Weapons Against China

NEW DELHI—Just one day after the breakthrough in the Cuban missile crisis, the United States finds itself involved in another Communist-related conflict. The Indian government, embroiled in a border war with Communist China, today asked the U.S. to supply the nation with weapons and ammunition. The U.S. agreed.

India, which has been independent since 1947, has not been aligned with either the Soviet Union or the Western powers. However, Prime Minister Jawaharlal Nehru and the United States are on good terms, and the Indian military is desperate for materiel. Over the last 10 days, Chinese troops have killed at least 2,000 Indians in fighting along the northern frontiers.

India also asked other Western nations for weapons. Britain agreed, and Canada and France are also expected to contribute. India is not asking the Western nations to commit troops to the cause.

Nov 2 Kennedy Says Missile Sites Being Dismantled

WASHINGTON—President Kennedy tonight told the American people what they have been waiting to hear for 11 tension-filled days. "[T]he Soviet missile bases in Cuba are being dismantled, their missiles and related equipment are being crated, and the fixed installations at these sites are being destroyed," he said.

A Soviet ship leaves Cuba loaded with three fuselages from IL-28 jet bombers.

What the President did not say is that the logistics of verifying the missiles' removal is turning into a challenge. Cuban Premier Fidel Castro has rejected the U.S.-Soviet plan to allow United Nations representatives to inspect the missile sites. Last night, a Soviet official flew to Havana to talk to Castro.

The good news, according to the White House, is that the U.S. has taken aerial photographs that prove that the Soviets are dismantling the missiles. All indications are that the Soviets are making good on their promise to remove the weapons.

Meanwhile, the U.S. will maintain its quarantine of the island until, Kennedy said, "the threat to peace posed by these offensive weapons is gone." The President has agreed to the Soviet offer of allowing the International Committee of the Red Cross to inspect Soviet ships bound for Cuba.

Nov 6 TED KENNEDY BREEZES TO VICTORY IN SENATE RACE

BOSTON—A third Kennedy brother is coming to Washington to help run the country, joining older brothers John and Robert. Edward "Ted" Kennedy, just 30 years old, was elected to the U.S. Senate today in an easy victory over George Cabot Lodge. With most of the returns in, Kennedy holds nearly a 2-1 advantage over his Republican opponent.

Kennedy, whose last job was assistant district attorney in Suffolk County, Massachusetts, had never run for public office before. His slogan, "I can do more for Massachusetts," also fell flat. But his state has long been dominated by fellow Irish Catholic Democrats. And with his brother in the White House—and riding an unprecedented wave of popularity after his success in the Cuban missile crisis—the younger brother's victory was all but assured. President Kennedy, himself a former a U.S. senator from Massachusetts, cast his ballot in Boston today.

Ted Kennedy almost seems predestined for greatness. When he was born, his brother John (who is also his godfather) wanted his parents to name him George Washington Kennedy. Moreover, Ted received his First Communion in the Vatican—from Pope Pius XII.

November

15 The President names Christian Herter, the secretary of state under Dwight Eisenhower, as a special representative for trade negotiations.

16 The federal district court in New Orleans orders the U.S. Justice Department to charge Mississippi Governor Ross Barnett and Lieutenant Paul Johnson for impeding the admission of James Meredith to the University of Mississippi.

17 Presidents Kennedy and Eisenhower participate in opening ceremonies for Washington's Dulles International Airport, which is designed to handle longer-range commercial jets and serve the capital's growing metropolitan area.

18 The President is reportedly considering a domestic version of the Peace Corps. He appoints a Cabinet-level committee to study the idea.

19 Alarmed by American military assistance for India, Pakistan is said to be reconsidering its policy of leaning toward Washington.

20 By executive order, Kennedy prohibits religious or racial discrimination in housing that is built or purchased with federal money.

21 China's announcement of a cease-fire on its border with India is met with skepticism in New Delhi, which believes the Communists are attempting to solidify key territorial gains in the region.

22 The superpowers further relax their military alerts in the aftermath of the Cuban crisis. The Air Force plans to release more than 14,200 reservists; Soviet bloc countries cancel various military alerts.

Nov 7 — KHRUSHCHEV: MISSILES OUT OF CUBA; PEACE NEEDED

Moscow, November 7, 1962—If Soviet Premier Nikita Khrushchev seemed to be rattling sabers during the Cuban missile crisis, he now seems to be embracing peaceful relations with the United States.

At a reception honoring the Bolshevik Revolution this evening, Khrushchev announced that the Soviets had removed all of their missiles from Cuba. Moreover, the Premier talked at length about how the U.S. and Soviets need to work to achieve a peaceful coexistence. He also said the Berlin crisis needs to be solved soon.

The seriousness of the Cuban ordeal seems to have profoundly affected Khrushchev. He said that "we were very, very close to a thermonuclear war.… If there had not been reason, then we would not be here tonight and there might not have been elections in the United States."

"…we were very, very close to a thermonuclear war."

— SOVIET PREMIER NIKITA KHRUSHCHEV

Eero Saarinen's Dulles Airport design included this distinctive control tower.

Nov 17 — JFK INAUGURATES JET-AGE AIRPORT

CHANTILLY, VA.—President Kennedy today inaugurated the Dulles International Airport, the first in the country designed for commercial jets. It bears the name of John Foster Dulles, secretary of state under President Eisenhower.

Thousands of onlookers arrived to see the fruition of a plan that had been in the works since 1950, when Congress passed the Washington Airport Act. The state-of-the-art airport, located 26 miles from Washington, D.C., sits on an enormous 10,000-acre site. It is the metropolitan area's second major airport, joining Washington National Airport.

Spectators were particularly enthralled with the main teminal building, whose white, concave roof soars high on one end. Architect Eero Saarinen, who died last year, said he wanted to capture "the soul of the airport."

The President referred to the airport as a "distinguished ornament of a great country and a great governmental system. This building, I think, symbolizes the aspirations of the United States in the 1950s and the 1960s."

Nov 18 PRESIDENT CONSIDERING DOMESTIC PEACE CORPS

WASHINGTON—Pleased with the success of his international Peace Corps program, President Kennedy yesterday named a seven-member committee, chaired by Attorney General Robert Kennedy, to study the possibility of launching a domestic version of the public service organization. The group is scheduled to deliver its findings to JFK by January 1. If they find in favor of establishing such an organization, the relevant legislation will likely be sent to Congress.

The program would likely be open to all Americans, from high school graduates to retirees, with a one-year term of service. Volunteers would receive living expenses and a small stipend.

Projected areas of service could include schools in slums and impoverished rural settings, Indian reservations, correctional institutions, mental hospitals, and migrant labor camps.

Nov 20 JFK BANS HOUSING DISCRIMINATION

WASHINGTON—President Kennedy made good on a campaign promise today by prohibiting racial discrimination in federally supported housing.

The President signed Executive Order 11063, stating: "I hereby direct all departments and agencies in the executive branch of the Federal Government, insofar as their functions relate to the provision, rehabilitation, or operation of housing and related facilities, to take all action necessary and appropriate to prevent discrimination because of race, color, creed, or national origin."

The order states that discrimination is prohibited in the sale, leasing, or renting of residential property that is owned or operated by the federal government. Even if the federal government is only peripherally involved—for example, with loans and grant money—discrimination cannot exist.

Housing discrimination has plagued the United States, even in "progressive" northern cities, for generations. In many communities, white homeowners, real estate agents, and banks have overtly and subtly refrained from selling homes to minorities. The President's executive order cannot prevent all housing discrimination, but the administration believes it is a strong and symbolic step in the right direction.

The President's 150th executive order is one of the few related to civil rights.

23 The Atomic Energy Commission projects that nuclear power will generate half of all electricity in the U.S. by the year 2000.

24 Capping a fierce competition, the Pentagon gives General Dynamics the contract to develop the F-111, the next-generation American fighter/bomber.

25 The administration plans to capitalize on its success in the Cuban situation by pressing NATO ministers to move troops eastward and provide more financial support for the Western alliance.

26 Despite appeals from nonaligned countries, Indian Prime Minister Nehru indicates that he will reject China's peace proposal unless it returns the disputed Ladakh region to Indian control.

27 JFK tours Georgia and Florida military bases that played key roles in the Cuban crisis.

28 NASA says that budget constraints have forced it to postpone for more than a year the first manned flight of the two-man Gemini spacecraft.

29 At the UN, the Soviets drop their opposition to the election of U Thant for a full term as secretary general. Previously, the Soviets had blocked the election until an agreement was reached on international inspections of former missile sites in Cuba.

30 The Pentagon reveals that the Cuban crisis prompted it to mobilize more than 300,000 troops and put crews handling nuclear weapons on maximum alert. During the crisis, the U.S. used uncoded radio transmissions to let Moscow listen in as U.S. forces moved to DEFCON 2 status for the first time ever.

JFK believes the Soviets have made good on their promise to remove the missiles.

Nov 20 KENNEDY ENDS WEEKS-LONG QUARANTINE OF CUBA

WASHINGTON—President Kennedy has ordered the termination of the naval quarantine of Cuba, in effect since October 24. The order puts an end to the last significant vestige of the Cuban missile crisis.

Kennedy made his decision after Premier Khrushchev informed him that all Soviet jet bombers would be removed from Cuba within 30 days. Considering that Khrushchev had made good on his promise to remove all of the Soviet missiles, Kennedy is making a good-faith gesture—accepting the Premier's word that the jet bombers will indeed be removed.

The jet bombers had been a sticking point with Cuban Premier Fidel Castro because, he insisted, they are Cuban property—unlike the missiles. It is believed that the Soviets persuaded the strong-willed dictator to change his mind.

Kennedy had ordered the quarantine four weeks ago to prevent the Soviets from shipping more weapons to Cuba. At the time, many nuclear missiles had already been transported to the island.

The President reiterated today that the Cuban nuclear threat is over. "The evidence to date indicates that all known offensive missile sites in Cuba have been dismantled," he said. "Their missiles and their associated equipment have been loaded on Soviet ships." He added that U.S. inspectors counted the number of missiles leaving Cuba, and that that figure "closely corresponded" to the number of missiles that the U.S. had believed to be on the island.

THE FIRST LADY

Jack and Jackie Kennedy had been married for seven years, and were the parents of two children, when they moved into the White House. By 1961, their relationship had survived his philandering and Jackie's realization that politics would keep her husband away from home far more often than she would like.

Friends said that Jackie interested her husband in ways that other women simply did not. But while he may have respected her more than he did other women, that respect did not translate to fidelity. And she knew it. Once, while giving a tour of the White House to a visiting journalist from France, Jackie pointed to a young female secretary. In French, she told the official that her husband supposedly was sleeping with her.

Jackie did not like playing the role of political wife, even when that role was enlarged to that of first lady. She made it plain that she did not consider herself a public official—she was, she said, a mother and a wife. Nevertheless, she took advantage of the perks of power. To her husband's cha-

grin, she accepted expensive gifts, such as horses, from foreign heads of state.

The President was reluctant to confront his wife when he was annoyed with her, as he often was about her spending. He relied on aides to relay his displeasure. But friends noticed that the death of the Kennedys' infant son, Patrick, in 1963, seemed to bond Jack and Jackie in the weeks before his assassination.

1 The Kennedy administration announces a 10 percent cut in oil imports to states east of the Rockies, a move that reduces profits for U.S. oil companies.

2 NASA is reportedly planning to open astronaut training to scientists, who would lead the research phase of future space missions—including planned lunar landings.

3 U.S. pilots observe the Russian freighter *Okhotsk* leaving Cuban waters with dismantled Ilyushin-28 bombers aboard. Removal of the bombers was a key sticking point in resolving the Cuban issue.

4 With less than three weeks left in a Taft-Hartley injunction against a nationwide dockworkers strike, the Kennedy administration sees little hope of a resolution. Some in Congress suggest the need for new laws against transportation strikes.

5 The Pentagon begins a reorganization of military reserves that will affect 40 percent of reservists and members of several National Guard divisions.

6 In an answer to reports that UN Ambassador Adlai Stevenson was out of favor with the White House for criticizing U.S. policy on Russia, the President expresses confidence in Stevenson.

7 British and U.S. sources indicate that the two countries would reconsider their commitment to the defense of Western Europe if France and Germany block Britain from entering the Common Market.

8 Kennedy tours the nuclear facilities in Los Alamos and Albuquerque.

The President tours the Nuclear Rocket Development Station in Nevada.

Dec 9
JFK VISITS NUCLEAR SITES; ASKS ABOUT MARS MISSION

PALM SPRINGS, CALIF.—President Kennedy is spending the night at the Southern California home of recording star Bing Crosby following a whirl-wind weekend tour of space development and nuclear sites in the Southwest. The purpose of the trip was to inform the President of the progress of the government's atomic propulsion program.

Kennedy began his travels Friday at the Strategic Air Command headquarters in Omaha, Nebraska. On Saturday morning, the President visited the Kirtland Air Force Base near Albuquerque, New Mexico. He then flew to the Nevada Testing Grounds near the Indian Springs Air Force Base. While there, the President toured the nuclear rocket station and saw a Kiwi nuclear reactor that was still radioactively "hot" from a test firing.

The President discussed the progress of Project Rover, the purpose of which is to develop the nuclear propulsion devices necessary to send man into space. Kennedy also questioned the top scientists on Project Rover about the likelihood of America sending a manned mission to Mars. The President and his advisers are trying to determine if an infusion of additional funds would help speed the progress toward both the planned moon missions and any potential future Mars missions.

It appears the matter will be subject to further discussion among administration officials. Nonetheless, the President found the trip to be valuable and informative.

Dec 12
SKYBOLT MISSILE PROJECT IS DEAD IN THE WATER

WASHINGTON—President Kennedy held a press conference today in which he clarified his administration's December 7 decision to cancel the joint U.S.-Britain Skybolt missile project. The cancellation came after the fifth round of tests ended in failure.

British leaders and press have reacted angrily to the news, accusing the United States of jeopardizing Britain's nuclear capabilities by eliminating the weapon that was to serve as the centerpiece of their nation's nuclear deterrence plan. The 1,000-mile range air-to-ground missile has yet to live up to its billing or its steep price tag, which will become prohibitively steep for the British should they continue the project without U.S. partnership.

Though the issue has the potential to set off a diplomatic crisis between the two long-standing allies, the President seemed resolved that the program was unsalvageable. He claimed that the engineering necessary to execute Skybolt "has been really, in a sense, the kind of engineering that's been beyond us."

THE SKYBOLT BUNGLE

In the weeks after the missile crisis, the Kennedy administration badly bungled a foreign policy issue, nearly resulting in the collapse of British Prime Minister Harold Macmillan's government.

At issue was Skybot, a U.S.-made guided nuclear missile system. Macmillan was eager to purchase Skybolt as the centerpiece of Britain's independent nuclear arsenal. But while Washington had approved the sale during the Eisenhower years, a series of failed tests led some Kennedy administration officials to consider scrapping the expensive system.

The Macmillan government, however, was kept in the dark about American doubts about Skybolt. Macmillan and Kennedy, while of different generations, also were close and were working hand-in-hand to win support for Britain's membership in the Common Market. Such a move would advance British and American interests, they believed.

But when Kennedy decided to cancel Skybolt because of high costs and poor performance in December 1962, the British were caught by surprise. Macmillan was embarrassed, and his government took a beating in the polls. Making matters worse, several weeks after Skybolt's cancellation, the system underwent a previously scheduled test—and this time, it worked. The British became deeply suspicious of Washington's agenda.

The Skybolt affair suggested that Kennedy still had much to learn about global diplomacy, even after his adept handling of the Cuban missile crisis.

Dec 15 JFK CALLS FOR TAX CUTS

NEW YORK—President Kennedy offered a double dose of good news in a speech to the Economic Club of New York today. The President reported that the economy is booming and that he will call for wide-ranging federal tax cuts to take effect next year.

"In the last two years," Kennedy said, "we have made great strides. Our gross national product has risen 11 percent while inflation has been arrested. Employment has been increased by 1.3 million jobs. Profits, personal income, living standards—all are setting new records. Most of the economic indicators for this quarter are up—and the prospects are for further expansion in the next quarter."

From there, the President called for cuts in corporate and personal tax rates in 1963, which would lead to an increase in business activity and greater consumer spending. To compensate for the decrease in tax revenue, Kennedy called for "long-needed tax reforms, a broadening of the tax base, and the elimination or modification of many special tax privileges." It is likely that the President will send a bill to Congress that includes proposals for tax cuts and tax reform.

9 The President spends Sunday relaxing at the home of singer Bing Crosby in Palm Springs, California.

10 In a meeting with national security advisers, Kennedy expresses his view that if Berlin were not an issue, nuclear deterrence alone could stabilize Europe.

11 Another protracted labor dispute develops when a federal court extends an initial 10-day injunction into an 80-day cooling-off period for International Association of Machinists members, who are threatening a strike against Lockheed.

12 The Air Force announces that 20 Minuteman intercontinental ballistic missiles are now in place in their silos, ready for firing against worldwide targets if needed.

13 Recalling the world's close brush with nuclear war over Cuba and the communication problem it highlighted, Kennedy supports the idea of creating a special hot line between the White House and the Kremlin.

14 Intelligence estimates from Southeast Asia show that North Vietnam has nearly 6,000 troops in Laos.

15 In New York, the President pledges to cut taxes to help the economy next year. But he does not repeat his previous intent to make tax cuts effective at the start of the New Year.

16 Before traveling to the Bahamas for talks with President Kennedy, British Prime Minister Macmillan and French President de Gaulle hold a contentious two-day meeting over the issue of British membership in the Common Market.

Dec 17
GRIM REALITY
Kennedy Paints Worst-Case Scenario During TV Special

WASHINGTON—Hoping to be uplifted by John F. Kennedy this evening, TV viewers instead heard some of the bleakest words ever spoken by a U.S. president. Kennedy said the United States and Soviet Union are "one major mistake" from nuclear war, and if that happens, Kennedy said, "you are talking about…150 million fatalities in the first 18 hours."

Below are excerpts from the President's interview with three network correspondents. The taped interview aired at 6:30 P.M. Eastern time on CBS.

Kennedy told reporters that once a nuclear war begins, 150 million people would die within 18 hours.

On the responsibilities of the U.S. as leader of the free world: "Well, I think in the first place the problems are more difficult than I had imagined they were…. I think our people get awfully impatient and maybe fatigued and tired, and saying, 'We have been carrying this burden for 17 years; can we lay it down?' We can't lay it down, and I don't see how we are going to lay it down in this century."

On nuclear war (speaking rhetorically): "Once [Khrushchev] fires his missiles, it is all over anyway, because we are going to have sufficient resources to fire back at him to destroy the Soviet Union. When that day comes, and there is a massive exchange, then that is the end, because you are talking about Western Europe, the Soviet Union, the United States, of 150 million fatalities in the first 18 hours."

On how the Cuban missile crisis worsened the Cold War: "The Cuban effort has made it more difficult for us to carry out any successful negotiations, because this was an effort to materially change the balance of power. It was done in secret. Steps were taken really to deceive us by every means they could, and they were planning in November to open to the world the fact that they had these missiles so close to the United States. Not that they were intending to fire them, because if they were going to get into a nuclear struggle, they have their own missiles in the Soviet Union. But it would have politically changed the balance of power. It would have appeared to, and appearances contribute to reality. So it is going to be some time before it is possible for us to come to any real understandings with Mr. Khrushchev. But I do think his [recent] speech shows that he realizes how dangerous a world we live in."

On USSR's and China's quest for expansion: "The real problem is the Soviet desire to expand their power and influence. If Mr. Khrushchev would concern himself with the real interests of the people of the Soviet Union—that

"Once [Khrushchev] fires his missiles, it is all over anyway, because we are going to have sufficient resources to fire back at him to destroy the Soviet Union." —KENNEDY

they have a higher standard of living, to protect his own security—there is no real reason why the United States and the Soviet Union, separated by so many thousands of miles of land and water, both rich countries, both with very energetic people, should not be able to live in peace. But it is this constant determination which the Chinese show in the most militant form, and which the Soviets also have shown, that they will not settle for that kind of a peaceful world, but must settle for a Communist world. That is what makes the real danger. The combination of these two systems in conflict around the world in a nuclear age is what makes the '60s so dangerous.

"Mr. Khrushchev and I are in the same boat in the sense of both having this nuclear capacity, and also both wanting to protect our societies. Where we are not on the same wave is that the Soviets expand their power and are determined to, and have demonstrated in Cuba their willingness to take great risks, which can only bring about a direct collision."

On the U.S. shouldering the burden: "Our troops in Western Europe are the best equipped, we have six divisions, which is about a fourth of all of the divisions on the Western front. They are the best equipped. They can fight tomorrow, which is not true of most of the other units. So we are doing our part there, and we are also providing the largest naval force in the world. We are also providing the nuclear force in the world, and we are also carrying out the major space program for the free world, as well as carrying the whole burden in South Vietnam. So the United States is more than doing its part."

On the responsibilities of European nations: "All we ask Western Europe to do is not look in and just become a rich, careful, secluded group, but to play their role in this great world struggle, as we have done it."

On why Americans should be proud: "Just because I think that this country, which as I say criticizes itself and is criticized around the world, 180 million people, for 17 years, really for more than that, for almost 20 years, have been the great means of defending first the world against the Nazi threat, and since then against the Communist threat. And if it were not for us, the Communists would be dominant in the world today, and because of us, we are in a strong position. Now, I think that is a pretty good record for a country with six percent of the world's population, which is very reluctant to take on these burdens. I think we ought to be rather pleased with ourselves this Christmas."

17 President Kennedy considers U.S. options for responding to the Congo crisis. General Maxwell Taylor tells the President he should not intervene. American military force, Taylor says, "won't bring military success, and the U.S. may well be blamed for the failure there."

18 *Look* magazine publishes "The Arts in America," an essay by President Kennedy. In it, Kennedy writes, "I have called for a higher degree of physical fitness in our nation. It is only natural that I should call, as well, for the kind of intellectual and spiritual fitness which underlies the flowering of the arts."

19 In Nassau, Bahamas, President Kennedy and Prime Minister Macmillan hold discussions on Europe, Africa, and other topics. Macmillan is under political pressure at home to secure Britain's status as an independent nuclear power.

20 American and British leaders agree to end the controversial Skybolt program and look for alternatives.

21 Prime Minister Macmillan agrees to support a cooperative nuclear command within NATO. Kennedy pledges to sell Britain the Polaris medium range missile to replace the Skybolt.

22 The administration approves a $5.7 billion fiscal-year budget for NASA, three-quarters of it for expenses related to a manned mission to the moon.

23 In exchange for $53 million worth of food and medicine, Cuban Premier Fidel Castro releases the first group of prisoners from the Bay of Pigs fiasco. They had been held in Cuba for 20 months.

Hoping for a guided nuclear missile system called Skybolt, British Prime Minister Harold Macmillan (right) will have to settle for submarine-based Polaris missiles.

Dec 21 KENNEDY, MACMILLAN SIGN THE NASSAU PACT

NASSAU—President Kennedy and British Prime Minister Harold MacMillan signed the Nassau Pact in the Bahamas today, reaching accord on the abandonment of the controversial and trouble-plagued Skybolt missile project. They also agreed on the sale of submarine-based U.S. Polaris missiles to Britain. Moreover, the leaders agreed on the creation of a nuclear force within the North Atlantic Treaty Organization (NATO), for which they will request assistance from France.

Response on both sides of the Atlantic was tempered. Some Britons remain concerned that the agreement forces Britain to relinquish its nuclear autonomy. Some Americans have implied that the Polaris missile deal was executed to buy Britain's cooperation with U.S. policy in the Congo.

While Kennedy appeared to consider the summit a success, the result was, at best, mixed. If, as some believe, Kennedy hoped to stymie Britain's push for a separate nuclear deterrent by canceling the Skybolt program, history may well regard the outcome of the tense Nassau negotiations as a diplomatic failure.

The Kennedy family managed to enjoy a traditional Christmas in a tropical climate.

Dec 25 KENNEDYS CELEBRATE HOLIDAYS IN PALM BEACH

PALM BEACH, Fla—The President, Mrs. Kennedy, and their children spent the Christmas holiday surrounded by family and friends in Palm Beach, Florida, as guests at the estate of businessman and philanthropist C. Michael Paul. Lee Radziwill, Jackie Kennedy's sister, was there with her young family, and on Christmas Eve, the President enjoyed a day cruise aboard the 92-foot presidential yacht *Honey Fitz* with brother-in-law Prince Stanislaus Radziwill.

The holiday festivities began in earnest when the children staged a production of a traditional Christmas pageant. Caroline played the part of Mary, and young John served as a shepherd along with his cousin Tony. This morning, the President and First Lady attended Christmas services at St. Ann's Church in Palm Beach.

As always, it will be a working vacation for the President. The holiday will be followed by a full schedule of meetings with members of his administration, Congress, and military leaders.

JFK said the brigade's flag will one day fly in a free Cuba.

Dec 29

KENNEDY GREETS MEMBER OF CUBAN INVASION BRIGADE

MIAMI—President Kennedy today received the flag of the Cuban Invasion Brigade from Erneido Oliva, the brigade's second in command. Kennedy thanked Oliva for giving the flag to the United States for safekeeping and added, "I can assure you that this flag will be returned to this brigade in a free Havana." Kennedy compared the members of the brigade to other Latin American heroes—including Bolivar, San Martin, and Juarez—many of whom were defeated and returned to their respective countries after a time in exile.

Released from prison to the United States, members of the brigade were welcomed by the President, who noted that they are leaving some six million of their countrymen behind, in a repressive Cuba. Under these circumstances, according to Kennedy, members of the brigade hold a special responsibility to their fellow Cubans. They must continue to focus on Cuban freedom with a single-minded purpose so that someday, when Cuba is again free, they will be ready to lead.

"I need not tell you how happy I am to welcome you here in the United States," Kennedy said. "I can assure you that it is the strongest wish of the people of this country, as well as the people of this hemisphere, that Cuba shall one day be free again, and when it is, this brigade will deserve to march at the head of the free column."

> *"I can assure you that this flag will be returned to this brigade in a free Havana."*
> — KENNEDY, TO ERNEIDO OLIVA OF THE CUBAN INVASION BRIGADE

24 As a cargo ship carrying $11 million of the Bay of Pigs ransom arrives in Havana, all 1,113 Cuban war prisoners reach freedom in Florida. Nearly two dozen Americans remain imprisoned in Cuba.

25 Congressional opponents of President Kennedy sharpen their criticism over moves they say have allowed the Soviets to open up a "missile gap" on the United States: cancellation of Skybolt, and failure to fund the Nike Zeus anti-missile program and other missile projects.

26 The labor dispute among dockworkers deepens, as the National Maritime Union's 50,000 members honor picket lines set up in ports by striking longshoremen.

27 The USSR continues a hectic pace of nuclear tests in advance of expected proposals for a New Year moratorium.

28 The President travels to Palm Beach, Florida, to meet privately with leaders of the Bay of Pigs invasion.

29 In Miami, President Kennedy tells a large crowd of Cuban exiles that the flag of the Bay of Pigs Brigade will one day fly in a "free Havana."

30 In a message to the Soviet Union, Kennedy pledges more efforts to preserve world peace in the new year.

31 In a year-end message in *Look* magazine, Kennedy says that history has "refuted the myth of the inevitability of Communist victory."

THE FINAL YEAR
President Kennedy Works for Peace Before He Himself Is Killed

John Kennedy entered the pre-election year of 1963 without much in the way of legislative achievements on which to build a successful reelection campaign. He remained popular, however, and as the year began, he still was basking in the glow of his successful handling of the Cuban missile crisis.

Voters seemed happy with JFK. In the midterm elections of 1962, the Democrats picked up four seats in the Senate and lost just four in the House. (Usually, the president's party loses many more House races in midterm elections.) One of the victorious Democratic Senate candidates in 1962 was the President's youngest brother, Edward.

Kennedy was eager to get a tax-cut bill past Congress as quickly as possible to jump-start the economy and spark his reelection campaign. Congress, however, remained skeptical, much to the President's frustration. He remarked that Congress seemed a lot more powerful to him than it did when he was in Congress himself.

Civil rights also demanded Kennedy's time. The new year marked the 100th anniversary of Abraham Lincoln's Emancipation Proclamation, and civil rights leader Martin Luther King, Jr., made it clear that the country had failed to deliver on the promise of equality for African Americans. King was arrested during a demonstration in Birmingham, Alabama, in the spring, and from his jail cell he wrote a letter criticizing white liberals for offering only words on behalf of the nation's black citizens. The letter didn't mention Kennedy by name, but King's words left little doubt that he was impatient with the President's approach to black demands for justice.

Kennedy, meanwhile, had a new priority. In the aftermath of the missile crisis, he sought to lower the temperature of the simmering conflict with the Soviet Union. In June, JFK delivered a speech that many historians regard as one of his best. Speaking to an audience at American University in Washington, D.C., Kennedy asked citizens to reexamine their attitudes toward the Cold War and toward the Russian people. It was the beginning of a less-confrontational approach to Moscow, an approach that would guide his immediate successors, Lyndon Johnson and Richard Nixon.

Early summer saw one of the highlights of his short presidency—a tour of Europe that included a stop in West Berlin, where hundreds of thousands cheered him as a champion of their freedom. The trip also included a nostalgic tour of Ireland, the land his great-grandparents had fled. The Irish greeted Kennedy as one of their own, making the trip a diplomatic, political, and personal triumph for the President.

As JFK prepared for his reelection campaign, he sought to repair a rift within the Democratic Party in the politically important state of Texas. In late November, he and his wife flew to Texas to help improve relations within the party. There, in Dallas on November 22, 1963, Kennedy's life came to an end.

In the years since JFK's assassination, the nation has learned much about its fallen leader, and many of the revelations have not been flattering. Nevertheless, John F. Kennedy remains one of the nation's most revered American presidents, a symbol of a generation that came of age in the 1960s.

Kennedy and daughter Caroline sail aboard the *Honey Fitz* in August 1963.

Katangese widows, one with a child on her back, weep at a graveside in Elisabethville, Congo.

Jan 1 UN Forces Reunify War-Torn Congo

Congo—United Nations troops officially united the politically fractured Central African nation of Congo today. The action came nearly three years after Belgium's grant of independence left the Leopoldville-based government of Patrice Lumumba and the self-declared independent government of Moise Tshombe (in mineral-rich Katanga in southern Congo) vying for dominance.

In 1961, under the looming threat of civil war, the United Nations sent a 10,000-man security force to the Congo. When the international body refused to take sides with Lumumba's government, he turned to the Soviet Union, which provided him with the means to attack Katanga. That attack failed, leaving dictator Colonel Mobutu in charge—and Lumumba dead.

When it became clear, in August 1961, that the UN's hands-off policy was a failure, some 5,000 UN troops attacked Katanga three times over the next year, until Tshombe finally fled Katanga.

Early analysis suggests that, in avoiding civil war and Soviet involvement, the UN operation was a success. However, it seems that the international body spent some political capital with the Soviets, Belgians, and French, and may have over-reached its own authority, though by how much remains to be seen.

Jan 3 SOUTH VIETNAMESE, U.S. FORCES DEFEATED AT AP BAC

AP BAC, VIETNAM—Vietcong guerrillas shocked South Vietnamese and American forces yesterday, emerging victorious from a skirmish in which they were badly outnumbered by a heavily mechanized opponent.

The Army of the Republic of Vietnam's premier Seventh Division encountered an entrenched enemy near the small village of Ap Bac, some 40 miles southwest of Saigon. Equipped with heavy artillery, armored personnel carriers, and American helicopter-based air support, the ARVN expected to make short work of the two Vietcong companies. However, the attack was delayed to allow troops to enjoy the New Year holiday. In the meantime, the Vietcong learned of the plan and successfully reinforced its positions.

A series of critical mistakes ensued. Artillery fire was misdirected, repeated communication failures led to critical mistakes, flamethrower fuel was mixed incorrectly, and ultimately the Vietcong succeeded in destroying or disabling five American helicopters, and subjecting APC gunners to high casualties. A final count revealed 18 Vietcong killed and 39 wounded while the ARVN forces lost 80 with 100 injured. The U.S. suffered three fatalities and eight injuries in a battle that will surely be remembered as a milestone victory for Communist North Vietnam.

Jan 8 THE *MONA LISA* COMES TO WASHINGTON

WASHINGTON—Leonardo da Vinci's *Mona Lisa* was unveiled today at the National Gallery of Art in a special showing for President and Mrs. Kennedy, members of Congress, the U.S. Supreme Court, Kennedy's Cabinet, and members of the diplomatic corps.

The enigmatic masterpiece, the most widely known and certainly among the world's most valuable works of art, is on loan to the people of the United States courtesy of the people of France. Andre Malraux, France's minister of Cultural Affairs, escorted the painting from its home at Paris's Musee du Louvre to the United States. She will spend 27 days in residence in the West Sculpture Hall, under the watchful eye of a round-the-clock detail of U.S. Marines. The gallery will offer extended viewing hours in order to accommodate expected crowds of nearly a half-million visitors.

Following the National Gallery engagement, the *Mona Lisa* will head north for a month-long special exhibition at New York's Metropolitan Museum of Art before returning to France aboard the SS *United States*.

1 The White House is surprised by the sudden advance of UN troops against the Katanga region of the Congo. Despite U.S. concerns, the troops secure the country within three days.

2 South Vietnamese forces fight a fierce battle with a Vietcong battalion in Ap Bac, 35 miles from Saigon. Despite having four times as many troops, as well as armor and air support, the South Vietnamese suffer heavy casualties. Three Americans die.

3 U.S. commanders reporting on Ap Bac express concern about the training and morale of South Vietnamese forces.

4 A day after Castro publicly ridiculed Kennedy for the Bay of Pigs ransom, National Security Adviser McGeorge Bundy privately advises the President on the potential benefits of "some form of accommodation with Castro."

5 French President Charles de Gaulle expresses limited interest in hosting Polaris missiles, according to U.S. Ambassador Charles Bohlen.

6 Brazilian President Joao Goulart gets a mandate for presidential powers from an overwhelming majority of 12 million voters in a plebiscite. (The CIA reportedly spends nearly $20 million in an unsuccessful attempt to defeat the proposal.)

7 The U.S. informs UN Secretary General U Thant that it considers the Cuban crisis closed.

8 The President attends the much-anticipated opening of a traveling exhibit of the *Mona Lisa,* loaned by France to the National Gallery of Art in Washington.

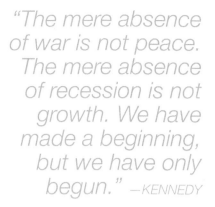

"The mere absence of war is not peace. The mere absence of recession is not growth. We have made a beginning, but we have only begun." —KENNEDY

Jan 14

KENNEDY TALKS TAX CUTS IN STATE OF THE UNION ADDRESS

Kennedy proposed $11 billion worth of tax cuts in order to spur economic growth.

WASHINGTON—President Kennedy delivered his annual State of the Union address tonight before a joint session of Congress. He reported progress on several foreign policy fronts—in Cuba, the Congo, Indochina, and Berlin. But the big message centered around tax cuts.

With the recession in recession and job creation on the rise, the President's tone was one of cautious optimism. "The mere absence of war is not peace," he said. "The mere absence of recession is not growth. We have made a beginning, but we have only begun."

Underscoring his commitment to economic recovery, the President delivered some very good news to American taxpayers, announcing his intention to phase in the biggest federal income tax cut in national history. Asserting that the current income tax burden is strangling growth and discouraging investment, Kennedy proposed reducing rates on individuals from the current range of 20 to 91 percent to a range of 14 to 65 percent, resulting in a total $11 billion annual cut. On the corporate side, rates will drop from 52 to 47 percent, a $2.5 billion change, if Kennedy's proposed changes are passed.

The President suggested phasing these changes in gradually over three years, as well as enacting measures to both broaden the tax base and shift corporate tax payment schedules to better regulate the federal income stream. If the President's initiative works according to plan, Americans will be able to keep, and spend, more of their hard-earned money—and stimulate the economy at the same time.

The President touched on many other issues of national concern, namely education, voting rights, transportation infrastructure, national security, and the creation of a multilateral nuclear force. But surely the easing of the collective tax burden is the message that most Americans will remember from tonight's uplifting address.

Jan 17 — JFK DELIVERS RECORD BUDGET TO CONGRESS

WASHINGTON—President Kennedy sent a record federal budget to Capitol Hill today, one that outlines a total budget of $98.8 billion and includes an $11.9 billion deficit. Half of the President's proposed budget is for military spending—a level unprecedented in peacetime.

The President's fiscal plan for the year ending June 30, 1964, which he claims will spur growth and speed economic recovery, is causing dissent on both sides of the aisle in the House and Senate. Kennedy has defended his plan, claiming it represents "the most powerful single tool the nation possesses for linking the private and public sectors of our economy in a common effort to achieve national prosperity." The proposed budget also reflects the massive income tax cuts that Kennedy outlined in his State of the Union address earlier this week.

One area that will see no reduction in costs is national defense, for which Kennedy asserted, "There is no discount price." In fact, funding of combat forces and nuclear weapons research will enjoy huge outlays, as will space exploration and the Apollo program.

DEALING WITH DE GAULLE

The Kennedy administration saw West Germany as the key to American influence in European affairs. If the West Germans aligned themselves closer with Washington and London, the President believed, the doors of the European Common Market might be thrown open to Britain—giving the U.S. a surrogate hand in running the continent's domestic affairs.

But there was a formidable obstacle in the way of JFK's shrewd strategy— Charles de Gaulle, the proud and famously difficult president of France. De Gaulle believed that the French and West Germans should control the future of European integration.

During a 1961 visit to France, it was Jackie Kennedy who charmed de Gaulle, much to the President's amusement. A year later, de Gaulle embarked on a charm offensive of his own, traveling to West Germany and delivering warm speeches that included several phrases in German. It was a remarkable gesture for a man proud of his native language and country, which he had fought to liberate from German occupation less than two decades before.

Kennedy worried about de Gaulle's sudden popularity in Germany, fearing that a de facto alliance between the two old enemies would block Anglo-American designs for the Common Market and other European initiatives. British Prime Minister Harold Macmillan confirmed those fears in late 1962 when he and de Gaulle argued over Britain's application to the Market.

To counter de Gaulle's growing influence in Europe, as well as to further other U.S. goals, Kennedy decided to visit West Berlin and West Germany in June 1963. It was no accident that his famous speech at the Berlin Wall contained a memorable phrase in German: *"Ich bin ein Berliner."*

9 As the 88th Congress begins work, Democrats control both the House and Senate.

10 The White House prepares to send Congress a record $98.8 billion budget proposal, with an expected $11.9 billion deficit.

11 In classified testimony before the Senate Foreign Relations Committee, Secretary of State Dean Rusk testifies that the United States reserves the right to invade Cuba if provoked by Cuban or Russian actions there.

12 In a meeting about Cuba, Kennedy and his advisers debate whether the situation merits continuation of round-the-clock reconnaissance flights, amid indications that Cuban forces may be preparing to shoot at American aircraft.

13 Unrest continues to ripple through former European colonies in West Africa when the Togolese military takes power and kills Togo's president, Sylvanus Olympio.

14 In his State of the Union address, Kennedy asks Congress for deep cuts in federal income tax levels. He calls current tax rates an obstacle to economic growth.

15 French President de Gaulle dismisses U.S. proposals for a shared Atlantic nuclear defense and British entry into the European Economic Community.

16 President Kennedy welcomes Italian Prime Minister Amintore Fanfani to the White House. The two men discuss a proposal to close American missile bases in Italy and defend the country with Polaris nuclear submarines.

Jan 20 JFK, KHRUSHCHEV WORK TOWARD NUCLEAR TEST BAN

WASHINGTON—The White House today released a letter from President Kennedy to Soviet Premier Khrushchev, dated December 28, 1962. The letter is a continuation of the ongoing dialogue between the two leaders on nuclear test-ban proposals.

In his letter, Kennedy responds to Khrushchev's last overture, dated December 19. The Soviet leader suggested that because the U.S. and Soviet Union had averted a violent confrontation in October, they should be able to come to an agreement on a test ban. Khrushchev's letter outlined a series of proposals toward that end.

Kennedy's response to Khrushchev indicates that the President is encouraged by Khrushchev's proposals and the forward momentum of their talks. Specifically, Kennedy expressed satisfaction that the Soviets are willing to accept some level of on-site inspections. According to Kennedy, "These seem to me to be essential not just because of the concern of our Congress but because they seem to us to go to the heart of a reliable agreement ending nuclear testing." Still, the two sides are in substantial disagreement about the number of annual tests, with Khrushchev agreeing to two to four while Kennedy anticipating eight to 10, down from a hoped-for 20.

In the just-released letter, Kennedy reassures Khrushchev: "I would certainly agree that we could accept any reasonable provision which you had in mind to protect against your concern that the on-site inspectors might engage in 'espionage' en route to the area inspection."

However, the number of annual inspections will likely remain a sticking point for some time. Kennedy, who has already received Khrushchev's reply, was told by the Soviet premier: "We believed and we continue to believe now that, in general, inspection is not necessary, and if we give our consent to an annual quota of two to three inspections, this is done solely for the purpose of removing the remaining differences for the sake of reaching agreement."

Kennedy found time to smile despite the weighty topics.

Jan 24 KENNEDY PRESSER FOCUSES ON DEFENSE, TAX CUTS

WASHINGTON—At President Kennedy's press conference today, national defense was an ongoing theme. In fact, the President opened with a statement about the importance of a strong Atlantic alliance to serve as a bulwark against the ever-present threat of communism.

The President fielded questions about the Soviet presence in Cuba, the failed Bay of Pigs invasion, and efforts toward completing a nuclear test-ban treaty. He also discussed the depth of America's nuclear arsenal in response to one reporter who expressed concern that the Polaris missile was shouldering a disproportionate share of the defensive burden.

Reporters asked the President to touch upon a range of issues, including congressional term limits, racial tension, the European Common Market, and a proposal on Capitol Hill to offer honorary citizenship to Sir Winston Churchill.

Jan 29 President Wants More Money for Education

WASHINGTON—President Kennedy today sent a message to Congress in which he outlined his goals for education in the United States. The message contained a multi-proposal spending package slated to cost taxpayers $1.2 billion over the next fiscal year.

Saying that "education is the keystone in the arch of freedom and progress," Kennedy claimed that the public education system in America—coupled with the availability of a college education—has been the single most important contributing factor to this nation's success.

The President noted several statistics that illustrate the importance of education in today's job market. He asserted that in "the new age of science and space, improved education is essential to give new meaning to our national purpose and power. In the last 20 years, mankind has acquired more scientific information than in all of previous history. Ninety percent of all the scientists that ever lived are alive and working today."

As in 1961 and 1962, Kennedy is proposing a sweeping, comprehensive bill that he is calling the National Education Improvement Act of 1963. As in years earlier, the bill is comprised of several interconnected proposals. Among them, Kennedy would like to see education become more widely available, with the expansion of existing loan programs and the addition of others. To address serious infrastructure shortfalls, he is calling for loans to institutions to construct new and improved academic facilities. In addition, the President hopes the final bill will include funding for an improvement of educational quality through increased teacher salaries and training, as well as the strengthening of vocational and special education programs.

In summary, Kennedy declared: "Today we need a new standard of excellence in education, matched by the fullest possible access to educational opportunities, enabling each citizen to develop his talents to the maximum possible extent."

> *"Education is the keystone in the arch of freedom and progress."* —KENNEDY

Due to the postwar baby boom, large numbers of young people are about to become college age.

McNamara believes U.S. troops can train the South Vietnamese to get the job done.

Kennedy wants to help mental health patients with upgraded care and the establishment of comprehensive community health centers.

Jan 31 McNamara Confident of Victory in Vietnam

WASHINGTON—Despite the discouraging news from Ap Bac earlier this month, Defense Secretary Robert McNamara is optimistic that the Army of the Republic of Vietnam will ultimately prevail against Ho Chi Minh's Vietcong. "The war in Vietnam is going well and will succeed," McNamara said. The statement echoes his report from a 1962 fact-finding mission that he "found nothing but progress and hope for the future."

Dissenters might justifiably counter with the proclamation made by French Deputy Rene Kuehn, when he said, "Victory is possible, certain, and almost immediate…." That cheerful assessment was delivered to the French Parliament on October 1953, less than seven months before France's defeat at Dien Bien Phu drove them from Vietnam.

Feb 5 Kennedy Announces Plan for Mental Health Crisis

WASHINGTON—President Kennedy today delivered a special message on Capitol Hill in which he announced his plan to deal with the scourge of mental illness and mental retardation in the United States.

The President asserted that these public health issues have been relatively ignored when compared to infectious disease, though their results are no less devastating. Presenting some stunning figures, Kennedy claimed that nearly 1.5 million Americans spend time residing in inadequate, antiquated, overcrowded, and understaffed mental institutions annually.

Until now, individual states have taken the lead in treating mental illness, and for a variety of reasons the result has been a dismal failure. To address this, the President has submitted a proposal calling for prevention, the establishment of comprehensive community mental health centers, and upgrading the care available in existing state institutions. He also wants to fund the research and development of new therapies for the mentally ill and mentally retarded.

Said Kennedy: "We as a nation have long neglected the mentally ill and the mentally retarded. This neglect must end if our nation is to live up to its own standards of compassion and dignity…." Kennedy's plan, if authorized by Congress, will go a long way toward righting these wrongs.

IRAQ AND JFK

On February 8, 1963, a group of ambitious Iraqis belonging to the Ba'athist Party overthrew the country's military ruler, Abd al-Karim Qasim, and installed its own regime. The coup was carried out with the encouragement and approval of the Kennedy administration, which feared that Qasim wished to become a powerful force in the volatile Middle East.

The U.S. saw Qasim as a possible threat to the West's oil supplies and a potential aggressor against Israel and Kuwait. In the late 1950s, America saw the Iraqi as a counterweight to another aggressive leader in the region, Egypt's Gamal Abdel Nasser. But by early 1963, JFK's advisers decided that Qasim was just as dangerous and potentially destabilizing as Nasser. American agents in the region drummed up opposition to Qasim in other Arab capitals, while the CIA kept in close touch with the coup plotters. Qasim was executed shortly after he was removed from power.

The new regime was no more merciful with hundreds of other Iraqis considered to be potential threats to the government. The Ba'athists murdered them, exhibiting the sort of cruelty that would lead the U.S., decades later, to seek the removal of coup participant Saddam Hussein.

The Kennedy administration's role in the Iraqi coup remains murky. Many of Kennedy's most authoritative biographers pay little attention to the episode.

Feb 9 IRAQI LEADER EXECUTED

BAGHDAD—Prime Minister Abd al-Karim Qasim's reign came to a violent end today. Following a summary trial, Qasim was executed along with several members of his cabinet. Today's executions came just one day after members of Iraq's Ba'athist Party seized control of the government.

Qasim, a nationalist and former Iraqi military officer, rose to power in the army and seized control with the July 14 Revolution of 1958, in which he and his followers abolished the monarchy and murdered most of the royal family. That coup was met with little resistance.

Qasim assumed the post of prime minister and immediately began instituting reforms that earned him favor with the Iraqi people while alienating the West. He formed an alliance with the Soviets and withdrew from the Baghdad Pact, the mutual security agreement with Great Britain. He also abandoned a treaty with the U.S. and expelled all British troops from Iraq.

Qasim earned the admiration of his people by undertaking massive public housing projects, particularly when he reclaimed vast tracts of Iraqi land that had been held by British petroleum interests and redistributed the land back to the Iraqi people. The Ba'athist claim that Qasim had fallen under Communist influence and would federalize the petroleum industry triggered the bloody coup, in which some 5,000 ordinary Iraqis lost they lives along with Qasim.

January

26 The administration uses the Taft Hartley Act to delay a planned labor strike against Boeing. On another front, striking longshoremen in the eastern United States prepare to return to work.

27 Kennedy suspends underground nuclear testing in Nevada in order to improve the mood at ongoing test-ban negotiations.

28 Britain refuses to contribute $43 million toward the cost of developing U.S. Polaris missiles, a key component of the administration's plan to defend Europe.

29 The President proposes $1.2 billion in funding for education in the next fiscal year. He calls education the "keystone in the arch of freedom and progress."

30 A simmering feud bursts into the open as Britain condemns France's veto of British membership in the Common Market. Macmillan accuses de Gaulle of "trying to dominate Europe."

31 Secretary of Defense Robert McNamara tells Congress that the war in Vietnam "is going well and will succeed."

Feb 14 PRESIDENT PITCHES DOMESTIC PEACE CORPS, CONSERVATION CORPS

WASHINGTON—Borrowing a phrase from late British Prime Minister Benjamin Disraeli, President Kennedy today told Congress that "the youth of a nation are the trustees of posterity." As such, he said, they need to have their interests promoted and protected. To that end, Kennedy is proposing a series of measures to provide growth and opportunities to America's youth.

The President presented several convincing statistics that illustrated the urgency of this situation. The baby boom that began with the end of World War II is manifesting itself with a staggering population increase in high school and college classrooms, as well as the entry levels of the workforce. Overcrowded facilities, unemployment, and decreased opportunity are the negative effects of such a dramatic development.

To address the crisis, Kennedy urged the enactment of the Youth Employment bill, which calls for the establishment of a Youth Conservation Corps to employ young men in projects designed to improve federal lands. He also proposed directing additional federal funds to help finance local, nonprofit community improvement projects.

Additionally, the President proposed the creation of a National Service Corps of educated and idealistic young people. He sees the corps not as a route to employment but rather as a volunteer public service post, similar to the international Peace Corps. The National Service Corps would focus on domestic needs, such as mental health institutions, Indian reservations, and areas of urban and rural poverty.

The President concluded his address by urging continued congressional support of existing initiatives, including the Peace Corps, measures to combat juvenile delinquency, child welfare, education, and physical fitness.

Feb 14 JFK PROPOSES $4 BILLION FOR OUTDOOR RECREATION

WASHINGTON—The White House today delivered a letter to Vice President (and Senate President) Lyndon Johnson and House of Representatives Speaker John McCormack, urging their support of President Kennedy's outdoor recreation spending package. The message included draft legislation that, if passed, would establish a Land and Water Conservation Fund.

Noting that as many as 90 percent of Americans engage in outdoor recreation annually, Kennedy asserted: "Today's resources are inadequate to today's needs, and the public demand for outdoor recreation opportunities is expected to triple by the turn of the century." His proposed fund calls for a federal land acquisition program as well as grants to individual states to upgrade and enhance their outdoor recreational facilities.

The newly created Bureau of Outdoor Recreation, within the Department of the Interior, will serve to execute the proposed disbursements, slated to cost approximately $4 billion over 10 years. Additional funding will come from user fees, the sale of surplus federal property, and existing taxes on marine fuels.

Feb 18 SOVIET TROOPS TO PULL OUT OF CUBA

Moscow—Soviet Premier Nikita Khrushchev today assured President Kennedy that his government will recall a significant number of troops from its bases in Cuba, further defusing tensions that nearly reached a boiling point last October.

The Soviets plan to begin repatriating several thousand troops immediately. They are aiming to complete the withdrawal by March 15.

The Soviets began arming Castro's Cuba following the failed U.S.-sponsored Bay of Pigs invasion in April 1961. A February 1962 economic embargo further strained relations between the U.S. and the small Soviet satellite. Late last year, U.S. intelligence detected the construction of missile bases on the island, precipitating a 13-day crisis that, by all appearances, led the two superpowers to the brink of nuclear war. President Kennedy left little room for doubt when, mid-crisis, he claimed that the U.S. would "regard any nuclear missile launched from Cuba against any nation in the Western Hemisphere as an attack on the United States, requiring a full retaliatory response upon the Soviet Union."

Today's announcement will certainly be met with relief, not only by American policy-makers but by nations worldwide who closely followed the events of last October.

JFK wants to enhance outdoor recreational facilities. Pictured is Balboa Park in San Diego.

Feb 21 | AMERICAN FISHERMEN ATTACKED BY SOVIET MIGs

FLORIDA STRAITS—Two American shrimp fishermen were surprised to find themselves on the front lines of the Cold War yesterday, when their craft, disabled in the Florida Straits, came under attack by a MIG fighter jet.

The boat *Ala* sustained no damage, though it was certainly a terrifying experience for the men on board. A protest was immediately filed with the Cuban government, whose leader, Fidel Castro, denied any knowledge of the incident.

Regardless, President Kennedy's response was immediate and decisive. He instructed the Department of Defense to revise its standing orders to call for an immediate military retaliation in the face of any further Cuban aggression against American shipping or commerce in the Caribbean.

It remains unclear if the attack was an impulsive act by the crew of the Russian-made MIG or if the orders came from somewhere up the chain of command. But, according to President Kennedy, "These planes came from Cuba and flew under a Cuban flag, and, therefore, unless the Soviet Union should claim they were flying them, we would hold the Cubans responsible."

"A proud and resourceful nation can no longer ask its older people to live in constant fear of a serious illness for which adequate funds are not available." —KENNEDY

Feb 21 | KENNEDY PITCHES FEDERAL HEALTH CARE PLAN FOR ELDERLY

WASHINGTON—President Kennedy delivered his proposal for federal health care for senior citizens to members of Congress today. It was part of a larger comprehensive aid package for the elderly.

Calling his address a "Special Message on Aiding Our Senior Citizens," Kennedy outlined no less than 39 legislative initiatives. The centerpiece of the legislation was the creation of Medicare, a federal insurance program designed to supplement private medical insurance coverage as well as cover catastrophic care.

The President said: "A proud and resourceful nation can no longer ask its older people to live in constant fear of a serious illness for which adequate funds are not available." Kennedy appears confident that resources can be found in the federal budget, despite recent tax cuts and other belt-tightening measures.

The President's proposal likely will encounter stiff resistance from those who believe that federalized health care is just another step down the slippery slope to socialism. The proposal will win passage if a congressional majority agrees with Kennedy's claim that America's elderly deserve "the right of dignity in sickness as well as in health."

Feb 28 KENNEDY INSISTENT ON CIVIL RIGHTS REFORM

WASHINGTON—In a written message to Congress today, President Kennedy sought support for the most substantial civil rights legislation of his administration. Noting that it has been 100 years since Lincoln signed the Emancipation Proclamation, Kennedy declared that we still have a long way to go before Negroes enjoy equal opportunity in American society.

"Equality before the law has not always meant equal treatment and opportunity," Kennedy stated. "And the harmful, wasteful, and wrongful results of racial discrimination and segregation still appear in virtually every aspect of national life, in virtually every part of the nation."

The President stated that legislation, existing and proposed, should be strengthened and created with the goal of racial equality. The first item on his agenda was voting rights. "The right to vote in a free American election is the most powerful and precious right in the world—and it must not be denied on the grounds of race or color," Kennedy asserted. Voting rights legislation, while on the books, is severely hampered by spotty enforcement and hostility, especially in the South.

Kennedy wants to address these problems with a multi-pronged attack, including federal voting referees, expedited lawsuits, and the prohibition of registration standards and literacy tests. The remainder of the President's message addressed other civil rights issues, including segregation and inequality in education, expansion of the Federal Commission on Civil Rights, employment opportunity and equality, and the desegregation of public accommodations.

"The centennial of the issuance of the Emancipation Proclamation is an occasion for celebration, for a sober assessment of our failures, and for rededication to the goals of freedom," Kennedy declared in the conclusion of his message. "Surely there could be no more meaningful observance of the centennial than the enactment of effective civil rights legislation and the continuation of effective executive action."

"The right to vote in a free American election is the most powerful and precious right in the world—and it must not be denied on the grounds of race or color." —KENNEDY

9 The President's physical fitness campaign gets a high-profile boost when Robert Kennedy completes a 50-mile hike along the banks of the Potomac River.

10 The administration calls on Moscow to withdraw from Cuba all combat forces, which the Soviets claim are on the island for a training mission.

11 The White House puts the final touches on its proposal for Congress to invest $4 billion over a decade in outdoor recreation facilities nationwide.

12 The Civil Rights Commission presents Kennedy with a 246-page report, "Freedom to Fail," with emphasis on the challenge of fighting subtle forms of discrimination in the North.

13 At a social gathering of Russian immigrants in Fort Worth, Texas, guests hear Lee Harvey Oswald denounce President Kennedy and General Edwin Walker, a Dallas-based anti-Communist and segregationist.

14 In a message to Congress, Kennedy proposes a new Youth Conservation Corps and a stateside version of the Peace Corps.

15 JFK assures NATO allies that American forces will defend Western Europe as long as desired and that allies will have a say in nuclear defense strategy.

16 Khrushchev reportedly says that Russian and Chinese communism together will "bury capitalism," an echo of his famous 1956 "we will bury you" remark to Western diplomats.

17 U.S. missile defense suffers a setback when the first Titan II fired from an underground silo explodes after launch.

Older Americans appreciate Kennedy's efforts on their behalf, be it senior health care reform or age discrimination in the workplace.

Mar 14 PRESIDENT WARNS AGAINST AGE DISCRIMINATION

WASHINGTON—President Kennedy sent a memo to the heads of all federal agencies and departments, warning them against discriminatory treatment of older employees. In the memo, Kennedy underscored a previous decree that the hiring policy under his administration be age-blind, in order to attract the best talent.

The President was pleased with the federal government's record on this issue, and the fact that there was no age restriction in place. Nonetheless, he clearly felt the need to restate this policy. It is not clear if the memo was in response to a specific incident of age-related bias.

"Personnel actions should be based, in accordance with merit principles, solely on the ability of candidates to meet qualification requirements and physical standards of the position to be filled," Kennedy wrote. Though he did allow that there might be exceptions, he requested that the department and agency leaders review their policies in practice and establish age limits only when "absolutely necessary."

Mar 16 | SENATE VOTES TO EXTEND MILITARY DRAFT

WASHINGTON—Following 10 minutes of debate, the U.S. Senate voted yesterday to extend the military draft for an additional four years. The measure, which passed the House of Representatives on March 12, will now go to the White House for President Kennedy's signature.

Though the bill passed quickly in the Senate, the House debated the length of the extension, with some Representatives vying for a shorter, two-year extension. As it stands, the military draft will make eligible males from 18.5 to 26 years of age subject to conscription.

The measure will also suspend the cap on the size of the armed services, a cap that has been suspended since 1950. Accordingly, the Army expects to draft an additional 75,000 young men this year alone. The bill will extend the government's ability to draft doctors, dentists, and veterinarians, but it also contains provisions for those drafted professionals to receive additional allowances and pay.

Coincidentally, this measure passed through Congress almost a century after the first U.S. conscription act—the Civil War Conscription Act—which was signed into law by President Lincoln on March 3, 1863.

Mar 18 | RIGHTS IMPROVE FOR INDIGENT DEFENDANTS

WASHINGTON—The U.S. Supreme Court today decided for the plaintiff in the case of *Gideon* v. *Wainwright*. The court suggested that, in the future, federal rules would require state courts to appoint public defenders for all defendants who cannot afford legal representation, regardless of the nature of the crime.

Clarence Earl Gideon was accused of larceny in June 1961, and he was convicted on circumstantial evidence. His inability to hire an attorney left him representing himself against a skilled prosecutor.

Gideon crafted his successful Supreme Court appeal from his Florida jail cell. Because of today's decision, the case will go back to the Florida court that convicted him—with the instruction that the Supreme Court agrees that states have a constitutional obligation to provide legal representation to all indigent defendants. Though the case still needs to play out in a Florida court, it would appear that Mr. Gideon has already won the key battle.

18 Kennedy tells congressional leaders that Khrushchev plans to withdraw several thousand combat troops from Cuba within a month.

19 Venezuela's President Romulo Betancourt meets with President Kennedy to discuss oil trade and American help against Communist insurgency in Venezuela.

20 Four Cuban MIG jets fire at a disabled American shrimp boat, the *Ala*, north of Havana in the Florida Straits. After a tense standoff with scrambled U.S. Phantom jets, the MIGs return to Cuba.

21 Congress receives an ambitious White House proposal for adding Medicare hospital insurance to the Social Security system.

22 The military receives orders from the President to prevent future attacks like the one by MIGs against the *Ala*.

23 Tensions flare over Cuba, as Washington demands an explanation for the MIG attack on a fishing boat. Moscow warns that any U.S. attack on Cuba will mean world war.

24 The Senate learns that U.S. military and economic aid to South Vietnam has reached $400 million annually. Some 12,000 U.S. troops and advisers are stationed in the country.

25 In *Edwards* v. *South Carolina*, the U.S. Supreme Court reverses the 1961 convictions of anti-segregation protesters in Columbia, South Carolina.

26 India refuses to recognize the validity of any agreement between Pakistan and China that establishes China's border with the portion of Kashmir controlled by Pakistan.

Kennedy praised the unity of the Central American states and promised to (figuratively speaking) "build a wall around Cuba."

Mar 18 KENNEDY, CENTRAL AMERICA STAND AGAINST COMMUNISM

SAN JOSE, COSTA RICA—President Kennedy issued a call to action against communism as he opened the Presidents' Conference today at the Teatro Nacional in San Jose, Costa Rica.

Addressing the presidents of Costa Rica, Guatemala, El Salvador, Honduras, Nicaragua, and Panama, as well as the archbishop of San Jose and other distinguished guests, Kennedy praised the alliance of American states as the "most enduring of international order in the history of the world." He noted that despite the occasional skirmish, the region remains one of the most stable on earth, almost universally committed to democracy, sovereignty, and peaceful resolution.

However, Kennedy emphasized that there is a serious challenge to peace in the Americas: the absorption of Cuba into the Soviet sphere of influence. Vowing that the Americas will never yield to foreign tyranny, and that the United States will support the Central American states in their efforts to fight communism, Kennedy promised that together "we will build a wall around Cuba—not a wall of mortar or brick or barbed wire, but a wall of dedicated men determined to protect their freedom and their sovereignty."

Mar 22 — JFK Pushes Anti-Poll Tax Amendment

WASHINGTON—President Kennedy today sent a telegram to the governors of states that have failed to ratify the 24th Amendment, which outlaws the collection of poll taxes.

Only 22 of the 50 states have signed off on the amendment. The delay is likely a procedural one in most states, as the measure passed overwhelmingly in both the House and the Senate. It also enjoys strong and vocal support from the executive branch.

Kennedy underscored the importance of ratifying the amendment as soon as possible in order to ensure a fair election in 1964. He noted, "Every effort should be made to broaden the base of citizen participation in national and local affairs through the voting process. One important contribution to this objective can be the elimination of the poll tax as an obstacle to voting."

KENNEDY AND HIS WORDSMITHS

President Kennedy had the good fortune of working with one of the greatest presidential speechwriters of the 20th century, Theodore Sorensen, along with a team of other superb writers that included Richard Goodwin. Nevertheless, JFK considered himself a writer and was an active partner in the speechwriting process.

Kennedy with speechwriter Ted Sorensen

Some speeches, including the inaugural address, went through draft after draft as the President and his speechwriters searched for poetic phrases and vivid language to make their points. Other speeches were put together quickly, like the President's address on June 11, 1963, which was finished just minutes before JFK spoke to the nation about civil rights. Kennedy had been prepared to go forward without a prepared text—he was that confident in his speaking ability.

Another memorable speech, the address at the Berlin Wall, was the product of presidential improvisation. Kennedy didn't like the speech he was supposed to give at the wall. He worked with his writers to come up with the passionate words, including the phrase in German that made the speech immortal.

Sorensen was among Kennedy's most trusted aides. JFK and his speechwriter secretly collaborated on a speech in the spring of 1963 that called for Americans to rethink their attitude toward the Cold War. The State Department and the Pentagon were kept out of the loop over what Kennedy would say until the last minute.

February

27 Despite its planned withdrawal of troops from Cuba, the Soviet Union has indicated that it will keep a residual force there indefinitely.

28 In his first significant civil rights legislative proposal, Kennedy calls for a significant strengthening of the voting rights provisions within existing civil rights acts.

March

1 A CIA official reports to Congress that Cuba was a training ground in subversive tactics for up to 1,500 Latin Americans the previous year.

2 The President and Robert Kennedy talk by phone about concerns that an investigation in the Senate could reveal details of President Kennedy's decisions on air cover for the abortive Bay of Pigs invasion.

3 Administration officials urge allies to join the U.S. in supplying an estimated $175 million to help the Congo, whose government is struggling to maintain order.

4 At a dinner marking the 50th anniversary of the Department of Labor, Kennedy laments the fact that social programs are often considered wasteful, while defense expenditures are "untouchable."

5 In a letter to Congress on national transportation policy, JFK writes, "Although our Nation enjoys one of the most highly developed and diversified transportation systems in the world, it has been severely handicapped by laws and regulations which have failed to keep pace with advancing technology."

King Hassan receives a royal greeting in Washington.

Billie Sol Estes (right) confers with his lawyers.

Mar 27 PRESIDENT WELCOMES MOROCCO'S KING HASSAN II

WASHINGTON—President and Mrs. Kennedy greeted King Hassan II of Morocco in Washington's Union Station today. The 33-year-old monarch arrived for an official state visit. He was accompanied by his 22-year-old sister, Princess Lalla Nezha, and bore gifts for the Kennedy children.

As the first sovereign nation to recognize American independence, Morocco has always enjoyed a special relationship with the United States—a relationship Kennedy highlighted in his welcoming remarks to the king.

Following an elegant state dinner, President and Mrs. Kennedy retired to the East Room with their honored guests and enjoyed a screening of *Brigadoon*. Hassan II and his entourage are expected to spend three days in Washington. The king will be treated to banquets and receptions and will sit down for wide-ranging policy discussions with President Kennedy.

Mar 28 LBJ ASSOCIATE ESTES GUILTY OF MAIL FRAUD

El Paso, Tex.—Billie Sol Estes, the Texas financier who was accused of perpetrating one of the biggest swindles in U.S. history, was convicted today on charges of mail fraud and conspiracy.

A player in Texas Democratic Party circles, Estes made several contributions to Lyndon Johnson's campaign fund in the late 1950s and early 1960s. In 1961 and 1962, the suspicious deaths of several of Estes associates led FBI investigators to closely investigate the business practices of Estes and members of his inner circle. The investigation led to an April 1962 indictment on dozens of counts of fraud. He was accused of swindling investors and institutions of some $24 million.

It is thought that perhaps the Estes-Johnson connection may cause President Kennedy to consider dropping Johnson from his ticket prior to next year's reelection bid.

Estes was released on bond and will be sentenced at a later date.

Kennedy Family Tours Gettysburg Battlefield

Apr 1

GETTYSBURG, PA.—President and Mrs. Kennedy, along with daughter Caroline, friends Paul and Anita Fay, and the Fay children, toured the Civil War battlefield at Gettysburg, Pennsylvania, yesterday.

The touring party drove up from the presidential retreat at Camp David, Maryland, and met with Park Service historian and decorated veteran Jacob Sheads, who conducted the informative tour. Highlights included Seminary Ridge, Little Roundtop, Devil's Den, the Wheatfield, and the High Water Mark, the site of Pickett's Charge.

Following the two-hour tour, the Kennedys and Fays returned to Camp David on board the presidential helicopter.

"We stood together, and because of that fact the free world now stands." —WINSTON CHURCHILL

JFK Names Churchill Honorary Citizen

Apr 9

WASHINGTON—President Kennedy issued a proclamation today granting honorary U.S. citizenship to Sir Winston Churchill. The former British prime minister, America's chief ally in the Second World War, is revered on both sides of the Atlantic.

The President declared that Churchill, 88, "has been throughout his life a firm and steadfast friend of the American people and the American nation." Kennedy mentioned an oft-forgotten fact about Churchill: His mother was American. The President offered praise of the highest order when he called Churchill "the most honored and honorable man to walk the stage of human history in the time in which we live."

Unable to accept the honor in person, Churchill sent his son Randolph to the White House ceremony. Randolph read a statement prepared by his father two days prior. Recounting the war that had led to the ironclad partnership between the two allies, Churchill remarked, "We stood together, and because of that fact the free world now stands." He also expressed his gratitude to the American people for this "unique distinction, which will always be proudly remembered by my descendants."

6 The President tells reporters that he supports a NATO nuclear defense system on board ships, a departure from his agreement with British Prime Minister Harold Macmillan at Nassau. He urges Latin American nations to stop the flow of their citizens to Cuba for guerrilla training.

7 U.S. unemployment reaches 6.1 percent, the highest level since 1961. The White House says that this is evidence that a tax cut is needed.

8 A costly strike by printers and engravers against New York newspapers, including *The New York Times,* reaches 90 days. The strike will last until April 1.

9 Kennedy appoints Senator William Benton of Connecticut as U.S. representative to the United National Educational, Scientific and Cultural Organization (UNESCO).

10 Khrushchev signals a move toward cultural repression when he praises Stalin's contributions to communism. Before these remarks, the late dictator was officially disgraced.

11 The President warns that without swift congressional action on tax reform, unemployment in the United States could reach 7 percent within four years.

12 A Soviet delegate in Geneva rejects American demands for nuclear ground inspections, adding that the USSR is able to explode a nuclear weapon "behind the moon" at will.

13 JFK telegrams union and company leaders in the Southern Pacific Railroad dispute, instructing them to submit items to a binding arbitration panel.

Apr 11 | PRESIDENT SAYS NO TO ANY STEEL PRICE INCREASES

WASHINGTON—President Kennedy issued a statement today outlining his opposition to any increase in the price of steel by American companies.

Citing competition from overseas steel imports and domestic steel substitutes, American steel manufacturers propose an across-the-board price increase. President Kennedy was adamant today that he opposes any increase. "It would reduce the gains of our economic growth and reduce job opportunities in this country," he noted.

The President made it clear that he understands the pressures facing American steel companies. He called out federal government efforts to support the industry and noted that steel-specific tax benefits enacted last year are enabling the industry to modernize its means of production. Kennedy also pointed to the current year's tax-reduction program, which offers further support for steel interests.

Kennedy conceded that the choice was ultimately up to steel industry leaders, but he urged them to avoid a price increase "in their own enlightened self-interest and in the public interest as well."

JACKIE AS "MINISTER OF CULTURE"

Those American citizens who are old enough to remember the Kennedy years vividly recall images of the glamorous President and First Lady opening the White House to famous artists, writers, and performers. World-famous cellist Pablo Casals and Russian composer Igor Stravinsky were among the cultural elite invited to the White House for elegant affairs of state. The President donned a tuxedo and the First Lady wore a stunning strapless gown for an unveiling of the *Mona Lisa,* which the French government loaned to the National Gallery of Art in Washington in 1963.

The Kennedy's cultural leadership was part of the Camelot myth. To a great extent, Jacqueline Kennedy was the myth's author, producer, director, and, of course, leading lady. *The New York Times* labeled Jackie the nation's "unofficial minister of culture." She certainly was more familiar with high culture than her husband, who preferred popular music and movies. He was, after all, friendly with Frank Sinatra and his Rat Pack—stylish performers for sure, but not exactly Jackie's idea of art.

Although Mrs. Kennedy shunned the political spotlight, she grew into the role of national patron of the arts. She supervised a display of paintings by French post-impressionist artist Paul Cezanne in the White House, and she was the driving force behind the high-profile visits from such artists as Russian choreographer George Balanchine.

President Kennedy once asked his wife to play host to a group of Girls Scouts visiting the White House. Jackie was reluctant to do so, but her husband made her an offer she couldn't refuse: He promised to sit through two symphonies.

Apr 12 JFK HONORS THOSE LOST IN *THRESHER* DISASTER

WASHINGTON—President Kennedy today ordered the American flag to be flown at half-staff on all federal buildings and facilities. The executive order, in ho or of those lost in the USS *Thresher* disaster, will expire at sunset on Monday the 15th.

Commissioned in August 1961, the 3,700-ton nuclear submarine was conducting exercises in the North Atlantic two days ago, following an overhaul at the Portsmouth Navy Shipyard. Escorted by the *Skylark,* a submarine rescue ship, *Thresher* was diving in extremely deep waters about 220 miles east of Boston when she suffered an unknown mechanical malfunction, causing her to sink.

Approximately five minutes after the first indication of trouble, the *Skylark*'s sonar received the sounds of the *Thresher* breaking apart under extreme pressure. She was lost with all hands. The 129 crewmembers included 16 officers, 96 sailors, and 21 civilians.

Apr 14 KENNEDY FAMILY ENJOYS EASTER IN PALM BEACH

PALM BEACH, FLA.—President and Mrs. Kennedy, Caroline, and John Jr. attended a private Easter mass today at the Palm Beach home of the President's father, Joseph Kennedy. Much of the rest of the holiday was spent on the water, as the Kennedys cruised Lake Worth aboard both the *Honey Fitz* and their sailboat *Pattycat.*

The First Family was accompanied by good friends Paul and Anita Fay and their children. The President is expected to spend several more days enjoying the balmy Palm Beach weather before returning to Washington.

The Kennedys pose outside Joe Sr.'s house.

14 The President orders federal agencies to ensure that older workers "receive fair and full consideration for employment and advancement in the competitive service."

15 After Kennedy rejected a death-row plea, convicted murderer Victor Feguer is executed in Iowa.

16 Congress extends the military draft law for four years—100 years to the month after the first U.S. conscription act during the Civil War. Kennedy will sign the extension later in the month.

17 Officials report that U.S. fighters intercepted but did not engage two Russian reconnaissance jets that flew 30 miles into U.S. airspace over Alaska.

18 In *Gideon* v. *Wainwright,* the U.S. Supreme Court decides that states are required to provide free legal counsel to criminal defendants who are unable to pay for their own defense.

19 Kennedy meets with Central American leaders in Costa Rica.

20 In a speech to students at the University of Costa Rica, JFK insists that the United States will not accept Cuba yielding its sovereignty to the USSR.

21 At a news conference focused on his trip to Costa Rica, Kennedy praises the region's presidents for pledging to fight subversive Soviet activity.

22 JFK telegrams governors of nearly two dozen states to urge ratification of the 24th Amendment, which prohibits state or federal voting taxes.

23 The President travels to Chicago for the formal dedication of the O'Hare International Airport, already the world's busiest.

An officer arrests Martin Luther King, Jr., for his participation in an anti-segregation march in Birmingham.

Apr 19 CIVIL RIGHTS LEADER KING RELEASED FROM BIRMINGHAM JAIL

BIRMINGHAM—Reverend Martin Luther King, Jr., was released from his Birmingham jail cell today. Incarcerated a week ago for violating an injunction against protests issued by the state circuit court, King spent much of his jail time in solitary confinement.

Birmingham officials even denied King's requests to call his wife, Coretta, recovering from childbirth in their Atlanta home. Fearing for her husband's welfare in isolation, Mrs. King appealed directly to President Kennedy and his brother, the attorney general. The Kennedy administration dispatched federal agents to Birmingham, with the immediate result of restoring King's communication with the outside world.

The Birmingham campaign, brainchild of King and SCLC colleague Ralph Abernathy, has been an unqualified success since it was launched on April 3. The effort to desegregate Birmingham's public facilities and businesses has drawn greater numbers of volunteers with each passing day. Peaceful protests have been held in churches, libraries, municipal buildings, and downtown businesses. Clearly, their message of nonviolent resistance has caught the attention of the highest levels of government.

Apr 22   JFK ORDERS WARSHIPS TO THE GULF OF SIAM

VIENTIANE, LAOS—American warships, including carriers *Ranger* and *Ticonderoga*, along with a three-ship amphibious group, entered the Gulf of Siam today. The ships have been deployed in response to recent victories by Communist Pathet Lao forces against the neutralists in Laos.

President Kennedy's hope for a lasting peace under an all-party coalition government came to a sudden end with the April 1 assassination of Foreign Minister Quinim Pholsema. With the dissolution of the months-old government, a resurgence of the Laotian civil war was assured.

Indeed, with the Soviets and the North Vietnamese supporting the Pathet Lao, and the Kennedy administration throwing U.S. support behind the neutralists, the situation appears to be paralleling that of neighboring Vietnam.

U.S. involvement in the region continues to be guided by the "domino theory" and an overriding commitment to the containment of communism. Still, Kennedy and his advisers maintain the hope that the situation in Laos, unlike that in Vietnam, can be managed without an American military presence on the ground.

May 7   TELSTAR II SATELLITE LAUNCHED INTO ORBIT

CAPE CANAVERAL, FLA.—The communications satellite Telstar II was launched from Cape Canaveral today. The product of a joint venture involving NASA, Bell Labs, and the American Telephone and Telegraph Company, Telestar II will pick up where Telstar I left off when it malfunctioned in February.

Built at Bell Labs, Telstar II is nearly identical to its predecessor, which was launched in July of last year. President Kennedy hailed the accomplishment of the international team that put Telstar in space, saying last year that the project was "an outstanding example of the way in which government and business can cooperate in a most important field of human endeavor."

The Telstar program brought America the first live transatlantic television signal two weeks after the launch of the first satellite. Although technical complications shortened the operational lifespan of Telstar I to less than eight months, it is hoped that Telstar II will function successfully for significantly longer.

24   To the dismay of administration officials, a Kennedy-appointed commission on American foreign aid recommends a nearly $500 million cut in aid and stricter conditions on countries that receive aid.

25   White House and Kremlin officials agree to establish a direct teletype and fax link to avoid the dangers of miscommunication that were revealed during the Cuban missile crisis.

26   Kennedy orders the State Department to seek ways of stopping nuclear weapons development programs that are believed to be in progress in Israel, Egypt, and Syria.

27   JFK welcomes Morocco's King Hassan II. During a state dinner at the White House, the President observes that Morocco was the first country to give the fledgling United States official recognition.

28   Tensions rise in the waters near Cuba throughout March. Cuban exiles harass cargo ships bound for Havana, and Cuban MIGs fire on another U.S. merchant ship.

29   U.S. and Moroccan officials announce that American forces will withdraw from the North African country by the end of the year.

30   After Castro apologizes for the MIG attack on an American ship, U.S. State and Justice department officials pledge "every step necessary" to stop attacks against Soviet ships and other Cuban targets.

31   The President, Mrs. Kennedy, and daughter Caroline tour the Civil War battlefield at Gettysburg, Pennsylvania.

Birmingham firefighters blast young black demonstrators with powerful fire hoses. This and similar images in Birmingham have stirred outrage across the nation.

May 8 WHITE HOUSE MONITORING HOT SPOTS IN HAITI AND BIRMINGHAM

WASHINGTON—The past several days have been challenging ones for the Kennedy administration, as the President has had federal troops on the brink of intervention in Haiti and Birmingham, Alabama.

Haitian President Francois Duvalier is in a tight spot. Both the United States and the Organization of American States are objecting to the dictator's harassment of foreign officials and his saber rattling toward the neighboring Dominican Republic. Duvalier, who seems to be under threat of overthrow by underground elements in Haiti, has put his nation under martial law.

Just yesterday, the Council of the Organization of American States urged the two island nations to exercise restraint and use diplomacy to settle their differences. Also yesterday, the United States ordered the evacuation of more than 200 nationals—family members of U.S. government employees stationed in Haiti.

Kennedy elaborated on the latest developments in Birmingham today during an afternoon press conference. He expressed measured relief at the limited progress made in negotiations between white and Negro citizens in the strife-torn city. Noting that he is willing to use any power at his disposal to uphold civil rights, Kennedy said: "We have, in addition, been watching the present controversy to detect any violation of the federal civil rights or other statutes." Having failed to find that, Kennedy's efforts have focused on getting the two sides to negotiate at the local level. Assistant Attorney General Burke Marshall has been in Birmingham, working with the community toward resolution.

Despite the challenges of recent days, Kennedy remains hopeful that the situation in Birmingham may soon be resolved. Near the end of his statement, he said: "While much remains to be settled before the situation can be termed satisfactory, we can hope that tensions will ease and that this case history, which has so far only narrowly avoided widespread violence and fatalities, will remind every state, every community, and every citizen how urgent it is that all bars to equal opportunity and treatment be removed as promptly as possible."

SHOWDOWN IN BIRMINGHAM

According to Martin Luther King, Jr., Birmingham, Alabama, was the most segregated city in the United States. King sought to draw attention to Birmingham's racist dynamics in the fall of 1962. He organized a campaign of peaceful agitation in "Bombingham," whose chief law enforcement official was notorious segregationist Eugene "Bull" Connor.

King stepped up the pressure in the spring of 1963, organizing a series of marches that included a children's march on May 2. Six hundred of the 1,000 marchers were arrested. The following day, as more children marched, Connor ordered the city's fire department to bring out their hoses. Film crews captured images of children being attacked by high-pressure water blasts as well as the police department's German shepherds.

African Americans fired back with rocks. King told television news reporters that the President had to take a stand.

Kennedy sent emissaries to Birmingham, and they helped broker a deal to desegregate the city's lunch counters and other private facilities. But after bombs exploded near King's motel room and in his brother's church in a suburb of Birmingham, the President at last decided that the time for negotiation was over. He put U.S. Army units in the vicinity on alert, and he prepared to send in airborne troops. Kennedy went on television to condemn those he called extremists.

JFK's actions eased tensions in Birmingham, but only for a while. Four months later, in September, white supremacists bombed a church in Birmingham, killing four African American girls.

May 8 — PRESIDENT OFFERS ASSURANCES TO ISRAEL

WASHINGTON—President Kennedy held a press conference at the White House today, touching on several topics of domestic and international concern during the afternoon session.

Notable was the President's stand on the balance of power in the Middle East. Responding to a question about U.S. policy on threats against Israel, Kennedy said, "In the event of aggression or preparation for aggression, whether direct or indirect, we would support appropriate measures in the United Nations, adopt other courses of action on our own to prevent or to put a stop to such aggression." While not a policy shift by any means, such assurances must go a long way toward bolstering Israel's position of strength in the region.

Kennedy also reiterated the United States' opposition to a regional arms race as well as the proliferation of communism in the Middle East.

Other issues covered in the lengthy session included Puerto Rico's status, U.S.-Canada relations, and the ongoing racial strife in Birmingham, Alabama.

1 In the first action resulting from a recent agreement between Washington and London to stop raids on Soviet ships, British sailors off the Bahamas seize a small contingent of Cuban exiles believed to be sailing toward Cuban waters.

2 Congress receives a White House proposal for $4.5 billion in foreign aid during the next fiscal year, down by more than $400 million from its original budget proposal.

3 In Birmingham, Alabama, Martin Luther King, Jr., and other leaders of the Southern Christian Leadership Conference begin a coordinated campaign to desegregate business and public facilities.

4 Kennedy acknowledges the work of his advisory committee on drug abuse, which recommended a concerted attack on importers and distributors of hard narcotics.

5 The President meets with advisers, including Secretary of Labor Willard Wirtz, about the economic impact of recent wage and price increases in the steel industry.

6 The New York Times reports a renewed effort by the United States to patrol the waters south of Florida to prevent provocative acts by anti-Castro raiders.

7 Political observers see the reelection this week of Chicago Mayor Richard J. Daley as a good sign for Kennedy's quest for a second term in 1964.

8 Kennedy continues a venerable Washington, D.C., tradition by throwing out the ceremonial first pitch at D.C. Stadium to open the 1963 baseball season.

May 10 BIRMINGHAM OFFICIALS REACH ACCORD WITH SCLC PROTESTERS

BIRMINGHAM—Business and civil leaders in Birmingham today finalized a peace agreement of sorts with members of the SCLC, a civil rights organization.

Mediated by Burke Marshall, Robert Kennedy's assistant attorney general, both sides agreed to stand down. The SCLC will cancel future protests and boycotts of Birmingham businesses, while the city has agreed to desegregate its stores and public facilities as well as release the jailed civil rights protesters.

President Kennedy continues to demonstrate his commitment to civil rights and racial justice, claiming in recent remarks to the press, "I have made it clear since assuming the presidency that I would use all available means to protect human rights and uphold the law of the land." Calling the scene in Birmingham a "spectacle which was seriously damaging the reputation of both Birmingham and the country," Kennedy has given notice to southern segregationist leaders that he is not afraid to support the legal and constitutional rights of all Americans with the power of the federal government.

May 11 KENNEDY, CANADA'S PEARSON CONCLUDE PRODUCTIVE SUMMIT

HYANNISPORT, MASS.—President Kennedy and Canadian Prime Minister Lester Pearson released a joint statement today in which they emphasized the strong U.S.-Canada relationship. The statement followed two days of talks at the Kennedy compound in Hyannisport.

Both leaders expressed their ongoing commitment to the North Atlantic Alliance, continental security, and a strong bilateral defense. To that end, the Prime Minister seems ready to accept the deployment of U.S. nuclear warheads on Canada-based missiles. This provision, regarded by the U.S. as a necessary part of the two nations' mutual defense, was a sticking point with Pearson's predecessor, former Prime Minister Diefenbaker.

In addition, the two leaders stressed their mutual interest in sharing resources, both natural and intellectual, and working together in defense production as well as scientific and technological endeavors.

International trade, border issues, and cooperative use of shared waterways, fishing rights, and aid to the Caribbean were some of the other issues that were laid on the table during the course of the talks. Conducted without an agenda, the meeting remained friendly and relaxed, as the President and Prime Minister worked together in a spirit of goodwill and cooperation.

May 13 JFK ADDRESSES NATION REGARDING BIRMINGHAM

BIRMINGHAM—Yesterday evening, President Kennedy addressed the nation from the Oval Office regarding the recent turn of events in Birmingham, Alabama. A resurgence of anti-Negro violence, the targeted bombings of the Gaston Motel (where Martin Luther King was staying), and rioting in the streets has once again turned back the progress of racial relations in the city.

In his address, Kennedy declared: "This government will do whatever must be done to preserve order, to protect the lives of its citizens, and to uphold the law of the land." Accordingly, the President has begun the process of federalizing the Alabama National Guard. Kennedy stated unequivocally: "The federal government will not permit it to be sabotaged by a few extremists on either side who think they can defy both the law and the wishes of responsible citizens by inciting or inviting violence."

The President is sending Assistant Attorney General Burke Marshall back to Birmingham, along with other Justice Department officials, to consult with city officials and residents in an effort to get the agreement back on track.

Kennedy underscored the fact that the preservation of peace is up to the people. He stated: "I call upon all the citizens of Birmingham, both Negro and white, to live up to the standards their responsible leaders set last week in reaching agreement, to realize that violence only breeds more violence, and that good will and good faith are most important now to restore the atmosphere in which last week's agreement can be carried out. There must be no repetition of last night's incidents by any group."

Emboldened youths in Birmingham jeer at police on May 7, 1963.

9 At the White House, Kennedy bestows honorary American citizenship on 88-year-old Sir Winston Churchill, who watches from London thanks to live satellite television relay.

10 Former Marine Lee Harvey Oswald shoots at but narrowly misses Major General Edwin Walker (Ret.). Off the coast of Cape Cod, the U.S. nuclear submarine *Thresher* sinks during sea trials, killing all 129 crewmembers.

11 Pope John XXIII releases an encyclical, *"Pacem in Terris,"* which includes an appeal for nations to end their nuclear arms race.

12 On Good Friday, police in Birmingham arrest Martin Luther King, Jr., Ralph Abernathy, and other civil rights leaders when they defy a state court's ban on their demonstrations.

13 In the immediate aftermath of the *Thresher* disaster, the Navy says it plans to continue building 22 more submarines of the same type, but will undertake a design review.

14 An AP wire photo published in newspapers around the country shows the Kennedy family after they attend a private Easter Mass at the Florida home of the President's father.

15 Yielding to protests by African nations and the Soviets, the Congolese government revises its plan to invite instructors from the West and Israel to train the young country's military.

16 Martin Luther King, Jr.'s "Letter from Birmingham Jail" responds to white ministers who argued that the fight against segregation should take place in the courts.

May 14 — KENNEDY CONCERNED ABOUT CIVIL RIGHTS EXTREMISTS

WASHINGTON—President Kennedy hosted 26 Alabama newspaper publishers and editors at the White House today to discuss the situation in Birmingham. The meeting, while timely, was in fact scheduled nearly two weeks ago, before the latest crisis flared up.

The Kennedy administration is currently engaged in a standoff with Alabama Governor George Wallace, who believes that the President overstepped his authority in ordering federal troops to the Birmingham area.

Kennedy, for his part, is hopeful that the situation can and will be handled by the local authorities. In a May 13 telegram that he wrote to Wallace, he stated that "I trust that we can count on your constructive cooperation" toward that end.

In his remarks to the assembled journalists, Kennedy reportedly expressed concern that if the nonviolent Negro civil rights movement failed, blacks might turn to the Black Muslims and other radical groups.

May 14 — NEVADA NUCLEAR TESTS CANCELED

WASHINGTON—The Atomic Energy Commission and the Department of Defense yesterday canceled an upcoming round of weapons tests originally scheduled for later this month. The series of three tests, including two nuclear detonations and one chemical explosion, were to be carried out at the Nevada test site.

Few details have been released about the decision, and White House sources deny that it bears any relationship to a note that President Kennedy allegedly received from Soviet Premier Khrushchev. There has been some speculation that the cancellation may be due to a thinly veiled threat broadcast on the Soviet state mouthpiece, Radio Moscow, which asserted that "the USSR is not going to stand by idly watching the U.S. perfect its nuclear weapons."

The United States, Britain, and the Soviet Union have attempted to draft an agreeable test-ban treaty for nearly six years, but they repeatedly have failed to reach terms on the issue of weapons inspections. It is unclear what impact yesterday's developments may have on that process.

May 16 — PRESIDENT WELCOMES ASTRONAUT BACK TO EARTH

WASHINGTON—Astronaut Gordon Cooper returned safely from Earth's orbit today. His space capsule, *Faith 7*, plunged into the Pacific Ocean and was quickly recovered, concluding the final Project Mercury mission.

President Kennedy wasted little time contacting Major Cooper and confirming the success of the flight. Afterward, the President made a congratulatory statement about the mission, saying "we take the greatest satisfaction as Americans in this extraordinary feat…. Peace has her victories as well as war, and this was one of the victories for the human spirit today."

> *"Peace has her victories as well as war, and this was one of the victories for the human spirit today."* — KENNEDY

Project Mercury was launched in 1959 with the objective of sending a human into Earth's orbit. That goal was achieved in February 1962 by astronaut John Glenn aboard *Friendship 7*. Major Cooper's flight, which lasted more that 34 hours, has earned him the distinction of being the first American to orbit Earth for more than a day.

JFK told Vanderbilt graduates: "of those to whom much is given, much is required."

May 18
JFK DELIVERS VANDERBILT ADDRESS

NASHVILLE—President Kennedy today delivered the address at the 90th commencement exercises of Tennessee's Vanderbilt University. He opened with kind words for the institution itself, which has grown from a small, local school to a nationally ranked university. The President also saluted the 30th anniversary of the New Deal-era Tennessee Valley Authority as well as the careers of Tennessee statesmen Cordell Hull and J. Percy Priest.

The bulk of Kennedy's speech, however, detailed the importance of personal responsibility. Using Commodore Vanderbilt, the school's benefactor, as an example, Kennedy reminded the graduates that "increased responsibility goes with increased ability, for 'of those to whom much is given, much is required.'" He further delineated three key obligations educated people have in society: to pursue education, serve the public, and uphold the law.

Acknowledging recent events in Birmingham, Kennedy concluded: "In these moments of tragic disorder, a special burden rests on the educated men and women of our country to reject the temptations of prejudice and violence, and to reaffirm the values of freedom and law on which our free society depends."

17 Lee Harvey Oswald decides to move to New Orleans, where he will become embroiled in controversy over his pro-Castro views.

18 South Vietnamese President Ngo Dinh Diem says he plans to destroy card-carrying Communists.

19 Kennedy denies reports that his administration promised Cuban exiles a second U.S.-backed invasion of Cuba.

20 The White House grudgingly praises the steel industry for having "acted with some restraint" in making only selective price increases.

21 The administration plans to expand the scope of Kennedy's June trip to West Germany to include discussion of French opposition to a nuclear defense pact with the United States.

22 Reacting to recent Communist successes in the fighting in Laos, the U.S. dispatches 22 ships from the Seventh Fleet to patrol the Gulf of Siam.

23 After receiving news that Havana has freed the last group of Bay of Pigs prisoners, Robert Kennedy calls on Cuban exiles to form a unified group for more effective interaction with the administration on Cuban policy.

24 JFK condemns the murder in Alabama of William Moore, an anti-segregationist activist who was marching alone from Tennessee to Mississippi.

25 Soviet leaders in Moscow initially refuse to meet with W. Averell Harriman on Laotian neutrality, but later agree to a joint statement underscoring U.S.-Soviet support for an independent Laos.

May 30 HAPPY BIRTHDAY, MR. PRESIDENT!

WASHINGTON—President Kennedy celebrated a festive 46th birthday yesterday, enjoying cake and good cheer with staff in the White House's Navy Mess Hall. In the evening, the President was joined by the First Lady, brothers Robert and Edward, and about 20 of his closest friends and associates on board the presidential yacht *Sequoia*. Guests enjoyed a feast of crabmeat ravigotte, roast beef, and asparagus hollandaise. The dessert, a special creation for the event, was Bombe President with chocolate sauce. Guests toasted the President's health with glasses of 1955 Cuvee Dom Perignon.

The day was not all play and no work, however. Civil rights issues remained at the top of Kennedy's agenda, as he organized a meeting with business leaders to sit down and discuss the difficulties minorities face with regard to equal employment and access to public facilities and services. The meeting is scheduled for June 4 at the White House.

May 30 KENNEDY, JOHN JR. LAY MEMORIAL DAY WREATH

ARLINGTON, VA.—President Kennedy attended a somber Memorial Day observance this morning at Arlington National Cemetery. Accompanied by young John Jr., General Maxwell Taylor, and General John S. Gleason, the President laid a wreath at the Tomb of the Unknowns. On his way out of the cemetery, Kennedy paid his respects at the grave of James Forrestal, America's first secretary of defense.

President Kennedy continued a long-standing Memorial Day tradition among sitting presidents by honoring the unknown soldiers interred at Arlington. The first soldier, a casualty of World War I, was interred on Armistice Day in 1921. Unknown soldiers from World War II and the Korean conflict were interred in the plaza on Memorial Day, 1958. The inscription on the main tomb in the plaza reads: "Here lies, in honored glory, an American soldier, known but to God."

JFK admires the shillelagh he received for his birthday.

JFK laid a wreath at the Tomb of the Unknowns.

Though many of his Cold War talks have been gloomy, Kennedy delivered a hope-filled message to the graduates.

26 The Mother's Day edition of *Life* magazine features a cover story entitled "Charming Album of Jackie Growing Up," a photo essay about the First Lady's childhood.

27 After Haitian troops occupy the Dominican Embassy in Port-au-Prince, the Dominican Republic is said to be threatening military action against its island neighbor.

28 A Gallup poll shows New York Governor Nelson Rockefeller leading among potential Republican challengers to Kennedy in 1964.

29 Yielding to the combined weight of Dominican troop deployments and U.S. diplomatic pressure, Haiti agrees to remove its forces from the Dominican Embassy.

30 Kennedy instructs Secretary of the Interior Stewart Udall to review federal mine safety regulations after two mining disasters killed 59 workers.

May

1 The White House hears criticism from its political right and left over Middle East policy. Senator Jacob Javits calls for a U.S. commitment to defend Israel; Senator Hubert H. Humphrey proposes an arms embargo to the entire region.

2 Violence erupts during a march by black students in Alabama. Nearly 1,000 are arrested.

3 The administration faces new domestic and international challenges. Birmingham police use batons, dogs, and fire hoses to quell civil rights demonstrations in the city. In Haiti, President Francois Duvalier declares martial law.

Jun 10 JFK CHEERS GRADUATES WITH UPBEAT SPEECH

WASHINGTON—President Kennedy, the keynote speaker at American University's commencement ceremonies today, delivered a frank and eloquent address on the always-timely topic of world peace.

In a sharp departure from standard Cold War rhetoric, the President spoke disarmingly of a sympathetic Soviet Union—a former ally that has suffered during much of the 20th century. Kennedy reminded the graduates that, despite our abhorrence of communism, "we can still hail the Russian people for their many achievements—in science and space, in economic and industrial growth, in culture and in acts of courage."

The President issued a call for "genuine peace," one that is not maintained by the threat of total war and mutually assured destruction. To that end, he announced upcoming talks in Moscow between the Soviet Union, Britain, and the United States. The three nuclear powers hope to reach agreement on a comprehensive test-ban treaty as soon as possible. Further, he declared that the United States would not resume atmospheric testing, provided that other states follow suit.

Kennedy left the graduates with an uplifting message of hope. Peace is an attainable goal, he implored, and as Americans, "confident and unafraid, we labor on—not toward a strategy of annihilation but toward a strategy of peace."

By signing the Equal Pay Act, Kennedy hopes to particularly help working mothers, especially those who are heads of households.

Jun 10 KENNEDY SIGNS EQUAL PAY ACT FOR WOMEN

WASHINGTON—President Kennedy today signed the Equal Pay Act of 1963, making it a violation of federal law to pay female employees less than males for performing the same job.

In America today, women are one-third of the workforce, and their numbers are growing. At the same time, women on average earn only 60 cents for each dollar earned by a man.

Speaking from the Oval Office, President Kennedy emphasized the importance of this legislation for all women, but especially for those from lower-income families. Nearly half of working women have young children, and some of these mothers are the heads of their households, he noted. Perpetuating a system that exploits these women has doomed many young families to poverty and public assistance.

President Kennedy also appealed to members of Congress for additional services to benefit working women. These include the expansion of day-care services as well as the addition of a federal tax deduction for child-care costs. He characterized the Equal Pay Act as a good first step, saying that it "affirms our determination that when women enter the labor force they will find equality in their pay envelopes."

Governor Wallace blocks a school door in a symbolic gesture: He is resisting integration in Alabama.

Jun 11 WALLACE STEPS ASIDE, UNIVERSITY DESEGREGATED

TUSCALOOSA, ALA.—Alabama Governor George Wallace blocked the doorway at the University of Alabama's Foster Auditorium today, expressing his displeasure at the university's admission of two Negro students, Vivian Malone and James Hood.

Wallace, whose inaugural speech featured the oath "Segregation now, segregation tomorrow, segregation forever," kept his promise to physically bar integration at Alabama's public schools. Still, his act was more symbolic than obstructionist. President Kennedy was prepared to federalize the Alabama National Guard, which was ready to physically remove the governor from the doorway if he refused to move.

Deputy Attorney General Nicholas Katzenbach politely asked Wallace to obey the wishes of the federal court, which had ordered the university to permit the matriculation of Malone and Hood. Citing states' rights, Wallace declined. Katzenbach then phoned President Kennedy, who federalized the Alabama National Guard.

National Guard General Henry Graham, who had served to protect civil rights Freedom Riders two years ago, accompanied Malone and Hood back to the door, initiating a confrontation with the governor. Ultimately, Wallace stepped back at Graham's request and allowed Malone and Hood to register for classes.

Jun 12 JFK ADDRESSES NATION ON CIVIL RIGHTS CRISIS

WASHINGTON—President Kennedy delivered a television and radio address to the American people yesterday evening in which there was clearly only one issue on the table: the continued injustices perpetrated against the American Negro.

The recent violence in Birmingham, Alabama, coupled with the need to send national guardsmen to desegregate the University of Alabama, seems to have clarified Kennedy's sense of purpose on this issue.

Saying that it is not enough that the federal government has banned discrimination in its employment practices, federal facilities, and publicly funded federal housing, the President asked Congress to enact broad-based civil rights legislation extending to the state, local, and private sector. Kennedy expects that this legislation will ban discrimination in all public facilities and accommodations as well as in employment and housing.

"One hundred years of delay have passed since President Lincoln freed the slaves," Kennedy said, "yet their heirs, their grandsons, are not fully free. They are not yet freed from the bonds of injustice. They are not yet freed from social and economic oppression. And this nation, for all its hopes and all its boasts, will not be fully free until all its citizens are free."

Kennedy made it clear that he expects to usher through landmark civil rights legislation, rectifying the generations of wrongs, this very year.

"And this nation, for all its hopes and all its boasts, will not be fully free until all its citizens are free."

—KENNEDY

Criticized for being lukewarm on civil rights issues, Kennedy now seems determined to attack segregation head-on.

4 The White House monitors a tense situation in Port-au-Prince as U.S. Marines wait aboard ships near Haiti for possible deployment in the crisis.

5 Kennedy tells members of the International Association of Machinists, "One of the great things about this country has been that our most extraordinary accomplishments have not come from the government down, or from the top down, but have come from the bottom up."

6 The U.S. Air Force displays the latest generation of its jet fighter, the F-105F, which will become a mainstay of the American combat operations in Vietnam.

7 NASA successfully launches Telstar II, the second prototype in a test of the feasibility of a global network of more than 100 satellites.

8 During a news conference, the President speaks against the use or threatened use of force in the Middle East, and offers Israel assistance against aggression.

9 South Vietnamese soldiers in Hue fire into a crowd of Buddhists who are protesting a ban on their display of the Buddhist flag. The death of one woman and injuries to eight children spark riots in the country throughout May.

10 After a hopeful day in which Birmingham leaders and civil rights leaders agree to the integration of stores and an end to demonstrations, the peace is shattered. Bombs explode near Martin Luther King, Jr.'s hotel and his brother's home, and riots ensue citywide.

Buddhist monk Thich Quang Duc immolates himself to protest the treatment of Buddhists in South Vietnam.

Jun 12 IN PROTEST, MONK IMMOLATES HIMSELF IN SOUTH VIETNAM

SAIGON—A shocking story and images are emerging from Vietnam, where a Buddhist monk deliberately set himself on fire yesterday in the middle of a busy Saigon intersection.

According to witnesses, some 350 monks and nuns were marching to protest the treatment of Buddhists by the South Vietnamese regime of Ngo Dinh Diem. Thich Quang Duc emerged from the crowd. He sat on a cushion in the middle of the street while another monk doused him with gasoline. Then he lit a match. He burned for several minutes before dying. Not once did he appear to move a muscle.

Western newspaper reporters supposedly had learned that there would be an event of some importance. Photographer Malcolm Browne took several disquieting images of the suicide.

Diem himself has expressed regret over the incident. President Kennedy learned of the suicide as many of us did—he saw the images in the morning paper. He was on the phone with his brother, Robert Kennedy, at the time and was reportedly shocked by the graphic photos.

Jun 13 NAACP LEADER EVERS GUNNED DOWN IN JACKSON

JACKSON, MISS.—Civil rights activist Medgar Evers died early yesterday after being cut down by a sniper's bullet outside his home.

The killing, which took place shortly after President Kennedy addressed the nation on the civil rights crisis, has shocked the nation and enraged the Negro community. Kennedy, who said he was "appalled by the barbarity" of Evers' killing, conferred with former President Eisenhower about the racial crisis, but the two made no statement about the result of their talks.

Evers was active in the civil rights movement and instrumental in desegregating the University of Mississippi. After he made an anti-segregation speech on local television earlier this month, threats on his life increased. Just five days before his

NAACP activist Medgar Evers (left) once said, "You can kill a man, but you can't kill an idea."

11 Kennedy and Canadian Prime Minister Lester Pearson announce a defense pact that will place U.S. nuclear missiles in Canadian territory.

12 The President orders federal troops to positions near Birmingham. Alabama Governor George Wallace responds that state and local police are best suited to handle the situation.

13 After Khrushchev signals his interest in a speedy solution to the nuclear testing stalemate, Kennedy cancels three planned U.S. nuclear tests.

14 The President tells newspaper editors at the White House that a failure of nonviolent civil rights leaders to achieve change could lead to the emergence of extremist black leaders less interested in conciliation.

15 Astronaut Gordon Cooper is launched into orbit. He will successfully orbit the Earth seven times and return safely the next day. For the first time, NASA transmits live television images from an orbiting spacecraft.

16 A report by the President's Science Advisory Committee warns about unknown dangers of widespread use of DDT and other pesticides.

17 As American warships patrol off the coast of Haiti, the U.S. prepares to break off diplomatic contact with the Duvalier government.

18 During a graduation address at Vanderbilt University in Nashville, Kennedy calls the struggle by black Americans for civil rights as being "in the highest traditions of American freedom."

death, he narrowly avoided being deliberately struck by a car as he left the Jackson office of the NAACP. Three weeks ago, someone targeted his home with a Molotov cocktail.

Evers had just returned home yesterday when he was shot in the back after exiting his car. The perpetrator is still at large. Evers died in the hospital less than an hour later. Evers leaves a wife, Myrlie, and three children.

Jun 16 SOVIETS LAUNCH A WOMAN INTO SPACE

Moscow—The Soviet government in Moscow has announced that the USSR has put the first female cosmonaut in space. Valentina Tereshkova was launched aboard *Vostok 6* early this morning.

Tereshkova is expected to remain in orbit for several days, along with fellow Soviet cosmonaut Valery Bykovsky, whose *Vostok 5* mission left Earth two days ago.

In the U.S., the Project Mercury-manned spaceflight that was scheduled for October was canceled late last week. It appears that NASA has no immediate plans to better Gordon Cooper's 22-orbit mission aboard *Faith 7* last month. Nonetheless, NASA is determined to make good on President Kennedy's 1961 vow to put a man on the moon before the close of the decade. It seems that the U.S. will be racing the Soviets every step of the way.

Valentina Tereshkova was the first woman in space. The U.S. has no female astronauts.

"Justice requires us to insure the blessings of liberty for all Americans and their posterity— not merely for reasons of economic efficiency, world diplomacy, and domestic tranquility, but above all, because it is right." — KENNEDY

Jun 19 KENNEDY SENDS CIVIL RIGHTS LEGISLATION TO CAPITOL HILL

WASHINGTON—President Kennedy today presented Congress with a mandate: Enact the Civil Rights Act of 1963, and do it before the congressional recess.

Claiming that the legislative branch has stalled the progress of Negro civil rights, Kennedy asserted that "the time has come for the Congress of the United States to join with the executive and judicial branches in making it clear to all that race has no place in American life or law."

The President outlined the key issues that he would like to see covered in this broad-based act. Namely, voting rights must be assured: Tests designed to block the vote must be abolished, and appropriate legal remedies must be employed when needed. Also, constitutionally mandated school desegregation must continue, with federal assistance if necessary. Equal access to public facilities, such as restaurants, hotels, and stores, must be guaranteed to all Americans.

Further, Kennedy called for expanded authority for the Commission on Civil Rights. He wants the commission to help advise those in both the public and private sectors and expedite compliance with civil rights issues. Finally, the President addressed the problem of Negro unemployment. He proposed a three-pronged attack consisting of job creation, training, and the eradication of racial discrimination in hiring and in the workplace.

Calling legislative action "imperative," Kennedy concluded: "Justice requires us to insure the blessings of liberty for all Americans and their posterity—not merely for reasons of economic efficiency, world diplomacy, and domestic tranquility, but above all, because it is right."

President Welcomes Civil Rights Leaders to White House

Jun 21

WASHINGTON—President Kennedy yesterday met with several prominent civil rights leaders at the White House. The issue on the table was the proposed "March on Washington for Jobs and Freedom."

March organizers are among the most prominent leaders of the civil rights movement, including A. Philip Randolph, Martin Luther King, Jr., James Farmer, Whitney Young, Roy Wilkins, and John Lewis. The event is scheduled for August 28, and organizers hope to draw 100,000 or more to the city.

Kennedy went into the meeting with grave reservations about the march, fearing that racial tensions could set off violence and rioting throughout the capital. However, event organizers successfully argued that the march would help further the President's agenda and passage of the Civil Rights Act. By the end of the meeting, the President had given reluctant approval to their plan.

JFK Moving Forward on Equal Rights Issues

Jun 22

WASHINGTON—President Kennedy today issued Executive Order 11114, entitled "Extending the Authority of the President's Committee on Equal Employment Opportunity." The order contains a provision that requires all contractors of federal projects to follow non-discriminatory employment practices. Otherwise, they will face such consequences as cancellation of their contract, withholding of payments, and legal action.

The executive order provides specific language that outlines the anti-discrimination policy that is to be followed by all contractors. Also, it requires that the policy be provided to all subcontractors as a condition of their employment.

Civil rights issues dominated the President's calendar today, as he also met with Martin Luther King and other movement leaders at the White House. The President expressed sincere concerns and misgivings about the massive march on Washington that civil rights leaders are organizing for August. Suggesting that "we want success in Congress, not just a big show at the Capitol," Kennedy appeared to be chiefly concerned with the security of the event, warning that rioting or other mayhem could seriously set back the movement.

Dr. King and his colleagues will not be deterred; they plan to hold the march with or without the President's support. Still, they seem to have successfully assuaged Kennedy's fears, as he is now said to be throwing his support behind the event.

19 Kennedy sends Israeli Prime Minister David Ben-Gurion a stern note expressing concern about Israel's nuclear weapons program. The President warns that failure to grant access by American inspectors to Israel's nuclear facilities could compromise U.S. support.

20 In *Lombard* v. *Louisiana*, the U.S. Supreme Court rules that governments cannot interfere with anti-segregation sit-in demonstrations. Also on this day, in *Wright* v. *Georgia*, the court invalidates breach-of-the-peace convictions of six black residents of Savannah, Georgia, for playing basketball in a whites-only park.

21 Despite heavy lobbying from the administration, American wheat farmers in a nationwide referendum surprisingly vote down a federal plan to control wheat crops.

22 After several political opponents claim that the administration plans to withdraw from Cuba, Kennedy tells reporters that abandoning Guantanamo Bay naval base "has never been considered."

23 NATO ministers agree to a U.S. and British proposal to set up an allied nuclear defense force drawn from 10 of NATO's 15 member nations. France does not object to the plan.

24 Worried about national unrest over the Birmingham riots, Attorney General Robert Kennedy meets privately with black intellectuals and artists, including Kenneth Clark, Clarence B. Jones, and Harry Belafonte.

Jun 23 — CATHOLICS HAVE A NEW LEADER IN POPE PAUL VI

VATICAN CITY—White smoke curled into the sky over the Vatican's Sistine Chapel yesterday, announcing that a new pontiff had been elected by the College of Cardinals.

After a 41-hour, five-ballot conclave, the 80-member college elected Giovanni Battista Cardinal Montini, archbishop of Milan. He will serve as the 262nd supreme pontiff, taking the name Pope Paul VI.

John Kennedy, the first Catholic president of the United States, offered his "heartiest congratulations" to the new pope and is looking forward to a formal introduction during a visit to Europe scheduled for July.

Pope Paul VI succeeds Pope John XXIII, who died earthier this month of complications from stomach cancer.

Jun 26 — JFK IN GERMANY: "I AM A BERLINER"

BERLIN—President Kennedy received a warm welcome in this divided German city today, as he visited Berlin on his final day of his state visit.

The Kennedy trip to Berlin came the day after he told a crowd in Frankfurt that "we will risk our cities to defend yours," underscoring America's continued commitment to security in postwar Germany.

In an unveiled swipe at the Soviet Union, the President referenced the quadripartite division of Berlin into American, French, British, and Soviet sectors. The President said today, "Real, lasting peace in Europe can never be assured as long as one German out of four is denied the elementary right of free men, and that is to make a free choice." The massive crowd roared its support.

The speech, delivered from the balcony of the Rathaus Schoneberg, also received an enthusiastic reception from the small number of East Berliners who were able to view the President from the other side of the wall.

White House Press Secretary Pierre Salinger said that Kennedy's reception in Berlin was "the greatest he has had anywhere."

> *"All free men, wherever they may live, are citizens of Berlin, and therefore, as a free man, I take pride in the words Ich bin ein Berliner [I am a Berliner]."* — KENNEDY

Kennedy's theme of freedom resonated strongly with the residents of West Berlin, a city that today is a virtual island surrounded by totalitarian East Germany. West Berliners live under the daily shadow of the possibility of occupation by a clearly failing state.

Kennedy's message, however, was clear, as he concluded by declaring his allegiance to the city: "All free men, wherever they may live, are citizens of Berlin, and therefore, as a free man, I take pride in the words *Ich bin ein Berliner* [I am a Berliner]."

The President will continue his European tour with a visit to Ireland.

HAILED IN BERLIN

President Kennedy's speech at the Berlin Wall on June 26, 1963, was one of the most stirring and memorable moments of his short presidency. It also was a high point of America's post-World War II popularity around the world. Not until Barack Obama would an American president be as revered abroad as John Kennedy was in the spring of 1963.

Kennedy's trip to West Berlin was designed, in part, to counter the sudden popularity of French President Charles de Gaulle, who was determined to forge an alliance between France and West Germany to counter Anglo-American influence. Kennedy was supposed to deliver a carefully worded ceremonial speech at a plaza near West Berlin's City Hall. But the sight of the infamous wall led Kennedy to put diplomacy aside. Instead, egged on by adoring crowds in West Berlin, he vented—about communism, about the wall, and about a system that treated ordinary citizens like prisoners.

In the most remembered line of the speech, he said that the proudest boast in the world of freedom was *"Ich bin ein Berliner"*—"I am a Berliner." The grammar wasn't perfect (the word *ein* was unnecessary), but the crowd roared its approval. On a platform within sight of the wall, he stated that those who didn't understand the struggle between East and West need only come to Berlin. Freedom was not perfect, he said, but the West didn't have to build a wall to keep its people from escaping.

The speech was raw and impolitic. But it made Kennedy a hero in a nation that had been America's enemy fewer than 20 years earlier.

25 Despite worries about a growing national debt, the administration believes the economy is improving. Kennedy plans to press for tax reform up to the last days of the congressional session.

26 African American writer James Baldwin calls the recent meeting between Robert Kennedy and black intellectuals "heated but significant." The problem, Baldwin says, is that RFK "does not understand the extent of growing racial strife" in the North.

27 The U.S. Supreme Court rules that Memphis, Tennessee, officials must move quickly to integrate the city's schools, parks, and playgrounds.

28 Administration officials work to dissuade Indonesian President Sukarno from moving to nationalize foreign oil companies, two of which are operated by U.S. companies.

29 President Kennedy celebrates his 46th birthday. He also invites business leaders to come to the White House soon to discuss problems of equal employment and public facilities access by minorities.

30 Accompanied by his son, the President observes Memorial Day by placing a wreath at the Tomb of the Unknowns in Arlington National Cemetery.

31 The Joint Chiefs of Staff evaluate a report prepared earlier in May by Admiral Harry Felt, commander-in-chief of U.S. Pacific forces. Felt is skeptical that Vietnam will be stable enough by the end of 1965 for a hoped-for withdrawal of American forces.

Kennedy was welcomed in Ireland as if he were a returning son. He hopes to return to the country in the spring of 1964.

Jun 30 JFK CONCLUDES POIGNANT TRIP TO THE EMERALD ISLE

WASHINGTON—President Kennedy has returned home after an emotional visit to Ireland. As the first Irish Catholic president of the United States, Kennedy was afforded a rousing welcome at every stop across the Emerald Isle. It was the first visit to Ireland by a sitting U.S. president.

Along with sisters Jean Kennedy Smith and Eunice Kennedy Shriver, the President attended a reunion at the family homestead in Dunganstown, County Wexford, enjoyed tea, and had the opportunity to meet some of his cousins.

He also delivered a warm-hearted address in Dublin's Leinster House before a joint session of the Irish Parliament. He told of the bravery of the Irish Brigade at the Battle of Fredericksburg during the American Civil War, and he presented his hosts with one of the flags the brigade carried into battle that day.

The President spoke at length about the special bond between Ireland and America, as well as Ireland's changing role as a peaceful and prosperous nation. "I sincerely believe," Kennedy said, "that your future is as promising as your past is proud…. Ireland's hour has come."

Yesterday, shortly before departing from the airport in Shannon, Kennedy briefly said his goodbyes, adding, "I am going to come back and see old Shannon's face again, and I am taking, as I go back to America, all of you with me."

Undoubtedly, this was one of the more pleasurable and poignant state visits ever embarked upon by an American president.

WELCOMED IN IRELAND

John Kennedy was certainly not the first Irish American to become president. Andrew Jackson, the son of Irish immigrants, holds that title. Many others had Irish blood, but they had descended from Ireland's Protestant minority, many of whom descended from British stock. Kennedy, as a Catholic, was perceived to be more authentically Irish.

Although he was several generations removed from the immigrant experience—his paternal great-grandparents had fled the famine in Ireland in 1849—Kennedy was well aware of his heritage. So, when aides began planning a tour of Europe in 1963, JFK insisted that they include a visit to Ireland. Kennedy arrived in Ireland on June 26, 1963, and traveled to the old Kennedy homestead near New Ross, County Wexford. He was greeted by a distant cousin, Mary Kennedy Ryan, who offered the President—she called him "Cousin Jack"—a cup of tea.

The presidential homecoming tour moved to Dublin, where Kennedy was greeted by the aging Irish president, Eamon de Valera, who had been born in New York. The Irish in Ireland shared Irish Americans' deep pride in Kennedy's election, and the crowds in Dublin cheered him as a returning hero. De Valera referred to Kennedy as a "distinguished scion of our race."

Kennedy relished the experience, and as he left, made a promise. He would return, he said, in the spring of '64.

Jul 2 KENNEDY MEETS THE POPE

VATICAN CITY—The first Roman Catholic president of the United States met with the new Pope, Paul VI, at the Vatican today. The historic meeting took place less than two weeks after the former Cardinal Giovanni Battista Montini took over as the head of the Catholic Church.

In his welcoming address to the President, the Pope touched on several issues, including America's sacrifices and contributions to world peace and space exploration. Kennedy, notably, failed to kiss the Pope's ring, as is customary for Catholics.

Kennedy is the third American president to sit down with a pope, following Woodrow Wilson's 1919 meeting with Pope Benedict XV and Dwight Eisenhower's 1959 meeting with Pope John XXIII.

Pope Paul VI meets Kennedy just two days after his coronation.

June

1 NAACP official Medgar Evers telegrams President Kennedy urging a Justice Department investigation into the treatment of jailed black protesters, including children, by Jackson, Mississippi, police.

2 Governor Wallace says he still plans to block the integration of the University of Alabama despite a federal injunction. Wallace says the state cannot guarantee the safety of two black students who plan to enroll.

3 After Pope John XXIII dies in Rome at age 81, President Kennedy says that the Pope's "wisdom, compassion, and kindly strength have bequeathed humanity a new legacy of purpose and courage for the future."

4 The President orders a review of federal construction projects to ensure that contractors do not practice hiring discrimination.

5 JFK leaves Washington for another tour through the West, including Colorado, California, and Texas. He tells graduates at the Air Force Academy in Colorado Springs, Colorado, that the U.S. plans to build a supersonic transport plane for commercial use.

6 San Diego State College confers an honorary degree on Kennedy, who tells graduates the country "must recognize that segregation in education—and I mean de facto segregation in the North as well as the proclaimed segregation in the South—brings with it serious handicaps to a large proportion of the population."

7 In California, the President reviews naval weaponry at the China Lake Station before attending a Democratic Party fundraising event in the evening.

Jul 6 KENNEDY SUMS UP HIS EUROPEAN TRIP

WASHINGTON—In a message broadcast yesterday evening, President Kennedy asserted about his recent trip overseas: "Today I can report an even deeper tie between the people of Europe and the people of the United States."

Calling his trip a "moving experience," Kennedy reported: "I heard expressions of confidence in the United States from the leaders of Germany and England, Italy and Ireland. And I felt the admiration and affection that their people had for the people of the United States."

All in all, it was a feel-good message for Americans, most of whom still recall the sacrifices U.S. citizens made on Europe's behalf just a generation ago, and the sacrifices that continue to be made by American men and women in uniform who remain stationed in Europe.

The President said that Europe itself is a changed continent—much different than the Europe that found itself at the center of two global wars over a 40-year span. In conclusion, Kennedy expressed much hope and optimism that Europe and the United States can move forward in peace.

Jul 8 KENNEDY ADMINISTRATION STRENGTHENS CUBAN EMBARGO

WASHINGTON—The Kennedy administration has further tightened the economic noose around the neck of the Castro regime. Issuing the Cuban Assets Control Regulations in response to the Cuban government's cooperation with the Soviets, the government has frozen all Cuban assets in the United States.

The embargo was officially launched in February 1962 in the form of trade restrictions. Travel restrictions, enacted in February of this year, followed.

The basis for the embargo is found in a 1917 federal law, the Trading with the Enemy Act, which was passed in the wake of the First World War.

Relations with Castro's Cuba, precarious from the outset, reached a new low last October when the discovery of Russian missile bases on the island triggered a tense, 13-day standoff between Kennedy and Soviet Premier Khrushchev. The crisis ended with a Soviet withdrawal from Cuba and U.S. concessions with missiles based in Turkey. The two superpowers came precariously close to a nuclear confrontation during the course of the standoff.

Jul 24 JFK APPEALS TO CONGRESS ON IMMIGRATION QUOTAS

WASHINGTON—President Kennedy sent a letter to Capitol Hill leaders yesterday in an effort to encourage Congress to revise U.S. immigration laws.

The letter, addressed to Senate President Lyndon Johnson and House Speaker John McCormack, specifically addresses the current system of quotas, whereby prospective immigrants' nation of origin determines how many will be admitted in a given year.

The letter asserts that the "use of a national origins system is without basis in either logic or reason. It neither satisfies a national need nor accomplishes an international purpose. In an age of interdependence among nations, such a system is an anachronism, for it discriminates among applicants for admission into the United States on the basis of accident of birth."

For that reason, Kennedy is seeking a complete restructuring of the system. He wants to eliminate the flaw that has resulted in lengthy waits for certain nationals while quotas allocated to some countries go unused.

The President recommends a new standard, one that prioritizes an individual's skill set and his ability to contribute positively to the national welfare, as well as any family relationship with existing American citizens or resident aliens.

LOOKING AHEAD TO 1964

A specter haunted John Kennedy as he contemplated his reelection campaign in 1964. The specter's name was Nelson Rockefeller, the successful Republican governor of New York. Polls in 1963 showed that Rockefeller would be the Republican Party's strongest candidate against Kennedy. Although the same polls showed Kennedy beating Rockefeller, JFK was uneasy about the prospect of facing the young, popular, and wealthy New Yorker.

Adding to the President's anxiety were polls that showed significant slippage in his popularity with white voters as civil rights became a more visible issue. Black voters seemed ambivalent about the Kennedy, but white Southerners fled his camp in droves.

Rockefeller's potentially tough challenge evaporated when the governor divorced his wife in 1962 and the following spring married Margaretta "Happy" Murphy only a month after she had divorced her husband, a close friend of Rockefeller's. Kennedy turned his attention to another prominent Republican governor, George W. Romney

Rockefeller (left), Goldwater (right)

of Michigan. Romney, however, was new to politics, and would not run for president until 1968.

Kennedy hoped Republicans would nominate Senator Barry Goldwater of Arizona. JFK believed the senator was too far to the right for most voters. Kennedy joked that if the Republicans went with Goldwater, there would be no need to campaign in 1964. He encouraged other Democrats to speak well of Goldwater to build up his credibility in the press.

For the reelection campaign, JFK told advisers that he wanted to emphasize peace and prosperity as his reelection theme. It was, he believed, a winning combination.

8 The President plans to sell NBC the television rights to his Pulitzer Prize-winning book, *Profiles in Courage*, and donate the proceeds to charity.

9 After flying to Hawaii, Kennedy urges the U.S. Conference of Mayors to support the "nationwide drive for full equality."

10 Kennedy signs the Equal Pay Act, which requires most employers to pay women equal pay for equal work.

11 Governor Wallace defies a presidential order delivered by Assistant Attorney General Nicholas Katzenbach designed to allow integration of the University of Alabama. Kennedy federalizes the Alabama National Guard and prevents Wallace from blocking the enrollment of two black students. In a prime-time national broadcast, JFK calls segregation a moral issue not confined to the South.

12 Just hours after Kennedy's televised speech on segregation, NAACP Field Secretary Medgar Evers is murdered in Jackson, Mississippi.

13 Kennedy holds a meeting on pending civil rights legislation with former President Truman, members of Congress, and nearly 300 union leaders including AFL-CIO President George Meany.

14 Worldwide reaction builds after a horrific news photo of Vietnamese Buddhist monk Thich Qaung Duc burning himself to death to protest religious persecution by the Diem regime.

15 Kennedy telegrams Governor Wallace to insist that the governor use state police to maintain order in Tuscaloosa, Alabama, after the administration withdraws federal troops from the city.

Emphasizing the importance of freedom, JFK told the boys that the U.S. "stands on guard all the way from Berlin to Saigon."

Jul 24 PRESIDENT WELCOMES AMERICAN LEGION DELEGATES

WASHINGTON—President Kennedy this morning welcomed the delegates of the American Legion Boys Nation to the White House Flower Garden. Along with the President, the young men were greeted by members of the Joint Chiefs of Staff, including Admiral Anderson, head of the Navy; General Wheeler, head of the Army; General LeMay, head of the Air Force; and General Shoup, head of the Marine Corps.

In his remarks, Kennedy congratulated Richard Stratton, the newly elected president of Boys Nation. Kennedy pointed out some of the trees planted by presidents John Adams and Andrew Jackson, and he once again mentioned the pride and admiration he felt for and toward America on his recent trip through Europe. Kennedy also expressed his admiration for the good works of the American Legion. "No group could be more appropriately visiting here now," he said. "We want you to feel very much at home."

Jul 24 CASTRO'S GOVERNMENT SEIZES AMERICAN EMBASSY

HAVANA—The Cuban government today released a decree expropriating the building and grounds of the U.S. Embassy in Havana. The Cubans took this action in retaliation for the U.S. government's freezing of Cuban assets earlier this month.

The decree, signed by Fidel Castro and two other senior members of his administration, is said to include the building on Havana's Malecon Drive as well as its contents. The embassy has been occupied by the Swiss since the 1961 U.S.-Cuba break in diplomatic relations. On that occasion, the Cubans assaulted the building, using a ball-and-crane assembly to knock an American eagle from the roof of the structure. The Castro administration has asked the Swiss to evacuate the property immediately.

This is thought to be the first case of a host nation seizing outright the embassy of another.

> *"Let us, if we can, step back from the shadows of war and seek out the way of peace."*
>
> *KENNEDY*

JFK still hopes for complete nuclear disarmament.

Jul 26 A NUCLEAR PEACE PLAN
U.S., U.K., Soviets Agree on Test-Ban Treaty

WASHINGTON—Speaking to the nation from the Oval Office this evening, President Kennedy announced an agreement on a nuclear weapons test-ban treaty. The President noted that it has been 18 years since nuclear weapons changed the face of warfare. Since then, he said, "each increase of tension has produced an increase of arms; each increase of arms has produced an increase of tension." For the first time, it seems, peace-loving people have reason to hope that this soon may change.

"Yesterday a shaft of light cut into the darkness," Kennedy said. On July 25, negotiations were concluded on a treaty that will ban all nuclear testing in the atmosphere, outer space, and under water. Principal authors and likely initial signatories include the United States, Great Britain, and the Soviet Union. The treaty, though somewhat limited, is the achievement of a major goal of President Kennedy's ever since he first took office.

The treaty does not preclude underground testing, and it allows for any nation to withdraw if it feels that its national interests are jeopardized. But, significantly, it will go a long way toward preventing the kind of atmospheric mushroom clouds that have so contaminated areas in the South Pacific and sent unknown amounts of radioactive fallout into the global environment. A comprehensive treaty banning all testing, along with complete disarmament, remains the ultimate, if lofty, goal. It remains out of reach for the foreseeable future, as the Soviets are unwilling to accept the inspections necessary to effectively ban all testing.

In conclusion, Kennedy told the American people that peace is within reach, and that the time to take action to achieve that peace is now. "Let us, if we can, step back from the shadows of war and seek out the way of peace," he said. "And if that journey is a thousand miles, or even more, let history record that we, in this land, at this time, took the first step."

June

16 The Russian space program records another notable first by launching into space the first female cosmonaut, Valentina Tereshkova.

17 The U.S. Supreme Court stuns religious conservatives in the country by ruling 8-1 that school-sponsored Bible reading in public schools is unconstitutional.

18 The President talks about his civil rights program at the White House with governors from Maryland, Virginia, Kentucky, Ohio, Pennsylvania, New Mexico, Colorado, and Oregon.

19 Kennedy tells Congress that passage of proposed civil rights legislation is "imperative" even if it requires extending the legislative session. The bill would mandate equal access to hotels, restaurants, and other facilities open to the public, and allow federal suits aimed at desegregating public schools.

20 In a meeting with key civil rights leaders, Kennedy approves their plan for a march on Washington to demand education and employment reforms.

21 French government sources indicate that President de Gaulle will withdraw French warships from the NATO fleet.

22 By executive order, Kennedy authorizes the withholding of federal funds from construction firms that practice racial discrimination. Also on this day, in a meeting with the vice president as well as Martin Luther King, Jr., and other civil rights leaders, Kennedy cautions against demonstrations that may work against passage of civil rights legislation.

Jul 26 DEFENSE DEPARTMENT ISSUES ANTI-DISCRIMINATION POLICY

WASHINGTON—The Department of Defense, under Secretary Robert McNamara, today issued Directive 5120.36 to address racial discrimination in military communities.

The new policy asserts that "every military commander has the responsibility to oppose discriminatory practices affecting his men and their dependents and to foster equal opportunity for them, not only in areas under his immediate control, but also in nearby communities where they may live or gather in off-duty hours."

For the first time, it is no longer enough that the military is integrated (a directive issued by President Truman in July 1948). This order empowers commanding officers to enforce a boycott against off-base businesses or organizations that discriminate. By forbidding military personnel and their substantial purchasing power from patronizing discriminating businesses, base commanders can foster racial inclusion throughout their communities.

NUCLEAR PEACE

From the very beginning of his administration, President Kennedy sought to persuade the Soviet Union to join the United States in banning tests of nuclear weaponry. He once described himself as a "great anti-tester," but he found a great skeptic in Soviet Premier Nikita Khrushchev, who believed JFK supported a ban on testing only because the U.S. was ahead of the Soviets in nuclear weaponry.

Both sides had stopped testing nuclear weapons in 1958, recognizing that they were unpopular and environmentally destructive. Kennedy first raised the possibility of a formal ban on nuclear testing at his summit meeting with Khrushchev in Vienna in 1961. While the Soviet leader told JFK in Vienna that he would not be the first to resume testing, the Soviets did just that on September 1, 1961, with the first of a series of nuclear explosions. "The bastards!" Kennedy said when aides told him of the Soviet detonations.

To counter the Soviet tests, the U.S. tested 40 nuclear weapons from April to September 1962. But Kennedy never gave up hope that he could bring Khrushchev to the bargaining table. After the Cuban missile crisis in October 1962, both sides stepped away from the politics of confrontation. After months of negotiation, Washington and Moscow agreed, in a treaty signed on July 26, 1963, to outlaw nuclear testing in the atmosphere, in outer space, and under the oceans. The treaty did not cover underground testing, which was common, but it marked an important victory for JFK—and for peace.

Left to right: Senators William Fulbright and Hubert Humphrey toast the signing of the treaty with UN Secretary General U Thant and Soviet Premier Nikita Khrushchev.

WORLD'S NUCLEAR POWERS SIGN TEST-BAN TREATY

Aug 5

Moscow—Representatives of the United States, the Soviet Union, and the United Kingdom met in Moscow today to sign the Nuclear Test Ban Treaty. Formally known as the Treaty Banning Nuclear Weapon Tests in the Atmosphere, in Outer Space, and Under Water, it expressly forbids nuclear test detonations above ground. The agreement is one that President Kennedy regards as a major achievement, and one of which he spoke hopefully earlier this year in a commencement address at American University.

The treaty, as written, twice underscores the fact that the signatories' ultimate goal is "the speediest possible achievement of an agreement on general and complete disarmament." Kennedy has been clear that this Nuclear Test Ban Treaty, while an important step toward disarmament, remains a means to an end.

In Article I, the treaty identifies the litmus test for an unacceptable detonation as any that "causes radioactive debris to be present outside the territorial limits of the State under whose jurisdiction or control such explosion is conducted." The rest of the articles cover technicalities such as ratification, amendments, and future signatories.

The treaty will take effect as soon as it is delivered to and ratified by President Kennedy, Prime Minister Macmillan, and Premier Khrushchev, likely sometime this fall.

John Kennedy greets his wife shortly after the death of their son.

Aug 10 KENNEDYS MOURN THE DEATH OF NEWBORN BABY

BOSTON—Patrick Bouvier Kennedy, the fourth child and second son of President and Mrs. Kennedy, lost his battle for life yesterday in Boston Children's Hospital.

Mrs. Kennedy underwent an emergency cesarean section on the 7th, at the Otis Air Force Base Hospital in Falmouth, Massachusetts. The infant, born more than five weeks prematurely, was diagnosed with hyaline membrane disease. The condition, not uncommon in premature infants, is characterized by respiratory distress of varying severity.

This is the second time that the President and First Lady have suffered the heartbreak of burying a child. Mrs. Kennedy's first pregnancy ended with the stillbirth of a daughter, Arabella, seven years ago this month. The family plans to hold a private funeral for Patrick today, in the chapel of Richard Cardinal Cushing, archbishop of Boston.

LOSS OF A SON

First Lady Jacqueline Kennedy became pregnant in early 1963, and in late summer of that year, the country joined the First Family in anticipation of a new arrival. But in early August, Jackie went into labor five weeks early while on vacation on Cape Cod. Concern was immediate, for Jackie had suffered a late-stage miscarriage in 1956.

Doctors delivered Patrick Bouvier Kennedy on August 7 by Caesarean section. He weighed four pounds, 10 ounces, but size was not the issue. The newborn had a life-threatening lung disease. President Kennedy was in Washington on August 7, but he rushed to Cape Cod to be with his wife and son.

Gravely ill, the baby was taken to Boston, where doctors attempted to clear his lungs. Their efforts were in vain. Patrick died on August 9. The baby was buried the following day, after his father gripped the child's little white coffin during a private funeral mass conducted by Cardinal Richard Cushing, the Roman Catholic archbishop of Boston. The grieving First Lady remained hospitalized during the mass and burial.

Friends and aides noticed that Patrick's death brought Jack and Jackie together. They seemed more affectionate with each other in the weeks afterward, during what proved to be the final months of the President's life. Patrick Kennedy's body was reburied in Arlington National Cemetery after his father died. Jackie would never overcome the trauma of losing her son and husband within the span of 15 weeks.

Buddhists stage a sit-down protest in Saigon.

Aug 22
SOUTH VIETNAMESE ARMY ATTACKS BUDDHIST PAGODAS

SAIGON—Special-forces soldiers with the Army of the Republic of Vietnam launched a series of raids against Buddhist pagodas in South Vietnam shortly after midnight yesterday.

The violent, well-coordinated attacks were especially severe in the cities of Saigon and Hue. Troops stormed the pagodas, most notably Xa Loi, the largest pagoda in Saigon, with firearms and explosives. Monks were beaten, religious objects were destroyed, and works of art were stolen. Even the miraculously intact heart of the recently self-immolated monk, Thich Quang Duc, was carried off in the plunder.

Monks and nuns, tipped off in advance about the impending raids, barricaded themselves inside their rooms. The fierce attacks were slowed, but not stopped, by their efforts. In the end, unknown hundreds lay dead, and hundreds more were injured. Some took refuge in the USAID compound adjacent to Xa Loi, while many others sought asylum at the U.S. Embassy.

Tensions between the Catholic government and Buddhist majority have long run high in South Vietnam. The belligerent act is troubling for the Kennedy administration, which is supporting the Republic of Vietnam in its war against Communist Vietcong insurgents.

June 1963

30 In England, JFK and British Prime Minister Macmillan meet for two days. They issue a statement that affirms their desire for a nuclear test-ban treaty with the Soviets.

July

1 Kennedy travels to Rome for meetings with Italian President Antonio Segni and Premier Giovanni Leone on NATO and economic issues. JFK tells Italian officials that the United States "will regard any threat to your peace and freedom as a threat to our own."

2 At the Vatican, Pope Paul VI welcomes President Kennedy, the first Roman Catholic U.S. president and third overall to meet with a head of the Catholic Church.

3 Reports circulate that some American officials would prefer a different leader in South Vietnam than embattled President Diem.

4 U.S. diplomats view with skepticism an offer from Moscow to sign a nuclear test-ban treaty in conjunction with a new East-West nonaggression treaty. It is seen by some as a Soviet attempt to drive a wedge between U.S. and European allies.

5 After his 10-day trip to Europe, the President uses a recorded TV and radio message to tell Americans that the U.S. and Western Europe have strengthened their alliance.

6 Government statistics reveal a mixed economic picture: Total jobs surpass 70 million for the first time ever, but unemployment among teens is 16 percent and overall unemployment is 5.7 percent.

Martin Luther King, Jr., said he dreams of the day when his children will be judged not "by the color of their skin but by the content of their character."

Aug 29 KING'S SPEECH HIGHLIGHTS MARCH ON WASHINGTON

WASHINGTON—By almost any account, yesterday's March on Washington for Jobs and Freedom was a tremendous success. A crowd estimated at a quarter of a million people descended on the National Mall virtually without incident. Witnesses claim that the massive crowd was so orderly that the 5,000 officers and guardsmen hired to keep the peace had little to do. The stirring keynote speech by civil rights leader Martin Luther King will long be remembered by Americans of all races.

When first apprised of plans for the March, President Kennedy was skeptical. Fearing an outbreak of violence in these racially charged times, Kennedy initially encouraged organizers to scuttle their plans. However, they successfully convinced the President that the event would remain peaceful and would summon support for the civil rights bill that Kennedy was eager to pass before the expiration of his first term.

What mention there was of the bill itself, however, was somewhat negative. More than one speaker suggested that Kennedy's bill was too watered-down and incomplete to bring about meaningful change. Most vocal was John Lewis, chair of the Student Nonviolent Coordinating Committee, who claimed the bill was "too little and too late."

Following the march, several civil rights leaders proceeded to the White House and met with President Kennedy. Vice President Lyndon Johnson, Secretary of Labor Willard Wirtz, and Burke Marshall, the chief of the administration's Civil Rights Division, were also in attendance.

Though President Kennedy let the focus of the day remain on Dr. King and the other speakers, he did issue a statement that "the cause of 20,000,000 negroes has been advanced."

KENNEDY AND KING

During the 1960 presidential campaign, Richard Nixon held high hopes of winning a sizeable portion of the black vote. But when a young civil rights leader named Dr. Martin Luther King, Jr., was arrested in Atlanta during a protest against segregated lunch counters, Nixon refused to defend King's actions. Conversely, John Kennedy called King's wife, Coretta, to express his sympathy. King's father and namesake, a formidable figure in his own right, publicly switched his support from Nixon to Kennedy.

King cast a large shadow over Kennedy's presidency. The President met with King in the White House in late April 1961, just after the Bay of Pigs fiasco. The meeting was carefully choreographed so that it seemed accidental: Kennedy knew that King was meeting with an aide, Harris Wofford, and King knew that the President knew. Kennedy happened to "stop by" Wofford's office, so the two men met face to face for first time since Kennedy's election.

For most of his presidency, John Kennedy saw civil rights as a distraction from the struggle with the Soviet Union. But as racial tensions grew in 1963, Kennedy defended King against attacks from southern politicians, including the accusation that King was a Communist sympathizer. And while JFK feared that the giant civil rights march on Washington in 1963 might exacerbate tensions, he recognized the brilliance of King's famous speech that day. When the rally was over, King went to the White House to meet JFK—this time officially. As Kennedy shook King's hand, he said, "I have a dream."

Aug 29 JFK BLOCKS RAIL STRIKE

WASHINGTON—The President today took action to prevent a threatened national railroad strike. He signed legislation designed to resolve the labor dispute shortly after the bill passed both houses of Congress.

The law calls for an impartial arbitration board to address the most contentious issues in the dispute. It also prohibits a walkout for 180 days while both sides make a good-faith effort to come to terms.

One of the key issues on the table is the elimination of yard and freight diesel firemen, a move supported by management and emphatically opposed by labor. The railroads have been trying to effect this change since early 1959, suggesting it was up to management to determine when it should be necessary to employ diesel firemen.

Several arbitration boards have been instated in the past several years, and all have found for management. However, H. E. Gilbert, president of the Brotherhood of Local Firemen and Enginemen, has refused to accept their findings.

Aug 30 WASHINGTON-MOSCOW HOTLINE NOW CONNECTED

WASHINGTON—The long-awaited "hot line" between Washington and Moscow was pressed into service today. The concept rose from the recognition that better communication between the superpowers could greatly reduce the chance of accidental nuclear war.

Both the United States and the Soviet Union have been actively pursuing safeguards against accidental war since the 1950s, but it was last year's Cuban missile crisis that underscored the need for an instant and unambiguous channel of communication. This past June, U.S. and Soviet officials met in Geneva and signed the Memorandum of Understanding Regarding the Establishment of a Direct Communication Link.

Unlike the conjured image of a red telephone, the actual hot line is in fact comprised of two terminals with teletype capabilities and a telegraph circuit. The line is routed from Washington to Moscow via London, Copenhagen, Stockholm, and Helsinki.

The hot line agreement is the first step in bilateral efforts to relieve tensions between the U.S. and the Soviet Union. It is hoped that this cooperation will manifest itself in further arms controls the next time the superpowers sit down at the bargaining table.

Sept 2 PRESIDENT ANALYZES VIETNAM SITUATION IN CRONKITE INTERVIEW

HYANNIS PORT, MASS.—Sitting down with television journalist Walter Cronkite, President Kennedy today discussed the war in Vietnam. The President provided a sobering assessment of the issues faced by the United States as it strives to support the Vietnamese in their struggle against communism.

Kennedy was clear that while the U.S. intends to continue its support of Vietnam and President Ngo Dinh Diem, the war can be won only if the Vietnamese people support their government. In fact, Kennedy asserted, "I don't think that unless a greater effort is made by the government to win popular support that the war can be won out there."

Rather than trying to connect with the people and shore up the badly needed popular support, the Catholic government has launched a series of violent attacks against Vietnam's Buddhist community. Kennedy suggested that without a dramatic shift in policy, and perhaps personnel, the government will continue to alienate the people and jeopardize the outcome of this struggle.

"I don't think that unless a greater effort is made by the [South Vietnamese] government to win popular support that the war can be won out there." —KENNEDY

17 JFK tells reporters that normal relations with Cuba will be impossible as long as the island functions as a "Soviet satellite."

18 The President proposes a new tax on foreign securities bought by Americans. It is part of the administration's attempt to reduce the U.S. deficit in balance of payments.

19 After Peru's military seizes power in Lima, the United States stops economic aid and suspends diplomatic relations with the country.

20 In a 90-minute address broadcast throughout Eastern Europe and watched with interest by Western diplomats, Khrushchev expresses hope for a partial nuclear testing agreement.

21 After learning that his negotiators have reached a tentative deal on nuclear testing, Kennedy flies back early from a vacation in Massachusetts to prepare for a busy schedule at the White House.

22 The President meets with union and railroad officials before asking Congress to empower the Interstate Commerce Commission to resolve the railroad work rules, which are at the heart of the labor dispute.

23 The White House sends a message to Congress in which it proposes an end within five years to the complex quota system that controls immigration to the United States.

24 At the White House, Kennedy greets 100 young delegates to the American Legion Boys Nation convention. Among the teenagers who shake hands with JFK is future president Bill Clinton.

Kennedy on Vietnam: "Forty-seven Americans have been killed in combat with the enemy, but this is a very important struggle even though it is far away."

Sept 9 KENNEDY OPENS UP ABOUT VIETNAM

WASHINGTON—President Kennedy appeared this evening on NBC's *Huntley-Brinkley Report*. The interview, conducted earlier in the day by correspondents Chet Huntley and David Brinkley at the Oval Office, touched on a number of different issues. The President discussed the proposed tax cuts to civil rights to the upcoming United Nations visit by Yugoslavian dictator Josef Tito. However, as is often the case these days, the primary issue on the table was Vietnam.

The President conceded that the way South Vietnam's government has handled the country's Buddhist population has, in recent months, led to some deterioration in U.S.-South Vietnamese relations. Nonetheless, Kennedy seems to feel that the situation needs to be given some time, and that the U.S. needs to influence South Vietnam's government to act in a way that will help regain the support of the people. However, that "influence" should not be financial. "I don't think that would be helpful at this time," Kennedy asserted. "If you reduce your aid, it is possible you could have some effect upon the government structure there."

Asked by Brinkley if he does, in fact, believe in the "domino theory"—that if one country fell under the influence of communism, its neighboring countries would follow—Kennedy unequivocally stated that he does. In fact, he made it clear that the theory will likely inform his decisions on Vietnam. "I believe it," Kennedy replied. "I think that the struggle is close enough. China is so large, looms so high just beyond the frontiers, that if South Vietnam went, it would not only give them an improved geographic position for a guerrilla assault on Malaya, but would also give the impression that the wave of the future in Southeast Asia was China and the Communists. So I believe it."

Nevertheless, the President said that the United States has to ward against imposing its will on Southeast Asian countries. "They have their own interest, their own personalities, their own tradition," Kennedy said. "We can't make everyone in our image, and there are a good many people who don't want to go in our image."

Kennedy was clear, though, that Americans need to guard against impatience with the situation in Southeast Asia. "I think we should stay," he said. "We should use our influence in as an effective way as we can, but we should not withdraw."

Brinkley asked President Kennedy if he would enlighten them as to what the CIA was up to in South Vietnam, to which the President offered a one-word reply: "No."

"I think we should stay. We should use our influence in as an effective way as we can, but we should not withdraw."

—KENNEDY, REFERRING TO U.S. MILITARY PRESENCE IN SOUTHEAST ASIA

Sept 10 PRESIDENT FEDERALIZES THE ALABAMA GUARD

WASHINGTON—President Kennedy today issued Executive Order No. 11118, entitled Assistance for Removal of Unlawful Obstructions of Justice in the State of Alabama. The proclamation was issued to force segregationist governor George Wallace to comply with federal regulations that mandate desegregation in schools.

The order authorizes the secretary of defense to federalize Alabama's Army and Air National Guard (and utilize other U.S. troops as needed) to help Alabama's Negro students enroll and gain access to desegregated schools. In addition, the troops are charged with preventing any violent protests or assaults that might result from this effort.

Governor Wallace has long been an opponent of Negro rights. He was elected to his office in a landslide victory last year following a campaign platform of states' rights and segregation. His "segregation now, segregation forever" inaugural speech, delivered this past January, earned him a national reputation. He made national news again in June when he physically blocked the door of the University of Alabama, preventing two Negro students from entering the building.

Governor Wallace is clearly determined to swim against the tide. However, it seems that President Kennedy is equally determined to use all resources to ensure that the governor complies with federal law, whether he agrees with it or not.

Sept 10 JFK GIVES MARRIED MEN DRAFT DEFERMENT

WASHINGTON—President Kennedy today signed Executive Order 11119, Amending the Selective Service Regulations. The amendment designates married men as a separate subcategory of draftee, with the selection of unmarried men taking precedence. Though not ironclad, the amendment effectively serves as a deferment for married men.

Though the wartime draft was established during the Civil War, the first peacetime draft began with President Franklin Roosevelt's signing of the Selective Service and Training Act in 1940. The Selective Service was established as an independent federal agency that same year.

The draft impacts young men ages 18.5 to 26. They are called up based on age, with the oldest getting selected first.

25 After years of off-and-on talks, scores of nuclear detonations, and doubts that any testing treaty is possible, the United States, Britain, and the Soviet Union initial a treaty that bans atmospheric, underwater, and outer space testing of nuclear weapons.

26 Kennedy speaks to the nation on television about the significance of the test-ban treaty. He calls it a step toward peace but cautions that it should not be considered a cure-all for war.

27 Inflation worries preoccupy the White House after a surge in prices for sugar and cigarettes raise the Consumer Price Index to a new record.

28 Undersecretary of State W. Averell Harriman briefs President Kennedy on the just-concluded nuclear test-ban talks. Initial signs indicate that Americans favor ratification of the treaty.

29 The Kennedys gather on Cape Cod for a day of swimming and sailing to celebrate Jacqueline Kennedy's 34th birthday.

30 A mass demonstration against the Catholic-dominated Diem government draws approximately 60,000 Buddhist protesters.

31 At a meeting with top U.S. nuclear scientists, Kennedy says he is pleased by the nuclear testing treaty. However, he fears that future detonations by China or other countries could soon force the United States to resume its own program.

Bob Hope thanked the President for his medal and kept everyone in stitches with a series of wisecracks.

Sept 11 COMEDIAN HOPE HONORED IN WHITE HOUSE CEREMONY

WASHINGTON—In a lighthearted Rose Garden ceremony today, comedian Bob Hope received the Congressional Gold Medal for his many years of service—specifically, entertaining American troops. President Kennedy presented the award before some 100 members of Congress and other distinguished guests.

With the medal's presentation, Kennedy acknowledged the "great affection that all of us hold for you." He praised Hope for "so many years going so many places to entertain the sons, daughters, brothers, and sisters of Americans who were very far from home."

Predictably, Hope's gracious response was laced with good humor. He accepted the honor while noting that "there is only one sobering thought: I received this for going outside the country. I think they are trying to tell me something."

Hope added: "I actually don't like to tell jokes about a thing like this because it is one of the nicest things that has ever happened to me, and I feel very humble.... I am thrilled that you invited all the senators and congressmen up here with us. For awhile it looked like a congressional investigation, but I really appreciate this very much."

Sept 16 — FOUR GIRLS DIE IN BIRMINGHAM BOMBING

BIRMINGHAM—A cowardly bomb attack on Birmingham's 16th Street Baptist Church claimed the lives of four Negro girls yesterday, and two more young people were killed in the ensuing rioting. Civil rights leaders (including Dr. Martin Luther King), Burke Marshall (the Kennedy administration's civil rights liaison), and some two dozen FBI agents have rushed to the chaotic city.

The four girls who died were Denise McNair, 11; Carole Robinson, 14; Addie Mae Collins, 14; and Cynthia Diane Wesley, 14. They were in the middle of their Sunday school classes when the wall to their classroom blew in due to the force of the blast. Distraught citizens poured into Birmingham's streets, and racial clashes, riots, and fires led to untold property damage. Two Negro boys, ages 13 and 16, were killed.

Dr. King wired President Kennedy before traveling to Birmingham for emergency meetings with Dr. Fred Shuttlesworth. King told the President he intended to issue a plea for a nonviolent response to the disaster. Nevertheless, he pointedly said that unless the federal government steps in, there would be "in Birmingham and Alabama the worst racial holocaust this nation has ever seen."

There was no doubt in King's mind who was truly to blame for the deaths. He sent another wire, this one to Governor George Wallace, stating, "Your irresponsible and misguided actions have created in Birmingham and Alabama the atmosphere that has induced continued violence and now murder."

Pallbearers transport the casket of one of the four girls who died in the bombing. Two Negro boys were later killed during rioting.

August

1. Kennedy rebuts claims by some in Congress that the test-ban treaty is a tacit U.S. recognition of East Germany, which signed the treaty. He also confirms that the U.S. will continue underground nuclear testing.

2. Washington suspends aid to Haiti after reports that the Duvalier government has increased the pace of political arrests in that country.

3. Despite France's rejection of the nuclear test-ban treaty, the White House is hopeful that the French can be coaxed to sign the pact through military aid and sharing of nuclear technology.

4. The administration considers retaliatory action in response to higher tariffs on U.S. poultry exports by European countries.

5. Delegates to the successful Moscow talks on nuclear testing formally sign the treaty documents, clearing the way for signatory countries to begin their ratification processes.

6. Despite the terms of the nuclear testing treaty, Kennedy authorizes the development of a Thor rocket system designed to use nuclear warheads in space to damage enemy satellites.

7. The First Lady gives birth to Patrick Bouvier Kennedy at an Air Force hospital on Cape Cod. The child, born five and a half weeks premature, suffers from a respiratory condition and will die two days later.

8. The White House formally transmits the nuclear treaty to the Senate for ratification.

Though liberal in his support of social programs, Kennedy bucks the stereotype with his calls for lower taxes.

Sept 18 JFK PUSHES CONGRESS TO REDUCE FEDERAL TAXES

WASHINGTON—President Kennedy this evening delivered a radio and television address to the nation from the Oval Office. He spoke of two issues coming before Congress in the next few days: the Senate vote on the test-ban treaty that outlaws atmospheric nuclear testing, and the House vote on the administration's proposed tax bill. Confident that the Senate will sign off on the test-ban treaty, Kennedy's address focused most heavily on taxes.

"No more important legislation will come before the Congress this year than the bill before the House next week to reduce federal taxes," Kennedy said. The President has good reason to drum up support for his tax initiative: It has been proven, most recently in Britain, that a lower tax rate spurs economic growth, job creation, and consumer spending. Moreover, the President sees a tax cut as sound insurance against another recession.

"I do not say it will solve all of our economic problems; no single measure can do that," Kennedy said. "We need to advance on many other fronts—on education, in job retraining, in area redevelopment, in youth employment, and the rest, but this bill is the keystone of the arch."

The House is scheduled to take up the bill next week.

"No more important legislation will come before the Congress this year than the bill before the House next week to reduce federal taxes." —KENNEDY

Sept 19

PRESIDENT TAKES STEPS TO HEAL BIRMINGHAM

WASHINGTON—President Kennedy today issued a statement outlining some of the measures his administration is taking in response to the bombings in Birmingham last Sunday, which killed four Negro girls.

The President has assured the public that the Federal Bureau of Investigation has agents working around the clock to bring the killers to justice. In addition, Kennedy intends to meet with civil rights leaders and white Birmingham business leaders to restore law and order to the city.

Kennedy also announced that he has appointed General Kenneth Royall and Colonel Earl Blaik to travel to Birmingham to participate in the city's recovery. They will take part in Birmingham's efforts to move past the climate of fear and distrust that has descended over the city since Sunday's tragedy.

TAKING A HIT IN THE POLLS

Racial tensions in 1963 forced John Kennedy to confront the forces of reaction in the South. His use of federal power to desegregate southern universities led to a public backlash among white Southerners, one of the Democratic Party's most reliable voting blocs since the Civil War.

In the late summer of 1963, after hundreds of thousands of African Americans and their white supporters gathered to hear Martin Luther King, Jr., deliver his "I Have a Dream" speech at a massive rally in Washington, 38 percent of Americans said that JFK was moving too fast on civil rights. Another survey, conducted by pollster Louis Harris, found that Kennedy had lost the support of more than four million white southern voters. Kennedy began 1963 with an approval rating of 76 percent, according to the Gallup poll. By early fall, that figure had fallen to 59 percent.

It was a startling reversal of fortune, but for the President and his aides, there was no mystery about Kennedy's loss of popularity. The civil rights struggle had cost him support among whites on his left and right. Conservative whites resented his administration's involvement in desegregation efforts, while white liberals thought he was not moving aggressively enough. Meanwhile, African Americans were not yet convinced that he was on their side in a meaningful way.

Still, as the election year of 1964 approached, polls also showed that JFK would have little problem defeating the frontrunner for the Republican presidential nomination, Barry Goldwater.

9 After the death of the Kennedys' newborn son, Patrick, expressions of sympathy pour in from around the world. News of the fatal condition (which will become known as respiratory distress syndrome) will help generate research into better treatment.

10 President Kennedy attends a private funeral mass for his son in Boston, then visits Jacqueline in the hospital.

11 Public health officials announce that atmospheric nuclear tests in 1962 were responsible for a doubling in one year of the levels of strontium-90 found in U.S. milk supplies.

12 The administration puts the final touches on revisions to its tax bill proposal. It aims to cut taxes in high tax brackets and, to a lesser extent, in lower tax brackets.

13 To counter impressions of a permanent division of Germany along East-West lines, West German officials plan to sign copies of the nuclear test-ban treaty in London, Moscow, and Washington on behalf of all Germans.

14 The President accompanies Jacqueline on a helicopter flight to their house in Hyannis Port after her release from the hospital.

15 U.S. commanders in Vietnam report that Communist guerrillas continue to make inroads in the Mekong Delta despite American-supported sweeps in the region by South Vietnamese troops.

16 Union leaders criticize the Kennedy tax proposals as being too generous to corporations and not sufficient to stimulate spending by most taxpayers.

Kennedy greets UN Secretary General U Thant, who was undoubtedly pleased by JFK's message of peace.

Sept 20 JFK Urges Cooperation with Soviets in UN Address

New York—President Kennedy traveled to New York City to address the United Nations General Assembly today. The President covered a number of issues in his wide-ranging speech, but U.S.-Soviet relations were central to his remarks.

Kennedy's tone was optimistic while noting that in the two years since his last UN appearance, the world has become a safer place. He hailed the limited nuclear test-ban agreement as one of the main contributing reasons for hope in international relations. He expressed confidence that it will receive Senate endorsement when it comes before that body next Tuesday.

Kennedy's enthusiasm was, as always, somewhat tempered. He issued a warning that we should not fail to take advantage of what he called a pause in the Cold War. He noted that we "have not been released from our obligations…and if we fail to make the most of this moment and this momentum…then the indictment of posterity will rightly point its finger at us all."

The President emphasized the need to build on this potential peace with the Soviets. He said that the nations should strive for comprehensive disarmament and common interests, and build "the institutions of peace as we dismantle the engines of war." One area in which Kennedy expressed hope that this might be accomplished was in a joint mission to the moon. It remains to be seen if relations between the two superpowers have changed enough to allow the space race to become a cooperative effort.

SENATE RATIFIES TEST-BAN TREATY

Sept 24

WASHINGTON—In one of the biggest victories of John F. Kennedy's presidency, the Senate has ratified the limited nuclear test-ban agreement, which bans all nuclear testing in the Earth's atmosphere, oceans, and space.

The treaty enjoys support from the majority of legislators on both sides of the aisle. Crediting the efforts of Arkansas Senator J. William Fulbright for the successful vote, Kennedy congratulated the Senate for representing the clear will of the people.

Awareness about nuclear testing fallout and environmental harm has intensified since two massive nuclear detonations brought the Second World War to a close in 1945. Even while the world's superpowers have been trying to build bigger bombs, they have also been striving to mitigate the effects of their research and development in times of relative peace.

It has been more than eight years since the United Nations Disarmament Commission's Subcommittee of Five began negotiating an international ban on nuclear testing. That group, which included the United States, the United Kingdom, the Soviet Union, France, and Canada, worked steadily toward consensus. They did so even while issues of monitoring, compliance, and changes in Cold War tensions threw up roadblocks along the way.

The Limited Nuclear Test Ban was signed on August 5 in a ceremony in Moscow. With its Senate ratification, it is one step closer to being entered into force.

KENNEDY HALTS AID TO DOMINICAN REPUBLIC

Sept 26

WASHINGTON—President Kennedy immediately cut of all aid to the Dominican Republic yesterday after receiving word that an early-morning military coup had taken down the government of President Juan Bosch.

Bosch's 1962 democratic election pulled the island nation's government out of chaos following the 1961 assassination of dictator Rafael Trujillo. Bosch instituted a series of reforms, permitted the creation of labor unions, and enacted a liberal constitution in his short, seven-month term of office.

While the United States was never entirely comfortable with Bosch's far-left leanings, and the Republic's powerful Catholic Church disliked his secularism, it is the military leadership who clearly resented their change in status since Trujillo's death.

In addition to canceling aid to the Dominican Republic, the Kennedy administration has also suspended diplomatic relations until further notice.

17 Lee Harvey Oswald appears on a New Orleans radio station to talk about his pro-Castro views. Four days later, he will participate in a heated radio debate with leaders of two anti-Communist organizations.

18 After an unsuccessful attempt by Mississippi Governor Ross Barnett to prevent it, James Meredith becomes the first African American to graduate from the University of Mississippi.

19 The U.S. balance of payments deficit continues to grow, reaching an annual rate of $5.2 billion.

20 As he prepares to leave for his new post in Saigon, U.S. Ambassador Henry Cabot Lodge gets classified instructions to signal that the U.S. would support a military coup against President Diem.

21 Kennedy tells reporters that economic aid is an essential part of effective foreign policy. In the first half of the fiscal year, $1.5 billion in agricultural commodities have been sent overseas under the Food for Peace program.

22 Tran Van Phuong, South Vietnam's ambassador in Washington, resigns in protest against his own government's harsh treatment of Buddhists.

23 Haiti's legislature suspends individual rights under its constitution and gives special powers to President Duvalier for at least six months.

24 The State Department cables Ambassador Lodge in Saigon confirming support for a regime change in South Vietnam. President Diem's brother, Ngo Dinh Nhu, has reportedly assumed de facto command and is increasing attacks against Buddhist interests in the country.

Though he once went deer hunting on Lyndon Johnson's ranch, Kennedy shows affection for this creature during his conservation tour.

Sept 28 JFK COMPLETES CONSERVATION TOUR OF MIDWEST AND WEST

LAS VEGAS—President Kennedy wrapped up a nine-state swing with an address at the Las Vegas Convention Center today. Traveling to conservation projects and federal lands from Wyoming's Grand Tetons to Nevada's Lake Mead, Kennedy was struck by both the bounty and beauty of America's natural resources as well as the importance of properly conserving them.

Kennedy spoke of building for the future. This is especially relevant in the city of Las Vegas, which will depend on Lake Mead's water and the Hoover Dam's power for its continued growth and development, he said. He also emphasized straight conservation and the need to preserve what is yet unspoiled in the Sierras and Lake Tahoe, as well as the region of the proposed Great Basin National Park.

The President underscored three major conclusions he has reached in his travels. They include the importance of a national campaign of environmental preservation, environmental education of our youth, and peace on Earth so that Americans can enjoy their land. "We want 'America the Beautiful' to be left for those who come after us," he said. "Our greatness today rests in part on this good piece of geography that is the United States, but what is important is what the people of America do with it."

KENNEDY MAKES NUCLEAR TEST-BAN TREATY A REALITY

Oct 7

WASHINGTON—President Kennedy today signed the Nuclear Test Ban Treaty, achieving a goal he set at the beginning of his administration. Noting that the 20 years since the advent of nuclear weaponry have been a fearful period in world history, Kennedy said: "Today the fear is a little less and the hope a little greater."

The treaty bans nuclear tests in the atmosphere, outer space, and under water, but nuclear nations can still test their weapons underground. The treaty falls short of the comprehensive test ban that Kennedy had hoped for, as the signatories were never able to agree on a framework that would allow for the necessary site inspections.

Still, Kennedy acknowledged, the treaty is an important first step. "Even this limited treaty, great as it is with promise, can survive only if it has from others the determined support in letter and in spirit which I hereby pledge on behalf of the United States."

The treaty will take effect three days from now. Along with Great Britain and the Soviet Union, the United States is one of the three principal architects of the agreement. Some 100 other nations have also signed, or signaled their intent to do so.

The President, who signed the treaty in the White House Treaty Room, concluded: "With our courage and understanding enlarged by this achievement, let us press onward in quest of man's essential desire for peace."

Kennedy signs the Nuclear Test Ban Treaty, which will ban nuclear tests everywhere except underground.

25 Attorney General Robert Kennedy announces that he will leave his job and run for U.S. Senate in New York.

26 The U.S. Interior Department releases a sweeping plan to spend $4 billion over three decades to improve the management of water resources in the Colorado River Basin.

27 As the political situation worsens in Saigon, the U.S. State Department releases a statement saying that it holds South Vietnamese military officers responsible for recent repression of Buddhists. The public statement is the latest in a series of American signals that favor a coup.

28 After a peaceful civil rights march in Washington by some 250,000 people, Martin Luther King, Jr., speaks from the steps of the Lincoln Memorial and delivers his memorable "I Have a Dream" address. King also meets with President Kennedy at the White House.

29 Railroads in the nation continue to operate a day after the President signed a bill that barred a strike for six months and required the two sides in the dispute to submit to binding arbitration of work rules. The bill marked the first time in U.S. history that Congress legislated compulsory labor arbitration.

30 The much anticipated "hot line" between the White House and the Kremlin, actually a dedicated teletype connection for use in times of crisis, becomes operational.

31 In *The Nation's Business*, Kennedy appeals to business leaders for support of his tax reforms.

Oct 11 — KENNEDY: WORKING WOMEN GETTING SHORT-SHIFTED

WASHINGTON—President Kennedy today endorsed the Peterson Report, issued by the President's Commission on the Status of Women. Established by Kennedy in 1961, the commission was charged with researching discrimination against American women, especially in the workplace. The President's Commission was initially chaired by former First Lady Eleanor Roosevelt, who served until her death last November.

The report, released after more than two years of study, is not encouraging. It revealed that American women, relative to men, endure a diminished status universally. Kennedy's concern was clear. "I think this is an extremely vital matter with which we are dealing," he said. "This used to be an old story, that a civilization could be judged on how it treated its elderly people. But I think it can also be judged on its opportunities for women."

The report points to several areas of particular concern, including poor access to child care and a lack of paid maternity leave. These factors make it difficult for women to be both mothers and competitive in the workforce. The result is a lack of opportunity for women, not only in terms of salary but also in terms of personal fulfillment. "I wonder whether," said Kennedy, "in our society, women have the chance to use their powers, their full powers, intellectual powers, emotional powers, and all the rest, along the lines of excellence."

Oct 20 — PRESIDENT'S APPROVAL RATING DROPS TO THE 50s

WASHINGTON—President Kennedy's presidential approval ratings are hovering at 59 percent this month after hitting a low of 56 percent in September. These numbers are far below his high of 83 percent in April 1961, when America was still enjoying its honeymoon phase with the new president. Kennedy's rating was 73 percent in November 1962 after his strong handling of the Cuban missile crisis.

Pundits seem to agree that Kennedy is taking a major hit for his supportive stance on civil rights. Polls reveal that for every Negro vote Kennedy earns, he loses about four white votes. Nowhere is that more apparent than in the Deep South, where there is talk that Kennedy may lose several southern states when he runs for a second term in November of next year.

Still, Republican strategists face a stiff challenge. In spite of the growing opposition to certain aspects of the President's domestic agenda among some of his white constituency, the other side does not seem to have a candidate to field who would pose much of a challenge to the incumbent. In addition, the President earns high marks for foreign policy, especially for the hard line he has taken against the Cubans and the Russians. Finally, the handsome young President and his glamorous First Lady and lovely children hold tremendous personal appeal for many Americans. Decreasing poll numbers aside, Kennedy's Republican challenger will be fighting an uphill battle should the President choose to run for a second term.

ASSESSING JFK'S LEGACY

John Kennedy's brief presidency remains the subject of endless fascination nearly a half-century after his death, in part because he touched a generation of Americans with his words and deeds, partly because he remains forever young in our collective memory, and, in part, because his personal life was so disorderly and contradictory.

Historians, who view presidents more dispassionately than voters do, continue to regard JFK as a charismatic and memorable leader, but they do not place him with presidential greats such as George Washington, Abraham Lincoln, and Franklin Roosevelt. In 11 significant polls taken since 1982, Kennedy has ranked anywhere from the sixth greatest president in U.S. history to the 18th best. His sixth-place showing came in a 2009 C-SPAN poll.

Kennedy was unable to pass important domestic legislation, such as a civil rights bill, elder care, and his tax cuts. His record on foreign affairs was mixed—the Bay of Pigs was an embarrassing failure, the Cuban missile crisis a triumphant success. Kennedy inspired the U.S. to go to the moon and Americans to volunteer in the developing world. But he was slow to grasp the importance of civil rights.

As his administration matured, however, JFK showed signs of what might have been. Two speeches, given on June 10 and June 11, 1963, offer historians insight into how a second term might have unfolded. In the first speech, given at American University in Washington, D.C., Kennedy called on Americans to reassess their opinions of the Russian people. The following night, he told a national television audience that the civil rights movement was a moral struggle that whites should support.

Historian Robert Dallek summed up President Kennedy's legacy by saying that JFK "inspired visions of a less-divisive nation and world, and demonstrated that America was still the last best hope of mankind."

1 After an expected military coup in Saigon fizzles, the U.S. State Department cables the U.S. ambassador. The State Department says that while Washington may support future Vietnamese efforts to change the regime, it has no intention of toppling the Diem regime directly.

2 In a recorded interview with CBS news anchor Walter Cronkite, President Kennedy defends his policy in Vietnam, comparing it to the U.S. commitment to the defense of Europe in World War II. "I don't agree with those who say we should withdraw," he says.

3 Administration officials echo the President's criticism of South Vietnamese government policies. Kennedy called the Diem regime's actions against Buddhist protesters "unwise."

4 Washington monitors reports from Saigon that South Vietnamese President Diem may resign and cede power to his brother.

5 As the Senate debates ratification of the nuclear test-ban treaty, presidential hopeful and Arizona Senator Barry Goldwater creates a stir when he proposes delaying ratification until all Soviet military personnel withdraw from Cuba.

6 The American Embassy in Saigon continues to harbor at least three Buddhists who sought refuge from arrest by the Diem government. The U.S. refuses a formal demand by Saigon to turn over the Buddhists, including protest leader Thich Tri-Quang.

7 For the second time in the new school year, Alabama Governor George Wallace uses state police to prevent attendance by white students at newly integrated public schools, this time in Huntsville.

With the new legislation, women will be able to receive prenatal care even if they can't afford it.

Oct 24 PRESIDENT SIGNS BILL TO PREVENT MENTAL RETARDATION

WASHINGTON—In the Cabinet Room at the White House, President Kennedy this morning signed important legislation designed to reduce the number of mentally retarded babies born in America each year.

The President noted that many cases of mental retardation are due to premature birth—an often-preventable event that may be dramatically reduced with proper prenatal care. Each year, nearly a half-million pregnant American women are unable to afford necessary prenatal medical assistance.

The passage of H.R. 7544, the Mills-Ribicoff Bill, will help provide prenatal care for needy women and thus go a long way toward reducing the number of children born mentally retarded in this country. Said Kennedy: "We can say with some assurance that, although children may be the victims of fate, they will not be the victims of our neglect."

Oct 26 U.S. MILITARY PULLS OFF OPERATION BIG LIFT IN BERLIN

BERLIN—Operation Big Lift, a major operation undertaken by the U.S. Military Air Transport Service, has been successfully executed. In just 63 hours (and at a cost of some $20 million) more than 15,000 soldiers with the Second Armored Division were airlifted to Europe, along with their support troops and 504 tons of battle equipment. The massive operation required the services of 204 aircraft and was accompanied by another 116 fighter and reconnaissance aircraft.

It was the most ambitious troop movement ever attempted, one that would have typically taken up to six weeks to accomplish. As many as 30 air bases in North America and Europe were involved, though the center of activity was the Fort Hood, Texas, home of the Second Armored Division. Once in Germany, the troops picked up pre-positioned hardware, making them fully combat ready.

The Big Lift is the manifestation of a directive that President Kennedy handed down in a May 1961 speech before a joint session of Congress. In that speech, he called for improvements in the Army's "tactical mobility" to ensure that the world's finest fighting force could be flexible enough to rapidly respond to threats worldwide.

Oct 28 CRITICS CALL MOON MISSION WASTE OF TIME

WASHINGTON—NASA announced a reshuffle of its manned spaceflight program today amid increasing criticism of the program by some members of Congress.

Austrian native George M. Low has been named second in command in the Office of Manned Space Flight, under director Dr. George E. Mueller. Dr. Walter C. Williams was named the number-three man in the office. Despite speculation that the reorganization was related to Soviet Premier Khrushchev's announcement on Saturday that the USSR is stepping back from the space race, NASA officials insist the changes were in the offing well in advance of that. Such speculation is hardly surprising in light of the fact that, on the heels of Khrushchev's announcement, NASA administrator James Webb noted that the Apollo program has "a brake as well as a throttle."

The anti-Apollo congressional contingent has a solid argument. They object to the mission's goal of putting a man on the moon because they feel the agency should be more focused on military applications of space exploration. Khrushchev's announcement has only intensified their objections. Republican Representative James D. Weaver, a member of the House Space Committee, has said that if Webb does not realign "our space program with national security as its prime objective, I shall call for his resignation."

None of this is likely to deter President Kennedy from his enthusiasm for the planned Apollo missions. He charged the nation to meet this accomplishment two years ago, and last year he eloquently explained why: "We choose to go to the moon. We choose to go to the moon in this decade and do the other things, not because they are easy, but because they are hard, because that goal will serve to organize and measure the best of our energies and skills, because that challenge is one that we are willing to accept, one we are unwilling to postpone, and one which we intend to win, and the others, too."

8 Former President Eisenhower speaks out on the continuing controversy in the U.S. Senate over ratifying the nuclear treaty. Eisenhower says he opposes new conditions for ratification that would require reopening negotiations with the Soviets.

9 In an interview with NBC anchors Chet Huntley and David Brinkley, President Kennedy denies that the CIA is involved in efforts to overthrow the Diem government in Saigon. Despite disagreement with South Vietnamese government actions, he says, he will not reduce American aid.

10 The President orders the secretary of defense to use federalized troops of the Alabama National Guard to enforce court-ordered integration of Alabama schools. Kennedy issues a proclamation that in effect orders Governor Wallace to cease his obstruction of the process.

11 Kennedy signs an order amending the draft that in effect stops the conscription of married men.

12 JFK holds a wide-ranging news conference in which he calls an invasion of Cuba "a most dangerous idea" that is not in American interests. He urges the Senate to complete debate and ratify the nuclear test-ban treaty.

13 UN Secretary General U Thant expresses concern that the political situation in South Vietnam is rapidly deteriorating.

14 U.S. scientists detonate two large nuclear bombs under the Nevada desert.

Kennedy's relationship with Lyndon Johnson has been cool but professional. JFK said he will retain LBJ as his vice president if reelected.

Oct 31 JFK DISCUSSES TROOP LEVELS, MOON RACE, HIS RUNNING MATE

WASHINGTON—In his 63rd news conference, President Kennedy uncharacteristically did not make an opening statement today. Instead, he immediately opened the floor to questions, which ranged from troop deployment to his level of happiness.

Asked about rumors regarding a reduction in forces stationed in Germany, the President clarified that he will not be reducing the size of his combat force (more than six combat divisions), though there may be some reduction in noncombat personnel. However, regarding troop withdrawal in the East, the President did suggest that the United States would be able to draw down its forces in Vietnam by the end of the year.

Asked if he thinks that Soviet Premier Khrushchev has really taken the USSR out of the race to the moon, Kennedy was highly skeptical. He also used it as an opportunity to take a shot at those critical of the Apollo program. "I think it is remarkable that some people who were so unwilling to accept our test-ban treaty, where there was a very adequate area of verification of whatever the Soviet Union was doing, were perfectly ready to accept Mr. Khrushchev's very guarded and careful and cautious remark that he was taking himself out of the space race, and use that as an excuse for us to abandon our efforts," he said.

Kennedy gave an unequivocal yes when asked if he intended to retain Johnson as his running mate in 1964. Asked whether Kennedy enjoys being president, he replied: "I have given before to this group the definition of happiness of the Greeks, and I will define it again. It is full use of your powers along lines of excellence. I find, therefore, the presidency provides some happiness."

Nov 3 COUP STAGED IN VIETNAM; PRESIDENT DIEM KILLED

WASHINGTON—President Kennedy received word yesterday that Ngo Dinh Diem's South Vietnam, a longtime American ally, is no more. A military coup has toppled the pro-U.S. government. Diem as well as his brother Nhu appeared to be casualties of the bloody upheaval.

The President was in a meeting with some of his senior advisers when he received the alarming cable from Saigon. He reportedly left the room in a hurry, visibly shaken.

The United States has long worked cooperatively with the Diem government in an effort to prevent the North Vietnamese from exporting communism to the South. It was an imperfect partnership, with the Kennedy administration often finding fault with Diem's handling of domestic issues. Diem's mistreatment of Vietnamese Buddhists, in particular, is thought to have severely harmed Diem's—

and by extension, Kennedy's—credibility with the South Vietnamese peasantry. In recent weeks, on the heels of a fact-finding mission by Defense Secretary Robert McNamara and General Maxwell Taylor, the United States withdrew its support of Diem.

South Vietnamese smash windows during the military coup that toppled the government of Ngo Dinh Diem.

That act clearly opened the door for what was to follow. Generals from Diem's own military ordered the president and his brother to vacate the presidential palace on the evening of November 1. Diem refused, and the palace was besieged. The Ngo brothers turned themselves in the following day. It is unclear what happened next. Coup leaders claim the brothers committed suicide, but that is doubtful given their strong Catholic faith.

It is unclear what role, if any, the United States may have played in the coup.

DIEM'S DEMISE

Ngo Dinh Diem was the elected leader of the government of South Vietnam, although his reelection in 1961 with 90 percent of the vote impressed few members of the Kennedy administration. They knew the vote was rigged. Diem was America's ally against communism in Southeast Asia, but he was a flawed ally. He ruled like a dictator, and his wife flaunted the family's presumably ill-gotten wealth.

Diem was not a popular figure in Washington, but Kennedy and his aides lacked an alternative. But after Diem, a member of the country's Catholic minority, ordered a brutal crackdown on the nation's Buddhists in early 1963, leading a monk to set fire to himself in protest, the Kennedy administration began to consider its options. Pictures of the monk's self-immolation were published around the world, drawing new attention to Diem's corrupt and repressive regime.

Rebels' plans to remove Diem from office were well underway in the middle of 1963, and Kennedy knew about them. American officials in Vietnam were in direct contact with would-be coup leaders, although Washington told the U.S. officials that they should not take an active role in promoting Diem's overthrow. In early October, Kennedy and some of his top advisers discussed the pros and cons of the imminent coup. Ever a pragmatist, Kennedy sought to figure out which side had the better chance of winning.

On November 1, the coup that JFK had tacitly approved unfolded in Saigon. Diem and his brother, Ngo Dinh Nhu, were murdered by rebel troops. The State Department denied any U.S. involvement.

Nov 17 — KENNEDY ENJOYING WEEKEND IN PALM BEACH

PALM BEACH, FLA.—President Kennedy passed a restful Sunday in Palm Beach today, beginning his day by attending mass at St. Ann's Church. He also signed a bill establishing a Coastal Engineering Research Center. The center will study near-shore oceanography as it relates to engineering issues, and serve as a central clearinghouse for all Army Corps of Engineers water resources projects.

The President has a busy week ahead of him, with several stops in Florida tomorrow before flying back to Washington. After a series of midweek meetings, the President and First Lady are scheduled to fly to Texas for a two-day visit at the end of the week.

Nov 19 — PRESIDENT ADDRESSES CROWDS ACROSS FLORIDA

WASHINGTON—President Kennedy returned to Washington late yesterday evening after spending the day delivering several speeches in Tampa and Miami.

The President's first stop was Tampa's Al Lopez Field, where he honored the achievements of aviation pioneer Captain Tony Jannus, who completed a historic flight from Tampa to St. Petersburg nearly 50 years ago.

From there, Kennedy proceeded to Tampa's Fort Homer Hesterly Armory, where he addressed members of the business community at the 47th annual meeting of the Florida State Chamber of Commerce. Not unexpectedly, the primary topic of the hour was the economy, and President Kennedy vigorously defended his administration against the pervasive perception that it is anti-business. He then opened up the

The President visits Cape Canaveral on November 16.

268

floor to questions, which ranged from Cuba to civil rights to whether he intends to run for a second term. The President then addressed a gathering of members of the United Steelworkers of America in the Crystal Room of Tampa's International Inn.

Kennedy then flew to Miami and held a Democratic rally upon his arrival at the airport. He declared: "I have been making nonpartisan speeches all day, and I am glad to come here as a Democrat and express my pleasure to speak as a Democrat. If there are any Republicans here, this is a Democratic message that I am about to give. I want to give them fair warning."

The last item on the President's lengthy agenda was an address, delivered at the Americana Hotel in Miami Beach, before an audience that included several prominent Latin American leaders. The topic was primarily the Alliance for Progress and inter-American relations and security.

Nov 19 KENNEDY MESSAGE READ AT GETTYSBURG

GETTYSBURG, PA.—A solemn ceremony was held today marking the 100th anniversary of President Lincoln's reading of the Gettysburg Address, at the Gettysburg National Cemetery. Lincoln had delivered his timeless words during the dedication of the cemetery in 1863.

President Kennedy was unable to attend personally, but former President Eisenhower, a resident of Gettysburg, Pennsylvania, lent plenty of presidential presence to the event. Kennedy did, however, send brief remarks to be delivered during the event.

Kennedy's statement read, in part: "Today, as we honor Lincoln's immortal eulogy to the dead on Cemetery Ridge, let us remember as well those thousands of American patriots whose graves at home, beneath the sea, and in distant lands are silent sentries of our heritage…. On this solemn occasion, let us all rededicate ourselves to the perpetuation of those ideals of which Lincoln spoke so luminously. As Americans, we can do no less."

22 NASA officials, surprised by JFK's proposal for a joint U.S.-Soviet moon mission, doubt such a mission could be executed by 1970. However, they suggest that a Soviet cosmonaut could travel with the crew of a U.S. mission.

23 Kennedy meets with business and religious leaders from Birmingham on the eve of arrival in Alabama by the President's personal representatives.

24 The U.S. Senate votes 80-19 to ratify the nuclear test-ban treaty. The treaty, which will remain open for future participation by other nations, will reach more than 120 signatories by the 21st century.

25 A three-man military junta overthrows Dominican Republic President Juan Bosch. In response, the Kennedy administration suspends diplomatic relations with the regime.

26 Lee Harvey Oswald travels to Mexico City. He tries unsuccessfully over four days to obtain a travel visa to Russia, where he and his wife, Marina, lived for nearly three years.

27 On the third day of his conservation-themed tour of 11 states, Kennedy tells an audience in Salt Lake City that he does not believe in formulating foreign policy rooted in "black-and-white choices of good and evil."

28 French President de Gaulle underscores his opposition to U.S. policies, telling a cheering crowd that his country will follow its own interests and not follow the will of the United Nations, NATO, or the United States.

29 Secretary of Defense McNamara and General Taylor tour key sites in Vietnam's Mekong Valley before holding lengthy talks with President Diem in Saigon.

Lena Horne (third from left) and Carol Lawrence (fifth from left) were among Kennedy's visitors.

Nov 20 — JFK DELIVERS STATEMENTS ON SPACE COMMUNICATIONS, UN

WASHINGTON—President Kennedy had a full agenda today, including a White House meeting with entertainers Lena Horne and Carol Lawrence as well as a talk with Democratic National Committee Chairman John M. Bailey.

Kennedy also made a statement regarding the recent, month-long Extraordinary Administrative Radio Conference to Allocate Frequency Bands for Space Radio Communication Purposes, held in Geneva, Switzerland. He called for international cooperation in the establishment of a global communications satellite system.

In addition, the President sent the annual report to Congress detailing the participation of the United States in the United Nations for calendar year 1962. After enumerating some of the major international issues the United Nations was engaged in during the year—including the confrontation between the United States and the Soviet Union over the missiles in Cuba, the crisis in the Congo, and issues in Palestine, Kashmir, and Korea—Kennedy's assessment was largely favorable.

The President stated: "[D]espite noncooperation from some members and wavering support from others, the organization moved significantly toward the goal of a peace system worldwide in scope. The United States will continue to lend vigorous support to the building of that system."

Afterward, the President and First Lady prepared for their trip to Texas. They leave tomorrow.

Nov 21 — JOHN, JACKIE BEGIN FIVE-CITY TOUR OF TEXAS

HOUSTON—President and Mrs. Kennedy landed in San Antonio today, their first destination on a whirlwind tour of Texas. They also plan to visit Houston, Fort Worth, Dallas, and Austin.

Their first destination was Brooks Air Force Base, where the President helped dedicate the Aerospace Medical Health Center with Texas dignitaries, including Vice President Lyndon Johnson, Air Force Secretary Eugene Zuckert, Texas Governor John Connally, and U.S. Senator Ralph Yarborough (D-TX). Noting the potential applications of medical space research here on Earth, Kennedy said: "This nation has tossed its cap over the wall of space, and we have no choice but to follow it. Whatever the difficulties, they will be overcome."

Mrs. Kennedy received yellow roses upon the First Couple's arrival in San Antonio, Texas.

The presidential entourage then continued to Houston. They stopped at the Rice Hotel, where Kennedy spoke before a meeting of the League of United Latin American Citizens. The President said a few words about how interested he is in developing a cooperative relationship with Latin America. He then handed over the dais to Mrs. Kennedy, whose fluent Spanish was presumably more understandable to many in the audience.

The Kennedys concluded the evening at the Coliseum in Houston, where the President delivered remarks at a dinner in honor of Texas Representative Albert Thomas.

"This nation has tossed its cap over the wall of space, and we have no choice but to follow it. Whatever the difficulties, they will be overcome."

—KENNEDY

Nov 21 PRESIDENT TO FIGHT THE "WAR ON POVERTY"

WASHINGTON—President Kennedy's economic advisers have been put on notice: The President intends to put poverty at the top of his legislative agenda for 1964.

Though it is too early to tell on what fronts this "War on Poverty" will be fought, it is likely to involve large expenditures on social service programs administered through the Department of Health, Education and Welfare. Medical aid to the elderly, a program that has long been a pet project of Kennedy's, would certainly be part of his administration's anti-poverty plan. Education, too, remains a key aspect of the President's agenda, and it is easy to see how improvements in America's educational system would naturally lend itself to reducing poverty.

One thing that remains unclear is how the President intends to cut taxes and continue to expand expensive social service programs. Regardless, fighting poverty has been an important goal of Kennedy's since his first day in office. He said in his inaugural speech: "If a free society cannot help the many who are poor, it cannot save the few who are rich."

September

30 The White House and several allied governments agree to special funding for keeping UN troops in the Congo for six more months.

October

1 American and West German officials will collaborate this month for Operation Big Lift, a training exercise in which an entire U.S. armored division is airlifted to West Germany for rapid deployment in a crisis.

2 Back from their fact-finding trip to Vietnam, Secretary of Defense McNamara and General Taylor recommend finding an exit strategy for U.S. forces. One proposal is for Canadians to replace American advisers.

3 Honduran military leaders overthrow the government of Ramon Villeda Morales and exile him to Costa Rica. The White House views with concern the fourth coup of the year in Latin America.

4 After hearing of strong disagreement between Ambassador Lodge and intelligence officials in South Vietnam, President Kennedy recalls to Washington the chief CIA officer in Saigon.

5 Basking in the glow of public response to President Kennedy during his 1963 trips to western and southern states, the reelection strategists in the administration are planning fall trips to key states, including New York, Florida, and Texas.

6 After weeks of wrangling over Kennedy's civil rights proposals, Congress prepares to approve a simple one-year extension of the Civil Rights Commission.

Nov 22 JFK ASSASSINATED
President Kennedy Is Shot and Killed in Dallas

DALLAS—The nation is in shock this evening as the horrible news out of Dallas, Texas, travels around the globe. Earlier today, John Fitzgerald Kennedy, the 35th president of the United States, was shot and killed. A suspect has been apprehended.

Upon arriving at Love Field following a stop in Fort Worth, the Kennedys, along with Texas Governor John Connally and his wife, Nellie, entered the presidential limousine for the 11-mile drive to the Dallas Trade Mart. Due to the warm and sunny weather and the President's preference, the protective "bubble top" was not in place. The 1961 Lincoln and the rest of the motorcade left Love Field at 11:50 A.M.

About forty minutes later, at 12:30 P.M., the motorcade turned onto Elm Street and passed the Texas School Book Depository, when shots rang out. Spectators reported seeing the President and Governor Connally slump in their seats after being struck by bullets. The First Lady inexplicably crawled onto the back of the car until she was redirected into the back seat by a Secret Service agent, who covered her and the President with his own body. Not soon enough, the motorcade sped off in the direction of Parkland Hospital.

> *"President John F. Kennedy died at approximately 1:00 P.M. Central Standard Time today here in Dallas. He died of a gunshot wound in the brain."*
>
> —ASSISTANT PRESIDENTIAL PRESS SECRETARY MALCOLM KILDUFF

Once there, doctors attempted to revive the mortally wounded Kennedy while Governor Connally was stabilized and sent into surgery to treat the gunshot wound to his back. Kennedy suffered a shot to the neck—a wound that might have been survivable—but it was the other wound, a massive injury to Kennedy's right temple, that proved fatal.

At about 12:50 P.M., Father Oscar Huber and Father James Thompson arrived to administer last rites. The President's time of death was set at 1:00 P.M. It was then that Assistant Presidential Press Secretary Malcolm Kilduff went to the press corps to deliver the news. "President John F. Kennedy died at approximately 1:00 P.M. Central Standard Time today here in Dallas," Kilduff said. "He died of a gunshot wound in the brain. I have no other details of the assassination."

Members of the President's family were immediately notified, as were members of the Cabinet. Of the latter, the secretaries of Agriculture, State, Labor, Interior, and Commerce, as well as Press Secretary Pierre Salinger, were all on a plane on their way to Tokyo when they received the news. They returned to Washington.

At approximately 2:40 P.M., Judge Sarah Hughes administered the Oath of Office to Vice President Lyndon B. Johnson, who was sworn in as the 36th president of the United States. A dazed Jacqueline Kennedy stood to his left, while the new first lady, Lady Bird Johnson, stood to his right.

Mrs. Kennedy and the Secret Service insisted upon returning immediately to Washington with the President's body, despite the fact that jurisdiction called for the autopsy to be performed in Dallas. By 3:00 P.M., Air Force One had departed Love Field with Mrs. Kennedy and the Johnsons accompanying the body.

Before the wheels were up on Air Force One, Dallas police had a suspect in custody: Lee Harvey Oswald, an employee of the Texas School Book Depository who left the building after the shooting and reportedly shot a police officer. A local merchant called police when he observed that Oswald appeared to be hiding from police cars.

7 President Kennedy signs the Nuclear Test Ban Treaty at the White House, commenting, "For the first time we have been able to reach an agreement which can limit the dangers of this age."

8 The UN General Assembly authorizes an investigation of claims by Buddhists in South Vietnam that the government there is engaged in a systematic campaign of religious oppression.

9 The President approves the sale of more than $250 million of American wheat to Soviet bloc countries, on condition that the supplies would not be resold to Cuba or China.

10 The President's Commission on the Status of Women details pervasive discrimination against women. It concludes that legal remedies are more likely to succeed than a constitutional amendment.

11 Soviet troops outside West Berlin block a U.S. military convoy from entering the city.

12 Cuba, Haiti, and the Dominican Republic begin a slow recovery from Flora, a Category 4 hurricane that killed more than 7,000 people and ravaged the agricultural economies of all three countries.

13 Kennedy signs a bill that expands the Junior Reserve Officer Training Corps, which uses federal military equipment and officers to train high school students interested in military careers.

14 The White House releases a letter from Kennedy to retiring West German Chancellor Adenauer. It reads in part: "you have created in your own land a stable, free and democratic society which stands in sharp contrast to the repression still enforced on so many of your countrymen."

Police believe that Lee Harvey Oswald, who has ties to both Russia and Cuba, assassinated the President.

Nov 22 POLICE ARREST OSWALD, THE ALLEGED ASSASSIN

DALLAS—Dallas police today had a suspect in custody almost immediately following the assassination of President Kennedy, and an indictment is expected to be handed down as soon as this evening.

Officers on the scene interviewed witnesses, who pointed to an upper floor of the Texas School Book Depository as the source of at least some of the shots fired. A witness, Howard Brennan, claimed to have seen a man fitting Lee Harvey Oswald's description with a rifle in a sixth-floor window of the depository. A search of the building uncovered empty cartridge cases and a Mannlicher-Carcano rifle that had been hastily hidden behind some boxes. Witnesses placed Oswald, a depository employee, in the vicinity, and he was spotted leaving the building immediately after the shootings.

Oswald returned home, where his landlady witnessed him behaving erratically and appearing to be in a hurry. Shortly thereafter, Oswald encountered Dallas police officer J. D. Tippit. Noticing Oswald's strange behavior, Tippit pulled over to question him. According to eyewitnesses, Oswald drew a weapon and fired four shots into Tippit at point-blank range. Oswald proceeded from the scene of Tippit's murder to a theater, where he attracted enough attention to trigger a call to the police. He was finally apprehended after officers stormed the theater. Oswald reportedly attempted to shoot his arresting officer.

Little is known about Oswald or what might have motivated his actions today. The 24-year-old Dallas resident is allegedly the chairman of the so-called Fair Play for Cuba Committee. He is a former resident of Russia and is married to a Russian national.

Nov 22 LYNDON JOHNSON SWORN IN AS PRESIDENT

DALLAS—Just 98 minutes after President Kennedy was pronounced dead at Dallas's Parkland Hospital, former Vice President Lyndon B. Johnson was sworn in as the 36th president of the United States.

Federal judge Sarah T. Hughes was brought on board Air Force One to administer the oath. A stunned Mrs. Kennedy stood alongside President Johnson, as did his wife, Lady Bird Johnson. Although the swearing-in of a president typically falls to the chief justice of the Supreme Court, on this sad day Justice Hughes became the first woman in American history to undertake the important duty.

Upon his return to Washington at around 6:00 P.M. this evening, President Johnson made the following statement to the American people: "This is a sad time for all people. We have suffered a loss that cannot be weighed. For me it is a deep personal tragedy. I know the world shares the sorrow that Mrs. Kennedy and her family bear. I will do my best. That is all I can do. I ask for your help—and God's."

Standing beside a shocked Jackie Kennedy, Lyndon Johnson is sworn in as president.

A Nation in Shock

In the hours after President Kennedy's murder, *Washington Star* columnist Mary McGrory wondered aloud if she and other grieving Americans would ever laugh again. A young Kennedy aide named Daniel Patrick Moynihan—later a four-term U.S. senator from New York—assured her that she and others surely would again find laughter and joy in their lives. But, he said, "we will never be young again."

For Americans who lived through the Depression and World War II, Moynihan's words captured the profound and very personal sense of loss. For these millions of Americans, Kennedy had been more than the nation's chief executive. He was a symbol of their hopes and aspirations. His murder was a shattering blow.

Americans of all ages and backgrounds followed the mourning rituals on television: the lying in state of the President's coffin, the funeral mass, the procession to Arlington National Cemetery. Network coverage of the rites brought the nation to a standstill for three days, although the National Football League went on with its schedule of games on Sunday, November 24, the day before JFK's funeral.

John Kennedy's assassination marked the turning point of the 1960s, which would devolve into a violent, disorderly period that would shake the country to its very core. Americans clung to the belief that somehow the 1960s would have been very different if John Kennedy had lived.

In the months after JFK's death, the nation rushed to memorialize him. New York's main airport was renamed in his honor, as were streets, bridges, schools, and other public venues around the country.

The President's body lay in state in the rotunda of the U.S. Capitol. More than 250,000 people would pay their respects.

Nov 23 AMERICA IN MOURNING
The President's Body to Lie in State; Oswald Questioned

WASHINGTON—America woke this morning to a national nightmare, and preparations to honor the life of John F. Kennedy, the 35th president of the United States, are underway.

Mrs. Kennedy has arranged to have the East Room decorated with black crepe, as it was for the funeral of assassinated president Abraham Lincoln. The original catafalque used to hold Lincoln's casket was brought to the White House and placed in the East Room.

After spending the night at a Washington mortuary, Kennedy's remains were transported back to the White House at around 4:30 A.M., with Mrs. Kennedy still by her late husband's side. The President's casket was carried to the East Room by a military honor guard, where his body will lie in state until it is taken to the Capitol rotunda tomorrow. Following Mrs. Kennedy's wishes, the casket will remain closed.

A private family mass was held at 10:00 A.M. today. Members of Congress, the Supreme Court, and other high-ranking government officials paid their respects throughout the afternoon. Defense Secretary Robert McNamara made several trips to Arlington National Cemetery, along with members of the Kennedy family, to make funeral arrangements.

Meanwhile, the business of running the government continued in other parts of the White House. While Evelyn Lincoln, Kennedy's longtime secretary, cleared the Oval Office of his personal effects, President Johnson met with members of his Cabinet, congressional leaders, and dignitaries, including former presidents Truman and Eisenhower. In addition, Johnson issued a proclamation making Monday, November 25, 1963, the day of Kennedy's funeral, a national day of mourning. "I invite the people of the world who share our grief to join us in this day of mourning and rededication," read Johnson's message.

Back in Dallas, suspected assassin Lee Harvey Oswald spent the day under interrogation by Dallas homicide chief Captain J. W. Fritz. Reportedly, Oswald denies the shootings of President Kennedy, Governor John Connally, and officer J. D. Tippit, but he does not deny that he is a member of the Communist Party.

An investigation into Oswald's U.S. Marine Corps records—he was given a dishonorable discharge in 1959—revealed an interesting clue. In 1961, Oswald penned a letter to Connally, then secretary of the Navy, requesting a reversal of the negative discharge. Connally refused, raising the question of whether Oswald was intentionally targeting Connally as well as the President.

A private mass was held on November 23, two days before the Low Mass and the burial.

Nov 23 WORLD GRIEVES OVER DEATH OF THE PRESIDENT

WASHINGTON—Feeling "profound grief" and retiring to his chapel to pray, Pope Paul VI is among millions of people around the globe who are saddened by the violent death of handsome and charismatic American president John F. Kennedy. People wept in the streets and traffic came to a halt as the news was broadcast around the world. Events have been canceled nationwide. Crowds gathered outside the White House while messages of condolence flooded in.

Soviet Premier Khrushchev, with whom Kennedy shared an often-contentious and mistrustful relationship, personally visited the U.S. Embassy in Moscow to express his "deep sadness" at Kennedy's assassination. Khrushchev also sent a telegram to President Johnson, which read in part: "John F. Kennedy's death is a serious blow to all people who cherish the cause of peace and Soviet-American cooperation." From Japan, Kohei Hanami, the captain whose warship almost claimed Kennedy's life in 1943, lamented: "The world has lost an irreplaceable man, for there is no other president who worked for peace like he did."

U.S. Senator Barry Goldwater (R-AZ), President Kennedy's presumptive challenger in the 1964 presidential election, said: "The President's death is a profound loss to the nation and the free world." Former presidents weighed in as well. "I am shocked beyond words at the tragedy that has happened to our country and to President Kennedy's family today," said Harry Truman. Former president Herbert Hoover noted: "He loved America and has given his life for his country." Dwight Eisenhower stated: "I share the sense of shock and dismay that all Americans feel at the despicable act that resulted in the death of our nation's president."

Sir Winston Churchill issued a statement that said that Kennedy's assassination has "taken from us a great statesman and a wise and valiant man." Perhaps General Douglas MacArthur best captured how we are all feeling today with the words expressed in a telegram to Mrs. Kennedy: "I realize the utter futility of words at such a time, but the world of civilization shares the poignancy of this monumental tragedy. As a former comrade in arms, his death kills something within me."

"The world has lost an irreplaceable man, for there is no other president who worked for peace like he did." —JAPANESE WAR VETERAN KOHEI HANAMI

Lee Harvey Oswald was pronounced dead less than two hours after being shot.

Nov 24 JFK "Admirer" Jack Ruby Murders Oswald

DALLAS—At 11:21 this morning, Lee Harvey Oswald, the suspected triggerman in the assassination of President John F. Kennedy, was himself shot in a bizarre incident broadcast live on NBC-TV.

Dallas detectives, including Jim Leavelle, who was handcuffed to Oswald, were transferring the suspect from the city jail to the Dallas County Jail. With television cameras rolling, a man named Jack Ruby fired a single bullet into Oswald's midsection. Oswald was transported unconscious to Parkland Hospital, where Kennedy had been pronounced dead on Friday. Doctors were unable to curb Oswald's internal bleeding, and he was pronounced dead at 1:07 P.M.

A picture is beginning to emerge of Ruby, born Rubenstein, who moved to Dallas from Chicago 15 years ago. Friends, enemies, and associates describe him as generous but vicious when crossed. A nightclub owner, he is said to be a tremendous admirer of President Kennedy and a proud American.

Dallas columnist Tony Zoppi, who has covered the Dallas nightlife beat for years, claims: "Kennedy was everything Rudy wasn't and would have liked to be: Polished, classy, articulate, educated, well mannered. Ruby wasn't any of these. When he talked to you he shouted." Police records indicate Ruby was arrested twice this year for carrying a concealed weapon.

In Washington, funeral preparations continued while Kennedy's body was brought to the Capitol rotunda to lie in state. The Kennedy family held another private mass in the East Room at 11 A.M. before escorting the President's casket to the Capitol rotunda. Prior to the hall being opened to the public, Mrs. Kennedy and her daughter, Caroline, approached the casket and kissed the flag with which it was draped.

Throughout the chilly November night, great throngs came to pay their respects. American citizens filed past President Kennedy's bier after standing in line for hours. At 9 P.M., Mrs. Kennedy returned for a few moments, and then the quiet procession resumed.

The procession will continue throughout the night, with tens of thousands of mourners expected to attend.

1 After the South Vietnamese military takes power, Kennedy orders the U.S. Seventh Fleet to prepare to assist Americans in Vietnam if needed.

2 During a White House briefing on the coup in Saigon, Kennedy pales when he learns that coup leaders had assassinated President Diem, Diem's brother, and other South Vietnamese officials.

3 An Associated Press poll of Republican voters finds Arizona's Barry Goldwater with a comfortable lead over Richard Nixon and Nelson Rockefeller for the 1964 Republican nomination.

4 Despite its distaste for the killing of the Diem brothers, the Kennedy administration signals it is still likely to recognize the new South Vietnamese government.

5 In a tape-recorded meeting that will not be made public until decades later, Kennedy and National Security Adviser McGeorge Bundy discuss a secret invitation by Fidel Castro to hold talks in Havana with a U.S. diplomat.

6 Despite his public denials that the United States "had nothing whatever to do with" the overthrow of the Diem government in Saigon, U.S. Ambassador Lodge writes Kennedy to say, "The ground in which the coup seed grew into a robust plant was prepared by us, and the coup would not have happened as it did without our preparation."

7 The U.S. officially recognizes the new regime in Saigon, which hopes Washington will follow through with a previously agreed $95 million annual economic aid commitment.

First Lady Jacqueline Kennedy holds the flag that draped the coffin of her late husband.

Nov 25 THE FINAL FAREWELL

WASHINGTON—The remains of President Kennedy were buried at Arlington National Cemetery today on a cold but sunny Monday afternoon.

At about 10 A.M., members of the Senate met and passed a resolution of sympathy for Mrs. Kennedy, who emerged from the White House about 20 minutes later. Escorted by her brothers-in-law, Mrs. Kennedy and members of the Kennedy family rode up Pennsylvania Avenue to the Capitol in a procession of black cars. As the Marine band played "Hail to the Chief," the casket was carried by servicemen to a horse-drawn caisson. It was followed by a riderless horse, boots backward in the stirrups.

The procession reached the White House, where it was joined by a large phalanx of visiting dignitaries from nations across the globe, including France's General de Gaulle, Germany's Chancellor Erhard, Ethiopian Emperor Haile Selassie, and the Duke of Edinburgh, husband of Queen Elizabeth. They followed President Johnson, who followed Mrs. Kennedy, who was flanked by Robert and Edward Kennedy for the procession to St. Matthew's Cathedral. The children, who were driven to the service, rejoined their mother on the steps of the cathedral.

Cardinal Richard Cushing, the archbishop of Boston who had performed the Kennedys' marriage ceremony and christened their children, conducted the Low Mass. Luigi Vena, who had sung at the Kennedys' wedding, sang "Ave Maria." As the mourners filed out of the cathedral, little John saluted his father's coffin—an indelible, heartbreaking image caught on film. The procession moved slowly to Arlington, where perhaps as many as a million spectators lined the route, with some 4,000 armed officers on hand to keep the peace.

At the gravesite, a peaceful, grassy slope overlooking Washington from beneath the Custis-Lee Mansion, the final elements of the service were played out. Mrs. Kennedy stood by the gravesite with her mother-in-law and other members of her husband's family. Members of the Irish Guard stood opposite the family. A flyover by 50 F-105 fighter jets, followed by Air Force One, appeared in the blue sky over Arlington. The burial service followed, and Mrs. Kennedy and her brothers-in-law lit an eternal flame at the gravesite. Mrs. Kennedy was presented with the colors from atop the President's casket as a 21-gun salute was fired and a bugler played Taps.

Following the services at Arlington, the visiting foreign dignitaries paid their respects to Mrs. Kennedy at the White House before joining President Johnson for a reception at the State Department.

An Unfinished Agenda

When John Kennedy died on November 22, 1963, most of his legislative agenda had yet to be realized. The great moments of his presidency were not so much about the meat-and-potatoes work of governance, but about crisis management, visionary rhetoric, and global leadership. He was less successful as an implementer of policy.

Three of Kennedy's most significant initiatives—a tax reform bill, medical insurance for the elderly, and a civil rights bill—were in legislative limbo when he died. As the nation prepared to enter a new election cycle in 1964, the fate of all three proposals was very much in question.

Kennedy's murder, however, offered a master legislator, his successor Lyndon B. Johnson, an opportunity to finish JFK's unfinished agenda. Johnson consciously played on the nation's grief to push for a

historic civil rights bill in 1964. LBJ persuaded legislators that support for the Civil Rights Act would be a fitting memorial to JFK, even though Kennedy had been cautious when it came to race issues. Once elected in his own right, Johnson pushed through another milestone, the Voting Rights Act of 1965. These two pieces of legislation would pretty much put an end to Jim Crow segregation.

The tax reform bill also required Johnson's formidable talent for horse-trading and political arm-twisting. Members of his own party were leery about cutting taxes, but the new president persuaded them to pass a bill in 1964 that cut the top marginal rate from 91 to 70 percent. Kennedy's health insurance plan, Medicare, was resuscitated after its near-death experience in Congress in 1962. Johnson got it passed in 1964.

8 Secretary of State Rusk tells reporters that the effort against Communists in Southeast Asia will improve under the military-civilian government that replaced President Diem.

9 White House officials quietly concede that Congress will not act on Kennedy's tax or civil rights proposals until 1964.

10 Administration officials scoff at published reports that Chinese troops are rotating in to replace Russian troops leaving Cuba. Washington believes only 5,000 Russians remain, with none of them functioning as combat units.

11 Across the Potomac River from Washington, President Kennedy observes Veterans Day by placing a wreath at the Tomb of the Unknowns in honor of U.S. veterans.

12 Concerned about spying by Soviet bloc agents, the U.S. State Department bans diplomats of several Eastern European nations from traveling to 355 counties in the United States.

13 The United States and its allies are reportedly exploring a plan to create a new international currency composed of dollars, pounds, francs, and marks in order to give Western Europe a bigger role in the monetary system.

14 At a news conference in Washington, Kennedy demands that Moscow immediately release accused spy Frederick Barghoorn. The President denies that the arrested Yale academic was gathering intelligence for the United States.

Nov 26 PRESIDENT JOHNSON GETS DOWN TO BUSINESS

WASHINGTON—President Lyndon Johnson has moved his belongings into the Oval Office. During the first day of his presidency not dominated by matters related to Kennedy's assassination and funeral, continuity was a recurring theme.

After talking with Soviet Deputy Premier Anastas Mikoyan for nearly an hour, the leaders left the meeting stressing that there is no change in U.S.-Soviet relations. The White House has already announced that a message went out to leaders worldwide that Kennedy's foreign policy will not be abandoned. Indeed, Johnson has pledged "continuity without confusion," and he made it clear that the tax cut and the civil rights bill—two cornerstones of the Kennedy domestic agenda—remain top priorities.

Johnson arranged meetings with several other foreign leaders, including General Charles de Gaulle. This could mean that there might be a thaw in U.S.-France relations, which have chilled of late.

Johnson also met with 35 state governors, to whom he expressed his concern over the transition. "Circumstances over which I had no control brought me into this position that I occupy tonight," he told them. "The difficulties and the tribulations are great, and this is the time when our whole system could go awry—not just the Republican Party and the Democratic Party, but the American system of government."

In other news today, Jack Ruby, the 52-year-old Dallas nightclub owner who murdered suspected Kennedy assassin Lee Harvey Oswald on live television, was indicted by a Dallas grand jury. Charged with murder with malice, Ruby faces the death penalty if convicted.

Nov 27 LBJ ADDRESSES CONGRESS, PLEDGES CONTINUITY

WASHINGTON—President Johnson delivered his first address to Congress today, less than a week after the assassination of his predecessor. It was a relatively brief speech, and it opened unlike any other presidential address to Congress in history when Johnson starkly stated: "All I have I would have given gladly not to be standing here today."

Johnson quickly reassured the assembled statesmen that Kennedy's agenda—in regards to space, international relations, education, the Peace Corps, elder care, and civil rights—did not die with him. Johnson also explicitly stated that the United States would stay the course in Vietnam and West Berlin. "We will carry on the fight," the President said, "against poverty and misery, and disease and ignorance, in other lands and in our own." Johnson also announced that Kennedy's policies of support for the United Nations, American military strength, and the Alliance for Progress will continue unabated.

Johnson urges Congress to work with him to help continue Kennedy's policies. He asserted that "no memorial oration or eulogy could more eloquently honor President Kennedy's memory that the earliest possible passage of the civil rights bill for which he fought so long." He likewise urged action on Kennedy's tax bill. "Let us here highly resolve," Johnson said, "that John Fitzgerald Kennedy did not live—or die—in vain."

"We will carry on the fight against poverty and misery, and disease and ignorance, in other lands and in our own." —PRESIDENT JOHNSON

Nov 29 NEW COMMISSION WILL EXAMINE ASSASSINATION

WASHINGTON—President Johnson announced today that he issued Executive Order No. 11130, which created a commission to investigate the circumstances of the Kennedy assassination as well as the killing of Lee Harvey Oswald.

The commission will examine the evidence uncovered by the Federal Bureau of Investigation and the Texas Court of Inquiry. All federal offices are to cooperate with the commission's efforts, and it is empowered to initiate its own investigations as it sees fit. At the conclusion of the investigation, the report is to be made public.

Members of the commission include Chief Justice Earl Warren, chair; senators Richard Russell and John Sherman Cooper; Representatives Hale Boggs and Gerald Ford; former CIA Director Allen Dulles; and Council on Foreign Relations Chairman John McCloy.

Supreme Court Chief Justice Earl Warren will head a commission that will investigate the assassination of President Kennedy.

15 Kennedy speaks to delegates at the AFL-CIO convention in New York, telling them that "no one gains from a fair employment practice bill if there is no employment to be had." He calls for Congress to pass his tax cuts and reforms.

16 The Soviets release Frederick Barghoorn in response to Kennedy's personal intervention in the case. Meanwhile, on his way to a family gathering in Florida, the President visits Cape Canaveral, which will be renamed Cape Kennedy shortly after his death.

17 The President rests in Palm Beach to prepare for upcoming tours of cities in Florida and Texas.

18 Kennedy delivers both policy and campaign speeches during a busy day in Florida, which includes multiple stops in Tampa and Miami. In the evening, he flies back to Washington to prepare for his tour through Texas.

19 Kennedy issues a statement for the centennial rededication of Gettysburg National Military Park. "The goals of liberty and freedom, the obligations of keeping ours a government of and for the people are never-ending," he writes.

20 The President proposes a global commercial satellite system in which foreign nations and companies could join the existing U.S. private space corporation. In the evening, Jack and Jacqueline Kennedy host a cocktail party.

21 President Kennedy begins a hectic schedule of rallies and speeches that are planned for Texas cities, including San Antonio, Houston, Fort Worth, Dallas, and Austin.

Dec 6 KENNEDYS ANNOUNCE PLANS FOR JFK LIBRARY

BOSTON—Robert and Edward Kennedy, the two surviving Kennedy brothers, held a press conference today announcing efforts to raise $6 million for the establishment of a John F. Kennedy Memorial Library in Boston, Massachusetts.

Attorney General Robert Kennedy announced that although the late president "has been deprived of the personal enjoyment of such a library…its speedy completion would be his dearest wish."

Plans for the library were in the works well in advance of Kennedy's assassination last month, and the late president himself had already inspected the proposed site—more than two acres of land donated by Harvard University.

The library's charitable corporation will, according to Harvard President Nathan M. Pusey, "provide a vehicle for the tangible expression of love and respect for the late president now evident in this country and abroad."

In other Kennedy news, the late president's two deceased children were re-interred alongside him in Arlington National Cemetery. They are a daughter who was stillborn in 1956 and a son who died shortly after birth earlier this year.

Dec 10 IDLEWILD RENAMED IN PRESIDENT KENNEDY'S HONOR

NEW YORK—The New York City Council voted today to rename the Idlewild Airport, located in the borough of Queens, in honor of President John F. Kennedy. There has been a virtual explosion of public facilities named after Kennedy since his death less than three weeks ago. Now known as the John F. Kennedy International Airport, it is among the busiest in the nation in terms of both passenger and freight flight.

Dec 22 MOURNING FOR JFK ENDS WITH CANDLELIGHT MEMORIAL

WASHINGTON—The end of the official 30-day mourning for slain President Kennedy ended tonight with a candlelight memorial service at the Lincoln Memorial. It was a fitting venue for a president who, like Lincoln, was struck down in the prime of his life and at a critical juncture in our nation's history. Speaking at the event, President Johnson declared: "As it was 100 years ago, so it is now. We have been bent in sorrow, but not in purpose. We buried Abraham Lincoln and John Kennedy, but we did not bury their dreams or their visions."

Several thousand people attended the memorial, despite the freezing cold weather. Mrs. Johnson and daughter Lucy Baines stood beside the President. The small candles that they held were lit by a torch that had been lit from the eternal flame at Kennedy's gravesite. Soon, the flame passed through the crowd, candle to candle, to create a sea of tiny lights in a final tribute.

"So let us here on this Christmas night determine that John Kennedy did not live or die in vain," President Johnson concluded, "that this nation under God shall have a new birth of freedom, and that we may achieve in our time and for all time the ancient vision of peace on earth, good will toward all men."

The White House flag returns to full staff with the conclusion of the 30-day period of mourning.

CONSPIRACY THEORIES

The public's fascination with John Kennedy's presidency did not end with his death. Conspiracy theorists and skeptical citizens have speculated for decades about who might have been involved in his assassination.

Lyndon Johnson believed there was a conspiracy, although the commission he put together—the famous Warren Commission—concluded that Lee Harvey Oswald acted alone. Johnson thought Fidel Castro's supporters were behind the murder, seeking to avenge Washington's attempts to kill the Cuban leader. Other theorists suggest that anti-Castro activists, embittered by the Bay of Pigs fiasco, were behind the killing.

Director Oliver Stone's 1991 movie *JFK* theorized that shadowy U.S. government agents conspired to kill President Kennedy because he was softening his attitude toward the Soviet Union and Vietnam. Still others believe that organized crime ordered the killing because of Robert Kennedy's crackdown on mob-run unions. Another theory posits that Kennedy was killed because of U.S. government complicity in the overthrow and murder of South Vietnamese leader Ngo Dinh Diem.

A poll taken in the early 1990s, not long after Stone's film was released, showed that more than two-thirds of Americans rejected the Warren Commission's finding of a lone gunman. Frame-by-frame examinations of the famous home movie of the assassination taken by Abraham Zapruder, shows, according to many, that Kennedy was shot from the front after being struck from the back.

Americans continue to wonder if an obscure man with a grievance could have ended such a memorable, privileged life. Because Oswald was shot and killed before he could stand trial, such speculation will inevitably continue.

November

22 At 12:30 P.M. in Dallas, gunfire stuns spectators who are cheering Kennedy's motorcade. Bullets strike the President and Texas Governor John Connally, who are rushed to Parkland Hospital. President Kennedy is pronounced dead. Lyndon Johnson is sworn in as the 36th U.S. president. Dallas police arrest Lee Harvey Oswald for the murder of President Kennedy.

23 On a rainy day in Washington, Jacqueline receives visitors and participates in a private funeral mass for her husband. President Johnson proclaims November 25 a national day of mourning.

24 Thousands wait in line for hours to view the President's casket in the rotunda of the Capitol. Late in the day, as viewers watch on live television, nightclub operator Jack Ruby shoots Lee Harvey Oswald in Dallas. Oswald is pronounced dead at Parkland Hospital.

25 After a state funeral and procession watched by millions in person and on television, President Kennedy is buried at Arlington National Cemetery. John Kennedy, Jr., watching the proceedings on his third birthday, salutes his father's casket.

29 President Johnson appoints a special commission to investigate the assassination of John F. Kennedy. U.S. Supreme Court Chief Justice Earl Warren chairs the commission, which will conclude that Lee Harvey Oswald was the lone assassin.

December

22 Thousands attend a candlelight memorial service at the Lincoln Memorial, which closes the official period of mourning.

INDEX

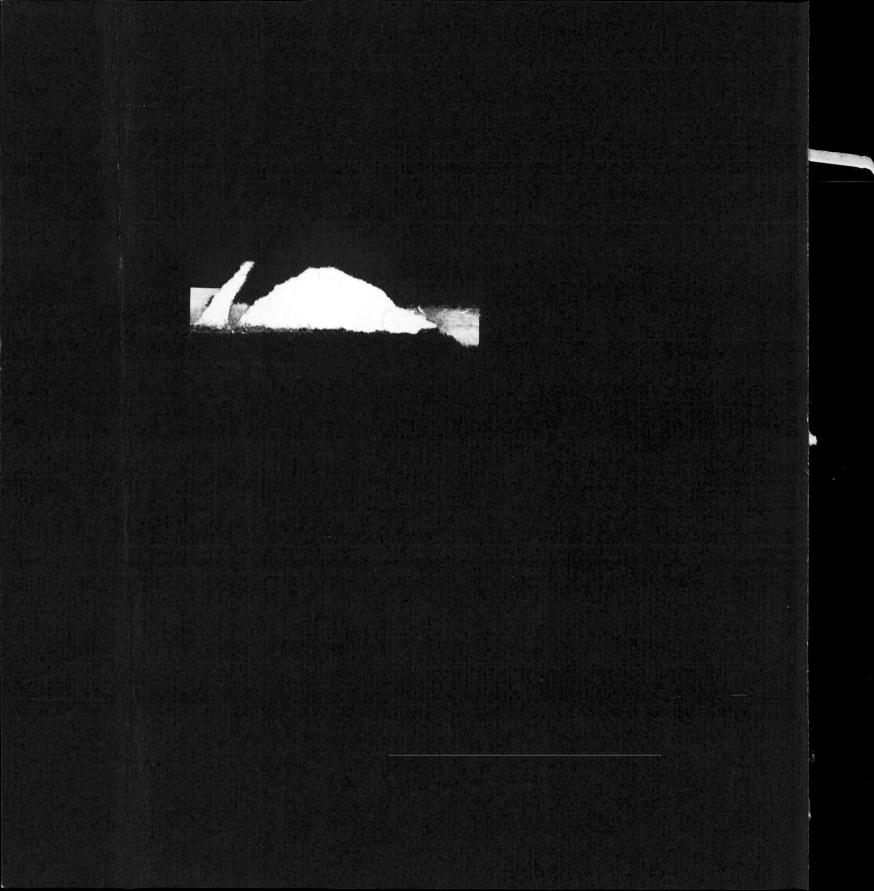